Leckie
the education publisher
for Scotland

Primary Maths

1st Level Maths

Teacher Guide

Series Editor: Craig Lowther

Authors: Antoinette Irwin, Linda Lapere,
Carol Lyon, Kirsten Mackay
and Scott Morrow

001/12022020

10 9 8 7 6 5 4 3 2 1

ISBN 9780008348946

Published by
Leckie & Leckie Ltd
An imprint of HarperCollins*Publishers*
Westerhill Road, Bishopbriggs, Glasgow, G64 2QT
T: 0844 576 8126   F: 0844 576 8131
leckieandleckie@harpercollins.co.uk   www.leckieandleckie.co.uk

Publisher: Fiona McGlade
Managing editor: Craig Balfour
Project editor: Peter Dennis

Special thanks
Copy editor: Peter Dennis
Layout: Jouve
Proofreader: Louise Robb

A CIP Catalogue record for this book is available from the British Library.

Acknowledgements

Images © Shutterstock.com

Whilst every effort has been made to trace the copyright holders, in cases where this has been unsuccessful, or if any have inadvertently been overlooked, the Publishers would gladly receive any information enabling them to rectify any error or omission at the first opportunity.

Printed by CPI Group (UK) Ltd, Croydon, CR0 4YY

Contents

Contents

Introduction

Primary Maths for Scotland programme overview

This Primary Maths for Scotland First Level Teacher Guide has been published in conjunction with the Primary Maths for Scotland First Level Maths Textbooks 1A, 1B and 1C. These titles complete a whole-school mathematics programme that also includes Early Level and Second Level.

This series has been written by a team of Scottish numeracy experts specially for Scottish schools and has been written to the Curriculum for Excellence Benchmarks to plan routes through the Experiences and Outcomes for Numeracy and Mathematics. They have been designed to develop conceptual understanding alongside procedural fluency whilst being easy to implement alongside existing plans and resources.

The team used researched informed pedagogy to guide the creation of these resources. The principle of social constructivism informed how teaching practices, resources and teaching ideas have been phrased. Pupils should be active participants in the learning process and be challenged and encouraged to talk about their ideas and share their strategies for solving mathematical problems. We also want our, and your, pupils to enjoy learning mathematics. This mindset and motivation makes learning and teaching a truly positive experience for everyone.

Primary Maths for Scotland programme components

Primary Maths for Scotland First Level Teacher Guide

At the beginning of the Teacher Guide is a suggested teaching plan for First Level. We have organised the curriculum into three parts: 1A, 1B and 1C, each of which correspond to a year's worth of work for children learning at the expected rate. The teaching plan can be used by teachers as their planning document or can be ignored in favour of an existing or different plan. The Teacher Guide and the Textbooks have been organised by Experiences and Outcomes, and not by suggested teaching plan, so that each topic can be found easily, and teachers can use the resources as they see fit.

Suggested Teaching Plan

1A Block	Textbook 1A Chapter	Textbook 1A Units	Benchmark/E&O
1	Number – order and place value	2.1 Reading and writing numbers (1) 2.2 Counting in tens 2.3 Reading and writing numbers (2) 2.4 Forward number sequences (1) 2.5 Forward number sequences (2) 2.6 Backward number sequences (1) 2.7 Backward number sequences (2)	MNU 1-02a • I have investigated how whole numbers are constructed, can understand the importance of zero within the system and can use my knowledge to explain the link between a digit, its place and its value. Benchmarks • Reads, writes, orders and recites whole numbers to 1000, starting from any number in the sequence. • Counts forwards and backwards in 2s, 5s, 10s and 100s. • Reads, writes, orders and recites whole numbers to 1000, starting from any number in the sequence.

This provides a suggested order of topics to follow. The resources are designed to be flexible and will fit with an established curriculum design, but if you are looking for a revised order then this is your starting point. The order is designed to support the pupils to progressively build knowledge and skills, whilst being able to return to previously learned topics as part of a spiral curriculum of deliberate spaced practice. This helps pupils to remember and practise old skills that they need to continue to learn. If you are working with a multi-stage class, it would be prudent to choose one sequence of topics for the class and then to differentiate to meet the needs of groups and individuals.

Chapters

Each chapter in the Teacher Guide is divided into three sections that correspond to the contents of Textbooks 1A, 1B and 1C. For each of the three sections within a topic, the following guidance is provided:

Section overview

Textbook 1A units	Review units	Prior learning	Benchmarks/Es&Os
Unit 1.1 Estimating and comparing collections	**1A** Unit 2.1	• I can count forwards to at least 20. • I can form and count a collection of up to 20 items. • I know number names and symbols up to at least 20.	**MNU 1-01a** • Uses strategies to estimate an answer to a calculation or problem; for example, doubling and rounding.
Unit 1.2 Estimating and describing collections	**1A** Unit 2.1	• I can count forwards to at least 20. • I can form and count a collection of up to 20 items. • I know number names and symbols up to at least 20.	**MNU 1-01a** • Uses strategies to estimate an answer to a calculation or problem; for example, doubling and rounding. • Rounds whole numbers to the nearest 10 and 100 and uses this routinely to estimate and check the reasonableness of a solution.

This table shows the Curriculum for Excellence Experiences and Outcomes and Benchmarks covered by each unit in this section. It is not our expectation that a child who successfully completes a single unit has demonstrated completion of a benchmark, rather it is through regularly returning to ideas and building skills and knowledge that ultimately a child will be able to demonstrate their understanding of each benchmark in new and unfamiliar contexts. This is when they, and you, know they are secure.

- Column 1 lists the Teacher Guide units in this section, which correspond to the Textbook units.
- Column 2 directs teachers to units that children can review if they are not yet ready to complete the work in the unit and do not possess the required pre-requisite knowledge.
- Column 3 describes the prior learning that children are expected to have mastered before embarking on the unit.
- Column 4 shows the coverage of the CfE and Benchmarks within this section.

Benchmarks and sections of benchmarks that are not relevant or covered within the section have been greyed out.

Conceptual context

Conceptual context

In daily life we routinely use estimating to help us make decisions, such as whether we have enough of something or not, sharing, or making quick approximations. Pupils first need to have a secure understanding of what we mean by a collection of objects and have wide experience of counting and sorting different objects to make collections. It is essential at this stage that they have knowledge of forward and backward number sequences to at least 20, and can read, write and sequence numerals to 20.

Pupils also need to understand the language used in comparing collections, such as bigger, smaller, greater, fewer, less than, or more than. It is important they have experience of using these terms when comparing a range of different concrete materials. This can easily be achieved through daily routines such as sorting pots of pencils or pens, as well as through maths activities.

This section provides an overview of the topic. It will include a brief explanation of key aspects of learning covered, including prior knowledge, calculation methods and next steps in learning.

Resources

Resources

- A range of different concrete counting materials, such as counters, dinosaurs, teddies, etc.
- Bead strings
- Blank ten frames
- Numeral cards 0–20
- Number lines 0–20
- Rekenreks

This section lists the physical resources that can be used to support the teaching and learning of the units in this topic.

We have listed resources that we use regularly with our own classes. We do not expect you to buy specific items of equipment; many objects, such as counters or cubes, will be available in a number of different forms. We do believe strongly that when pupils first encounter new ideas, they should have access to and be encouraged to use concrete materials. As pupils become more confident, they can move on to imaging the materials in their minds and then move on to using the number facts and skills without the help of manipulatives.

Key vocabulary

Key vocabulary

- **Approximately**
- **Collection**
- **Estimate**
- **Fewer**
- **Guess**
- **Less**
- **More**
- **Roughly**
- **Round**

The main mathematical terms relating to the units in this section are listed.

A full glossary of all the key mathematical terms and definitions from each topic can be found on our website here Collins.co.uk/primarymathsforscotland. The key vocabulary is listed and defined to promote the use of correct mathematical words and consistency across classes.

Misconceptions

Potential misconception	Addressing the misconception
Unit 1.1 Pupils may lack understanding of the terms bigger, smaller, more and less.	Ensure pupils are given lots of opportunities to count different types of collections of materials. Discuss meaning of which has more or less, or which is bigger or smaller by physically comparing the collections.

We have listed many of the common misconceptions that pupils will reveal to you when they have an opportunity to talk about their ideas. The left-hand column indicates the units where the potential misconceptions are most likely to occur.

Where errors or misconceptions are highlighted, it is important to address these immediately to support the pupil to change their thinking.

Teaching ideas

Unit 1.1 Estimating and comparing collections

- Show pupils two collections of counting objects: one that contains 12 elephants grouped randomly, the other that contains 14 dinosaurs grouped randomly. **Which collection is bigger?** Encourage pupils to make a prediction. Discuss why it is hard to tell which has more. **How could we sort them to make it easier to see which is bigger?**

These suggested activities add breadth, depth and challenge to the textbook resource. They can be used to introduce a topic prior to pupils practicing new skills or as part of the reinforcement of learning. The team have highlighted key questions in bold that you can use with individuals or groups of pupils. These questions are carefully constructed to provoke thought and to help reveal the pupils' current understanding and any misconceptions. The answers and explanations that the pupils offer will provide feedback that will help you and them to decide on the next steps in their learning.

Resource sheets – where worksheets are listed in the text, you can download them from Collins.co.uk/primary mathsforscotland to use with your pupils.

Glossaries

Glossary of Resources

A full glossary of all physical resources listed in the Teacher Guide, alongside a description and a photograph can be found on our website here Collins.co.uk/primarymathsforscotland.

Glossary of Key vocabulary

A full glossary of all the key mathematical terms and definitions from each topic can be found on our website here Collins.co.uk/primarymathsforscotland.

Primary Maths for Scotland First Level Textbooks

We have organised the curriculum into three parts; 1A, 1B and 1C, each of which correspond to a year's worth of work for children learning at the expected rate. There are three Textbooks covering First Level: 1A, 1B and 1C. Each Textbook is organised by Experiences and Outcomes, and not by suggested teaching plan. The Textbooks are progressive and should be used in sequence until the child has mastered the learning from each book.

The features of the Textbooks include:

What we are learning

We are learning to compare the size of collections by estimating.

Familiar characters introduce the learning intention so that the pupil knows what they are learning and can use this to reflect on their progress.

Before we start

Before we start

Can you draw this number of flowers? 12

This contains a diagnostic question that will help you find out what knowledge and strategy the pupil knows and can remember. This will help you to pitch the start point of your teaching.

Let's learn

Let's learn

Look at these collections. Which collection has more – the teddies or the dinosaurs?

We can make it easier to estimate which collection is bigger by organising them like this:

These worked examples can be used by you and/or the pupils to help understand the intended learning and the skills and knowledge required for the unit. The teaching ideas section in the Teacher Guide provides more ideas for introducing and extending this initial learning phase.

Let's practise

Let's practise

1) 

Put one counter onto every object.

Sort the fish and shell counters into two lines.

These exercises can be used for group, pair or individual practice. You will note that the exercises are not long and repetitive. They are designed to help the pupil to embed the learning in the unit in the initial phase of learning. Deep memory comes from pupils being motivated to learn and through regular, deliberate spaced practice over days, weeks and months. We advocate that pupils regularly return to, and build on, previously learned skills and knowledge as part of a spiral curriculum. Also, we are happy for our pupils to choose the questions they want to start at, if they feel confident with the topic. There are answers at the back of the Textbooks so that pupils can get immediate feedback on their solutions that you can then follow up by providing feedback on what they need to do next to improve their learning.

Challenge

CHALLENGE!

Draw between 10–20 circles on a piece of paper or a whiteboard for a partner. Do not tell your partner how many circles you have drawn.

Ask them to estimate how many circles you have drawn.

Now use counters and tens frames to work out how many circles there really were. Whose estimate was the closest?

This final section can be used as an extension to the Let's practise section or as the main part of the learning. These questions are usually written for pairs of pupils to work on together so that they are supported to talk and share their ideas.

Further resources and ideas are available from https://collins.co.uk/primarymathsforscotland

We welcome your thoughts and feedback, please contact the team here:
leckieandleckie@harpercollins.co.uk

Suggested Teaching Plans

Primary Maths for Scotland 1A scope and sequence

Chapter	Block	Units
Number – order and place value	1	2.1–2.7
Time	2	7.1, 7.2
Number – order and place value	3	2.8–2.13
Estimation and rounding	4	1.1–1.3
Mathematics, its impact on the world, past, present and future	5	9.1
Measurement	6	8.1–8.4
Number – addition and subtraction	7	3.1–3.5
Angles, symmetry and transformation	8	13.1–13.3
Number – addition and subtraction	9	3.6–3.10
Data handling and analysis	10	14.1–14.3
Measurement	11	8.5–8.8
Number – multiplication and division	12	4.1–4.5
Patterns and relationships	13	10.1–10.2
2D shapes and 3D objects	14	12.1–12.4
Number – addition and subtraction	15	3.11–3.15
Expressions and equations	16	11.1
Money	17	6.1–6.3
Number – multiplication and division	18	4.6–4.8
Fractions, decimal fractions and percentages	19	5.1–5.3
Time	20	7.3–7.4
Fractions, decimal fractions and percentages	21	5.4–5.6
Ideas of chance and uncertainty	22	15.1

Note: Sections of the benchmarks/Es&Os not covered in a 1A block have been highlighted grey in the table. These will be covered in 1B and 1C.

1A Block	Textbook 1A Chapter	Textbook 1A Units	Benchmark/E&O
1	Number – order and place value	2.1 Reading and writing numbers (1) 2.2 Counting in tens 2.3 Reading and writing numbers (2) 2.4 Forward number sequences (1) 2.5 Forward number sequences (2) 2.6 Backward number sequences (1) 2.7 Backward number sequences (2)	MNU 1-02a • I have investigated how whole numbers are constructed, can understand the importance of zero within the system and can use my knowledge to explain the link between a digit, its place and its value. Benchmarks • Reads, writes, orders and recites whole numbers to 1000, starting from any number in the sequence. • Counts forwards and backwards in 2s, 5s, 10s and 100s. • Reads, writes, orders and recites whole numbers to 1000, starting from any number in the sequence.
2	Time	7.1 Days of the week 7.2 Measuring time	MNU 1-10a MNU 1-10b MNU 1-10c • I can tell the time using 12-hour clocks, realising there is a link with 24-hour notation, explain how it impacts on my daily routine and ensure that I am organised and ready for events throughout my day. • I can use a calendar to plan and be organised for key events for myself and my class throughout the year. • I have begun to develop a sense of how long tasks take by measuring the time taken to complete a range of activities using a variety of timers. Benchmarks • Orders the months of the year and relates these to the appropriate seasons. • Selects and uses appropriate timers for specific purposes.
3	Number – order and place value	2.8 Number before, after and in-between 2.9 Counting in tens 2.10 Base ten for teen numbers 2.11 Counting in tens and ones 2.12 Counting in twos and fives 2.13 Ordinal numbers	MNU 1-02a • I have investigated how whole numbers are constructed, can understand the importance of zero within the system and can use my knowledge to explain the link between a digit, its place and its value. Benchmarks • Reads, writes, orders and recites whole numbers to 1000, starting from any number in the sequence. • Identifies the value of each digit in a whole number with three digits; for example, 867 = 800 + 60 + 7. • Counts forwards and backwards in 2s, 5s, 10s and 100s.

1A Block	Textbook 1A Chapter	Textbook 1A Units	Benchmark/E&O
4	Estimation and rounding	1.1 Estimating and comparing collections 1.2 Estimating and describing collections 1.3 Estimating and grouping collections	MNU 1-01a • I can share ideas with others to develop ways of estimating the answer to a calculation or problem, work out the actual answer, then check my solution by comparing it with the estimate. Benchmarks • Uses strategies to estimate an answer to a calculation or problem; for example, doubling and rounding. • Rounds whole numbers to the nearest 10 and 100 and uses this routinely to estimate and check the reasonableness of a solution.
5	Mathematics, its impact on the world, past, present and future	9.1 Ways numbers are used in real life	MTH 1-12a • I have discussed the important part that numbers play in the world and explored a variety of systems that have been used by civilisations throughout history to record numbers. Benchmarks • Investigates and shares understanding of the importance of numbers in learning, life and work. • Investigates and shares understanding of a variety of number systems used throughout history.

1A Block	Textbook 1A Chapter	Textbook 1A Units	Benchmark/E&O
6	Measurement	8.1 Comparing and ordering lengths and heights 8.2 Comparing and ordering mass 8.3 Comparing and ordering area 8.4 Comparing and ordering capacity	MNU 1-11a MNU 1-11b • I can estimate how long or heavy an object is, or what amount it holds, using everyday things as a guide, then measure or weigh it using appropriate instruments and units. • I can estimate the area of a shape by counting squares or other methods. Benchmarks • Uses knowledge of everyday objects to provide reasonable estimates of length, height, mass and capacity. • Makes accurate use of a range of instruments including rulers, metre sticks, digital scales and measuring jugs when measuring lengths, heights, mass and capacities using the most appropriate instrument for the task. • Records measurements of length, height, mass and capacity to the nearest standard unit; for example, millimetres (mm), centimetres (cm), grams (g), kilograms (kg), millilitres (ml), litres (l). • Compares measures with estimates. • Uses knowledge of relationships between units of measure to make simple conversions; for example, 1 m 58 cm = 158 cm. • Reads a variety of scales on measuring devices including those with simple fractions; for example, ½ litre. • Uses square grids to estimate then measure the areas of a variety of simple 2D shapes to the nearest half square. • Creates shapes with a given area to the nearest half square using square tiles or grids. Recognises that different shapes can have the same area (conservation of area).
7	Number – addition and subtraction	3.1 Addition bonds to 10 3.2 Fact families within 10 3.3 Doubles to 20 3.4 Ten plus facts 3.5 Five plus facts	MNU 1-03a • I can use addition, subtraction, multiplication and division when solving problems, making best use of the mental strategies and written skills I have developed. Benchmarks • Uses correct mathematical vocabulary when discussing the four operations including subtract, add, sum of, total, multiply, produce, divide and shared equally. • Demonstrates understanding of the commutative law; for example, $6 + 3 = 3 + 6$ or $2 \times 4 = 4 \times 2$. • Adds and subtracts multiples of 10 or 100 to or from any whole number to 1000. • Applies knowledge of inverse operations (addition and subtraction; multiplication and division).

1A Block	Textbook 1A Chapter	Textbook 1A Units	Benchmark/E&O
8	Angles, symmetry and transformation	13.1 Using positional language 13.2 Using directions 13.3 Symmetry	MTH 1-17a MTH 1-18a MTH 1-19a • I can describe, follow and record routes and journeys using signs, words and angles associated with direction and turning. • I have developed an awareness of where grid reference systems are used in everyday contexts and can use them to locate and describe position. • I have explored symmetry in my own and the wider environment and can create and recognise symmetrical pictures, patterns and shapes. Benchmarks • Uses technology and other methods to describe, follow and record directions using words associated with angles, directions and turns including: full turn, half turn, quarter turn, clockwise, anticlockwise, right turn, left turn, right angle. • Knows that a right angle is 90°. • Knows and uses the compass points, north, south, east and west. • Uses informal methods to estimate, compare and describe the size of angles in relation to a right angle. • Finds right angles in the environment and in well-known 2D shapes. • Identifies where and why grid references are used. • Describes, plots and uses accurate two-figure grid references, demonstrating knowledge of the horizontal and vertical location. • Identifies symmetry in patterns, pictures, nature and 2D shapes. • Creates symmetrical pictures and designs with more than one line of symmetry.
9	Number – addition and subtraction	3.6 Addition bonds to 20 3.7 Subtraction within 20 3.8 Counting on and counting back 3.9 Adding two one-digit numbers using a number line 3.10 Subtracting using a number line	MNU 1-03a • I can use addition, subtraction, multiplication and division when solving problems, making best use of the mental strategies and written skills I have developed. Benchmarks • Uses correct mathematical vocabulary when discussing the four operations including subtract, add, sum of, total, multiply, produce, divide and shared equally. • Solves addition and subtraction problems with three-digit whole numbers. • Demonstrates understanding of the commutative law; for example, $6 + 3 = 3 + 6$ or $2 \times 4 = 4 \times 2$. • Adds and subtracts multiples of 10 or 100 to or from any whole number to 1000.

1A Block	Textbook 1A Chapter	Textbook 1A Units	Benchmark/E&O
10	Data handling and analysis	14.1 Understanding data and information 14.2 Understanding data and information 14.3 Using data	MNU 1-20a MNU 1-20b MTH 1-21a • I have explored a variety of ways in which data is presented and can ask and answer questions about the information it contains. • I have used a range of ways to collect information and can sort it in a logical, organised and imaginative way using my own and others' criteria. • Using technology and other methods, I can display data simply, clearly and accurately by creating tables, charts and diagrams, using simple labelling and scale. Benchmarks • Asks and answers questions to extract key information from a variety of data sets including charts, diagrams, bar graphs and tables. • Selects and uses the most appropriate way to gather and sort data for a given purpose; for example, a survey, questionnaire or group tallies. • Uses a variety of different methods, including the use of digital technologies, to display data; for example, as block graphs, bar graphs, tables, Carroll diagrams and Venn diagrams. • Includes a suitable title, simple labelling on both axes and an appropriate scale where one unit represents more than one data value in graphs.

1A Block	Textbook 1A Chapter	Textbook 1A Units	Benchmark/E&O
11	Measurement	8.5 Estimating and measuring length (non-standard units) 8.6 Estimating and measuring mass (non-standard units) 8.7 Estimating and measuring area (non-standard units) 8.8 Estimating and measuring capacity (non-standard units)	MNU 1-11a MNU 1-11b • I can estimate how long or heavy an object is, or what amount it holds, using everyday things as a guide, then measure or weigh it using appropriate instruments and units. • I can estimate the area of a shape by counting squares or other methods. Benchmarks • Uses knowledge of everyday objects to provide reasonable estimates of length, height, mass and capacity. • Makes accurate use of a range of instruments including rulers, metre sticks, digital scales and measuring jugs when measuring lengths, heights, mass and capacities using the most appropriate instrument for the task. • Records measurements of length, height, mass and capacity to the nearest standard unit; for example, millimetres (mm), centimetres (cm), grams (g), kilograms (kg), millilitres (ml), litres (l). • Compares measures with estimates. • Uses knowledge of relationships between units of measure to make simple conversions; for example, 1 m 58 cm = 158 cm. • Reads a variety of scales on measuring devices including those with simple fractions; for example, ½ litre. • Uses square grids to estimate then measure the areas of a variety of simple 2D shapes to the nearest half square. • Creates shapes with a given area to the nearest half square using square tiles or grids. Recognises that different shapes can have the same area (conservation of area).
12	Number – multiplication and division	4.1 Making equal groups 4.2 Using arrays 4.3 Skip counting in twos 4.4 Skip counting in tens 4.5 Skip counting in fives	MNU 1-03a • I can use addition, subtraction, multiplication and division when solving problems, making best use of the mental strategies and written skills I have developed. Benchmarks • Counts forwards and backwards in 2s, 5s, 10s and 100s. • Demonstrates understanding of the commutative law; for example, $6 + 3 = 3 + 6$ or $2 \times 4 = 4 \times 2$. • Applies strategies to determine multiplication facts; for example, repeated addition, grouping, arrays and multiplication facts.

1A Block	Textbook 1A Chapter	Textbook 1A Units	Benchmark/E&O
13	Patterns and relationships	10.1 Continuing patterns 10.2 Recognise and continue number sequences	MTH 1-13a MTH 1-13b • I can continue and devise more involved repeating patterns or designs, using a variety of media. • Through exploring number patterns, I can recognise and continue simple number sequences and can explain the rule I have applied. Benchmarks • Counts forwards and backwards in 2s, 5s and 10s from any whole number up to 1000. • Describes patterns in number; for example, in the multiplication tables and hundred square. • Continues and creates repeating patterns involving shapes, pictures and symbols. • Describes, continues and creates number patterns using addition, subtraction, doubling, halving, counting in jumps (skip counting) and known multiples.
14	2D shapes and 3D objects	12.1 2D shapes 12.2 Sorting 2D shapes 12.3 Sorting 3D objects 12.4 3D objects	MTH 1-16a MTH 1-16b • I have explored simple 3D objects and 2D shapes and can identify, name and describe their features using appropriate vocabulary. • I can explore and discuss how and why different shapes fit together and create a tiling pattern with them. Benchmarks • Names, identifies and classifies a range of simple 2D shapes and 3D objects and recognises these shapes in different orientations and sizes. • Uses mathematical language to describe the properties of a range of common 2D shapes and 3D objects including side, face, edge, vertex, base and angle. • Identifies 2D shapes within 3D objects and recognises 3D objects from 2D drawings. • Identifies examples of tiling in the environment and applies knowledge of the features of 2D shapes to create tiling patterns incorporating two different shapes.

1A Block	Textbook 1A Chapter	Textbook 1A Units	Benchmark/E&O
15	Number – addition and subtraction	3.11 Missing addend 3.12 Missing subtrahend 3.13 Representing and solving word problems (1) 3.14 Representing and solving word problems (2) 3.15 Representing and solving word problems (3)	MNU 1-03a • I can use addition, subtraction, multiplication and division when solving problems, making best use of the mental strategies and written skills I have developed. Benchmarks • Uses correct mathematical vocabulary when discussing the four operations including subtract, add, sum of, total, multiply, produce, divide and shared equally. • Solves addition and subtraction problems with three-digit whole numbers. • Applies knowledge of inverse operations (addition and subtraction; multiplication and division).
16	Expressions and equations	11.1 Equations	MTH 1-15a MTH 1-15b • I can compare, describe and show number relationships, using appropriate vocabulary and the symbols for equals, not equal to, less than and greater than. Benchmarks • When a picture or symbol is used to replace a number in a number statement, I can find its value using my knowledge of number facts and explain my thinking to others. Benchmarks • Understands and accurately uses the terms 'equal to', 'not equal to', 'less than', 'greater than', and the related symbols (=, ≠ ,) when comparing quantities. • Applies understanding of the equals sign as a balance, and knowledge of number facts, to solve simple algebraic problems where a picture or symbol is used to represent a number; for example: ♦ + 17 = 30 and ♦ × 6 = 30.

1A Block	Textbook 1A Chapter	Textbook 1A Units	Benchmark/E&O
17	Money	6.1 Making amounts 6.2 Adding amounts 6.3 Calculating change	MNU 1-09a MNU 1-09b • I can use money to pay for items and can work out how much change I should receive. • I have investigated how different combinations of coins and notes can be used to pay for goods or be given in change. Benchmarks • Identifies and uses all coins and notes to £20 and explores different ways of making the same total. • Records amounts accurately in different ways using the correct notation; for example, 149p = £1·49 and 7p = £0·07. • Uses a variety of coin and note combinations, to pay for items and give change within £10. • Applies mental agility number skills to calculate the total spent in a shopping situation and is able to calculate change. • Demonstrates awareness of how goods can be paid for using cards and digital technology.
18	Number – multiplication and division	4.6 Multiplying using skip counting 4.7 Sharing equally 4.8 Grouping	MNU 1-03a • I can use addition, subtraction, multiplication and division when solving problems, making best use of the mental strategies and written skills I have developed. Benchmarks • Counts forwards and backwards in 2s, 5s, 10s and 100s. • Demonstrates understanding of the commutative law; for example, 6 + 3 = 3 + 6 or 2 × 4 = 4 × 2. • Applies strategies to determine multiplication facts; for example, repeated addition, grouping, arrays and multiplication facts. • Applies strategies to determine division facts; for example, repeated subtraction, equal groups, sharing equally, arrays and multiplication facts. • Uses multiplication and division facts to solve problems within the number range 0 to 1000. • Multiplies and divides whole numbers by 10 and 100 (whole number answers only). • Applies knowledge of inverse operations (addition and subtraction; multiplication and division). • Solves two-step problems.

1A Block	Textbook 1A Chapter	Textbook 1A Units	Benchmark/E&O
19	Fractions, decimal fractions and percentages	5.1 Make and identify halves 5.2 Make and identify quarters 5.3 Counting in halves and quarters	MNU 1-07a MNU 1-07b MTH 1-07c • Having explored fractions by taking part in practical activities, I can show my understanding of: o how a single item can be shared equally o the notation and vocabulary associated with fractions o where simple fractions lie on the number line. • Through exploring how groups of items can be shared equally, I can find a fraction of an amount by applying my knowledge of division. • Through taking part in practical activities including use of pictorial representations, I can demonstrate my understanding of simple fractions that are equivalent. Benchmarks • Explains what a fraction is using concrete materials, pictorial representations and appropriate mathematical vocabulary. • Demonstrates understanding that the greater the number of equal parts, the smaller the size of each share. • Uses the correct notation for common fractions to tenths; for example, $\frac{1}{2}$, $\frac{2}{3}$ and $\frac{5}{8}$. • Compares the size of fractions and places simple fractions in order on a number line. • Uses pictorial representations and other models to demonstrate understanding of simple equivalent fractions; for example, $\frac{1}{2} = \frac{2}{4} = \frac{3}{6}$. • Explains the role of the numerator and denominator. Uses known multiplication and division facts and other strategies to find unit fractions of whole numbers; for example, $\frac{1}{2}$ or $\frac{1}{4}$.
20	Time	7.3 Read o'clock and half past 7.4 Change o'clock and half past from analogue to digital	MNU 1-10a MNU 1-10b MNU 1-10c • I can tell the time using 12-hour clocks, realising there is a link with 24-hour notation, explain how it impacts on my daily routine and ensure that I am organised and ready for events throughout my day. • I can use a calendar to plan and be organised for key events for myself and my class throughout the year. • I have begun to develop a sense of how long tasks take by measuring the time taken to complete a range of activities using a variety of timers. Benchmarks • Tells the time using half past, quarter past and quarter to using analogue and digital 12-hour clocks.

<table>
<tr><th>1A Block</th><th>Textbook 1A Chapter</th><th>Textbook 1A Units</th><th>Benchmark/E&O</th></tr>
<tr><td>21</td><td>Fractions, decimals fractions and percentages</td><td>5.4 Sharing and grouping equally
5.5 Finding equivalent fractions
5.6 Share equally</td><td>MNU 1-07a
MNU 1-07b
MTH 1-07c
• Having explored fractions by taking part in practical activities, I can show my understanding of:
o how a single item can be shared equally
o the notation and vocabulary associated with fractions
o where simple fractions lie on the number line.
• Through exploring how groups of items can be shared equally, I can find a fraction of an amount by applying my knowledge of division.
• Through taking part in practical activities including use of pictorial representations, I can demonstrate my understanding of simple fractions that are equivalent.

Benchmarks
• Explains what a fraction is using concrete materials, pictorial representations and appropriate mathematical vocabulary.
• Demonstrates understanding that the greater the number of equal parts, the smaller the size of each share.
• Uses the correct notation for common fractions to tenths; for example, $\frac{1}{2}$, $\frac{2}{3}$ and $\frac{5}{8}$.
• Compares the size of fractions and places simple fractions in order on a number line.
• Uses pictorial representations and other models to demonstrate understanding of simple equivalent fractions; for example, $\frac{1}{2} = \frac{2}{4} = \frac{3}{6}$.
• Explains the role of the numerator and denominator.
Uses known multiplication and division facts and other strategies to find unit fractions of whole numbers; for example, $\frac{1}{2}$ or $\frac{1}{4}$.</td></tr>
<tr><td>22</td><td>Ideas of chance and uncertainty</td><td>15.1 Understanding chance</td><td>MNU 1-22a
• I can use appropriate vocabulary to describe the likelihood of events occurring, using the knowledge and experiences of myself and others to guide me.

Benchmarks
• Uses mathematical vocabulary appropriately to describe the likelihood of events occurring in everyday situations including, probable, likely/unlikely, certain/uncertain, possible/impossible, and fair/unfair.
• Interprets data gathered through everyday experiences to make reasonable predictions of the likelihood of an event occurring.</td></tr>
</table>

Primary Maths for Scotland 1B scope and sequence

Chapter	Block	Units
Number – order and place value	1	2.1–2.6
Mathematics, its impact on the world, past, present and future	2	9.1
Number – order and place value	3	2.7–2.10
Estimation and rounding	4	1.1
Number – addition and subtraction	5	3.1–3.3
Number – order and place value	6	2.11–2.14
Number – addition and subtraction	7	3.4–3.9
Number – multiplication and division	8	4.1–4.3
2D shapes and 3D objects	9	12.1–12.4
Number – addition and subtraction	10	3.10–3.12
Number – multiplication and division	11	4.4–4.7
Ideas of chance and uncertainty	12	15.1
Time	13	7.1–7.3
Number – multiplication and division	14	4.8–4.9
Patterns and relationships	15	10.1–10.2
Fractions, decimal fractions and percentages	16	5.1–5.4
Angles, symmetry and transformation	17	13.1–13.4
Time	18	7.4–7.5
Expressions and equations	19	11.1
Estimation and rounding	20	1.2
Number – addition and subtraction	21	3.13–3.15
Measurement	22	8.1–8.4
Money	23	6.1–6.3
Data handling and analysis	24	14.1–14.4
Fractions, decimal fractions and percentages	25	5.5–5.8
Measurement	26	8.5–8.9

Note: Sections of the benchmarks/Es&Os not covered in a 1B block have been highlighted grey in the table. These will be covered in 1A and 1C.

<table>
<tr><th>1B Block</th><th>Textbook 1B Chapter</th><th>Textbook 1B Units</th><th>Benchmark/E&O</th></tr>
<tr><td>1</td><td>Number – order and place value</td><td>2.1 Reading and writing two-digit numbers
2.2 Naming and ordering the hundreds
2.3 Reading and writing three-digit numbers
2.4 Counting forwards in ones
2.5 Counting backwards in ones
2.6 Before, after and in-between</td><td>MNU 1-02a
• I have investigated how whole numbers are constructed, can understand the importance of zero within the system and can use my knowledge to explain the link between a digit, its place and its value.

Benchmarks
• Reads, writes, orders and recites whole numbers to 1000, starting from any number in the sequence.
• Counts forwards and backwards in 2s, 5s, 10s and 100s.</td></tr>
<tr><td>2</td><td>Mathematics, its impact on the world, past, present and future</td><td>9.1 Ways numbers are used in work</td><td>MTH 1-12a
• I have discussed the important part that numbers play in the world and explored a variety of systems that have been used by civilisations throughout history to record numbers.

Benchmarks
• Investigates and shares understanding of the importance of numbers in learning, life and work.
• Investigates and shares understanding of a variety of number systems used throughout history.</td></tr>
<tr><td>3</td><td>Number – order and place value</td><td>2.7 Counting forwards in tens and hundreds
2.8 Counting backwards in tens and hundreds
2.9 Counting forwards and backwards in twos and fives
2.10 Counting in hundreds, tens and ones</td><td>MNU 1-02a
• I have investigated how whole numbers are constructed, can understand the importance of zero within the system and can use my knowledge to explain the link between a digit, its place and its value.

Benchmarks
• Counts forwards and backwards in 2s, 5s, 10s and 100s.</td></tr>
<tr><td>4</td><td>Estimation and rounding</td><td>1.1 Rounding</td><td>MNU 1-01a
• I can share ideas with others to develop ways of estimating the answer to a calculation or problem, work out the actual answer, then check my solution by comparing it with the estimate.

Benchmarks
• Rounds whole numbers to the nearest 10 and 100 and uses this routinely to estimate and check the reasonableness of a solution.</td></tr>
</table>

1B Block	Textbook 1B Chapter	Textbook 1B Units	Benchmark/E&O
5	Number – addition and subtraction	3.1 Compatible numbers: pairs to ten 3.2 Doubles and near doubles 3.3 Fact families	MNU 1-03a • I can use addition, subtraction, multiplication and division when solving problems, making best use of the mental strategies and written skills I have developed. Benchmarks • Uses correct mathematical vocabulary when discussing the four operations including subtract, add, sum of, total, multiply, produce, divide and shared equally. • Demonstrates understanding of the commutative law; for example, $6 + 3 = 3 + 6$ or $2 \times 4 = 4 \times 2$. • Solves addition and subtraction problems with three-digit whole numbers.
6	Number – order and place value	2.11 Standard place value partitioning 2.12 Comparing numbers 2.13 Ordering numbers 2.14 Ordinal numbers	MNU 1-02a • I have investigated how whole numbers are constructed, can understand the importance of zero within the system and can use my knowledge to explain the link between a digit, its place and its value. Benchmarks • Identifies the value of each digit in a whole number with three digits; for example, $867 = 800 + 60 + 7$. • Reads, writes, orders and recites whole numbers to 1000, starting from any number in the sequence.
7	Number – addition and subtraction	3.4 Complements to the next multiple of 10 3.5 Adding 0, 1 and 10 3.6 Subtracting 0, 1 and 10 3.7 Adding and subtracting single and double-digit numbers 3.8 Adding and subtracting multiples of 10 to and from two-digit numbers 3.9 Partitioning through 10	MNU 1-03a • I can use addition, subtraction, multiplication and division when solving problems, making best use of the mental strategies and written skills I have developed. Benchmarks • Uses correct mathematical vocabulary when discussing the four operations including subtract, add, sum of, total, multiply, produce, divide and shared equally. • Demonstrates understanding of the commutative law; for example, $6 + 3 = 3 + 6$ or $2 \times 4 = 4 \times 2$. • Solves addition and subtraction problems with three-digit whole numbers. • Adds and subtracts multiples of 10 or 100 to or from any whole number to 1000.

1B Block	Textbook 1B Chapter	Textbook 1B Units	Benchmark/E&O
8	Number – multiplication and division	4.1 Multiplying by skip counting 4.2 Understanding multiplication as repeated addition 4.3 Arrays	MNU 1-03a I can use addition, subtraction, multiplication and division when solving problems, making best use of the mental strategies and written skills I have developed. Benchmarks • Counts forwards and backwards in 2s, 5s, 10s and 100s. • Demonstrates understanding of the commutative law; for example, $6 + 3 = 3 + 6$ or $2 \times 4 = 4 \times 2$. • Applies strategies to determine multiplication facts; for example, repeated addition, grouping, arrays and multiplication facts. • Applies strategies to determine division facts; for example, repeated subtraction, equal groups, sharing equally, arrays and multiplication facts.
9	2D shapes and 3D objects	12.1 Properties of 2D shapes 12.2 2D shapes in 3D objects 12.3 Recognising 3D objects 12.4 Tiling patterns	MTH 1-16a MTH 1-16b • I have explored simple 3D objects and 2D shapes and can identify, name and describe their features using appropriate vocabulary. • I can explore and discuss how and why different shapes fit together and create a tiling pattern with them. Benchmarks • Names, identifies and classifies a range of simple 2D shapes and 3D objects and recognises these shapes in different orientations and sizes. • Uses mathematical language to describe the properties of a range of common 2D shapes and 3D objects including side, face, edge, vertex, base and angle. • Identifies 2D shapes within 3D objects and recognises 3D objects from 2D drawings. • Identifies examples of tiling in the environment and applies knowledge of the features of 2D shapes to create tiling patterns incorporating two different shapes.

1B Block	Textbook 1B Chapter	Textbook 1B Units	Benchmark/E&O
10	Number – addition and subtraction	3.10 Adding two-digit numbers 3.11 Subtracting two-digit numbers 3.12 Inverse relationships	MNU 1-03a • I can use addition, subtraction, multiplication and division when solving problems, making best use of the mental strategies and written skills I have developed. Benchmarks • Uses correct mathematical vocabulary when discussing the four operations including subtract, add, sum of, total, multiply, produce, divide and shared equally. • Demonstrates understanding of the commutative law; for example, $6 + 3 = 3 + 6$ or $2 \times 4 = 4 \times 2$. • Solves addition and subtraction problems with three-digit whole numbers. • Adds and subtracts multiples of 10 or 100 to or from any whole number to 1000.
11	Number – multiplication and division	4.4 Repeated addition 4.5 Multiplying using known facts 4.6 Dividing by sharing 4.7 Dividing by grouping	MNU 1-03a I can use addition, subtraction, multiplication and division when solving problems, making best use of the mental strategies and written skills I have developed. Benchmarks • Counts forwards and backwards in 2s, 5s, 10s and 100s. • Demonstrates understanding of the commutative law; for example, $6 + 3 = 3 + 6$ or $2 \times 4 = 4 \times 2$. • Applies strategies to determine multiplication facts; for example, repeated addition, grouping, arrays and multiplication facts. • Applies strategies to determine division facts; for example, repeated subtraction, equal groups, sharing equally, arrays and multiplication facts. • Uses multiplication and division facts to solve problems within the number range 0 to 1000.
12	Ideas of chance and uncertainty	15.1 Understanding chance and uncertainty	MNU 1-22a • I can use appropriate vocabulary to describe the likelihood of events occurring, using the knowledge and experiences of myself and others to guide me. Benchmarks • Uses mathematical vocabulary appropriately to describe the likelihood of events occurring in everyday situations including, probable, likely/unlikely, certain/uncertain, possible/impossible, and fair/unfair. • Interprets data gathered through everyday experiences to make reasonable predictions of the likelihood of an event occurring.

1B Block	Textbook 1B Chapter	Textbook 1B Units	Benchmark/E&O
13	Time	7.1 Time word problems 7.2 Finding durations 7.3 Recording time	MNU 1-10a MNU 1-10b MNU 1-10c • I can tell the time using 12-hour clocks, realising there is a link with 24-hour notation, explain how it impacts on my daily routine and ensure that I am organised and ready for events throughout my day. • I can use a calendar to plan and be organised for key events for myself and my class throughout the year. • I have begun to develop a sense of how long tasks take by measuring the time taken to complete a range of activities using a variety of timers. Benchmarks • Records the date in a variety of ways, using words and numbers. • Uses and interprets a variety of calendars and 12-hour timetables to plan key events. • Knows the number of seconds in a minute, minutes in an hour, hours in a day, days in each month, weeks and days in a year. • Orders the months of the year and relates these to the appropriate seasons. • Selects and uses appropriate timers for specific purposes.
14	Number – multiplication and division	4.8 Multiplying by 10 4.9 Dividing by 10	MNU 1-03a I can use addition, subtraction, multiplication and division when solving problems, making best use of the mental strategies and written skills I have developed. Benchmarks • Counts forwards and backwards in 2s, 5s, 10s and 100s. • Demonstrates understanding of the commutative law; for example, $6 + 3 = 3 + 6$ or $2 \times 4 = 4 \times 2$. • Applies strategies to determine multiplication facts; for example, repeated addition, grouping, arrays and multiplication facts. • Applies strategies to determine division facts; for example, repeated subtraction, equal groups, sharing equally, arrays and multiplication facts. • Uses multiplication and division facts to solve problems within the number range 0 to 1000. • Multiplies and divides whole numbers by 10 and 100 (whole number answers only). • Applies knowledge of inverse operations (addition and subtraction; multiplication and division). • Solves two-step problems.

1B Block	Textbook 1B Chapter	Textbook 1B Units	Benchmark/E&O
15	Patterns and relationships	10.1 Investigate repeating patterns 10.2 Recognise and continue number sequences	MTH 1-13a MTH 1-13b • I can continue and devise more involved repeating patterns or designs, using a variety of media. • Through exploring number patterns, I can recognise and continue simple number sequences and can explain the rule I have applied. Benchmarks • Counts forwards and backwards in 2s, 5s and 10s from any whole number up to 1000. • Describes patterns in number; for example, in the multiplication tables and hundred square. • Continues and creates repeating patterns involving shapes, pictures and symbols. • Describes, continues and creates number patterns using addition, subtraction, doubling, halving, counting in jumps (skip counting) and known multiples.
16	Fractions, decimal fractions and percentages	5.1 Making and naming equal parts 5.2 Identifying equal parts 5.3 Naming fractions 5.4 Counting fractions	MNU 1-07a MNU 1-07b MTH 1-07c • Having explored fractions by taking part in practical activities, I can show my understanding of: o how a single item can be shared equally o the notation and vocabulary associated with fractions o where simple fractions lie on the number line. • Through exploring how groups of items can be shared equally, I can find a fraction of an amount by applying my knowledge of division. • Through taking part in practical activities including use of pictorial representations, I can demonstrate my understanding of simple fractions that are equivalent. Benchmarks • Explains what a fraction is using concrete materials, pictorial representations and appropriate mathematical vocabulary. • Demonstrates understanding that the greater the number of equal parts, the smaller the size of each share. • Uses the correct notation for common fractions to tenths; for example, $\frac{1}{2}$, $\frac{2}{3}$ and $\frac{5}{8}$. • Compares the size of fractions and places simple fractions in order on a number line. • Explains the role of the numerator and denominator.

1B Block	Textbook 1B Chapter	Textbook 1B Units	Benchmark/E&O
17	Angles, symmetry and transformation	13.1 Making turns 13.2 Right angles 13.3 Grid references 13.4 Symmetry	MTH 1-17a MTH 1-18a MTH 1-19a • I can describe, follow and record routes and journeys using signs, words and angles associated with direction and turning. • I have developed an awareness of where grid reference systems are used in everyday contexts and can use them to locate and describe position. • I have explored symmetry in my own and the wider environment and can create and recognise symmetrical pictures, patterns and shapes. Benchmarks • Uses technology and other methods to describe, follow and record directions using words associated with angles, directions and turns including, full turn, half turn, quarter turn, clockwise, anticlockwise, right turn, left turn, right angle. • Knows that a right angle is 90°. • Knows and uses the compass points, north, south, east and west. • Uses informal methods to estimate, compare and describe the size of angles in relation to a right angle. • Finds right angles in the environment and in well-known 2D shapes. • Identifies where and why grid references are used. • Describes, plots and uses accurate two-figure grid references, demonstrating knowledge of the horizontal and vertical location. • Identifies symmetry in patterns, pictures, nature and 2D shapes. • Creates symmetrical pictures and designs with more than one line of symmetry.

1B Block	Textbook 1B Chapter	Textbook 1B Units	Benchmark/E&O
18	Time	7.4 Telling the time 7.5 Five-minute intervals	MNU 1-10a MNU 1-10b MNU 1-10c • I can tell the time using 12-hour clocks, realising there is a link with 24-hour notation, explain how it impacts on my daily routine and ensure that I am organised and ready for events throughout my day. • I can use a calendar to plan and be organised for key events for myself and my class throughout the year. • I have begun to develop a sense of how long tasks take by measuring the time taken to complete a range of activities using a variety of timers. Benchmarks • Tells the time using half past, quarter past and quarter to using analogue and digital 12-hour clocks. • Records 12-hour times using a.m. and p.m. and is able to identify 24-hour notation; for example, on a mobile phone or computer. • Knows the number of seconds in a minute, minutes in an hour, hours in a day, days in each month, weeks and days in a year.
19	Expressions and equations	11.1 Solve simple equations	MTH 1-15a MTH 1-15b • I can compare, describe and show number relationships, using appropriate vocabulary and the symbols for equals, not equal to, less than and greater than. • When a picture or symbol is used to replace a number in a number statement, I can find its value using my knowledge of number facts and explain my thinking to others. Benchmarks • Understands and accurately uses the terms 'equal to', 'not equal to', 'less than', 'greater than', and the related symbols (=, ≠ ,) when comparing quantities. • Applies understanding of the equals sign as a balance, and knowledge of number facts, to solve simple algebraic problems where a picture or symbol is used to represent a number; for example, ♦ + 17 = 30 and ♦ × 6 = 30.

1B Block	Textbook 1B Chapter	Textbook 1B Units	Benchmark/E&O
20	Estimation and rounding	1.2 Estimating the answer by rounding	MNU 1-01a • I can share ideas with others to develop ways of estimating the answer to a calculation or problem, work out the actual answer, then check my solution by comparing it with the estimate. Benchmarks • Uses strategies to estimate an answer to a calculation or problem; for example, doubling and rounding. • Rounds whole numbers to the nearest 10 and 100 and uses this routinely to estimate and check the reasonableness of a solution.
21	Number – addition and subtraction	3.13 Strategies for solving number puzzles 3.14 Representing and solving word problems (1) 3.15 Representing and solving word problems (2)	MNU 1-03a • I can use addition, subtraction, multiplication and division when solving problems, making best use of the mental strategies and written skills I have developed. Benchmarks • Uses correct mathematical vocabulary when discussing the four operations including subtract, add, sum of, total, multiply, produce, divide and shared equally. • Demonstrates understanding of the commutative law; for example, $6 + 3 = 3 + 6$ or $2 \times 4 = 4 \times 2$. • Solves addition and subtraction problems with three-digit whole numbers. • Solves two-step problems.

1B Block	Textbook 1B Chapter	Textbook 1B Units	Benchmark/E&O
22	Measurement	8.1 Estimating, measuring and recording length (standard units) 8.2 Estimating, measuring and recording mass (standard units) 8.3 Estimating, measuring and recording area (squares) 8.4 Estimating, measuring and recording capacity	MNU 1-11a MNU 1-11b • I can estimate how long or heavy an object is, or what amount it holds, using everyday things as a guide, then measure or weigh it using appropriate instruments and units. • I can estimate the area of a shape by counting squares or other methods. Benchmarks • Uses knowledge of everyday objects to provide reasonable estimates of length, height, mass and capacity. • Makes accurate use of a range of instruments including rulers, metre sticks, digital scales and measuring jugs when measuring lengths, heights, mass and capacities using the most appropriate instrument for the task. • Records measurements of length, height, mass and capacity to the nearest standard unit; for example, millimetres (mm), centimetres (cm), grams (g), kilograms (kg), millilitres (ml), litres (l). • Compares measures with estimates. • Reads a variety of scales on measuring devices including those with simple fractions; for example, $\frac{1}{2}$ litre. • Uses square grids to estimate then measure the areas of a variety of simple 2D shapes to the nearest half square. • Creates shapes with a given area to the nearest half square using square tiles or grids. • Recognises that different shapes can have the same area (conservation of area).

1B Block	Textbook 1B Chapter	Textbook 1B Units	Benchmark/E&O
23	Money	6.1 Making and recording amounts 6.2 Adding amounts 6.3 Calculating change	MNU 1-09a MNU 1-09b • I can use money to pay for items and can work out how much change I should receive. • I have investigated how different combinations of coins and notes can be used to pay for goods or be given in change. Benchmarks • Identifies and uses all coins and notes to £20 and explores different ways of making the same total. • Records amounts accurately in different ways using the correct notation; for example, 149p = £1·49 and 7p = £0·07. • Uses a variety of coin and note combinations, to pay for items and give change within £10. • Applies mental agility number skills to calculate the total spent in a shopping situation and is able to calculate change. • Demonstrates awareness of how goods can be paid for using cards and digital technology.
24	Data handling and analysis	14.1 Understanding data and information 14.2 Bar graphs 14.3 Investigate and interpret information 14.4 Drawing conclusions from data and graphs	MNU 1-20a MNU 1-20b MTH 1-21a • I have explored a variety of ways in which data is presented and can ask and answer questions about the information it contains. • I have used a range of ways to collect information and can sort it in a logical, organised and imaginative way using my own and others' criteria. • Using technology and other methods, I can display data simply, clearly and accurately by creating tables, charts and diagrams, using simple labelling and scale. Benchmarks • Asks and answers questions to extract key information from a variety of data sets including charts, diagrams, bar graphs and tables. • Selects and uses the most appropriate way to gather and sort data for a given purpose; for example, a survey, questionnaire or group tallies. • Uses a variety of different methods, including the use of digital technologies, to display data; for example, as block graphs, bar graphs, tables, Carroll diagrams and Venn diagrams. • Includes a suitable title, simple labelling on both axes and an appropriate scale where one unit represents more than one data value in graphs.

1B Block	Textbook 1B Chapter	Textbook 1B Units	Benchmark/E&O
25	Fractions, decimal fractions and percentages	5.5 Comparing fractions 5.6 Equivalent fractions 5.7 Counting in fractions 5.8 Finding part of a set	MNU 1-07a MNU 1-07b MTH 1-07c • Having explored fractions by taking part in practical activities, I can show my understanding of: o how a single item can be shared equally o the notation and vocabulary associated with fractions o where simple fractions lie on the number line. • Through exploring how groups of items can be shared equally, I can find a fraction of an amount by applying my knowledge of division. • Through taking part in practical activities including use of pictorial representations, I can demonstrate my understanding of simple fractions that are equivalent. Benchmarks • Explains what a fraction is, using concrete materials, pictorial representations and appropriate mathematical vocabulary. • Demonstrates understanding that the greater the number of equal parts, the smaller the size of each share. • Uses the correct notation for common fractions to tenths; for example, $\frac{1}{2}$, $\frac{2}{3}$ and $\frac{5}{8}$. • Compares the size of fractions and places simple fractions in order on a number line. • Uses pictorial representations and other models to demonstrate understanding of simple equivalent fractions; for example, $\frac{1}{2} = \frac{2}{4} = \frac{3}{6}$. • Explains the role of the numerator and denominator. • Uses known multiplication and division facts and other strategies to find unit fractions of whole numbers; for example, $\frac{1}{2}$ or $\frac{1}{4}$.

1B Block	Textbook 1B Chapter	Textbook 1B Units	Benchmark/E&O
26	Measurement	8.5 Converting standard units of length/height 8.6 Converting standard units of mass 8.7 Reading scales – length 8.8 Reading scales – mass 8.9 Reading scales – capacity	MNU 1-11a MNU 1-11b • I can estimate how long or heavy an object is, or what amount it holds, using everyday things as a guide, then measure or weigh it using appropriate instruments and units. • I can estimate the area of a shape by counting squares or other methods. Benchmarks • Uses knowledge of everyday objects to provide reasonable estimates of length, height, mass and capacity. • Makes accurate use of a range of instruments including rulers, metre sticks, digital scales and measuring jugs when measuring lengths, heights, mass and capacities using the most appropriate instrument for the task. • Records measurements of length, height, mass and capacity to the nearest standard unit; for example, millimetres (mm), centimetres (cm), grams (g), kilograms (kg), millilitres (ml), litres (l). • Compares measures with estimates. • Uses knowledge of relationships between units of measure to make simple conversions' for example, 1 m 58 cm = 158 cm. • Reads a variety of scales on measuring devices including those with simple fractions; for example, ½ litre. • Uses square grids to estimate then measure the areas of a variety of simple 2D shapes to the nearest half square. • Creates shapes with a given area to the nearest half square using square tiles or grids. Recognises that different shapes can have the same area (conservation of area).

Primary Maths for Scotland 1C scope and sequence

Chapter	Block	Units
Number – order and place value	1	2.1–2.6
Estimation and rounding	2	1.1
Mathematics, its impact on the world, past, present and future	3	9.1
Time	4	7.1–7.3
Number – order and place value	5	2.7–2.11
2D shapes and 3D objects	6	12.1–12.3
Number – addition and subtraction	7	3.1–3.7
Data handling and analysis	8	14.1–14.4
Ideas of chance and uncertainty	9	15.1
Number – addition and subtraction	10	3.8–3.13
Number – multiplication and division	11	4.1–4.3
Patterns and relationships	12	10.1–10.2
Time	13	7.4–7.5
Number – multiplication and division	14	4.4–4.8
Expressions and equations	15	11.1
Angles, symmetry and transformation	16	13.1–13.5
Fractions, decimal fractions and percentages	17	5.1–5.4
Estimation and rounding	18	1.2
Number – addition and subtraction	19	3.14–3.15
Number – multiplication and division	20	4.9
Money	21	6.1–6.3
Fractions, decimal fractions and percentages	22	5.5–5.8
Measurement	23	8.1–8.9

Note: Sections of the benchmarks/Es&Os not covered in a 1C block have been highlighted grey in the table. These will be covered in 1A and 1B.

1C Block	Textbook 1C Chapter	Textbook 1C Units	Benchmark/E&O
1	Number – order and place value	2.1 Recognising and writing three-digit numbers 2.2 Zero as a place holder 2.3 Number sequences (1) 2.4 Number sequences (2) 2.5 Number sequences (3) 2.6 Representing and describing three-digit numbers	MNU 1-02a • I have investigated how whole numbers are constructed, can understand the importance of zero within the system and can use my knowledge to explain the link between a digit, its place and its value. Benchmarks • Reads, writes, orders and recites whole numbers to 1000, starting from any number in the sequence. • Counts forwards and backwards in 2s, 5s, 10s and 100s. • Identifies the value of each digit in a whole number with three digits; for example, 867 = 800 + 60 + 7. • Adds and subtracts multiples of 10 and 100 to or from any whole number to 1000. • Demonstrates understanding of zero as a place holder in whole numbers to 1000.
2	Estimation and rounding	1.1 Rounding	MNU 1-01a • I can share ideas with others to develop ways of estimating the answer to a calculation or problem, work out the actual answer, then check my solution by comparing it with the estimate. Benchmarks • Rounds whole numbers to the nearest 10 and 100 and uses this routinely to estimate and check the reasonableness of a solution.
3	Mathematics, its impact on the world, past, present and future	9.1 Mathematicians and early number systems	MTH 1-12a • I have discussed the important part that numbers play in the world and explored a variety of systems that have been used by civilisations throughout history to record numbers. Benchmarks • Investigates and shares understanding of the importance of numbers in learning, life and work. • Investigates and shares understanding of a variety of number systems used throughout history.

1C Block	Textbook 1C Chapter	Textbook 1C Units	Benchmark/E&O
4	Time	7.1 Use a calendar to plan events 7.2 Recording time 7.3 Convert digital to analogue	MNU 1-10a MNU 1-10b MNU 1-10c • I can tell the time using 12-hour clocks, realising there is a link with 24-hour notation, explain how it impacts on my daily routine and ensure that I am organised and ready for events throughout my day. • I can use a calendar to plan and be organised for key events for myself and my class throughout the year. • I have begun to develop a sense of how long tasks take by measuring the time taken to complete a range of activities using a variety of timers. Benchmarks • Tells the time using half past, quarter past and quarter to using analogue and digital 12-hour clocks. • Records 12-hour times using a.m. and p.m. and is able to identify 24-hour notation; for example, on a mobile phone or computer. • Records the date in a variety of ways, using words and numbers. • Uses and interprets a variety of calendars and 12-hour timetables to plan key events. • Knows the number of seconds in a minute, minutes in an hour, hours in a day, days in each month, weeks and days in a year. • Orders the months of the year and relates these to the appropriate seasons. • Selects and uses appropriate timers for specific purposes.
5	Number – order and place value	2.7 Standard place value partitioning of three-digit numbers 2.8 Non-standard place value partitioning of two-digit numbers 2.9 Comparing two- and three-digit numbers 2.10 Ordering two- and three-digit numbers 2.11 Ordinal numbers	MNU 1-02a • I have investigated how whole numbers are constructed, can understand the importance of zero within the system and can use my knowledge to explain the link between a digit, its place and its value. MTH 1-15a I can compare, describe and show number relationships, using appropriate vocabulary and the symbols for equals, not equal to, less than and greater than. Benchmarks • Identifies the value of each digit in a whole number with three digits; for example, 867 = 800 + 60 + 7. • Demonstrates understanding of zero as a place holder in whole numbers to 1000. • Reads, writes, orders and recites whole numbers to 1000, starting from any number in the sequence. • Understands and accurately uses the terms 'equal to', 'not equal to', 'less than', greater than', and related symbols (=, ≠, <, >) when comparing quantities.

1C Block	Textbook 1C Chapter	Textbook 1C Units	Benchmark/E&O
6	2D shapes and 3D objects	12.1 Sorting 3D objects 12.2 Plan drawings 12.3 Tiling patterns	MTH 1-16a MTH 1-16b • I have explored simple 3D objects and 2D shapes and can identify, name and describe their features using appropriate vocabulary. • I can explore and discuss how and why different shapes fit together and create a tiling pattern with them. Benchmarks • Names, identifies and classifies a range of simple 2D shapes and 3D objects and recognises these shapes in different orientations and sizes. • Uses mathematical language to describe the properties of a range of common 2D shapes and 3D objects including side, face, edge, vertex, base and angle. • Identifies 2D shapes within 3D objects and recognises 3D objects from 2D drawings. • Identifies examples of tiling in the environment and applies knowledge of the features of 2D shapes to create tiling patterns incorporating two different shapes.

1C Block	Textbook 1C Chapter	Textbook 1C Units	Benchmark/E&O
7	Number – addition and subtraction	3.1 Adding and subtracting a one-digit number to and from a three-digit number 3.2 Adding and subtracting 10 and 100 3.3 Adding and subtracting multiples of 10 and 100 3.4 Number bonds to 100 3.5 Doubling and halving 3.6 Adding a string of numbers 3.7 Adding and subtracting 8 or 9 using round and adjust	MNU 1-02a • I have investigated how whole numbers are constructed, can understand the importance of zero within the system and can use my knowledge to explain the link between a digit, its place and its value. MNU 1-03a • I can use addition, subtraction, multiplication and division when solving problems, making best use of the mental strategies and written skills I have developed. Benchmarks • Count forwards and backwards in 2s, 5s, 10s, 100s. • Identifies the value of each digit in a whole number with three digits; for example, 867 = 800 + 60 + 7. • Identifies the value of each digit in a whole number with three digits; for example, 867 = 800 + 60 + 7. • Uses correct mathematical vocabulary when discussing the four operations including subtract, add, sum of, total, multiply, produce, divide and shared equally. • Demonstrates understanding of the commutative law; for example, 6 + 3 = 3 + 6 or 2 × 4 = 4 × 2. • Adds and subtracts multiples of 10 or 100 to or from any whole number to 1000. • Applies knowledge of inverse operations (addition and subtraction; multiplication and division). • Use multiplication and division facts to solve problems within the number range 0 to 1000. • Solves addition and subtraction problems with three-digit whole numbers.

<table>
<tr><th>1C Block</th><th>Textbook 1C Chapter</th><th>Textbook 1C Units</th><th>Benchmark/E&O</th></tr>
<tr><td>8</td><td>Data handling and analysis</td><td>14.1 Collect, organise and display data
14.2 Use data to create Carroll and Venn diagrams
14.3 Use data to check and verify information
14.4 Solve problems using data, graphs and diagrams</td><td>MNU 1-20a
MNU 1-20b
MTH 1-21a
• I have explored a variety of ways in which data is presented and can ask and answer questions about the information it contains.
• I have used a range of ways to collect information and can sort it in a logical, organised and imaginative way using my own and others' criteria.
• Using technology and other methods, I can display data simply, clearly and accurately by creating tables, charts and diagrams, using simple labelling and scale.

Benchmarks
• Asks and answers questions to extract key information from a variety of data sets including charts, diagrams, bar graphs and tables.
• Selects and uses the most appropriate way to gather and sort data for a given purpose; for example, a survey, questionnaire or group tallies.
• Uses a variety of different methods, including the use of digital technologies, to display data; for example, as block graphs, bar graphs, tables, Carroll diagrams and Venn diagrams.
• Includes a suitable title, simple labelling on both axes and an appropriate scale where one unit represents more than one data value in graphs.</td></tr>
<tr><td>9</td><td>Ideas of chance and uncertainty</td><td>15.1 Using data to predict the outcome</td><td>MNU 1-22a
• I can use appropriate vocabulary to describe the likelihood of events occurring, using the knowledge and experiences of myself and others to guide me.

Benchmarks
• Uses mathematical vocabulary appropriately to describe the likelihood of events occurring in everyday situations including, probable, likely/unlikely, certain/uncertain, possible/impossible, and fair/unfair.
• Interprets data gathered through everyday experiences to make reasonable predictions of the likelihood of an event occurring.</td></tr>
</table>

1C Block	Textbook 1C Chapter	Textbook 1C Units	Benchmark/E&O
10	Number – addition and subtraction	3.8 Solving number problems 3.9 Solving word problems 3.10 Adding two- and three-digit numbers 3.11 Subtracting two-digit numbers from three-digit numbers 3.12 Adding three-digit numbers 3.13 Subtracting three-digit numbers	MNU 1-02a • I have investigated how whole numbers are constructed, can understand the importance of zero within the system and can use my knowledge to explain the link between a digit, its place and its value. MNU 1-03a • I can use addition, subtraction, multiplication and division when solving problems, making best use of the mental strategies and written skills I have developed. Benchmarks • Identifies the value of each digit in a whole number with three digits; for example, 867 = 800 + 60 + 7. • Uses correct mathematical vocabulary when discussing the four operations including subtract, add, sum of, total, multiply, produce, divide and shared equally. • Solves addition and subtraction problems with three-digit whole numbers. • Adds and subtracts multiples of 10 or 100 to or from any whole number to 1000. • Demonstrates understanding of the commutative law; for example, 6 + 3 = 3 + 6 or 2 × 4 = 4 × 2. • Applies knowledge of inverse operations (addition and subtraction; multiplication and division).

1C Block	Textbook 1C Chapter	Textbook 1C Units	Benchmark/E&O
11	Number – multiplication and division	4.1 Dividing by skip counting 4.2 Dividing with remainders 4.3 Solving multiplication problems	MNU 1-03a I can use addition, subtraction, multiplication and division when solving problems, making best use of the mental strategies and written skills I have developed. Benchmarks • Counts forwards and backwards in 2s, 5s, 10s and 100s. • Demonstrates understanding of the commutative law; for example, $6 + 3 = 3 + 6$ or $2 \times 4 = 4 \times 2$. • Applies strategies to determine multiplication facts; for example, repeated addition, grouping, arrays and multiplication facts. • Applies strategies to determine division facts; for example, repeated subtraction, equal groups, sharing equally, arrays and multiplication facts. • Uses multiplication and division facts to solve problems within the number range 0 to 1000. • Multiplies and divides whole numbers by 10 and 100 (whole number answers only). • Applies knowledge of inverse operations (addition and subtraction; multiplication and division). • Solves two-step problems.
12	Patterns and relationships	10.1 Continue number patterns and sequences 10.2 Explain the rules for simple number sequences	MTH 1-13a MTH 1-13b • I can continue and devise more involved repeating patterns or designs, using a variety of media. • Through exploring number patterns, I can recognise and continue simple number sequences and can explain the rule I have applied. Benchmarks • Counts forwards and backwards in 2s, 5s and 10s from any whole number up to 1000. • Describes patterns in number; for example, in the multiplication tables and hundred square. • Continues and creates repeating patterns involving shapes, pictures and symbols. • Describes, continues and creates number patterns using addition, subtraction, doubling, halving, counting in jumps (skip counting) and known multiples.

1C Block	Textbook 1C Chapter	Textbook 1C Units	Benchmark/E&O
13	Time	7.4 Use a.m. and p.m. correctly 7.5 12-hour and 24-hour time	MNU 1-10a MNU 1-10b MNU 1-10c • I can tell the time using 12-hour clocks, realising there is a link with 24-hour notation, explain how it impacts on my daily routine and ensure that I am organised and ready for events throughout my day. • I can use a calendar to plan and be organised for key events for myself and my class throughout the year. • I have begun to develop a sense of how long tasks take by measuring the time taken to complete a range of activities using a variety of timers. Benchmarks • Tells the time using half past, quarter past and quarter to using analogue and digital 12-hour clocks. • Records 12-hour times using a.m. and p.m. and is able to identify 24-hour notation; for example, on a mobile phone or computer. • Records the date in a variety of ways, using words and numbers. • Uses and interprets a variety of calendars and 12-hour timetables to plan key events. • Knows the number of seconds in a minute, minutes in an hour, hours in a day, days in each month, weeks and days in a year. • Orders the months of the year and relates these to the appropriate seasons. • Selects and uses appropriate timers for specific purposes.

1C Block	Textbook 1C Chapter	Textbook 1C Units	Benchmark/E&O
14	Number – multiplication and division	4.4 Multiplying by 100 4.5 Dividing by 100 4.6 Linking multiplication and division 4.7 Recalling multiplication and division facts for 2, 5 and 10 4.8 Multiplying and dividing using known facts	MNU 1-03a I can use addition, subtraction, multiplication and division when solving problems, making best use of the mental strategies and written skills I have developed. Benchmarks • Counts forwards and backwards in 2s, 5s, 10s and 100s. • Demonstrates understanding of the commutative law; for example, $6 + 3 = 3 + 6$ or $2 \times 4 = 4 \times 2$. • Applies strategies to determine multiplication facts; for example, repeated addition, grouping, arrays and multiplication facts. • Applies strategies to determine division facts; for example, repeated subtraction, equal groups, sharing equally, arrays and multiplication facts. • Uses multiplication and division facts to solve problems within the number range 0 to 1000. • Multiplies and divides whole numbers by 10 and 100 (whole number answers only). • Applies knowledge of inverse operations (addition and subtraction; multiplication and division). • Solves two-step problems.
15	Expressions and equations	11.1 Completing number sentences	MTH 1-15a MTH 1-15b • I can compare, describe and show number relationships, using appropriate vocabulary and the symbols for equals, not equal to, less than and greater than. • When a picture or symbol is used to replace a number in a number statement, I can find its value using my knowledge of number facts and explain my thinking to others. Benchmarks • Understands and accurately uses the terms 'equal to', 'not equal to', 'less than', 'greater than', and the related symbols (=, ≠ ,) when comparing quantities. • Applies understanding of the equals sign as a balance, and knowledge of number facts, to solve simple algebraic problems where a picture or symbol is used to represent a number; for example: ♦ + 17 = 30 and ♦ × 6 = 30.

1C Block	Textbook 1C Chapter	Textbook 1C Units	Benchmark/E&O
16	Angles, symmetry and transformation	13.1 Identifying angles 13.2 Half and quarter turns 13.3 Using compass points 13.4 Grid references 13.5 Symmetry	MTH 1-17a MTH 1-18a MTH 1-19a • I can describe, follow and record routes and journeys using signs, words and angles associated with direction and turning. • I have developed an awareness of where grid reference systems are used in everyday contexts and can use them to locate and describe position. • I have explored symmetry in my own and the wider environment and can create and recognise symmetrical pictures, patterns and shapes. Benchmarks • Uses technology and other methods to describe, follow and record directions using words associated with angles, directions and turns including, full turn, half turn, quarter turn, clockwise, anticlockwise, right turn, left turn, right angle. • Knows that a right angle is 90°. • Knows and uses the compass points, north, south, east and west. • Uses informal methods to estimate, compare and describe the size of angles in relation to a right angle. • Finds right-angles in the environment and in well-known 2D shapes. • Identifies where and why grid references are used. • Describes, plots and uses accurate two-figure grid references, demonstrating knowledge of the horizontal and vertical location. • Identifies symmetry in patterns, pictures, nature and 2D shapes. • Creates symmetrical pictures and designs with more than one line of symmetry.

1C Block	Textbook 1C Chapter	Textbook 1C Units	Benchmark/E&O
17	Fractions, decimals fractions and percentages	5.1 Finding part of a set 5.2 Making a whole 5.3 Ordering fractions 5.4 Adding and subtracting fractions	MNU 1-07a MNU 1-07b MTH 1-07c • Having explored fractions by taking part in practical activities, I can show my understanding of: o how a single item can be shared equally o the notation and vocabulary associated with fractions o where simple fractions lie on the number line. • Through exploring how groups of items can be shared equally, I can find a fraction of an amount by applying my knowledge of division. • Through taking part in practical activities including use of pictorial representations, I can demonstrate my understanding of simple fractions which are equivalent. Benchmarks • Explains what a fraction is using concrete materials, pictorial representations and appropriate mathematical vocabulary. • Demonstrates understanding that the greater the number of equal parts, the smaller the size of each share. • Uses the correct notation for common fractions to tenths; for example, $\frac{1}{2}$, $\frac{2}{3}$ and $\frac{5}{8}$. • Compares the size of fractions and places simple fractions in order on a number line. • Uses pictorial representations and other models to demonstrate understanding of simple equivalent fractions; for example, $\frac{1}{2} = \frac{2}{4} = \frac{3}{6}$. • Explains the role of the numerator and denominator. • Uses known multiplication and division facts and other strategies to find unit fractions of whole numbers; for example, $\frac{1}{2}$ or $\frac{1}{4}$.
18	Estimation and rounding	1.2 Estimating the answer by rounding	MNU 1-01a • I can share ideas with others to develop ways of estimating the answer to a calculation or problem, work out the actual answer, then check my solution by comparing it with the estimate. Benchmarks • Uses strategies to estimate an answer to a calculation or problem; for example, doubling and rounding. • Rounds whole numbers to the nearest 10 and 100 and uses this routinely to estimate and check the reasonableness of a solution.

1C Block	Textbook 1C Chapter	Textbook 1C Units	Benchmark/E&O
19	Number – addition and subtraction	3.14 Representing and solving word problems 3.15 Two-step word problems	MNU 1-03a • I can use addition, subtraction, multiplication and division when solving problems, making best use of the mental strategies and written skills I have developed. Benchmarks • Uses correct mathematical vocabulary when discussing the four operations including subtract, add, sum of, total, multiply, produce, divide and shared equally. • Demonstrates understanding of the commutative law; for example, $6 + 3 = 3 + 6$ or $2 \times 4 = 4 \times 2$. • Solves addition and subtraction problems with three-digit whole numbers. • Adds and subtracts multiples of 10 or 100 to or from any whole number to 1000. • Applies knowledge of inverse operations (addition and subtraction; multiplication and division). • Solves two-step problems.
20	Number – multiplication and division	4.9 Solving number problems	MNU 1-03a I can use addition, subtraction, multiplication and division when solving problems, making best use of the mental strategies and written skills I have developed. Benchmarks • Counts forwards and backwards in 2s, 5s, 10s and 100s. • Demonstrates understanding of the commutative law; for example, $6 + 3 = 3 + 6$ or $2 \times 4 = 4 \times 2$. • Applies strategies to determine multiplication facts; for example, repeated addition, grouping, arrays and multiplication facts. • Applies strategies to determine division facts; for example, repeated subtraction, equal groups, sharing equally, arrays and multiplication facts. • Uses multiplication and division facts to solve problems within the number range 0 to 1000. • Multiplies and divides whole numbers by 10 and 100 (whole number answers only). • Applies knowledge of inverse operations (addition and subtraction; multiplication and division). • Solves two-step problems.

1C Block	Textbook 1C Chapter	Textbook 1C Units	Benchmark/E&O
21	Money	6.1 Recording amounts 6.2 Adding amounts 6.3 Calculating change	MNU 1-09a MNU 1-09b • I can use money to pay for items and can work out how much change I should receive. • I have investigated how different combinations of coins and notes can be used to pay for goods or be given in change. Benchmarks • Identifies and uses all coins and notes to £20 and explores different ways of making the same total. • Records amounts accurately in different ways using the correct notation; for example, 149p = £1·49 and 7p = £0·07. • Uses a variety of coin and note combinations, to pay for items and give change within £10. • Applies mental agility number skills to calculate the total spent in a shopping situation and is able to calculate change. • Demonstrates awareness of how goods can be paid for using cards and digital technology.

1C Block	Textbook 1C Chapter	Textbook 1C Units	Benchmark/E&O
22	Fractions, decimals fractions and percentages	5.5 Creating equivalent fractions 5.6 Comparing fractions 5.7 Find a fraction of an amount 5.8 Sharing one whole	MNU 1-07a MNU 1-07b MTH 1-07c • Having explored fractions by taking part in practical activities, I can show my understanding of: o how a single item can be shared equally o the notation and vocabulary associated with fractions o where simple fractions lie on the number line. • Through exploring how groups of items can be shared equally, I can find a fraction of an amount by applying my knowledge of division. • Through taking part in practical activities including use of pictorial representations, I can demonstrate my understanding of simple fractions that are equivalent. Benchmarks • Explains what a fraction is using concrete materials, pictorial representations and appropriate mathematical vocabulary. • Demonstrates understanding that the greater the number of equal parts, the smaller the size of each share. • Uses the correct notation for common fractions to tenths; for example, $\frac{1}{2}$, $\frac{2}{3}$ and $\frac{5}{8}$. • Compares the size of fractions and places simple fractions in order on a number line. • Uses pictorial representations and other models to demonstrate understanding of simple equivalent fractions; for example, $\frac{1}{2} = \frac{2}{4} = \frac{3}{6}$. • Explains the role of the numerator and denominator. • Uses known multiplication and division facts and other strategies to find unit fractions of whole numbers; for example, $\frac{1}{2}$ or $\frac{1}{4}$.

1C Block	Textbook 1C Chapter	Textbook 1C Units	Benchmark/E&O
23	Measurement	8.1 Reading and recording measurements – length 8.2 Measuring and recording length – millimetres 8.3 Converting length – millimetres and centimetres 8.4 Reading and recording measurements for mass 8.5 Reading and recording measurements for capacity 8.6 Converting standard units 8.7 Area of shapes 8.8 Creating areas 8.9 Area and arrays	MNU 1-11a MNU 1-11b • I can estimate how long or heavy an object is, or what amount it holds, using everyday things as a guide, then measure or weigh it using appropriate instruments and units. • I can estimate the area of a shape by counting squares or other methods. Benchmarks • Uses knowledge of everyday objects to provide reasonable estimates of length, height, mass and capacity. • Makes accurate use of a range of instruments including rulers, metre sticks, digital scales and measuring jugs when measuring lengths, heights, mass and capacities using the most appropriate instrument for the task. • Records measurements of length, height, mass and capacity to the nearest standard unit; for example, millimetres (mm), centimetres (cm), grams (g), kilograms (kg), millilitres (ml), litres (l). • Compares measures with estimates. • Uses knowledge of relationships between units of measure to make simple conversions; for example, 1 m 58 cm = 158 cm. • Reads a variety of scales on measuring devices including those with simple fractions; for example, ½ litre. • Uses square grids to estimate then measure the areas of a variety of simple 2D shapes to the nearest half square. • Creates shapes with a given area to the nearest half square using square tiles or grids. • Recognises that different shapes can have the same area (conservation of area).

1 Estimation and rounding

Estimation and rounding 1A

Section overview

Textbook 1A units	Review units	Prior learning	Benchmarks/Es&Os
Unit 1.1 Estimating and comparing collections	**1A** Unit 2.1	• I can count forwards to at least 20. • I can form and count a collection of up to 20 items. • I know number names and symbols up to at least 20.	**MNU 1-01a** • Uses strategies to estimate an answer to a calculation or problem; for example, doubling and rounding.
Unit 1.2 Estimating and describing collections	**1A** Unit 2.1	• I can count forwards to at least 20. • I can form and count a collection of up to 20 items. • I know number names and symbols up to at least 20.	**MNU 1-01a** • Uses strategies to estimate an answer to a calculation or problem; for example, doubling and rounding. • Rounds whole numbers to the nearest 10 and 100 and uses this routinely to estimate and check the reasonableness of a solution.
Unit 1.3 Estimating and grouping collections	**1A** Units 2.1, 2.2 and 2.4	• I can count forwards to 100. • I can count backwards from 100. • I know number names and symbols up to 100.	**MNU 1-01a** • Uses strategies to estimate an answer to a calculation or problem; for example, doubling and rounding. • Rounds whole numbers to the nearest 10 and 100 and uses this routinely to estimate and check the reasonableness of a solution.

Conceptual context

In daily life we routinely use estimating to help us make decisions, such as whether we have enough of something or not, sharing, or making quick approximations. Pupils first need to have a secure understanding of what we mean by a collection of objects and have wide experience of counting and sorting different objects to make collections. It is essential at this stage that they have knowledge of forward and backward number sequences to at least 20, and can read, write and sequence numerals to 20.

Pupils also need to understand the language used in comparing collections, such as bigger, smaller, greater, fewer, less than, or more than. It is important they have experience of using these terms when comparing a range of different concrete materials. This can easily be achieved through daily routines such as sorting pots of pencils or pens, as well as through maths activities.

Unit 1.1 explores the idea of sorting collections into rows to enable them to be easily compared. At this stage, the focus is on the ideas of bigger/smaller rather than on counting the collections. This is extended in Unit 1.2 using ten frames and number lines to estimate if numbers are closer to 10 or to 0, which introduces an early concept of rounding. Using ten frames and concrete materials allows pupils to develop an idea of number size and to physically see if a number is closer to 10 or 0; using a number line helps them to see this idea in a linear way. Equipment, such as bead strings, can also be useful to further help develop this idea.

In Unit 1.3, the idea of grouping objects into fives and tens is introduced as a way of quickly estimating amounts. Ten frames are an ideal resource to develop this using concrete materials. For example, using ten frames to represent numbers such as 14 or 22, pupils can quickly use their knowledge of fives and tens to estimate the size of the collection.

Resources

- A range of different concrete counting materials, such as counters, dinosaurs, teddies, etc.
- Bead strings
- Blank ten frames
- Numeral cards 0–20
- Number lines 0–20
- Rekenreks

Key vocabulary

- **Approximately**
- **Collection**
- **Estimate**
- **Fewer**
- **Guess**
- **Less**
- **More**
- **Roughly**
- **Round**

Misconceptions

Potential misconception	Addressing the misconception
Unit 1.1 Pupils may lack understanding of the terms bigger, smaller, more and less.	Ensure pupils are given lots of opportunities to count different types of collections of materials. Discuss meaning of which has more or less, or which is bigger or smaller by physically comparing the collections.
Unit 1.2 Pupils may lack understanding of number order when trying to estimate if a number is closer to 10 or 0.	**Review Unit 2.1** Ensure pupils are given lots of practice with number word sequences, both forwards and backwards. Practise sequencing numeral cards in order from smallest to biggest and vice versa.
Unit 1.3 Pupils might not be able to efficiently group into fives and tens.	Ensure pupils have lots of practice with five frames and ten frames to allow them to group collections into fives and tens.

Teaching ideas

Unit 1.1 Estimating and comparing collections

- Show pupils two collections of counting objects: one that contains 12 elephants grouped randomly, the other that contains 14 dinosaurs grouped randomly. **Which collection is bigger?** Encourage pupils to make a prediction. Discuss why it is hard to tell which has more. **How could we sort them to make it easier to see which is bigger?**
- Sort the two collections into rows. **Which do you think is bigger now?** Discuss how sorting into rows makes it easier to compare the collections.
- Repeat with a wide range of examples using different materials.

Unit 1.2 Estimating and describing collections

- Show pupils a numeral card: '8'. **Is this number closer to 10 or 0?** Explain that we can use ten frames to help us to decide. Count out 8 counters. Show a blank ten frame and ask a pupil to fill out the top row first with 5 counters. Now put the remaining counters on the bottom row. **Do you think 8 is closer to 10 or to 0? How do we know?** Ask the pupils: **How many counters would we need to be half way between 0 and 10?** Check pupils' understanding that the answer is 5. Explain that if we have half, or more, we can say that the number is closer to 10; if we have less than half, the number is closer to 0. Repeat with different examples using numbers up to 10.
- Explain that we can also use a number line to help us to decide. Show a number line from 0 to 10 and point to different numbers. **Is 2 closer to 10 or to 0? What about 4? 6?** A large number line could be made that would allow pupils to physically stand on the number line and decide if they are closer to 10 or to 0 for a fun alternative.

Unit 1.3 Estimating and grouping collections

- Show pupils a collection of 18 counting objects, such as teddy bears, arranged randomly. **Can you estimate how many there are?** Explain that we can arrange them into groups of 5 and 10 to make it easier. Show two blank ten frames and model sorting the teddies into rows of 5 using the ten frames.

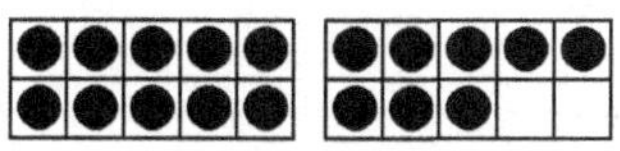

Is it easier to estimate how many now? How many can you see? Why is it easier now?

Explain that grouping collections into fives or tens helps us to estimate quickly. Repeat with a wide range of examples.

Estimation and rounding 1B

Section overview

Textbook 1B units	Review units	Prior learning	Benchmarks/Es&Os
Unit 1.1 Rounding to the nearest 10	**1A** Units 1.1, 1.2 and 1.3 Units 2.2, 2.3, 2.5 and 2.7	• I can count forwards and backwards to 100. • I know number names and symbols up to 100. • I can read and write decade numbers up to 100. • I can sequence decade numbers up to 100.	**MNU 1-01a** • Uses strategies to estimate an answer to a calculation or problem; for example, doubling and rounding. • Rounds whole numbers to the nearest 10 and 100 and uses this routinely to estimate and check the reasonableness of a solution.
Unit 1.2 Estimating the answer by rounding	**1A** Units 1.1, 1.2 and 1.3 Units 2.2, 2.3,2.5 and 2.7	• I can count forwards and backwards to 100. • I know number names and symbols up to 100. • I can read and write decade numbers up to 100. • I can sequence decade numbers up to 100.	**MNU 1-01a** • Uses strategies to estimate an answer to a calculation or problem; for example, doubling and rounding. • Rounds whole numbers to the nearest 10 and 100 and uses this routinely to estimate and check the reasonableness of a solution.

Conceptual context

At this stage, pupils should have a secure understanding of estimating the size of collections, as well as forward and backward number sequences to 100, and reading, writing and sequencing numerals to 100. It is also important that they understand decade numbers and can count, sequence and order decade numbers to 100.

Rounding the nearest 10 is introduced in Unit 1.1. Pupils should have lots of experience using number lines to find 2-digit numbers and be able to identify the multiples of 10 on either side to allow them to develop this understanding. They should also have opportunities to draw their own empty number lines for given multiples of 10 and have practice of finding half-way points between them:

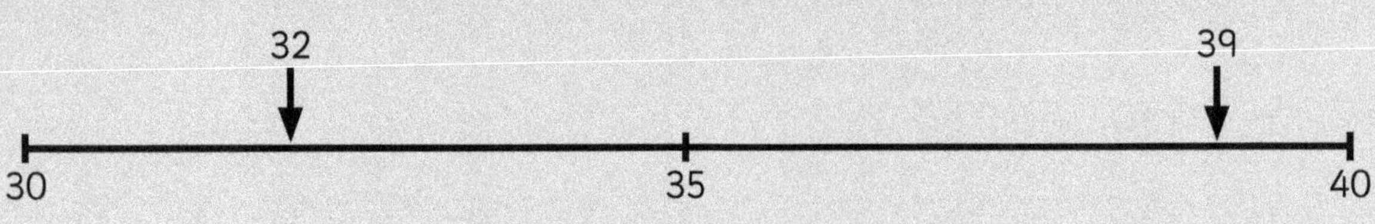

This experience is vital to ensure that pupils use their knowledge of number size and value to round, rather than following a rule to round up or down without a deeper understanding.

At this stage, pupils should also be introduced to the idea that the context of a problem affects whether we round up or down. Explain that we usually follow the convention of rounding up for numbers that end in 5 or more; however, there are some contexts where we might round down or up. Examples, such as budgeting with money, where we have £59 and we want to estimate the number of £10 tickets that can be bought, illustrate that in this case it is best to round down because we can't use the excess. Estimating the number of egg boxes needed for 62 eggs illustrates that in this case it is best to always round up because a box is needed even where it is not full. Pupils should understand that the context of the problem matters and that they should therefore not blindly follow a rule when rounding.

Pupils then apply their knowledge of rounding to the nearest 10 to estimate the answer to problems in Unit 1.2. It is important that pupils gain confidence in estimating and value this skill in checking answers, rather than worrying about 'guessing right or wrong'. Modelling examples where an answer is worked out incorrectly and pupils can use estimating to identify the mistake, or where there are two possible answers for pupils to evaluate, are very useful in building this confidence and sense of the value in developing rounding and estimating as a skill that can be used routinely in all areas of maths.

Resources

- Arrow cards
- Money – £10 notes and £1 coins
- Number lines 0–100
- Numeral cards 0–100
- Place value materials, such as bundles of sticks

Key vocabulary

- **Approximately**
- **Collection**
- **Estimate**
- **Fewer**
- **Guess**
- **Less**
- **More**
- **Roughly**
- **Round**

Misconceptions

Potential misconception	Addressing the misconception
Units 1.1 and 1.2 Pupils may be unclear of multiples of 10 on either side of a 2-digit number, or they may be unable to accurately estimate where the number would be placed on a number line. They might not understand where the half-way point between two multiples of 10 lies.	Ensure pupils have lots of experience with number lines or numeral rolls to find numbers and identify the multiples of 10 on either side of a 2-digit number. Model finding the half-way point for lots of examples and make sure pupils make the connection that the half-way point ends in 5 each time. Allow lots of opportunities for pupils to draw their own empty number lines and place numbers between multiples of 10. For example, draw a number line from 20 to 30 and place numbers such as 28 or 24 on their number line.
Units 1.1 and 1.2 Pupils might not understand what each digit in a number represents.	Use materials to represent the amounts, such as sticks bundled into tens and loose ones.

Teaching ideas

Unit 1.1 Rounding to the nearest 10

- Show a number line to 100. **Where is 40? Where is 50? What number is exactly half way between 40 and 50?** Check understanding this is 45. **Where would I find 48? Is it closer to 40 or 50? How do you know?** Check understanding that 48 is closer to 50 because it is more than half way. Explain that when we round to the nearest 10 we find the multiples of 10 on either side, then decide which 10 the number is closer to. In this case we round up to 50.

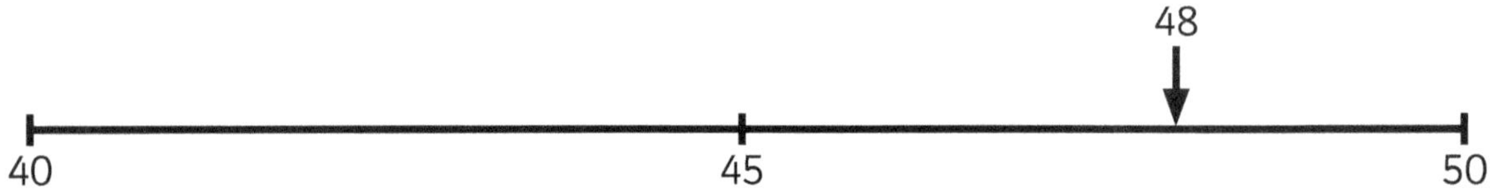

- Ask pupils to draw an empty number line on mini whiteboards that starts at 60 and finishes at 70. Ask them to write in the number that is half way between 60 and 70. Check understanding that 65 is half way between 60 and 70. **Can you write in the number 62 on your number line?** Check placement of 62 and ask pupils to check they are right by counting on their empty number line. **Is 62 closer to 60 or 70? What would 62 be rounded to the nearest 10?** Check understanding that in this case we round down to 60. **What would 65 be rounded to the nearest 10?** Explain that we usually round up when the number is 5 or more, but there might be some contexts where we might round down. Give an example such as: **If we had £65, and it cost £10 each to go to the cinema, how many tickets could we buy?** Check understanding that in this case we can't use the extra £5 so we would round down to £60.
- Repeat for a wide range of examples, ensuring that pupils are using their understanding of number size, rather than just following a rule for rounding up or down. Asking the pupils to place the number on an empty number line is a good way of assessing this understanding.

Unit 1.2 Estimating the answer by rounding

- Give a problem such as: **Amman has £51 and he wants to buy a game that costs £18. He estimates he will have approximately £30 left. Is he correct?** Explain that rounding to the nearest 10 is a useful way to quickly estimate the answer. **What is £51 rounded to the nearest 10?** Check understanding and record 50. **What is £18 rounded to the nearest 10?** Check understanding and record 20. Work out 50 – 20 to get an estimate of £30. Amman was correct.
- Repeat with a wide range of different examples, checking pupils' understanding of rounding to quickly estimate answers.

Estimation and rounding 1C

Section overview

Textbook 1C units	Review units	Prior learning	Benchmarks/Es&Os
Unit 1.1 Rounding	**1B** Unit 1.1 Units 2.2, 2.3, 2.4 and 2.6	• I can count forwards and backwards to 1000. • I know number names and symbols up to 1000. • I can read and write decade numbers up to 1000. • I can sequence tens and hundreds up to 1000.	**MNU 1-01a** • Uses strategies to estimate an answer to a calculation or problem; for example, doubling and rounding. • Rounds whole numbers to the nearest 10 and 100 and uses this routinely to estimate and check the reasonableness of a solution.
Unit 1.2 Estimating the answer by rounding	**1B** Unit 1.2 Units 2.2, 2.3, 2.4 and 2.6	• I can count forwards and backwards to 1000. • I know number names and symbols up to 1000. • I can read and write decade numbers up to 1000. • I can sequence tens and hundreds up to 1000.	**MNU 1-01a** • Uses strategies to estimate an answer to a calculation or problem; for example, doubling and rounding. • Rounds whole numbers to the nearest 10 and 100 and uses this routinely to estimate and check the reasonableness of a solution.

Conceptual context

At this stage, pupils should have a secure understanding of rounding to 10 and understand that we can apply rounding to quickly estimate the answer to a problem. It is important that pupils have a sound knowledge of forward and backward number sequences and can read, write and sequence numerals up to 1000. They also need to be able to count and sequence tens and hundreds up to 1000.

Unit 1.1 introduces rounding to the nearest 100. A strong knowledge of place value is needed at this point, with pupils able to clearly explain the value of each digit in 3-digit numbers. When rounding to the nearest 100, pupils should have wide experience using number lines to identify the multiples of 100 on either side of a given number. It is useful to give pupils lots of practice drawing their own empty number lines, identifying the half-way point and placing given numbers on the number line to ensure that they have a strong understanding of number value. They need to understand that they find the multiple of 100 that is closest when making the decision to round up or round down. Experience with number lines ensures that pupils base their decision on their knowledge of number size and value, rather than simply following a rule without understanding why they are doing so. It is also important that they understand that the context of a problem matters and may affect the decision to round up or down, rather than always following the convention of rounding up for numbers ending in 50 or more without thinking more deeply about the problem involved.

In Unit 1.2, pupils apply their knowledge of rounding to the nearest 10 or 100 to estimate if answers are reasonable or not. Again, pupils should be encouraged to look at the context of the problems they are estimating to think about the level of accuracy required, and the ease and speed of estimating. For instance, if estimating how many people attended a concert each evening for a week, rounding to the nearest 100 would probably give reasonable levels of accuracy, but when working out a bill it would be more useful to round to the nearest 10. Pupils should be encouraged to use rounding and estimating to quickly check their answers as a matter of routine at this point, and understand that estimating is an important skill in many aspects of daily life.

Resources

- Arrow cards
- Money – mock £100 and £10 notes and £1 coins
- Number lines 0–100
- Numeral cards 0–100
- Place value materials

Key vocabulary

- **Approximately**
- **Collection**
- **Estimate**
- **Fewer**
- **Guess**
- **Less**
- **More**
- **Roughly**
- **Round**

Misconceptions

Potential misconception	Addressing the misconception
Units 1.1 and 1.2 The pupil might not understand which digit in the number to look at to determine whether to round up or down. For example, 362 rounded down to 300 (pupil is using last digit to round incorrectly).	Write number on an empty number line and ask them which multiple of 100 the number is between and how they decide which multiple is nearer to the number. Ask them which digit helps them decide.
Units 1.1 and 1.2 Pupils might not understand what each digit in a number represents.	Use place value materials to represent the amounts. Review understanding of place value.
Units 1.1 and 1.2 Pupils may not understand that the context matters when rounding.	Give a problem based on a real-life context, such as 'Finlay has £47 and is estimating how many friends he can take on a trip if tickets cost £10 each.' In this problem he can't use the extra £7 as it's not enough for a ticket, so rounds down to £40 rather than the usual convention of rounding up for numbers ending in 5 or over.

Teaching ideas

Unit 1.1 Rounding to the nearest 100

- Give examples of 2-digit numbers and check understanding of rounding to the nearest 10. Write the number 362 on the board. Draw an empty number line from 300 to 400. Point to the half-way point between 300 and 400 on the number line. **What number would this be?** Check understanding that this would be 350. Ask pupils to count in tens from 300 to 400, pointing to the number line to indicate the placing of each ten as they count. **Where would 362 be?** Check understanding of placement of number on number line. **Which hundred is it closest to?**

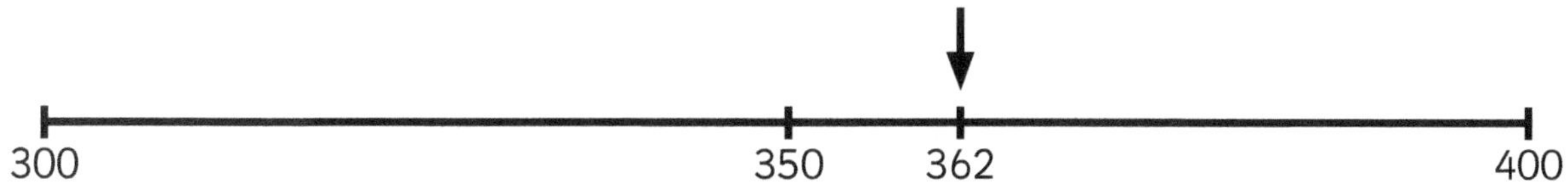

Check understanding that it is closer to 400. Explain that when we round to the nearest 100 we find the multiples of 100 on either side, then find the 100 to which the number is closest to decide whether to round up or down. In this case we round up to 400.

- Ask pupils to draw their own empty number line on mini whiteboards. **Which multiples of 100 are on either side of this number?** Show '519'. Check understanding that 500 and 600 are multiples of 100 on either side. Ask pupils to mark the half-way point. **What is this number?** Check understanding this is 550. **Which hundred is 510 closest to? Would we round up or round down?**
- Repeat for a wide range of examples. Ask pupils to think of examples in daily life when we might need to round to the nearest 100 (for example, budgeting or converting measurements). Remind them that if a number ends in 50 or above the convention is that we usually round up, but that the context of the problem is important and affects whether we round up or round down.

Unit 1.2 Estimating the answer using rounding

- Give an example of a problem, such as checking a bill in a restaurant. **Isla's mum took Isla and her sister to lunch. They ordered pasta, which cost £9; steak and chips, which cost £18; and fish, which cost £12. Their drinks cost £8. The total cost of the bill was £119. Isla thinks this is too much!**

  Ask the pupils to estimate the cost of the bill by rounding to the nearest 10. Check understanding that this comes to £10, £20, £10 and £10 with a total estimate of £50. The bill is clearly too much!
- Try another problem, such as: **Nuria investigates the price of a holiday. It costs £482 per adult and £235 per child. How much would it cost for 2 adults and 2 children?** Ask the pupils what the best way would be to estimate the total cost. They could estimate by rounding to the nearest 100 to get 2 × £500 and 2 × £200 with a total estimate of £1400. Or they could estimate to the nearest 10 to get £490 × 2 and £240 × 2 giving an estimate of £1460. Discuss which estimate is more accurate and which estimate was easier and quicker to work out. In this case, it was probably easier to round to the nearest 100 to give a useful estimate, but remind pupils that the context of the problem and the numbers involved matter when deciding.
- Repeat with a wide range of relevant examples linked to daily life. Explain that rounding and estimating is a valuable skill to use to work out if an answer is reasonable or not.

Number – order and place value 1A

Section overview

Textbook 1A units	Review units	Prior learning	Benchmarks/ Es&Os
Unit 2.1 Reading and writing numbers (1)	**Early – B** Units 1.2, 1.9 and 1.10	• Recognise the numerals 0–20. • Identify (find within a group) the numerals 0–20. • Read and write the number words (0–10).	**MNU 1-02a** • Reads, writes, orders and recites whole numbers to 1000, starting from any number in the sequence.
Unit 2.2 Counting in tens (1)	**Early – B** Units 1.5, 1.6, 1.7, 1.8, 1.11 and 1.12	• Recall the forward number word sequence (range 0–20). • Recall the backward number word sequence from 10. • Order the numerals from 0 to 9, both forwards and backwards.	**MNU 1-02a** • Counts forwards and backwards in 2s, 5s, 10s and 100s.
Unit 2.3 Reading and writing numbers (2)	**Early – B** Unit 1.9 **1A** Units 2.1 and 2.2	• Read and write the numbers from 0 to 20 in words. • Identify and order the decade numbers in numerals.	**MNU 1-02a** • Reads, writes, orders and recites whole numbers to 1000, starting from any number in the sequence.
Unit 2.4 Forward number sequences (1)	**1A** Unit 2.2	• Count forwards and backwards in tens, from 0 to 100 and from 100 to 0. • Recognise the 1 to 9 sequence within the decade numbers.	**MNU 1-02a** • Reads, writes, orders and recites whole numbers to 1000, starting from any number in the sequence.
Unit 2.5 Forward number sequences (2)	**Early – B** Unit 1.6 **1A** Units 2.1 and 2.4	• Recall the forward number word sequence within the range 0–20. • Recognise and use the 1 to 9 sequence to count in ones between consecutive decade numbers (range 0–100).	**MNU 1-02a** • Reads, writes, orders and recites whole numbers to 1000, starting from any number in the sequence.
Unit 2.6 Backward number sequences (1)	**Early – B** Unit 1.5 **1A** Unit 2.2	• Recall the backward number word sequence from 20 to 0. • Recognise and use the 9 to 1 sequence to count backwards in tens from 100 to 0.	**MNU 1-02a** • Reads, writes, orders and recites whole numbers to 1000, starting from any number in the sequence.

Unit 2.7 Backward number sequences (2)	**Early – B** Unit 1.5 **1A** Unit 2.6	• Recall the backward number word sequence within the range 20–0. • Recognise and use the 9 to 1 sequence to count backwards in ones between consecutive decade numbers (range 100–0).	**MNU 1-02a** • Reads, writes, orders and recites whole numbers to 1000, starting from any number in the sequence.
Unit 2.8 Number before, after and in-between	**Early – B** Units 1.7, 1.8 and 1.13	• Identify the number before, the number after and the missing numbers in a sequence within 20. • Use the language of before, after and in-between.	**MNU 1-02a** • Reads, writes, orders and recites whole numbers to 1000, starting from any number in the sequence.
Unit 2.9 Counting in tens (2)	**1A** Units 2.2, 2.4, 2.5, 2.6 and 2.7	• Count forwards in ones within the range 0–100. • Count backwards in ones within the range 50–0. • Count forwards and backwards in tens on the decade (range 0–100).	**MNU 1-02a** • Counts forwards and backwards in 2s, 5s, 10s and 100s.
Unit 2.10 Base ten for teen numbers	**Early – B** Units 1.11, 1.12 and 1.14	• Read, write and sequence all numerals from 0 to 20. • Explain that zero means there is none of a particular quantity and is represented by the numeral 0.	**MNU 1-02a** • Identifies the value of each digit in a whole number with three digits, for example, 867 = 800 + 60 + 7.
Unit 2.11 Counting in tens and ones	**1A** Units 2.4, 2.5, 2.6, 2.7 and 2.9	• Count forwards in ones within the range 0–100. • Count backwards in ones within the range 50–0. • Count forwards and backwards in tens off the decade (range 0–100).	**MNU 1-02a** • Counts forwards and backwards in 2s, 5s, 10s and 100s. • Identifies the value of each digit in a whole number with three digits; for example, 867 = 800 + 60 + 7.
Unit 2.12 Counting in twos and fives	**Early – B** Units 1.1, 1.2, 1.3 and 1.4 **1A** Units 2.8, 2.11, 4.3 and 4.5	• Use one-to-one correspondence to count a set of up to 20 objects. • Count in tens and ones to find how many in a collection (range 0–100). • Read, write and sequence all numerals within the range 0–50. • Say the forward number word sequence in 2s and 5s.	**MNU 1-02a** • Counts forwards and backwards in 2s, 5s, 10s and 100s.
Unit 2.13 Ordinal numbers	**Early – B** Unit 1.15	• Use ordinal numbers in real-life contexts; for example, 'I am third in the line'. • Recognise and continue simple shape patterns.	**MNU 1-02a** • Reads, writes, orders and recites whole numbers to 1000, starting from any number in the sequence.

Conceptual context

At Early Level, the focus is on reading, identifying (saying the number displayed), recognising (choosing from a set of numbers) and naming the numerals from 0 to 20. Reciting forward number word sequences within the range 0–30 and reciting backward number word sequences within the range 0–20 also feature prominently. All of these ideas are now extended to include numbers within the range 0–100. The decade number names (10, 20, 30, 40, 50, 60, 70, 80, 90, 100) are introduced. Most of these number names do not naturally arise from the number names one to ten and so need to be memorised. Thereafter, an initial focus on the repeating 1–9 pattern within each decade is developed to include examples that cross a decade, for example 49, **50**, 51. Pupils are introduced to reading and writing number words, and previous experiences of ordinal numbers in real-life contexts are extended to include ordinal numbers written in words and symbols within the range first (1st) to tenth (10th).

Place value underpins effective mental and written calculation. At Early Level, the foundations are laid through a focus on the five Counting Principles created by Gelman and Gallistel in 1978 and on the way that numbers are structured, using five and ten as reference points. Pupils are now introduced to counting in twos, fives and tens, both on the decade (20, 30, 40, 50) and off the decade (63, 73, 83, 93), as more efficient ways to determine the total when counting a large quantity. Ten plus facts (for example $10 + 2 = 12$, $10 + 7 = 17$) are also introduced and pave the way for further work on conceptual place value in Books 1B and 1C.

Resources

- 0–100 number line with decade numbers labelled
- 100-bead string per pupil
- A 100-square grid per pupil (numbered 1–100 with 1 in the top-left corner)
- Beads and string for threading
- Bingo cards with decade numbers written in words
- Blank number tracks
- Bundles of straws grouped in tens
- 'Feely bag' or empty box
- Interlocking cubes
- Large 100-bead bar
- Flashcards displaying each of the number words from eleven to twenty
- Flashcards displaying each of the numerals 11–20
- Flashcards displaying each of the decade numbers from 0 to 100
- Flashcards displaying each of the numerals 21–100
- Mini whiteboards
- Place value arrow cards for the numbers 1–10
- Set of five-wise and pair-wise ten frames per pupil
- Set of full (i.e. 10-dot) ten frames
- Washing line and pegs

Key vocabulary

- **After**
- **Backwards**
- **Bead string**
- **Before**
- **Forwards**
- **In-between**
- **Number square**
- **Number line**
- **Number track**
- **Numeral**
- **Order**
- **Pattern**
- **Ten frame**

Misconceptions

Potential misconception	Addressing the misconception
Units 2.1, 2.2 and 2.3 Pupils may confuse '-teen' and '-ty' numerals and number names. For example, they may read or say 15/fifteen as 50/fifty.	Show pupils a number track with the numerals 13–19 on it. Point to each numeral in turn while saying the number name. Count again, inviting the child to repeat after you. Emphasise the 'teen' in each word. **What is the same about the way we say these numbers? What is the same about the way they are written? What number am I pointing at? Can you point to number fif<u>teen</u>?** (note the stress on the 'teen'), etc. Show the numerals 13–19 and decade numbers 30–90 written in words. **Can you find the words with 'teen' at the end? Can you match each 'teen' word to the correct number?** Repeat the above activity for the decade numbers 30–90 before progressing to mixed examples.
Units 2.4 and 2.5 Pupils may 'reverse' two-digit numbers. For example, they may read or write 93 as 39 and vice-versa.	Provide pupils with lots of opportunities to explore and discuss the repeating patterns in a hundred square. Practise reading number sequences out loud, pointing to each number as it is said. **What do you hear? What do you see/notice?** Ask pupils to look away while you remove or hide numbers. **What number is missing? How will we say it? How will we write it?** Once pupils are confident with the above, provide practice in recognising and identifying the numbers from 1 to 100 in isolation, i.e. from flashcards.
Units 2.5, 2.7 and 2.8 Pupils may be unsure of the patterns in the way we say number sequences and so have difficulty crossing the decade numbers. For example, when asked to complete the sequence 85, 84, 83, 82 … may say or write 82, 81, **70**, 69, 68 or 82, 81, 80, **89, 88**	Provide pupils with lots of opportunities similar to those described above but use a 1–100 number track rather than a hundred square.
Unit 2.9 Pupils may be unable to combine their knowledge of counting in ones with counting in tens and so make errors similar to the following when counting in tens off the decade: 32, 40, 42, 50, 52, 60 … 58, 48, 38, 28, 8 … 58, 48, 38, 28, 10, 1	Provide pupils with lots of opportunities to read and say number sequences from a hundred square. Focus discussion around the patterns pupils see and on the concepts of ten more and ten less.
Unit 2.10 Pupils may not realise that the '1' in a teens number (for example 13) has a value of ten.	Provide pupils with lots of opportunities to count out sets of between 11 and 19 objects, make a group of ten objects and count how many left over, record as 10 + * = * then match to corresponding place value arrow cards. Discuss what happens to zero when the arrow cards are overlapped.

Potential misconception	Addressing the misconception
Unit 2.11 Pupils may not change from tens to ones when counting a set of objects grouped in tens and ones, e.g. for 'Let's Learn' page 32 (3 bundles of 10 and 7 ones) says '10, 20, 30, 40, 50, 60, 70, 80, 90, 100' rather than '10, 20, 30, 31, 32, 33, 34, 35, 36, 37'.	Provide pupils with sets of between 21 and 99 objects (for example 37 straws) and ask them to make as many groups of ten as possible. Pause after 30. **How many groups of ten have you made? How many straws is that? What would ten more make? Do you have enough straws to make another group of 10? The answer must therefore be less than 40. What does 30 and one more make? And another one ... and another one ... ?**
Unit 2.12 Pupils may be able to recite the forward number word sequence in twos and fives but do not equate this with counting to find 'how many' and so do not trust it as a strategy that can be used to determine a quantity.	Provide pupils with lots of opportunities that are similar to those described above, but change the focus on grouping the objects in twos or fives. Check solutions by counting in ones.

Teaching ideas

Unit 2.1 Reading and writing numbers (1)

- On a table or on the floor, scatter ten flashcards randomly. Each flashcard should display a number word from eleven to twenty. Invite pupils to draw a numeral from 11 to 20 from a feely bag or box and find the corresponding number word on the table. Pupils may work with a partner to help them. Display each pair of flashcards (word and numeral) on the wall and discuss. **What helped you decide which word to choose? What clues did you use to help you?**
- Hide the number words. Randomly call out the number names from 11 to 20. Ask pupils to work in pairs to write the corresponding word on a mini whiteboard. Compare answers with another pair. **Which words are easiest/trickiest to spell? Why is that? What advice would you give someone who was finding, for example, the word 'twelve' hard to spell?**
- Label jars/boxes/trays with 'tricky words', for example: 'eleven paintbrushes'; 'twenty pencils'; 'twelve pairs of scissors'. Ask pupils to count out the number of items in each container. **Is the label correct? How many brushes/pencils/pairs of scissors will we need to add/take away to make the label match what is in the container?**
- Invite pupils to write their own labels for collections of between 11 and 20 objects (for example, beads, cubes, shells) and ask a partner to check their spelling of the number word.

Unit 2.2 Counting in tens

- If available, display a 100-bead bar; alternatively, display a 100-bead string. **Does anyone know how many beads there are altogether?** Tell pupils you want to count them/check the answers provided but that it would take too long to count the beads one at a time. Ask pupils to suggest how the beads could be counted. **Which idea is best? Why? Let's count in tens from left to right.** Model counting the beads in tens. Hang the numerals 0, 10, 20, 30, 40, 50, 60, 70, 80, 90, 100 on the bar/string as you say each number name. Say each number name in sequence (from 0 to 100) as you point to the corresponding numeral. **What do you notice? Which number names are easy to remember? Which are harder to remember? Why is that?** Repeat the sequence several times ('Say with me'). Focus on 'sticky areas' and gradually withdraw the support until pupils are reciting the sequence, or parts of it, independently.
- Ask pupils to count in tens to find the total number of dots, displayed as a set of 'full' ten frames. Repeat for bundles of straws grouped in tens. **How many groups of ten? How many dots/straws altogether? How will we write that number? What do you notice?**
- Ask pupils to count out a requested number of items (dots or straws grouped in tens) and ask them to check their answer by counting out loud in tens.
- If available, ask pupils to 'show you' a multiple of ten on a 100-bead string.
- Use the bead bar/bead string to practise reading and saying the sequence of decade numbers backwards from 100 to 0.
- Display a set of 10-dot ten frames or straw bundles. For example:

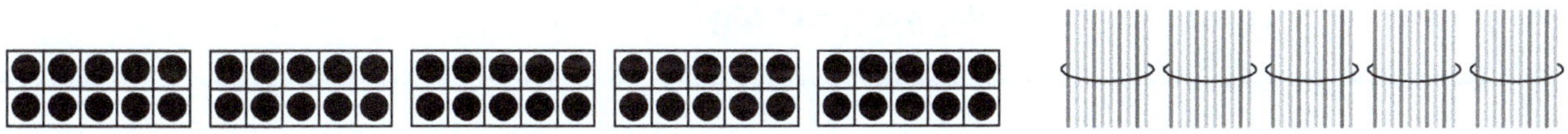

Ask: **How many dots/straws?** Practise counting backwards in tens by removing each ten frame/straw bundle one at a time until there are none left. If appropriate, link this action with subtraction, i.e. 50 – 50 = 0, etc.

Unit 2.3 Reading and writing numbers (2)

- Scatter ten flashcards (each displaying a decade number word from ten through to one hundred) randomly on a table or on the floor. Invite pupils to draw from a set of corresponding numeral flashcards and to match the numeral to the correct number word. They may work with a partner to help them. Display each pair of flashcards on the wall and discuss. **What helped you decide which word to choose? What clues did you use to help you?**
- Hide the number words. Randomly call out the decade number names from 10 to 100. Ask pupils to work in pairs to write the corresponding word on a mini whiteboard. Compare answers with another pair of pupils. **Which words are easiest/trickiest to spell? Why is that? What advice would you give to someone who was finding, for example, the word 'eighty' hard to spell?**
- Play 'Number Word Bingo'. Give each pupil a bingo board that displays decade numbers within the range 0–100 written in words. Call out the numbers in a random order. If pupils have the corresponding word on their boards, they cover it with a counter. The first player to cover all of the words on their board is the winner. Increase the challenge by extending the activity to include the number words from 1 to 20.

Unit 2.4 Forward number sequences (1)

- Display a 0–100 number line graduated in tens with every tenth graduation labelled, i.e. 10, 20, 30, etc. Tell pupils that there are numbers that lie in-between each pair of 'tens' numbers. **Can you name the numbers that come in-between 0 and 10? What about the numbers that come in-between 11 and 20?** Point to each graduation between 20 and 30 in turn and invite the children to count with you: 20, 21, 22, 23, 24, 25, 26, 27, 28, 29, 30. Repeat for 30–40, 40–50, 50–60, etc. **What do you notice about what you hear? Which parts of the 'forties numbers' sound the same as the 'fifties numbers'?**
- Introduce a *completed* hundred square of the same layout as the one on page 16 of the Pupil Book. Invite pupils to count in unison from 1 to 100. **What do you notice about what you see? Which parts of the 'eighties numbers' look the same as the 'nineties numbers'? What changes from one row to the next? What stays the same? Can you explain this? What other patterns can you see?**
- Discuss the partially completed hundred square on page 16 of the Pupil Book. **What number is missing? How do you say it? How would you write it?**
- Flash a series of two-digit numbers written in numerals and ask pupils to say the number shown. The range can be extended as confidence increases. For example, start with 31–39, 71–79, 91–99, then progress to 21–49, 21–69, 21–99. **How did you work it out?**
- Pose questions such as: **Finlay thinks 67 says sixty-seven but Isla thinks it says seventy-six. Who is correct? Why?**
- Call out a series of two-digit numbers and ask the pupils to 'show you' the number on their mini whiteboard. **Have we all written the same? If not, who is correct? Why?**

Unit 2.5 Forward number sequences (2)

- Practise reading number word sequences out loud from a hundred square or number line. Vary the starting number and focus on sequences that cross a decade number, for example 55–65.
- Draw a number track on the playground or create one by laying sheets of paper on a non-slip surface. Choose numbers that cross a decade; (for example, 64 to 73). Invite a pupil to stand on a given number on the track and take a specified number of jumps. The rest of the class should predict the number that he or she will finish on. For example: **Amman, can you please stand on the number sixty-eight? I'd like Amman to take four jumps forwards. What number will he land on?** Amman checks the prediction by taking four jumps forwards. Repeat, varying the starting number and the number of jumps.
- Invite pupils to work in pairs to create their own number track that crosses a decade number (range 0–99) and provide instructions for each other. Swap number tracks with another pair and repeat.
- Repeat the above activity but have pupils 'jump' their finger along a desktop number track.
- Compare the Snakes and Ladders board on page 18 of the Pupil Book with the hundred square on page 16. **What is the same? What is different? Why do you think the numbers are arranged in this way? Which square makes it easier to see the number patterns?** Highlight how the repeating 1–9 pattern remains the same regardless of the layout.
- Ask pupils to work in pairs to identify the missing numbers on the Snakes and Ladders board (in the 'Let's Learn' section on page 18 of the Pupil Book). **What number comes next? How do you say it? How will you write it?** Invite pupils to compare their completed board with another pair and play the game!

Unit 2.6 Backward number sequences (1)

- Invite a group of eleven pupils to stand in a row in front of the class. 'Name' the first pupil in the row with a decade number (for example, '40'). Count forwards in ones in unison naming each pupil in turn, i.e. 40, 41, 42, 43, 44, 45, 46, 47, 48, 49, 50. Count backwards down the line from 50 to 40. Repeat for different pairs of decade numbers between 0 and 100.
- Invite a different group of eleven pupils to stand in a row in front of the class. 'Name' the last pupil in the row with a decade number (for example, '100'). Invite pupils to count backwards from 100 in their heads to 'number' a chosen pupil. For example, **If Nuira is number 100, what number is Finlay?**
- Compare the hundred square on page 21 of the Pupil Book with the hundred square on page 16. **What is the same? What is different?**
- Introduce a *completed* hundred square of the same layout as the one on page 21 of the Pupil Book. Invite pupils to count in unison from 100 to 1. **What patterns can you see?**
- Discuss the partially completed hundred square on page 21 of the Pupil Book. **What numbers are missing? How would you say them? How would you write them?**

Unit 2.7 Backward number sequences (2)

- Line the class up around the room to make a 'human number line'. Give the last pupil in the line a number between fifty and zero. Pupils count back from the starting number one at a time until every pupil has called out a number. Pupils required to call out a 'tens' number jump as high as they can to alert the next pupil that the pattern is about to change. For example, a class of twenty-five pupils may be asked to count back from 46 to 22. Pupils numbered 40 and 30 would be required to jump up. Repeat for different starting numbers.
- Invite a group of pupils to stand in a row in front of the class. 'Name' the last pupil in the row with a number lower than fifty-five. Invite pupils to count backwards from the starting number in their heads to work out the first person's number. For example: **If Isla is number 53, what number is Nuria? Who is number 50/40/30? If Finlay is number 40, what will the next pupil's number be?**
- Draw a number track on the playground or create one by laying sheets of paper on a non-slip surface. Choose a pair of two-digit numbers that cross a decade (for example, 35 and 45). Invite a pupil to stand on a given number on the track and jump backwards a specified number of times. The rest of the class should predict the number that he or she will finish on. For example: **Nuria, can you please stand on the number forty-two. I'd like Nuria to take three jumps backwards. What number will she land on?** Nuria checks the prediction by taking three jumps backwards. Repeat, varying the starting number and the number of jumps.
- Repeat the above activity but have pupils 'jump' their finger along a desktop number track.
- Discuss Amman and Isla's game board (see 'Let's Learn' on page 23). Ask pupils to work in pairs to complete the board then 'play the game'. Each player should place a counter on 50, roll a dice and count back the correct number of jumps, saying the numbers out loud as they go. **Amman and Isla need some help to write rules for their game. What rules should they have? How will you decide who starts? What should happen if your counter is on number 3 and you roll a six? Etc.**

Unit 2.8 Number before, after and in-between

- Display two numbers at either end of a washing line (for example, 62 and 82). Scatter a set of flashcards that each display a two-digit number within the chosen range (e.g. 63 to 81) face down on a table or on the floor. Invite pupils to choose a card, name the number and place it on the washing line. **Where should your number go? Why? Does everyone agree?** Read the completed sequence out loud. **Are the numbers in the correct order?** Repeat for different starting and finishing numbers.
- Display the numbers 10 and 100 at either end of a washing line. Give each pupil a flashcard with a two-digit number written on it or ask them to write their own two-digit number on a piece of paper. Peg your own two-digit number on the washing line. **Who has a number that comes before my number? Who has a number that comes after my number?** Invite pupils to take turns to position their number on the washing line. **Which numbers come in-between Amman's number and Finlay's number? Which numbers need to be moved so that Isla's number can be pegged up in the correct place?** Compare the numbers in different sections of the number line. **What is the same? What is different? Are all of the numbers that come between 50 and 60 there? Which number(s) is/are missing?**
- Play 'Guess my Number'. Deal a collection of non-sequential numbers (for example, 36, 44, 47, 53, 58, 31) written on flashcards to a small group of pupils. These pupils should keep their numbers hidden from the class. Select two different pupils. Give one a number that is smaller than any of the 'secret numbers' (for example, 29). Give the other a number that is larger than any of the 'secret numbers' (for example, 62). Invite these pupils to stand apart, leaving sufficient space for the other six pupils. **What number is this? What about this number?** Tell the class that all of the 'secret numbers' lie in-between 29 and 62. Invite one pupil holding a 'secret number' to stand in-between 29 and 62. **What could the number be?** Establish that the secret number must come after 29 and before 62. Ask the child holding the secret number to reveal it. Repeat until all secret numbers have been revealed and are in the correct order.

Unit 2.9 Counting in tens

- Show pupils a hundred square similar to the one from the 'Let's Learn' section on page 28 (i.e. with the numbers arranged from 1 to 100 reading across each row from the top-left corner). **Can you find the 'tens' numbers?** Recap reciting the sequence of decade numbers from 0 to 100 both forwards and backwards, i.e. 10, 20, 30, 40 … 100, 90, 80, 70 …
- Repeat the above activity, linking each number name with the action of laying out or removing bundles of ten straws or completed ten frames. **Why do you think we call these numbers the 'tens numbers'?** Highlight the link between the action of counting forwards/backwards in tens to ten more/ten less than the previous number said.
- Discuss the 'Let's Learn' section on page 28. Read down each column from top to bottom. **What patterns do you notice?** Practise reading these forwards number word sequences. Link each sequence with laying out concrete materials (straw bundles or ten frames), i.e. 3 and 10 more is 13 … and 10 more is 23 … and 10 more is 33 … up to 93. Challenge more able pupils by asking: **What would 10 more than 93 be?**
- Repeat the above activity for counting backwards in tens off the decade, i.e. read up each column from bottom to top. Practise reading these backwards number work sequences. Link each sequence with removing concrete materials (straw bundles or ten frames), i.e. 97 and 10 less is 87 … and 10 less is 77 … and 10 less is 67 … down to 7.
- Invite a group of ten pupils to come to the front of the class. Give each pupil a flashcard (one of a set of ten flashcards displaying the numbers 9, 19, 29, 39, 49, 59, 69, 79, 89, 99) and ask them to arrange themselves in order from smallest to largest. Ask the class to read the number sequence in unison, forwards and backwards. Repeat for other sets of 'off decade' numbers: for example 2, 12, 22, 32, 42, 52, 62, 72, 82, 92, etc.
- Using the number sets described above, ask pupils to close their eyes whilst one or more of the children turn their flashcard over. **Open your eyes. Which number(s) is/are missing?** Ask children to practise saying the whole sequence forwards and backwards with eyes closed.

Unit 2.10 Base 10 for teen numbers

- Invite pupils to count out more than 10 but fewer than 20 beads or interlocking cubes (for example, 16). **Thread ten beads onto a string or make a tower of ten cubes. How many beads/cubes are not on/in the string/tower?** Record 10 and 6 makes 16 on a flipchart or whiteboard. Repeat for other teen numbers.
- Show pupils a bundle of ten straws. **There are ten straws in the bundle. I want to have nineteen straws. How many more straws do I need?** Record 10 and 9 makes 19 on a flipchart or whiteboard. Repeat for other teen numbers.
- Show pupils a number between 11 and 20 made from a full ten frame and a partially completed ten frame (for example, 14).

  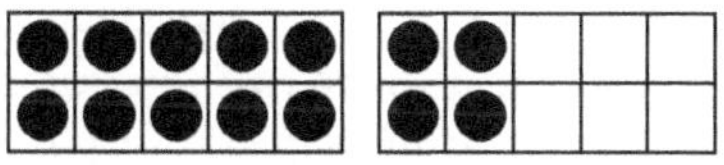

  How many dots altogether? How did you work it out? Encourage pupils to count on from ten to find the total. Record 10 and 4 makes 14 on a flipchart or whiteboard. Repeat for other teen numbers.
- If available, ask pupils to 'show you' a number between 11 and 20 on a bead string (for example, 15). **Did you need to count from one to find the correct number of beads? If not, why not?** Record 10 and 5 makes 15 on a flipchart or whiteboard. Repeat for other teen numbers.
- Write a number between 11 and 20 on a flipchart or whiteboard or list the examples used previously, e.g. 10 and 6 makes 16. Point to the '1' in the number sixteen. **What does it mean?** Demonstrate 10 + 6 = 16 with place value arrow cards.

Unit 2.11 Counting in tens and ones

- Invite pupils to suggest ways that we could arrange a set of between 21 and 99 items (for example, 74 interlocking cubes) to make them easier to count. **Is there more than one way to count the cubes?** Focus on any suggestions that use tens. **Which way is easier: 10, 20, 30, 40, 50, 60, 70, 71, 72, 73, 74 or 4, 14, 24, 34, 44, 54, 64, 74?** Encourage starting with the sticks of ten, i.e. count the 'tens' then the ones.
- Show a jar filled with a number of beads (for example, 96 beads). Ask the pupils to estimate the total. Introduce a set of paper cups. Have the pupils count the beads into paper cups (10 per cup) to find how many altogether. **How can we keep track of which beads have been counted and which have not? Does it matter which cup we start with?**
- If available, display a 1–100 bead bar or bead string with each tenth bead labelled. Point to one of the beads (for example, the thirty-sixth bead). **How many beads to here? How do you know? Do you need to count the beads one at a time? Why not?** Emphasise that when there are lots of things to count, counting in tens and ones is a more efficient strategy to use. Repeat for different numbers between 21 and 99.
- Repeat the above activity using straws, ten frames and money (10p and 1p coins). Note that the latter is more challenging, as the ten individual '1ps' with the same value as one 10p coin are not visible, and may therefore be inappropriate for some pupils.

Unit 2.12 Counting in twos and fives

- Revise reciting the number word sequence in twos. Present pupils with a collection of nine objects, displayed randomly. **Can we count in twos to find how many there are? Why might we do this?** Model counting the objects in twos whilst saying the number sequence aloud: 2, 4, 6, 8 and one more makes 9. Repeat for other odd numbers within the range 10–30.
- Ask the pupils to line up in twos. **Count in twos with me. How many people are in the line? Will we get the same answer if we arrange ourselves into groups of five? How else could we count to find out how many people are in the class today? Does it matter who we count first? Why not?**
- Revise reciting the number word sequence in fives. Present pupils with a collection of 28 objects displayed randomly. **Can we count in fives to find how many there are?** Model counting the objects in fives whilst saying the number sequence aloud. Pause at 25. **Can we count five more? Why not? What should we do?** Encourage responses such as, 'Change to counting in ones', 'Count 26, 27, 28'. More able pupils may realise there are 28 because 5 add 3 equals 8. Repeat for other numbers, within the range 20–50, which are not multiples of five.
- Present pupils with a collection of 31 objects (for example, shells) and ask them to vote on how they should be counted (for example, in ones, twos, fives or tens). **Who thinks it might be best to count the shells in ones/twos/fives/tens? What makes you say that?** Discuss the advantages and disadvantages of each method and steer pupils towards counting in twos or fives. Count the objects in twos/fives. **How many shells are there altogether? Will we get the same answer if we count the shells in fives/twos? Why is that?** Re-count the shells in fives/twos. **Did you get the same answer? If not, why not?**
- Invite pupils to work in pairs to arrange a set of objects (for example, interlocking cubes, shells, counters, etc.) to make counting easier. **Will you count in twos or fives? Why?**

Unit 2.13 Ordinal numbers

- Invite ten pupils to stand in a row. **If Amman is first in the line, who is third/sixth/seventh/tenth etc.?** Ask the class to close their eyes whilst the group is reshuffled. **Who is first/second/fourth/eighth now?**
- Create a simple pattern with different coloured counters; (for example, red, blue, red, blue, red). **What colour is the fifth/first/fourth counter? If we were to continue the pattern, what colour would the sixth/eighth/tenth counter be?** Continue the pattern to check predictions.
- Pupils work in pairs. Ask each pupil to create their own pattern with ten objects/shapes and to ask each other questions about the pattern they have created (for example, 'What colour is my ninth triangle?')
- Discuss the 'Let's Learn' section on page 36 of the Pupil Book. **Who can read the words written under the children? Which of these words have you seen before? Which words are new? Which words do you think might be easiest/trickiest to spell? Why is that?** Invite pupils to look at the symbols written underneath the words. **What is the same? What is different?** Invite pupils to compare words and symbols. **What might help you decide which letters to write after the number?**
- Randomly scatter ten flashcards (each displaying an ordinal number word from *first* through to *tenth*) on a table or on the floor. Invite pupils to draw an ordinal number written in symbols (1st – 10th) from a feely bag or box and to find the corresponding word. They may work with a partner to help them. Display pairs of flashcards on the wall and discuss. **What helped you decide which word to choose? What clues did you use to help you?**

Number - order and place value 1B

Section overview

Textbook 1B units	Review units	Prior learning	Benchmarks/ Es&Os
Unit 2.1 Reading and writing two-digit numbers	**1A** Units 2.1 and 2.3	• Recognise the numerals 0–99. • Identify (find within a group) the numerals 0–99. • Read and write the number words from 0 to 20. • Read and write the decade/tens numbers in words.	**MNU 1-02a** • Reads, writes, orders and recites whole numbers to 1000, starting from any number in the sequence.
Unit 2.2 Naming and ordering the hundreds	**1A** Units 2.2, 2.4, 2.6 and 2.9	• Say, read and write the number sequence from 0 to 20. • Name the decade/tens numbers in sequence. • Repeat the 1 to 9 sequence within each decade, e.g. 51, 52, 53, 54, 55, 56, 57, 58, 59.	**MNU 1-02a** • Counts forwards and backwards in 2s, 5s, 10s and 100s.
Unit 2.3 Reading and writing three-digit numbers	**1B** Units 2.1 and 2.2	• Read and write 2-digit numbers in numerals and in words. • Name the hundreds numbers in sequence.	**MNU 1-02a** • Reads, writes, orders and recites whole numbers to 1000, starting from any number in the sequence.
Unit 2.4 Counting forwards in ones	**1A** Units 2.4 and 2.5 **1B** Unit 2.3	• Count forwards in ones from any 2-digit number, including those that cross a decade. • Read and write 3-digit numbers in numerals	**MNU 1-02a** • Reads, writes, orders and recites whole numbers to 1000, starting from any number in the sequence.
Unit 2.5 Counting backwards in ones	**1A** Units 2.6 and 2.7 **1B** Unit 2.3	• Count backwards in ones from any 2-digit number, including those that cross a decade. • Read and write 3-digit numbers in numerals.	**MNU 1-02a** • Reads, writes, orders and recites whole numbers to 1000, starting from any number in the sequence.
Unit 2.6 Number before, after and in-between	**1A** Unit 2.8	• Identify the number after/1 more than/2 more than any 2-digit number. • Identify the number before/1 less than/2 less than any 2-digit number. • Identify missing 2-digit numbers on a number line. • Name all numbers that lie between a given pair of 2-digit numbers.	**MNU 1-02a** • Reads, writes, orders and recites whole numbers to 1000, starting from any number in the sequence.

Textbook 1B units	Review units	Prior learning	Benchmarks/ Es&Os
Unit 2.7 Counting forwards in tens and hundreds	**1A** Units 2.2, 2.4, 2.5, 2.9 and 2.11 **1B** Units 2.2 and 2.4	• Count forwards in tens, on and off the decade, e.g. 7, 17, 27, 37, etc. • Count forwards in hundreds on the hundred/centuple, i.e. 100, 200, 300, etc. • Count forwards in ones from any 3-digit number, appreciating the 1–9 and 1–99 patterns. • Identify missing numbers on a hundred square.	**MNU 1-02a** • Counts forwards and backwards in 2s, 5s, 10s and 100s.
Unit 2.8 Counting backwards in tens and hundreds	**1A** Units 2.2, 2.6, 2.7 and 2.9 **1B** Units 2.2 and 2.5	• Count backwards in tens, on and off the decade, e.g. 37, 27, 17, 7. • Count backwards in hundreds on the hundred/centuple, e.g. 300, 200, 100, 0. • Count backwards in ones from any 3-digit number, appreciating the 9–1 and 99–1 patterns. • Identify missing numbers on a hundred square.	**MNU 1-02a** • Counts forwards and backwards in 2s, 5s, 10s and 100s.
Unit 2.9 Counting forwards and backwards in twos and fives	**1A** Unit 2.12	• Count in 2s to find a total of up to 20 objects. • Count in 5s to find a total of up to 50 objects.	**MNU 1-02a** • Counts forwards and backwards in 2s, 5s, 10s and 100s.
Unit 2.10 Counting in hundreds, tens and ones	**1A** Units 2.10 and 2.11	• Group objects in tens to find a total up to 100. • Count in 10s and 1s to find how many (amounts up to 99). • Represent 2-digit numbers in ways that clearly show that 10 units of one = 1 unit of 10, e.g. bundles of straws, ten frames, bead string.	**MNU 1-02a** • Counts forwards and backwards in 2s, 5s, 10s and 100s.
Unit 2.11 Standard place value partitioning	**1A** Unit 2.10 **1B** Unit 2.1	• Read and write 2-digit numbers in numerals and in words. • Count in 10s and 1s to find how many (amounts up to 99). • Represent 2-digit numbers in ways that clearly show that 10 units of one = 1 unit of 10, e.g. bundles of straws, ten frames, bead string. • Partition the numbers from 11 to 20 into '10 + ?'.	**MNU 1-02a** • Identifies the value of each digit in a whole number with three digits; for example, 867 = 800 + 60 + 7.
Unit 2.12 Comparing numbers	**1A** Units 1.1, 1.2 and 2.8 **1B** Units 1.1, 2.2, 2.4, 2.5, 2.6, 2.7 and 2.8	• Compare numbers up to 20 using appropriate vocabulary, e.g. bigger, more. • Place 2-digit numbers on a number line. • Place 3-digit numbers on a number line.	**MNU 1-02a** • Reads, writes, orders and recites whole numbers to 1000, starting from any number in the sequence.

Textbook 1B units	Review units	Prior learning	Benchmarks/ Es&Os
Unit 2.13 Ordering numbers	**1B** Unit 2.12	• Arrange the numerals from 0 to 20 in order from smallest to largest and from largest to smallest. • Compare pairs of 2-digit numbers by looking at the first digit. • Compare pairs of 3-digit numbers by looking at the first digit.	**MNU 1-02a** • Reads, writes, orders and recites whole numbers to 1000, starting from any number in the sequence.
Unit 2.14 Ordinal numbers	**1A** Units 2.13 and 10.1	• Use ordinal numbers up to tenths in real-life contexts, for example, 'Finlay was eighth in the race.' • Read and write ordinal numbers to tenths in words and symbols.	**MNU 1-02a** • Reads, writes, orders and recites whole numbers to 1000, starting from any number in the sequence.

Conceptual context

Book 1B sees the introduction of three-digit numbers with a focus on reading, writing and sequencing numbers (forwards and backwards) within the range 100–1000. The recurring 1 to 9 pattern within each decade, and hundred, is emphasised, and particular attention is given to crossing a decade or hundred (for example, 568, 569, **570,** 571 and 798, 799, **800**, 801). As familiarity with these recurring patterns increases, and as pupils develop the ability to visualise the number line, they will be able to identify the numbers before, after and in-between a widening number range and be able to use this knowledge to compare and order pairs or sets of numbers.

Deep *conceptual* place value understanding equips pupils with the knowledge and skills to manipulate numbers flexibly. This is developed through a focus on counting forwards and backwards in tens and hundreds, both on and off the decade or hundred, and through linking these ideas to the concepts of 10 more than/less than and 100 more than/less than. Base 10 for teen numbers, introduced in Book 1A, is extended to include standard place value partitioning of two-digit numbers (for example, $54 = 50 + 4$, $89 = 80 + 9$). Initially, pupils should be provided with opportunities to form their own groups of ten when counting a set of objects. For example, counting a set of 36 counters by making 3 sets of ten (30) and having 6 left over $\longrightarrow 30 + 6 = 36$ or counting a set of 27 interlocking cubes by making two sticks of ten (20) and having 7 left over $\longrightarrow 20 + 7 = 27$.

It is vital that pupils are provided with lots of opportunities to represent quantities with concrete materials that show the individual units of one that make up each unit of ten (for example, ten frames, bundles of straws, base 10 blocks) before being introduced to more abstract units such as place value counters. This will help the pupils to realise that 1 ten has the same value as 10 ones.

Resources

- Base 10 blocks (hundreds, tens and ones)
- Bingo boards, each displaying a different set of numerals within the number range 11–99
- Blank 10 × 10 grid per pupil
- Calculators
- Counters
- Empty box or 'feely bag'
- Flashcards, each displaying a number word within the range 11–99
- Flashcards, each displaying a numeral that corresponds with the number words described above
- Flashcards displaying a random set of three-digit numbers
- Hundred dot squares, ten dot strips, 1–9 dot strips
- Hundred square per pupil
- Interlocking cubes
- Large 0–1000 number line graduated in hundreds for demonstration purposes
- Large blank 10 × 10 grid for demonstration purposes
- Mini whiteboard per pupil
- Numeral dice showing the digits 0–5 or 1–6
- One 0–1000 number line graduated in hundreds per pupil
- Place value arrow cards (TO) for demonstration purposes
- Place value house per pair (enlarged to A3 size)
- Post-it notes
- Set of digit cards 0–9 per pupil
- Set of place value arrow cards per pupil (tens and ones)
- Standard 1–6 spot dice per pair
- Straws: pre-bundled in tens and ones
- Ten frames: multiple 'tens' plus at least one set showing the quantities 1–9
- Un-numbered graduated number line per pupil

Key vocabulary

- **After**
- **Before**
- **Column**
- **Compare**
- **Digit**
- **Equal**
- **Greater than**
- **In-between**
- **Less than**
- **More than**
- **Number sentence**
- **Numerals**
- **Order**
- **Ordinal number**
- **Partition**
- **Position**
- **Pattern**
- **Sequence**
- **Three-digit number**
- **Two-digit number**

Misconceptions

Potential misconception	Addressing the misconception
Unit 2.1 Pupils may 'reverse' two-digit numbers; for example, a pupil may read or write 93 as 39 and vice-versa.	Provide pupils with lots of opportunities to explore and discuss the repeating patterns in a hundred square. Practise reading number sequences out loud, pointing to each number as it is said. **What do you hear? What do you see/notice?** Ask pupils to look away while you remove or hide numbers. **What number is missing? How will we say it? How will we write it?** Once pupils are confident with the above, provide practice in recognising and identifying the numbers from 1 to 100 in isolation, i.e. from flashcards.
Units 2.3 and 2.11 Pupils may include extra zeros when writing numbers in numerals. For example, a pupil may write three hundred and sixty-seven as 30067.	Firstly, ask the pupil to write a two-digit number (for example, forty-seven) in numerals. Ask the pupil to say the number they have written quietly to themselves then select from a set of place value arrow cards the two cards that best describe what they hear: 40 … 7. Demonstrate how the cards 40 and 7 can be overlapped to make the number 47. Focus the resulting conversation on the meaning of the digits. Tell pupils that in a two-digit number such as 47 the four means 4 lots of 10 or 40. Say a three-digit number aloud; for example, 347. Ask pupils to repeat the number quietly to themselves and find the three place value arrow cards that best describe what they hear: 300 and 40 … 7. Demonstrate how the cards 300 and 40 and 7 can be overlapped to make the number 347. Focus the resulting conversation on the meaning of the digits. Tell pupils that in a three-digit number such as 347 the three means 3 lots of 100 or 300. Repeat for other three-digit numbers.
Units 2.4, 2.5 and 2.6 Pupils may encounter difficulties with number word sequences that cross a decade or hundred. For example, pupils may: • believe that the number after 100 is 200, after 400 is 500, etc. • believe the number after 109 is 200, after 409 is 500, after 809 is 900, etc. • jump to the next 'hundred' number when counting backwards and so say, for example, 502, 501, 400, 499, 498 • omit the hundreds number and so say, for example, 702, 701, 699, 698, 697.	In Book 1A, pupils learned that the one to nine pattern is repeated within each pair of decade numbers. For example, the numbers 81, 82, 83, 84, 85, 86, 87, 88, 89 all come in-between 80 and 90. Through lots of oral practice, they come to realise that this same repeating pattern occurs in three-digit numbers (for example, 580, 581, 582, 583, 584, 585, 586, 587, 588, 589, 590) and that the one to ninety-nine pattern must be repeated between each of pair of hundreds numbers. Particular emphasis should be given to short sequences that cross a decade or hundred. Once pupils can confidently recite these sequences, they can be introduced to reading and writing them.
Units 2.7 and 2.8 Pupils may encounter one or more of the following difficulties when counting forwards or backwards in tens within the range 0–1000. For example, pupils may: • count by 100s rather than by tens and so say 116, 216, 316 not 116, 126, 136 • fail to increase the hundreds digit when crossing a hundred, i.e. say 371, 381, 391, 301, 311 • jump to the next 'hundred' number when counting backwards and so say, for example, 720, 710, 600, 690, 680 or 720, 710, 600, 590, 580.	Pupils should be given lots of opportunities to look for and explain number patterns (such as those in the tables on pages 21, 22 and 24 of Pupil Book 1B) before being introduced to written work.

Potential misconception	Addressing the misconception
Unit 2.9 Pupils may have difficulty counting to find 'how many' when presented with collections where the individual items that make up each unit of 'two' or 'five' cannot be seen; for example, 2p and 5p coins.	Present collections of 1p coins, grouped in twos or fives and ask the pupil to skip count to find the total. Cover the collections with semi-opaque screens so that the coins are still visible and ask the pupil to repeat the count. When pupils are confident with the number word sequence, hide the coins with opaque screens and repeat the count. Finally, progress to abstract units such as 2p and 5p coins.

Teaching ideas

Unit 2.1 Reading and writing two-digit numbers

- Discuss the 'Let's Learn' section on page 8 of Pupil Book 1B. **Which words do you find trickiest to spell? Why is that? Who finds this word easy to spell? What spelling tips can you give those who find the word difficult? What do you notice about the way the numbers 26, 43 and 84 are written in words?** Call out a number between 11–99 and ask pupils to 'show you' the number in words on a mini whiteboard. They may use the 'Let's Learn' section to help them with tricky spellings.
- Ask pupils to work in pairs. Each pupil needs a mini whiteboard. Pupil A writes a number between 11–99 in numerals and shows it to Pupil B, who writes the same number in words. **Do the words and numerals match? If not, why not? Who is correct?** Swap roles.
- Randomly scatter a set of flashcards on a table or on the floor. Each flashcard should show a number within the range 11–99 written in words. Include some 'tricky words.' Invite pupils to take turns to draw from a set of corresponding numerals and match it to the correct number word. They may ask a partner to help them. Display pairs of flashcards and discuss. **What helped you decide which word to choose? What clues did you use to help you?**
- Play 'Number Word Bingo'. Give each pupil a bingo board displaying a random set of numerals within the range 0–100. Call out the number names in random order and/or write the words on a flipchart or whiteboard. If pupils have the corresponding number on their board, they should cover it with a counter. The first player to cover all of the numbers on their board is the winner.

Unit 2.2 Naming and ordering the hundreds

- Discuss the 'Let's Learn' section on page 10. **What patterns do you notice? Why do you think we call these numbers the 'hundreds' numbers?** Practise reading the number sequence aloud, forwards and backwards. **If each number written is 100 more than the number before it, what is 100 more than 300, 700, 100, 500, etc.? Does anyone know the number that is 100 more than 900?** *We say 'one thousand' and we write 1000.* **Counting backwards, each number is 100 less than the number before it. What is 100 less than 400, 800, 100, 500, etc.?**
- Ask pupils to count in hundreds to find the total number of dots displayed as a set of one hundred dot squares. **How many sets of one hundred? How many dots altogether?** *Five lots of 100 dots makes 500 dots altogether,* etc.
- Ask pupils to count out a requested number of dots grouped in hundreds and check their answer by counting out loud in hundreds.

- Display a set of hundred dot squares. **How many dots?** Practise counting backwards in hundreds by removing the squares one at a time until there are none left.
- Introduce a number line from 0 to 1000 graduated in hundreds. Read the numbers forwards and backwards. Ask pupils to close their eyes whilst one or more of the numbers are covered. **Open your eyes. Which number(s) is/are missing?** Ask children to practise saying the complete sequence forwards and backwards with eyes closed.
- Give each pupil a number line graduated in hundreds. Call out instructions such as: **Start at 400. Take four jumps of one hundred forwards. Which number did you land on? Start at 900. Take two jumps of one hundred backwards. Which number are you on now?** If appropriate, make links with addition and subtraction; for example, 400 + 400 = 800 and 900 – 200 = 700.

Unit 2.3 Reading and writing three-digit numbers

- Display five 10-dot strips and one 2-dot strip; for example:

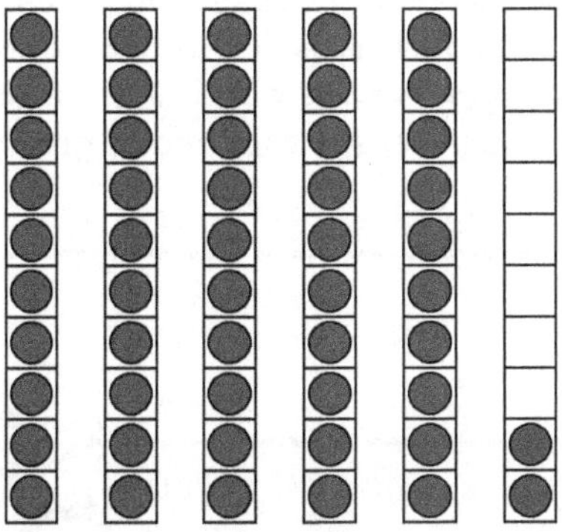

How many dots are there altogether? Introduce a one hundred dot square. **How many dots in the square?** Lay the hundred dot square to the left of the ten dot strips. *One hundred dots plus 52 dots makes one hundred and fifty-two dots altogether.* Write one hundred and fifty-two in words on a flipchart or whiteboard. Tell pupils that one hundred and fifty-two is a three-digit number. **How many digits does the number fifty-two have? How might we use this information to help us work out how to write one hundred and fifty-two in numerals?** Stress that when writing a three-digit number in numerals we always begin by writing the number of 'hundreds' (hundred dot squares), then the number of 'tens' (ten dot strips) then the number of 'ones'.

- Introduce three more hundred dot squares. **How many dots altogether now? What makes you say that? How will we write this new number in numerals? Which three digits do we need? How will we write this number in words?** Stress that when writing a three-digit number in words we start by writing down how many 'hundreds' there are (i.e. the number of hundred dot squares) followed by the word 'and', then the rest of the number.
- Repeat the above activities for different three-digit numbers.
- Display a range of three-digit numbers written in words on a flipchart or whiteboard. Ask pupils to 'show you' the number written in numerals on their mini whiteboards and to compare their answer with a partner. **Have you both written the same? If not, who is correct? Why?**
- Display a range of three-digit numbers randomly, each made up of the same three digits (for example, 182, 812, 821, 218, 128, 281). **Which number says two hundred and eighteen? How do you know? Why can't it be the first one?** Repeat for different sets of three-digit numbers.

Unit 2.4 Counting forward in ones

- Play 'Number Ping Pong'. Start by reciting the forward number word sequence from 90. Pupils say the next number in unison. Continue the sequence, alternating between teacher and class. For example: 90 (teacher), 91 (pupils), 92 (teacher), 93 (pupils), 94 (teacher). Pause after 99. **What number will I say next? What number will you say?** Continue the sequence. Pause at numbers that bridge a decade; for example, 129. **What number will I say next? What number will you say?** Repeat the activity several times, changing the starting number each time. Focus on sequences that bridge a 10 or 100. For example, count from 511 to 531 or from 689 to 709.
- Ask pupils to key the number 100 into a calculator. **Which keys will you press? What number is one more than 100? Which keys will you need to press to change one hundred into one hundred and one? What digits do you expect to come up on the screen? Try it. What number comes after one hundred and one? What will 102 look like in numerals?** Ask pupils to check their predictions by keying '+ 1 =' into their calculator. Continue the sequence to at least 111. Repeat the activity several times, changing the starting number each time. Focus on numbers with zero in the tens place.
- Ask pupils to imagine a number line. Tell them that you are going to start at a three-digit number (for example, 296). Say the number 296 out loud as you clap your hands. Continue clapping slowly. Pupils should count forwards in their heads in time to each clap. After several claps, stop and ask: **What number did you reach? Did everyone reach the same number? If not, what might have happened?** Repeat for different starting numbers.
- Discuss the 'Let's Learn' section on page 14 of the Pupil Book. Focus the discussion on the repeating patterns in the way we say, read and write three-digit numbers. If appropriate, discuss columns as well as rows. **Read the numbers from top to bottom. What do you notice? How much bigger is each number than the number above it? What makes you say that?** Note that counting forwards in tens is explored in greater depth in Unit 2.7.

Unit 2.5 Counting backwards in ones

- Play 'Ping Pong Backwards'. Start by reciting the backward number word sequence from 111. Pupils say the next number in unison. Continue the sequence, alternating between teacher and class. For example: 111 (teacher), 110 (pupils), 109 (teacher), 108 (pupils), 107 (teacher). Pause after the number 101. **What number will you say next? What number will I say?** Repeat the activity several times, changing the starting number each time. Focus on sequences that bridge a 10 or 100. For example, count back from 984 to 964 or from 203 to 183.
- Ask pupils to imagine a number line. Tell them that you are going to start at a three-digit number (for example, 809). Say the number 809 out loud as you clap your hands. Continue clapping slowly. Pupils should count backwards in their heads in time to each clap. After several claps stop and ask: **What number did you reach? Did everyone reach the same number? If not, what might have happened?** Repeat for different starting numbers.
- Draw a ladder on a flipchart or whiteboard. Write a three-digit number on the top rung. Ask pupils to count backwards in ones to work out which numbers go on the rungs below. **Which number will go here? Why?** Ask pupils to 'show you' each number, written in numerals and/or words on their mini whiteboards. **Has everyone written the same thing? If not, who is correct?**
- Discuss the 'Let's Learn' section on page 16 of the Pupil Book. Focus the discussion on the repeating patterns in the way we say, read and write three-digit numbers. If appropriate, discuss columns as well as rows. **Which digit changes each time? Why is that?** Please note, counting backwards in tens is explored in greater depth in Unit 2.8.

Unit 2.6 Number before, after and in-between

- Invite one pupil to draw from a class set of flashcards, displaying any number within the range 100–999 written in numerals. They should read the number out loud but keep it hidden from the rest of the class. The other pupils write the number read in the centre of their mini whiteboards. The number on the flashcard is then revealed so that answers can be checked. **Does the number on your whiteboard match the number written on the flashcard?** Discuss incorrect answers. **What number has (Isla) written? Which digit(s) does she need to change to make her answer correct?** Draw a graduated number line on a flipchart or whiteboard. Choose a range that includes the number on the flashcard. For example, if the flashcard reads 289, an appropriate range might be 285–294. Point to the first graduation on the number line. **If this is 285, where will 289 go?** Write 289 in the correct position. Point to each of the other graduations in turn. **What number will go here? How will I write it? Which digits will I need?** Ask pupils to read the numbers on the completed number line aloud. Emphasise how the numbers 286, 287, 288, 289, 290, 291, 292 and 293 all come *in-between* 285 and 294. **What number(s) come in-between 289 and 293 … 287 and 292 … 290 and 292 etc.? What number comes just after … ? What number comes just before … ?** Repeat for different three-digit numbers. Focus on numbers that cross a decade or hundred.
- Call out a pair of three-digit numbers and write them on a flipchart or whiteboard. Ask pupils to imagine a number line and to write down all of the numbers that come in-between those displayed. They should compare answers with a partner. **Have you both written the same set of numbers? If not, who is correct? Did anyone miss any numbers out? Did anyone add any extra numbers? Why aren't these numbers needed? Which number comes after ____? Which number comes before ____?** Repeat for different pairs of three-digit numbers. Focus on numbers that cross a decade or hundred.
- Pupils work in pairs. Pupil A writes a three-digit number in the centre of their mini whiteboard and shows it to Pupil B. Pupil B reads the number and tells Pupil A the numbers that come just before and just after the number displayed. Pupil A writes these numbers to the left and right of their chosen number. **Do you both agree with the order?** Swap roles.

Unit 2.7 Counting forwards in tens and hundreds

- Discuss the 'Let's Learn' section at the bottom of page 21 of the Pupil Book. **Look down each column, what patterns can you see? What would ten more than 191 be? How can we check?** Encourage responses such as, 'Count on from 200', 'Add another row', 'The number after 200 is 201', '200 add one more makes 201'. Ask pupils to visualise the next row in their heads. **What number is ten more than 199/194/197/192, etc.?**
- Ask pupils to key the number 201 into a calculator. **Which keys will you press? What number is ten more than 201? How can we use our calculators to check?** Ask pupils to check their prediction by keying '+ 10 =' into their calculator. Predict then check the next ten numbers in the sequence. Insert the numbers 221–311 in the left-hand column of a blank 10 × 10 grid. Invite pupils to help you complete the grid. **What numbers will we write in the top row? How can we use the completed boxes to help us fill in the missing numbers? What number will go here? Why?** Ask questions about the completed grid; for example: **What number is ten more than 266/289/249/310?**
- Discuss the 'Let's Learn' section at the top of page 22 of the Pupil Book. **Look down each column, what patterns can you see? How much more is each number than the number above it? What is one hundred more than 605/701/208/305, etc.?**
- Ask pupils to key a three-digit number into their calculator; for example, 528. **Which keys will you press? What number is one hundred more than 528? How can we use our calculators to check?** Ask pupils to check their prediction by keying '+ 100 =' into their calculator. Repeat for different three-digit numbers.

- Make simple 'number generators' from strong paper or card.

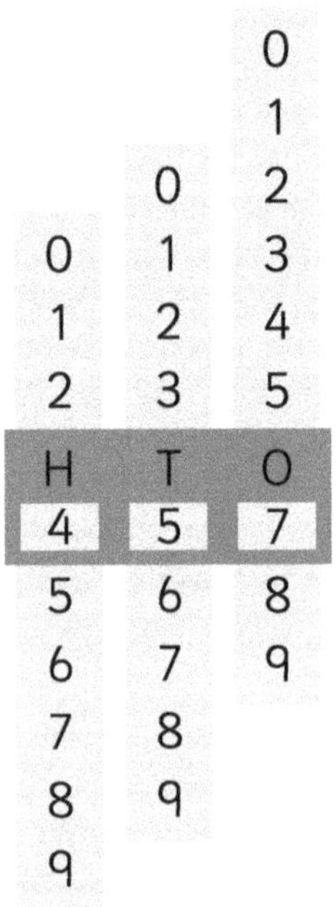

Have pupils use these to investigate '10/100 more than' with a variety of three-digit numbers. **How will you make the number 608 on your number generator? Which digits will you need? What number is 10 more than 608? Show me. What number is 100 more than 618? Show me. Which digit changes when we add 10? Which digit changes when we add 100? Is it ever necessary to change two digits? Why?** Encourage pupils to use a calculator to check examples that cross a hundred; for example, ten more than 297.

Unit 2.8 Counting backwards in tens and hundreds

- Discuss the first table in the 'Let's Learn' section on page 24 of the Pupil Book. **Look down each column. What is happening to each number?** Encourage responses such as, 'The numbers are getting bigger', 'Each number is ten more than the number above it,' 'Add ten each time'. **Let's start at the bottom and read up to the top, what is happening to the numbers now?** Encourage responses such as 'The numbers are getting smaller', 'Take away ten each time', 'Each number is ten less than the number below it'.
- Pupils work in pairs. Give each pair a blank 10 × 10 grid. Ask them to write the number 451 in the top left-hand corner and work together to complete the grid, then compare grids with another pair. **Have you written the same numbers? If not, who is correct? How can we check?** Ask questions about the completed grid; for example: **What number is ten less than 478/491/517/549?**
- Discuss the second table in the 'Let's Learn' section on page 24 of the Pupil Book. **Look down each column, what is happening to each number?** Encourage responses such as, 'The numbers are getting bigger', 'Each number is one hundred more than the number above it', 'Add one hundred each time'. **Let's start at the bottom and read up to the top, what is happening to the numbers now?** Encourage responses such as 'The numbers are getting smaller', 'Take away one hundred each time', 'Each number is one hundred less than the number below it'.
- Ask pupils to key a three-digit number into their calculator (for example, 727). **Which keys will you press? What number is one hundred less than 727? How can we use our calculators to check?** Ask pupils to check their prediction by keying '– 100 =' into their calculator. Repeat for different three-digit numbers.

- Make simple 'number generators' from strong paper or card.

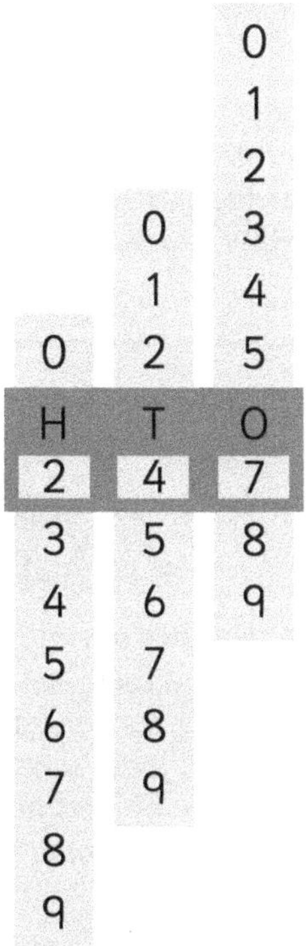

Have pupils use these to investigate '10/100 less than' using a variety of three-digit numbers. **How will you make the number 945 on your number generator? Which digits will you need? What number is 10 less than 945? Show me. What number is 100 less than 945? Show me. Which digit changes when we subtract 10? Which digit changes when we subtract 100? Is it ever necessary to change two digits? Why?** Encourage pupils to use a calculator to check examples that cross a hundred; for example, ten less than 807.

Unit 2.9 Counting forwards and backwards in twos and fives

- Display a collection of 38 cubes. Tell pupils that you are fairly certain that there are 38 but need them to help you check. **Who can count the cubes for me?** If the pupil chosen counts in ones, ask: **How else might we count the cubes?** Invite a different pupil to group the same collection in twos. **Will we get the same answer if we skip count in twos?** Ask pupils to skip count in twos in unison to check. Watch and listen carefully for any errors in the sequence and practise these.
- Display a collection of 65 counters. Tell pupils that you are fairly certain that there are 65 but need them to help you check. **How might we count the counters? Is counting in ones or twos a good idea this time? If not, why not? How else might we count the cubes?** Invite two or three pupils to work together to group the counters in fives, then invite the class to skip count in fives in unison to find the total. Watch and listen carefully for any errors in the sequence and practise these. **Will we get the same answer if we skip count in tens? Let's check. How can we rearrange the counters to make groups of ten?** Encourage suggestion of 'doubling up' groups. Skip count in tens in unison. Pause after 90. **What will we need to do now? Why?**

- Discuss the 'Let's Learn' section on page 26 of the Pupil Book then repeat the above activities for different collections of objects within the number ranges shown. Increase the challenge by screening the objects; (for example, by hiding the counters under sheets of paper or paper cups).
- Once pupils are confident with the number sequence in twos from 0 to 40 and in fives from 0 to 100, ask them to skip count collections of 2p and 5p coins to find how much money altogether. Stress that the 2p coin has the same value as two 1p coins, and the 5p coin has the same value as five 1p coins. Increase the challenge by extending the ranges beyond 40 and 100, respectively. For amounts over 100p, ask: **How much is that in pounds and pence?**

Unit 2.10 Counting in hundreds, tens and ones

- Introduce a large collection of objects (for example, 343 art straws/beads/paper clips). Invite pupils to suggest ways in which the objects can be counted that will make it easy to see and check how many there are. **Is counting in ones a good idea? Why/why not? How about counting in twos/fives/tens?** Steer conversation towards bundling ten groups of ten together to make groups of one hundred. Ask pupils to suggest ways in which the class can work together to group the objects so that they are easy to count. Once the objects have been grouped, count together as a class: *One hundred and one hundred more equals 200. Add another hundred makes 300. Add ten makes 310 … 320 … 330 … 340 … 341 … 342 … 343.*
- Discuss the 'Let's Learn' section on page 28 of the Pupil Book. Introduce pre-grouped place value materials such as those shown (i.e. dot squares and strips or base 10 blocks). Represent an amount from 100 to 999 and invite pupils to count in hundreds, tens and ones to find the quantity represented. **How many dots/small cubes? How will we write this number in numerals? What do you notice?** Focus discussion on the first digit representing the number of 'hundreds', the middle digit representing the number of 'tens' and the final digit representing the number of ones. Repeat for different three-digit numbers. Include numbers with no tens and/or no ones.
- Ask pupils to close their eyes whilst you represent a three-digit number (for example, 452) with base 10 blocks in the conventional way:

  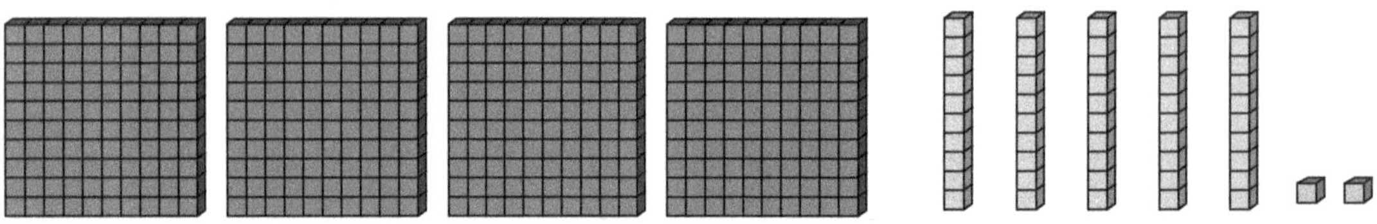

  Cover the blocks with a large sheet of paper, then invite pupils to open their eyes. Reveal the blocks one at a time whilst pupils keep a running total: 100, 200, 300, 400, 410, 420, 430, 440, 450, 451, 452. Repeat for different three-digit numbers. Include numbers with no tens and/or no ones.
- Repeat the above activity but this time display the base 10 blocks in an unconventional way; for example:

  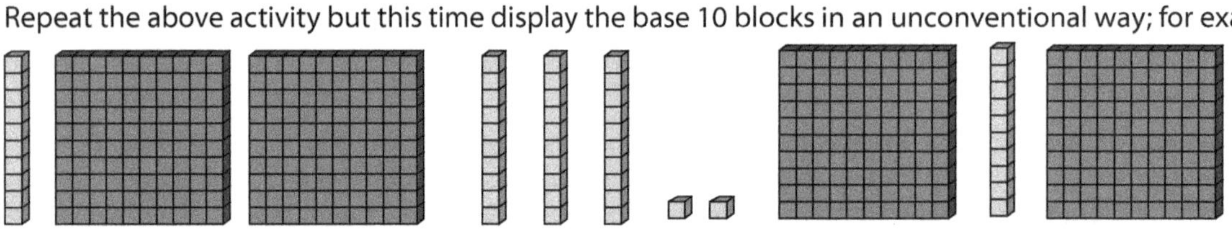

  Cover the blocks with a large sheet of paper, then invite pupils to open their eyes. Reveal the blocks one at a time whilst pupils keep a running total: 10, 110, 210, 220, 230, 240, 241, 242, 342, 352, 452. **Which way makes counting easier? Does everyone agree?** Encourage pupils to justify their answer.

Unit 2.11 Standard place value partitioning

- Pupils work in pairs. Give each pair a bundle of between 20 and 50 straws. Ask them to count the straws then come to the front of the class and record their total on a flipchart or whiteboard. Discuss each total in turn in the following way: *Nuria and Isla have 35 straws.* Point to the 3. **What does this digit mean?** Ask Nuria and Isla to separate out that number of straws. Record 30 + 5 = 35.
- Pupils work in pairs. Using base ten blocks, full and partially completed ten frames, or straws bundled in tens and ones, ask each pair to prove that, for example, 73 = 70 + 3.
- Spread a set of place value arrow cards, displaying the decade numbers 10–90 and the digits 1–9, on a table or the floor. Ask one pupil to find the number 80 and another to find the number 9. Demonstrate how the cards can be overlapped to make the number 89. Pick up two different cards (for example, 1 and 90). **I have 1 and 90, what number does this make?** Repeat for other pairs of cards. Note: it is important that pupils learn to appreciate that 90 and 1 is the same as 1 and 90.
- Give pupils their own set of place value arrow cards. **Using two cards each time, can you make the number 65/82/53/77 etc.? Is it possible to make a two-digit number using only one place value arrow card? Why is that?**
- Show pupils a two-digit number (for example, 84) on a place value house.

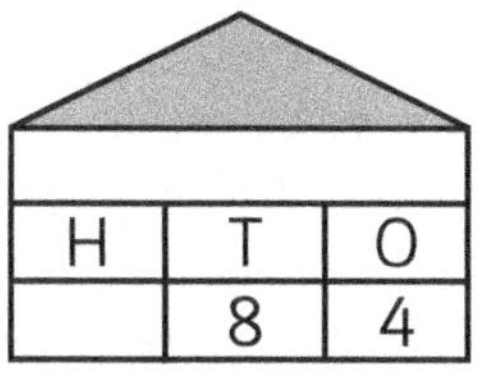

What number is this? Tell pupils that the number 84 has 8 in the tens place and 4 in the ones place. *It has 8 tens and 4 ones.* **What do 8 tens make? What do 4 ones make?** *8 tens and 4 ones is the same as 80 + 4.* Ask pupils to make the number 84 with place value arrow cards. **Which is the tens digit? Which is the ones digit? How many ones? How many tens?** Repeat for other two-digit numbers.

- Pupils work in pairs. Each pair needs a large place value house like the one below

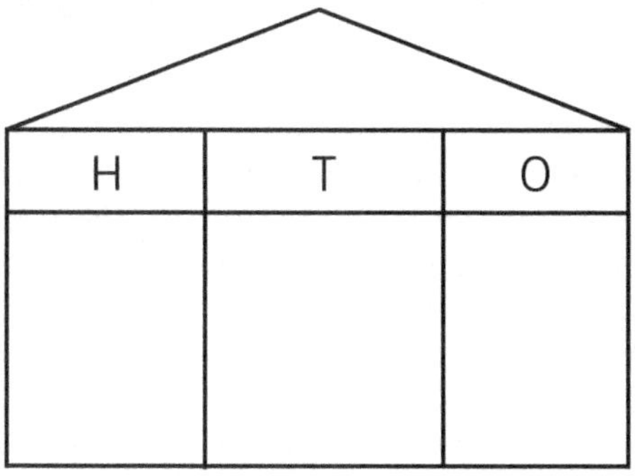

a dice, a bundle of straws and some rubber bands.

Pupils agree on a target number; for example, 50. They take turns to roll the dice and collect the corresponding number of straws that are placed in the ones column on the place value house. Play continues with each player declaring their new total. For example, *I had five ones. I rolled a four. Now I have nine ones.* Every time a player collects ten straws these are bundled together with a rubber band and placed in the tens column. For example, *I had nine ones and rolled a six. Now I have 15 ones. 15 is 10 and 5. I can make one ten and move these straws to the tens column. Now I have 1 ten and 5 ones, which equals 15.* The first player to reach or exceed the target number is the winner.

Unit 2.12 Comparing numbers

- Ask two pupils to each scoop up a pile of straws from a tray and group them in tens. Invite the class to say who has more and who has fewer by comparing the number of tens. **If Nuria has more tens than Finlay, do we still need to count the ones to find out who has more straws? If they both have the same number of tens, what could we do to find out who has more/less?**
- Ask pupils to choose from and use bundles of straws, ten frames, base 10 blocks or dot squares and strips to prove that, for example, 84 is more than 48 and 112 is less than 211.
- Ask pupils to place any pair of numbers used in the previous activity on a number line (for example, 84 and 48). Remind pupils that we already know that 84 is more than 48. *We can say that 84 is greater than (larger than) 48 and 48 is less than (smaller than) 84.* **Think about the numbers 725 and 527. Which do you think is greater and which is less? Prove it! Amman thinks 817 is less than 871 but Isla disagrees. Who is correct? What could Amman do to convince Isla that he is correct?**
- Pupils work in pairs. Each pair needs three dice. Pupil A rolls the dice to create a three-digit number (for example, 163) then writes the number chosen on a mini whiteboard. Pupil B must instruct Pupil A to change *one digit* to create a three-digit number that is greater than the number written, for example the instruction could be 'change the hundreds digit to a 4', 'change the tens digit to an 8' or 'change the ones digit to a 9'. Repeat to create a number less than the start number. For example, 'change the tens digit to a 2' or 'change the ones digit to a 0'. Pupils work together to place all numbers created on a number line and write comparative statements about them, for example 163 is less than 263 but greater than 143. Pupils swap roles. **Can one ever be replaced by zero? Which digits can replace the 6 to make a number greater than 163? Which digits can replace the 3 to make a number less than 163?** Ask pupils to justify their answers.

Unit 2.13 Ordering numbers

- Ask pupils to choose a number between 100 and 999 and write it on their mini whiteboard. **Compare numbers with the others at your table. Can you arrange yourselves in order from smallest to largest?** Ask two groups to join together and rearrange themselves so that the numbers remain in order from smallest to largest. Invite these pupils to line up at the front of the room and show their numbers to the rest of the class. **Is the order correct so far? If not, what changes need to be made? How many people have a number greater than/less than ____? Whose number is less than ____ but greater than ____?** Ask the pupils who are still seated to think about where their number might come in the sequence. **Who has a number that comes in-between _____ and ____?** Invite these pupils to fit themselves into the sequence. Repeat until the whole class is arranged in order from smallest to largest. **Does anyone have a number that is equal to yours? If so, how will you arrange yourselves?** Read the completed sequence aloud from smallest to largest and from largest to smallest.
- Ask pupils to choose a number that comes in-between 0 and 1000 and write it on a piece of card or paper. Invite pupils to take turns to peg their numbers in order from largest to smallest on a washing line. Read the completed sequence aloud from largest to smallest and from smallest to largest. Next, give each pupil another piece of paper or card and challenge them to write a second number that comes in-between their number and the number after or before it. **How do you know which number is greater and which is less?** Discuss any consecutive numbers; for example: **What number could come in-between 35 and 36?** Encourage suggestions such as 'thirty-five and a half' or 'thirty-five and three quarters'.

Unit 2.14 Ordinal numbers

- Discuss the top two tables in the 'Let's Learn' section on page 38 of the Pupil Book. **Which of these number order words have you seen before? Which number order words are new? What patterns do you notice? How can we use this information to help us read and say the numbers written in the table at the bottom of the page?** Once pupils are confident with reading and saying the ordinal numbers 21st–30th, ask them to work in pairs to write the same set of ordinal numbers in words.
- Create a pattern with twenty objects or shapes. **Which shape is thirteenth / eleventh / nineteenth in the pattern? If we were to continue the pattern, what colour would the twenty-first / twenty-seventh / thirtieth / twenty-second shape be?** Continue the pattern to check predictions.
- Pupils work in pairs. Each pupil creates their own pattern with up to 31 objects. Pairs take turns to ask each other questions about the pattern they have created (for example: **What colour is my twenty-sixth counter?**)
- Discuss a simple calendar. **If today is the 21st of November, what was yesterday's date? What date will tomorrow be? What date will it be one week from today?** Discuss the date of the month on which pupils were born. These could be displayed in a table or as a graph. **How many people were born on the first / twenty-second / thirtieth of the month? Was anyone born on the eleventh / fifteenth / thirty-first?**

Number - order and place value 1C

Section overview

Textbook 1C units	Review units	Prior learning	Benchmarks/ Es&Os
Unit 2.1 Recognising and writing three-digit numbers	**1B** Units 2.1, 2.2, 2.3 and 2.11	• Recognise the numerals 0–999. • Identify (find within a group) the numerals 0–999. • Read and write 2- and 3-digit numbers in numerals and in words. • Know the value of each digit in a 2-digit number.	**MNU 1-02a** • Reads, writes, orders and recites whole numbers to 1000, starting from any number in the sequence.
Unit 2.2 Zero as a place holder	**1B** Units 2.10 and 2.12 **1C** Unit 2.1	• Count in hundreds, tens and ones. • Recognise and write 3-digit numbers. • Compare 2- and 3-digit numbers by considering the values of the digits.	**MNU 1-02a** • Demonstrates understanding of zero as a place holder in whole numbers to 1000.
Unit 2.3 Number sequences (1)	**1B** Units 2.2, 2.4, 2.5, 2.6, 2.7 and 2.8	• Count forwards and backwards in hundreds on the hundred. • Count forwards and backwards in ones to or from a 3-digit number (no bridging or bridging a ten). • Say the number before or after a 3-digit number. • Count forwards and backwards in tens and hundreds to or from any 3-digit number (no bridging or bridging a ten). • Say the number 10 more/less or 100 more/less than a 3-digit number (simple examples).	**MNU 1-02a** • Counts forwards and backwards in 2s, 5s, 10s and 100s. • Demonstrates understanding of zero as a place holder in whole numbers to 1000.
Unit 2.4 Number sequences (2)	**1A** Units 4.3, 4.4 and 4.5 **1B** Units 2.9 and 4.8	• Skip count forwards in 2s, 5s and 10s. • Know that 20 is ten times bigger than 2. • Know that 50 is ten times bigger than 5.	**MNU 1-02a** • Adds and subtracts multiples of 10 and 100 to or from any whole number to 1000.
Unit 2.5 Number sequences (3)	**1A** Units 4.3, 4.4 and 4.5 **1B** Units 2.9 and 4.9	• Skip count backwards in 2s, 5s and 10s. • Know that 2 is ten times smaller than 20. • Know that 5 is ten times smaller than 50.	**MNU 1-02a** • Adds and subtracts multiples of 10 and 100 to or from any whole number to 1000.

Textbook 1C units	Review units	Prior learning	Benchmarks/ Es&Os
Unit 2.6 Representing and describing three-digit numbers	**1B** Units 2.10 and 2.11 **1C** Units 2.1 and 2.3	• Identify the value of each digit in a two-digit number. • Count in hundreds, tens and ones to find the value of a collection of base 10 materials. • Read and write 3-digit numbers.	**MNU 1-02a** • Identifies the value of each digit in a whole number with three digits; for example, $867 = 800 + 60 + 7$. • Demonstrates understanding of zero as a place holder in whole numbers to 1000.
Unit 2.7 Standard place value partitioning of three-digit numbers	**1B** Units 2.10 and 2.11 **1C** Units 2.2 and 2.6	• Partition 2-digit numbers into standard component parts, e.g. $34 = 30 + 4$. • Count in hundreds, tens and ones to find the value of a collection of base 10 materials. • Understand zero as a place holder in whole numbers. • Represent 3-digit numbers with base 10 materials and describe what they have made.	**MNU 1-02a** • Identifies the value of each digit in a whole number with three digits; for example, $867 = 800 + 60 + 7$. • Demonstrates understanding of zero as a place holder in whole numbers to 1000.
Unit 2.8 Non-standard place value partitioning of two-digit numbers	**1A** Unit 3.6 **1B** Unit 2.11	• Understand that the same total can be represented in different ways, e.g. 20 can be $10 + 10$, $17 + 3$, $5 + 15$, etc. • Partition 2-digit numbers into standard component parts, e.g. $34 = 30 + 4$.	**MNU 1-02a** • Identifies the value of each digit in a whole number with three digits; for example, $867 = 800 + 60 + 7$.
Unit 2.9 Comparing two- and three-digit numbers	**1B** Unit 2.12 **1C** Unit 2.8	• Compare two 2-digit numbers by considering the value of the tens digits. • Compare two 3-digit numbers by considering the value of the hundreds digit. • Use the words 'greater than', 'less than' and 'equal to' when comparing pairs of numbers.	**MNU 1-02a** • Reads, writes, orders and recites whole numbers to 1000, starting from any number in the sequence. **MTH 1-15a** • Understands and accurately uses the terms 'equal to', 'not equal to', 'less than', 'greater than', and related symbols ($=, \neq, <, >$) when comparing quantities.

Textbook 1C units	Review units	Prior learning	Benchmarks/ Es&Os
Unit 2.10 Ordering two- and three-digit numbers	**1B** Unit 2.13 **1C** Units 2.2 and 2.6	• Order sets of 3-digit numbers from smallest to largest by comparing the hundreds digits. • Order sets of 3-digit numbers from largest to smallest by comparing the hundreds digits. • Understand that the value of a digit is determined by its place.	**MNU 1-02a** • Reads, writes, orders and recites whole numbers to 1000, starting from any number in the sequence.
Unit 2.11 Ordinal numbers	**1B** Unit 2.14	• Read and write ordinal numbers up to 31st in words and symbols. • Use ordinal numbers up to 31st in real-life contexts; for example, 'Nuria was born on the thirtieth of July'.	**MNU 1-02a** • Reads, writes, orders and recites whole numbers to 1000, starting from any number in the sequence.

Conceptual context

Place value *underpins* mental calculation. Deep *conceptual* place value understanding allows us to manipulate numbers flexibly and to choose the most efficient method in order to solve a problem. In Book 1C this skill is developed through a continuing focus on counting in hundreds, tens and ones and extended to include counting in 20s, 25s and 50s.

Another contributing factor to the development of sound mental agility is the ability to *partition* numbers in different ways according to their place values. In Book 1B, pupils were introduced to standard place value partitioning of two-digit numbers (for example, 46 = 40 + 6). This is now extended to include standard place value partitioning of three-digit numbers; (for example, 329 = 300 + 20 + 9) and non-standard place value partitioning of two-digit numbers; (for example, 46 can also be 30 + 16, 20 + 26 or 10 + 36).

In Book 1B, pupils were introduced to reading, writing, comparing and ordering three-digit numbers. Book 1C sees a focus on building and describing three-digit numbers. Through opportunities to represent whole numbers with concrete materials and pictorially, pupils will develop a sense of the relative sizes of numbers and begin to understand that the value of each digit is determined by its place. They will also begin to appreciate zero as a place holder. This, along with an understanding of the patterns in the way we say, read and write whole numbers, will enable pupils to compare and order numbers with varying numbers of digits.

Through investigating quantities within the context of addition and subtraction, pupils learn that the equals sign (=) represents balance in a number sentence. Book 1C sees the introduction of the terms and symbols for 'not equal to' (≠), 'less than' (<) and 'greater than' (>). Finally, ordinal numbers are extended to include first (1st) up to and beyond one hundredth (100th).

Resources

- 10 × 10 square gird
- Base 10 blocks (hundreds, tens and ones)
- Calculators
- Empty number line
- Graduated number line per pupil (un-numbered)
- Hundred dot squares, ten dot strips, 1–9 dot strips
- Large place value house for demonstration purposes
- Mini whiteboard per pupil
- Numeral dice or spinners
- Place value counters
- Set of digit cards 0–9 per pupil
- Set of place value arrow cards per pupil (hundreds, tens and ones)
- Straws or interlocking cubes for counting

Key vocabulary

- **Compare**
- **Digit**
- **Equal**
- **Even number**
- **Greater than**
- **Less than**
- **More than**
- **Numerals**
- **Order**
- **Ordinal numbers**
- **Partition**
- **Place holder**
- **Place value**
- **Position**
- **Pattern**
- **Sequence**
- **Symbol**
- **Three-digit number**
- **Value**
- **Zero**

Misconceptions

Potential misconception	Addressing the misconception
Unit 2.1 Pupils may include extra zeros when writing numbers in numerals. For example, a pupil may write three hundred and sixty-seven as 30067.	Ask the pupil to say a chosen number (for example, 367) quietly to themselves then to select from a set of place value arrow cards the three cards that best describe what they hear. They should then say slowly to themselves: 300 and … 60 … 7. Have the pupil repeat this phrase faster whilst you combine the arrow cards. **What has happened to the zeros?** Focus the resulting conversation on the meaning of the digits. Emphasise that 367 is a 3-digit number made up of hundreds, tens and ones. When writing a 3-digit number we write the number of hundreds, then the number of tens, then the number of ones.

Potential misconception	Addressing the misconception
Units 2.1, 2.2, 2.6 and 2.7 Pupils may confuse numbers that contain a zero. For example, the pupil may read the number 470 as four *hundred and seven*. They may also write 417 when asked to write *four hundred and seventy* in numerals.	Say a three-digit number aloud (for example, 470). Ask pupils to repeat the number quietly to themselves and find the two place value arrow cards that best describe what they hear: 400 and 70. Demonstrate how the cards 400 and 70 can be overlapped to make the number 470. Write 470 on a flipchart or whiteboard. Repeat for the number 407. Compare the numbers written (i.e. 470 and 407). **What is the same and what is different?** Focus the resulting conversation on the meaning of the digits. Repeat for other pairs of three-digit numbers; for example, 109 and 190; 560 and 516. The following supplementary questions may be required in the latter example: **Which two numbers make up sixteen? How many place value arrow cards will you need to make 516?**
Unit 2.3 Pupils may encounter one or more of the following difficulties when counting forwards or backwards in tens within the range 0–1000. For example, the pupil may: • count by 100s rather than by tens and so say 116, 216, 316 not 116, 126, 136. • fail to increase the hundreds digit when crossing a hundred, i.e. says 371, 381, 391, 301, 311. • jump to the next 'hundred' number when counting backwards and so say, for example, 720, 710, 600, 690, 680 or 720, 710, 600, 590, 580.	Pupils should be given lots of opportunities to look for and explain number patterns in a number square or grid before being introduced to written work.
Units 2.1, 2.6, 2.9 and 2.10 Pupils may be able to name the places as 'hundreds, tens and ones' without fully understanding the meaning of the digits. For example, a pupil may say that 937 has nine hundreds, 3 tens and 7 ones but not equate this with '9 lots of one hundred', '3 lots of ten' and '7 lots of one'.	It is important that pupils see, and are helped to visualise, the individual units of one that make up one unit of ten and one unit of one hundred, respectively. They need lots of opportunities to build 3-digit numbers with base 10 equipment such as base 10 blocks, or dot squares and strips, before progressing to work with abstract units such as place value counters.
Units 2.9 and 2.10 Pupils may be able to name the places as hundreds, tens and ones without fully understanding the value of the digits, so disregard this when comparing a 2-digit number with a 3-digit number or when ordering a mixed set of 2- and 3-digit numbers. For example, when ordering the following set of numbers from smallest to largest, the pupil thinks that 317 should come first as '3' is the smallest first digit: 71, 640, 317, 96.	Provide lots of opportunities for pupils to build the numbers with concrete materials and place them on a number line.

Teaching ideas

Unit 2.1 Recognising and writing three-digit numbers

- Call out a range of three-digit numbers or write them in words on a flipchart or whiteboard. Ask pupils to 'show you' the number written in numerals on a mini whiteboard or calculator display, then compare their answer with a partner. **Have you both written the same? If not, who is correct? Why? How did the words help you decide which digits to write and the order to write them in? How did you know to write a three-digit number?**
- Show the same set of numbers on place value houses. Emphasise the hundreds, tens and ones structure (for example, 218 has 2 hundreds, 1 ten and 8 ones). **How many hundreds in the number 716? What does the zero mean in the number 970? Etc.**
- Display a range of three-digit numbers, each made up of the same three digits, on place value houses (for example, 329, 392, 923, 932, 239, 293). **What is the same and what is different?** Ask pupils to work with a partner to choose one of the six numbers and represent it with base 10 materials. They should swap places with another pair, count in hundreds, tens and ones to work out the number represented, and write the number in numerals and in words beside the model. Compare and discuss the models. **Did you have to count all of the hundreds, tens and ones? Why not? Which number can't this model show? Why not? Which number is largest/smallest? How do you know?**

Unit 2.2 Zero as a place holder

- Show the number 100 on a place value house. One hundred has 1 hundred, 0 tens and 0 ones.
- Show 200, 500, 900, etc. on place value houses. Discuss the purpose of the zeros (i.e. they keep the hundreds digit in place). **How would we write the numbers represented by these place value houses in words and in numerals?**
- **What about these numbers?** Represent a series of 3-digit numbers with none, one or two zeros on place value houses. Ask pupils to say the number represented. Where appropriate, discuss the position of the place holder(s).
- Give individuals/pairs of pupils a numeral dice or spinner and ask them to generate a list of ten 3-digit numbers. They should write each number down in numerals and in words then swap with another individual/pair. **Has 'and' been used correctly? Has zero been used correctly? Are answers such as 026 acceptable? Justify your answer.**
- Play 'Guess my Number'. Ask a pupil to write down a three-digit number in numerals without letting anyone see it. The rest of the class try to guess the number by asking questions to which the response can only be 'yes' or 'no'. For example, the questions 'Does your number have a zero in it?' and 'Is the zero in the ones place?' are permissible whereas 'How many zeros does your number have?' is not. Encourage pupils to keep track of what they find out about the number on a mini whiteboard. **Can you guess the number in less than 20 questions? What question will you ask first? Why? What sorts of questions are best asked early? Why? Why isn't it a good idea to guess the number too soon?**
- Play 'Guess my Number Name'. Pupils play in pairs. Pupil A thinks of a number between 100 and 1000 and draws a dash to represent each letter on a mini whiteboard. A slash separates words and hyphens are 'free'. For example, Pupil A may choose the number word *four hundred and sixty-nine* and represent it as follows: _ _ _ _ / _ _ _ _ _ _ _ / _ _ _ / _ _ _ _ _ - _ _ _ _. Pupil B asks for a letter; for example, Are there any 'd's? Pupil A writes all ds in the correct spaces. Pupil B keeps guessing letters to try to work out the number name. **Can you name the number in 10 guesses or less? Which letters did you ask for first? Why? Which letters are 'safe bets' and therefore a wasted guess?** For example, a hyphen indicates that the second last word will end in 'y'. As no other number names within this range contain a 'y', y is a wasted guess.

Unit 2.3 Number sequences (1)

- Revise counting forwards and backwards aloud in ones from a range of three-digit numbers. Focus on sequences that cross a decade and/or hundred (for example, counting from 277 up to 307 or from 807 down to 780). Add variety by having pupils respond to instructions or carry out actions as they count. For example, 'loud voice', 'quiet voice', 'stand on one leg', 'march on the spot' etc. A simple pendulum could also be made from a ball and string to control the pace of the count. Emphasise crossing decades and hundreds by asking follow up questions such as: **What number did you say just after 299/500/659/999, etc.? What comes just before 400/711/901/140, etc.?**
- Display a partially completed 10 × 10 grid, similar to the one shown below

50						59			
	61								69
			73					78	
80				84					
		92							99
		112							119
					125				
130							137		
					145				149

Have pupils take turns to help you complete it. Practise counting forwards and backwards in tens from various starting numbers. **What happens to the digit in the tens place each time you count forwards/backwards?** Challenge pairs to work together to extend one column of the grid. **How far can you go?**

- Display a graduated number line, similar to the one below

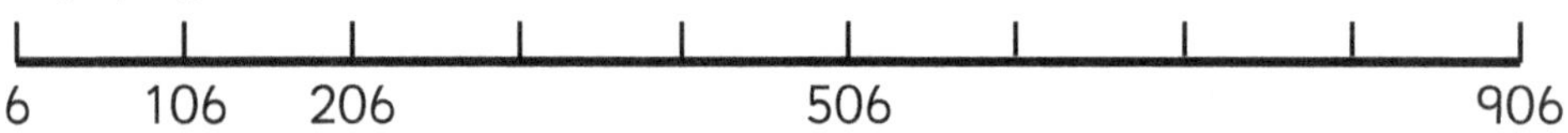

Have pupils count forwards in hundreds to find the missing numbers. **What happens to the digit in the hundreds place each time you count forwards?**

- Display a graduated number line, similar to the one below

Have pupils count backwards in hundreds to find the missing numbers. **What happens to the digit in the hundreds place each time you count backwards?**

- Give each pupil a sheet of blank number lines, each with ten graduations. Call out instructions such as 'Write 66 at the start and count forwards in hundreds', 'Write 911 at the end and count backwards in hundreds'. **What number goes at the end/start?**
- Lay a set of flashcards, each displaying a two- or three-digit number, face down on a table or on the floor. Pupils take turns to turn over a card and must say the number 10 more/less than and/or 100 more/less than the number displayed. **How will we write each new number? Which digit changes when we add/subtract 10/100? Is it ever necessary to change both the tens and hundreds digits? When?**

Unit 2.4 Number sequences (2)

- Ask pupils to work in pairs to investigate what happens when they key the following numbers and symbols into a calculator: 20+=========. **What do you notice? Can you explain this?** Encourage responses such as 'You keep adding 20', '20 add 20 add 20 add 20 makes 80', 'The numbers are going up in twenties'. Ask pupils to record the sequence on their mini whiteboards. Challenge them to write the next ten numbers in the sequence without using their calculator. Repeat for 25+========= and 50+=========. Ask pupils to compare the +25 and +50 sequences. **What do you notice? Can you explain this?**
- Give three groups of pupils a pile of 100 straws or interlocking cubes each. Ask one group to make sets of 20, another to make sets of 25 and the third group to make sets of 50. Have the class skip count in unison to find the totals, i.e. 20, 40, 60, 80, 100; 25, 50, 75, 100; 50, 100. **How many groups of 20? How many 25s in 100? What does 50 plus 50 make? How many straws altogether?** (100, 200, 300).
- Display three number lines graduated in 20s, 25s and 50s respectively. Point to each number in turn and have pupils recite each number word sequence aloud. Ask pupils to close their eyes while you hide or cover one or more number. **Which number(s) is/are missing? How do you know?**
- Ask pupils to imagine the +20 pattern in their heads. Tell them that you are going to start counting in 20s. Say the number zero out loud as you clap your hands. Continue clapping slowly. Pupils should count forwards in 20s in their heads in time to each clap. After several claps stop and ask: **What number did you reach? Did everyone reach the same number? If not, what might have happened?** Repeat for the +50 and +25 skip counting patterns.

Unit 2.5 Number sequences (3)

- Draw a number line, similar to the one below, on a flipchart or whiteboard.

A 'counting stick' (if available) provides a suitable alternative. **If this is zero (point to the start) and this is 200 (point to the end), what does each mark represent (20)?** Practise counting forwards and backwards in 20s along the number line/counting stick. **What number is halfway (100)? If this is one hundred, what is this number?** Point to graduations in random order. Repeat for counting in 50s (0–500) and 25s (0–250).

- Increase the challenge in the above activity by counting backwards in twenties from numbers that are not multiples of 20 (for example, 210) and in fifties from numbers that are not multiples of 50 (for example, 380).
- Play Ping Pong Backwards. Start counting backwards in 20s from a chosen number; for example, 860. Pupils say the next number in unison. Continue the sequence, alternating between teacher and class. For example: 860 (teacher), 840 (pupils), 820 (teacher), 800 (pupils). Pause after the number 800. **What number will I say next? What number will you say?** Repeat the activity several times, changing the starting number each time. Repeat for counting backwards in 50s and 25s. If appropriate, repeat for numbers that are not multiples of 20 or 50.
- Tell pupils that you are going to start at 480 and count backwards in 20s. Say the number 480 out loud as you clap your hands. Continue clapping slowly. Pupils should count backwards in 20s in their heads in time to each clap. After several claps, stop and ask: **What number did you reach? Did everyone reach the same number? If not, what might have happened?** Repeat for counting backwards in 50s and 25s. If appropriate, repeat for numbers that are not multiples of 20 or 50.

Unit 2.6 Representing and describing three-digit numbers

- Discuss the 'Let's Learn' section on page 18 of the Pupil Book. Show a different three-digit number on a place value house (for example, 518). Ask pairs or small groups to represent the number shown with base 10 blocks or dot squares and strips. **Can you 'see' the individual ones that make up each hundred/ten? How many 'hundreds'? how many ones is that? How many 'tens'? How many ones is that?** Highlight how 518 can be 5 hundreds, 1 ten and 8 ones or 500 + 10 + 8. Repeat for other three-digit numbers. Include numbers with zero in the tens and/or ones place.
- Write a three-digit number on a flipchart or whiteboard (for example, 777). **How many hundreds? How many tens? How many ones?** Scatter a set of hundreds, tens and ones arrow cards on a table or the floor. **Who can find three arrow cards to make the number 777? Has he/she chosen the correct cards? How can we check? Which card would we need to swap to make the number 797/377/772? Why is that?** Compare the original number with the new numbers. **What did you need to do to change 777 into 797?** (swap the 70 card for the 90 card). **What does the 'tens' digit say now?** Highlight the link between adding 20 and adding 2 tens.
- Challenge pupils to work in small groups to represent a 3-digit number using everyday objects such as paper clips, pasta shapes, beads, straws, plastic cups, rubber bands, etc. Their model should clearly show the values of the digits, i.e. the individual ones that make up each hundred and ten. **Can you work out the number represented by other groups' models? Can they guess your number?**

Unit 2.7 Standard place value partitioning of three-digit numbers

- Show the smallest base 10 block (1). **How many cubes?** Tell pupils that the cube has a value of one, i.e. it is worth one. Then show the next largest base 10 block (10). **If the cube has a value of one, what is the value of this 'rod'? What makes you say that? Can you see the ten ones that make up one ten?** Show the next largest base 10 block (100). **If the cube has a value of one, what is the value of this 'flat'? Can you see the one hundred ones? How many tens make 100? Can you see them? We have 1 hundred, 1 ten and 1 one, what number have we made?** Illustrate on a place value house.

H	T	O
1	1	1

- Scatter a set of hundreds, tens and ones place value arrow cards face-up on a table or on the floor. **Which cards do we need to make the number one hundred and eleven?** Write on a flipchart or whiteboard: 100 + 10 + 1 = 111. Record a different three-digit number on a place value house (for example, 254). Ask one pupil to make the number with base 10 materials and another to make the same number with place value arrow cards. Arrange the resources to highlight the relationship between the different representations.

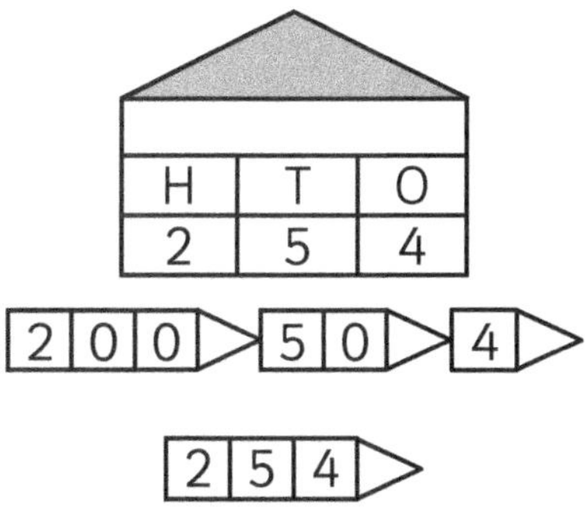

Repeat for different three-digit numbers. Include examples that have zero in the tens or ones place. **Can you think of a different three-digit number that can be built with only hundreds and ones/hundreds and tens? Can you think of a different three-digit number that can be made using only two place value arrow cards?** Discuss zero as a place holder.

- Represent the same set of numbers with place value counters. **Can you see the individual ones that make up each ten/hundred this time?** Each 10 counter has the same value as ten 1s counters. It is worth 10 ones. **How many 1s counters have the same value as one 10s counter? How many 1s counters have the same value as one 100s counter?**
- Make simple odometers out of Styrofoam cups. Pupils work in pairs. Pupil A makes a three-digit number on their odometer and shows it to Pupil B. Pupil B records the partitions on a mini whiteboard; for example, Pupil A makes the number 669. Pupil B writes 600 + 60 + 9. The cups are then pulled apart so that the answer can be checked.

Unit 2.8 Non-standard place value partitioning of two-digit numbers

- Display 35 counters as a 5 × 7 array (double-sided counters are ideal).

How many dots? How did you count them? Write the number 35 on a flipchart or whiteboard. Point to the 3. **What does this part of the number mean? Which part of the array shows that number of counters?** Point to the 5. **What does this part of the number mean?** If using double-sided counters, turn the last column of five over and display 35 = 30 + 5 underneath the array.

30 + 5 = 35

Repeat for different arrays. Alternatively, use collections of objects where the tens and ones are less obvious; for example, 4 bundles of ten straws and 16 single straws.

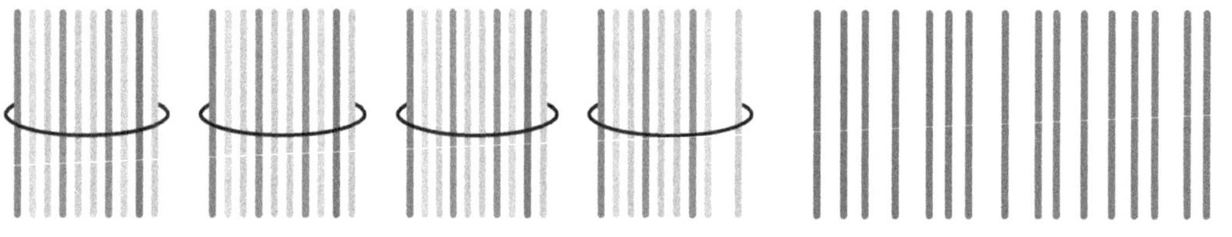

How many straws? How did you count them? Write the number 56 on a flipchart or whiteboard. Point to the 5. **What does this part of the number mean?** Point to the 6. **What does this part of the number mean?**

- Invite one pupil to make the number 35 with base 10 materials and/or place value counters. Pupils will most likely collect 3 tens and 5 ones to show 30 + 5. Rearrange the base 10 blocks/place value counters to show that 35 can also be partitioned into 20 + 15; 10 + 15; 10 + 10 + 5. Repeat for different two-digit numbers. **How many different ways can you find? Is 20 + 15 the same as 15 + 20?**
- Present the following scenario to the class: *Mrs Walker wants to buy some new felt pens for her classroom. Pens are sold in packs of ten and singly. Packs of ten may not be broken up.* Ask pupils to work in pairs to show all the different ways that Mrs Walker could buy 62 pens. They may choose to represent the pens with concrete materials and/ or make drawings on a mini whiteboard. **How many different ways are there? How did you work it out? How can you be sure you have found all of the possibilities?** Encourage systematic working, i.e. 6 packs of 10 plus 2 single pens; 5 packs of 10 plus 12 single pens; 4 packs of 10 plus 22 single pens, etc.

Unit 2.9 Comparing two- and three-digit numbers

- Write the following statements on a flipchart or whiteboard: 75 = 40 + 35; 16 + 30 = 36; 1 + 90 = 91; 91 = 41 + 40; 20 + 57 = 77; 12 + 80 = 82. Ask pupils to work in pairs to decide if each statement is true or false. Write the headings 'True' and 'False' on a flipchart/whiteboard. Invite pupils to take turns to write each statement in the correct column. **Which statements are true and which are false? Do we all agree?** Ask pupils to suggest ways to change each false statement to make it true. Introduce the 'not equal to' symbol (≠) as a straightforward way to make every statement in the false column true. Change the column headings to 'equal to' and 'not equal to' then invite pupils to take turns to add to either list. Encourage a focus on non-standard partitioning by setting ground rules. For example, the number statement should contain at least two 2-digit numbers, one of which must be a multiple of ten.

- Discuss the 'Let's Learn' section on page 26. Display different pairs of numbers and have pupils compare them. Include examples that require pupils to compare numbers with the same number of digits (for example, 193 and 319) and examples that require pupils to compare numbers with a different number of digits; for example, 75 and 705. **Which number is greater? Which number is less? What helped you decide?** Focus discussion on the value of the digits.
- Pupils work in pairs. Each pupil writes ten 3-digit numbers on pieces of card (a different number on each card) and places them face down in a pile. The first card in each pile is turned over. Pupils compare the two numbers displayed and use the symbols $<$, $>$, $=$, $\neq$ to write as many mathematical statements about the numbers as possible. For example, the numbers 619 and 642 would generate the following statements: $619 < 642$; $642 > 619$ and $619 \neq 642$. **Are three statements always possible? When might there only be one possible solution? Do you notice anything interesting about the direction of the less than and greater than symbols? Can you think up a rule to help you remember which symbol is which?**

Unit 2.10 Ordering two- and three-digit numbers

- Discuss the 'Let's Learn' section on page 28 of the Pupil Book. Focus the discussion on the value of the digits.
- Ask a group of pupils to each choose a 3-digit number within a given range, write it on a post-it note, estimate the position of their number on an empty number line and attach it. **Are the numbers in the correct order? If not, what needs to change?** Challenge all pupils to write a number that would fit in-between a given pair and 'show you' on a mini whiteboard.
- Ask all pupils to each write a 3-digit number on their mini whiteboard. They should then work together to compare numbers and arrange themselves in a given order around the room, i.e. smallest to largest or largest to smallest. **How did you work out the correct order? What strategy did you use? How many people have a number greater than/less than ____? Whose number is less than ____ but greater than ____?**
- Give each pupil a piece of paper or card. Ask half the class to write down any 2-digit number and the other half to write down any 3-digit number. Pupils take turns to peg their numbers in order from largest to smallest on a washing line. Read the completed sequence out loud. Next, give each pupil another piece of paper or card and challenge them to write a second number that comes in-between their number and the number after or before it. **How do you know which number is greater and which is less?** Discuss any consecutive numbers; for example: **What number could come in-between 289 and 290?** Encourage suggestions such as 'two hundred and eighty-nine and a half' or 'two hundred and eighty-nine and three quarters'.

Unit 2.11 Ordinal numbers

- Discuss the 'Let's Learn' section on page 30 of the Pupil Book. **What do you notice?** If necessary, draw pupils' attention to the fact that the last two letters of the ordinal number word are always written after the numeral. **How could we use this information to help us write fifty-first/forty-second/eighty-eighth/seventy-third? etc.** Call out an ordinal number word and ask pupils to 'show you' the word in symbols on a mini whiteboard. Write an ordinal number in symbols on a flipchart or whiteboard. Ask pupils to write the ordinal number in words then compare answers with a partner. **Have you both written *exactly* the same? If not, who is correct?**
- Write a list of ordinal number words within the range 'first – one hundredth' on a flipchart or whiteboard. Each word should contain at least one spelling error. Tell pupils that Nuria and Isla have been writing ordinal number words but have made some mistakes. Pupils should discuss each example with a partner, agree what needs to be done to correct each example, then write the ordinal number correctly in words and symbols. **What have the girls done wrong? What did you need to change? What tips do you have for the girls to help them avoid making the same mistake again?**
- Pose word problems such as the following:

  Eighty runners took part in a marathon. Finlay's mum finished six places behind the runner in thirty-third place. In what position did Finlay's mum finish?

  Amman's dad came first in a cycle race. The person who came last finished in forty-second place. How many cyclists were in the race?

  How will you work it out? Would a number line help? Ask pupils to write their own ordinal number problems for a partner or the class to solve.

Number – addition and subtraction 1A

Section overview

Textbook 1A units	Review units	Prior learning	Benchmarks/ Es&Os
Unit 3.1 Addition bonds to 10	**Early – B** Units 3.5 and 3.14	• Partition collections of up to 10 items in different ways (part-part-whole). • Recognise and correctly use the + and = symbols.	**MNU 1-03a** • Uses correct mathematical vocabulary when discussing the four operations including subtract, add, sum of, total, multiply, produce, divide and shared equally. • Demonstrates understanding of the commutative law, for example, 6 + 3 = 3 + 6 or 2 × 4 = 4 × 2.
Unit 3.2 Fact families within 10	**Early – B** Units 3.1, 3.6, 3.11 and 3.14	• Subitise five-wise patterns shown on ten frames. • Partition collections of up to 10 items in different ways (part-part-whole). • Recognise and describe concrete and pictorial representations of addition and subtraction facts within 10. • Recognise and correctly use the +, – and = symbols.	**MNU 1-03a** • Uses correct mathematical vocabulary when discussing the four operations including subtract, add, sum of, total, multiply, produce, divide and shared equally. • Demonstrates understanding of the commutative law; for example, 6 + 3 = 3 + 6 or 2 × 4 = 4 × 2. • Applies knowledge of inverse operations (addition and subtraction; multiplication and division).

Unit 3.3 Doubles to 20	**Early – B** Units 3.1, 3.2 and 3.3	• Subitise pair-wise patterns shown on ten frames. • Recall the doubles from 1 + 1 to 5 + 5.	**MNU 1-03a** • Uses correct mathematical vocabulary when discussing the four operations including subtract, add, sum of, total, multiply, produce, divide and shared equally. • Applies knowledge of inverse operations (addition and subtraction; multiplication and division).
Unit 3.4 Ten plus facts	**Early – B** Unit 2.3 **Early – B** Units 3.1 and 3.13 **1A** Unit 2.10 and Unit 3.2	• Read and write the numerals from 0–20. • Subitise to say 'how many' for regular dot patterns displayed on bead strings and ten frames. • Recognise that the same total can be represented in different ways. • Partition the numbers from 11 to 19 into '10 and ?'.	**MNU 1-03a** • Uses correct mathematical vocabulary when discussing the four operations including subtract, add, sum of, total, multiply, produce, divide and shared equally. • Demonstrates understanding of the commutative law, for example, 6 + 3 = 3 + 6 or 2 × 4 = 4 × 2. • Adds and subtracts multiples of 10 or 100 to or from any whole number to 1000.
Unit 3.5 Five plus facts	**Early - B** Units 3.2, 3.6, 3.14 and 3.15 **1A** Unit 2.10	• Subitise five-wise and pair-wise patterns on ten frames. • Combine and partition numbers using 5 and 10 as reference points. For example, can use the fact that 7 is 2 more than 5 on a ten frame to work out 5 + 2 =, or that 9 is 1 less than 10 to work out 10 – 1 =. • Recall addition bonds to 10 by visualising regular and irregular dot patterns. • Partition the numbers from 11 to 19 into '10 and ?'.	**MNU 1-03a** • Uses correct mathematical vocabulary when discussing the four operations including subtract, add, sum of, total, multiply, produce, divide and shared equally. • Solves addition and subtraction problems with three-digit whole numbers.

Unit 3.6 Addition bonds to 20	**Early - B** Units 3.6, 3.14 and 3.15 **1A** Unit 2.10 and Units 3.1 and 3.4	• Recall addition bonds to 10 by visualising dot and finger patterns. • Understand that the same amount can be partitioned in different ways. • Partition the numbers from 11 to 19 into '10 and ?'. • Know that amounts can be added in any order, e.g. 3 + 10 will give the same answer as 10 + 3. • Subitise ten plus facts on bead bars and/or double ten frames.	**MNU 1-03a** • Uses correct mathematical vocabulary when discussing the four operations including subtract, add, sum of, total, multiply, produce, divide and shared equally. • Solves addition and subtraction problems with three-digit whole numbers. • Adds and subtracts multiples of 10 or 100 to or from any whole number to 1000.
Unit 3.7 Subtraction within 20	**Early – B** Units 3.4, 3.6, 3.13, 3.14 and 3.15 **1A** Unit 2.10 Units 3.2, 3.4 and 3.5	• Combine and partition numbers using 5 and 10 as reference points. • Recall subtraction facts to 10 by visualising dot and finger patterns. • Understand that the same amount can be partitioned in different ways. • Partition the numbers from 11 to 19 into '10 and ?'. • Know some double facts to 20. • Subitise ten plus facts on bead bars and/or double ten frames.	**MNU 1-03a** • Uses correct mathematical vocabulary when discussing the four operations including subtract, add, sum of, total, multiply, produce, divide and shared equally. • Solves addition and subtraction problems with three-digit whole numbers.
Unit 3.8 Counting on and counting back	**Early - A** Unit 2.3 **Early – B** Units 2.1 and 2.7 and Unit 3.6	• Sequence the numbers 0–20 forwards and backwards. • Count to find the sum of two quantities. • Count to find how many left.	**MNU 1-03a** • Uses correct mathematical vocabulary when discussing the four operations including subtract, add, sum of, total, multiply, produce, divide and shared equally. • Solves addition and subtraction problems with three-digit whole numbers.

Unit 3.9 Adding two one-digit numbers using a number line	**Early – B** Units 3.8, 3.9 and 3.10 **1A** Unit 2.10 and Units 3.1, 3.4, 3.5 and 3.8	• Know all complements to 10. • Count on in ones to add on a numbered track and write an addition number sentence to match. • Recall ten plus facts.	**MNU 1-03a** • Uses correct mathematical vocabulary when discussing the four operations including subtract, add, sum of, total, multiply, produce, divide and shared equally. • Demonstrates understanding of the commutative law, for example, $6 + 3 = 3 + 6$ or $2 \times 4 = 4 \times 2$. • Solves addition and subtraction problems with three-digit whole numbers.
Unit 3.10 Subtracting using a number line	**Early – B** Units 3.6, 3.11 and 3.12 **1A** Unit 2.10 and Units 3.1, 3.4, 3.5, 3.7 and 3.8	• Know all complements to 10. • Subtract from a teen number to make 10. • Count back in ones to subtract on a numbered track and write a subtraction number sentence to match.	**MNU 1-03a** • Uses correct mathematical vocabulary when discussing the four operations including subtract, add, sum of, total, multiply, produce, divide and shared equally. • Solves addition and subtraction problems with three-digit whole numbers.
Unit 3.11 Missing addend	**Early – B** Unit 3.16 **1A** Units 3.2, 3.4, 3.5, 3.6, 3.8 and 3.9	• Solve simple missing number problems within the range 0–10. • Combine and partition sets of visible objects (for example, dots on ten frames or beads on a string/bar) to work our fact families within 10. • Combine and partition sets of visible objects (for example, dots on ten frames or beads on a string/bar) to add within 20. • Count on from a one-digit number on a numbered line to find a total.	**MNU 1-03a** • Uses correct mathematical vocabulary when discussing the four operations including subtract, add, sum of, total, multiply, produce, divide and shared equally. • Solves addition and subtraction problems with three-digit whole numbers. • Applies knowledge of inverse operations (addition and subtraction; multiplication and division).

Unit 3.12 Missing subtrahend	**Early – B** Unit 3.16 **1A** Units 3.2, 3.4, 3.5, 3.7, 3.8, 3.10 and 3.11	• Solve simple missing number problems within the range 0–10. • Combine and partition sets of visible objects (for example, dots on ten frames or beads on a string/bar) to work our fact families within 10. • Partition a set of visible objects to subtract from numbers up to 20. • Count back from a number in the range 11–20 to find the difference between two numbers.	**MNU 1-03a** • Uses correct mathematical vocabulary when discussing the four operations including subtract, add, sum of, total, multiply, produce, divide and shared equally. • Solves addition and subtraction problems with three-digit whole numbers. • Applies knowledge of inverse operations (addition and subtraction; multiplication and division).
Unit 3.13 Representing and solving word problems (1)	**Early – B** Unit 3.16 **1A** Units 3.11 and 3.12	• Solve simple missing number problems within the range 0–10. • Represent addition and subtraction situations with concrete materials and pictorially.	**MNU 1-03a** • Solves addition and subtraction problems with three-digit whole numbers. • Applies knowledge of inverse operations (addition and subtraction; multiplication and division).
Unit 3.14 Representing and solving word problems (2)	**Early** Unit 3.16 **1A** Units 3.11, 3.12 and 3.13	• Solve simple missing number problems within the range 0–10. • Represent addition and subtraction situations with concrete materials and pictorially and write number sentences to match their thinking (part-part-whole).	**MNU 1-03a** • Solves addition and subtraction problems with three-digit whole numbers. • Applies knowledge of inverse operations (addition and subtraction; multiplication and division).

Unit 3.15 Representing and solving word problems (3)	**Early – B** Unit 3.16 **1A** Units 3.11, 3.12, 3.13 and 3.14	• Solve simple missing number problems within the range 0–10. • Represent addition and subtraction situations with concrete materials and pictorially and write number sentences to match their thinking (part-part-whole). • Appreciate that the same word problem can be represented and solved in different ways.	**MNU 1-03a** • Solves addition and subtraction problems with three-digit whole numbers. • Applies knowledge of inverse operations (addition and subtraction; multiplication and division).

Conceptual context

An Early Level focus on mental addition and subtraction within 10 is extended to include number bonds to 20. Central to the development of sound mental agility within this number range is the ability to visualise quantities using five and ten as reference points. For example, the pupil who can subitise the number 18 on a double ten frame appreciates that 18 is two less than 20 so 18 add 2 must equal 20 and 20 minus 2 must equal 18.

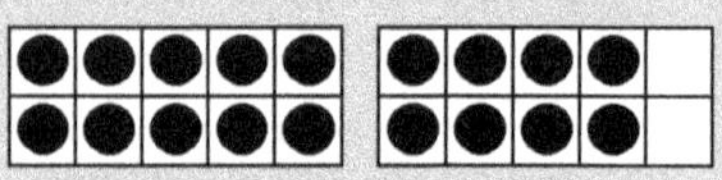

Likewise, the pupil who appreciates that 11 is one more than 10, and also that 4 is one less than 5, can use this knowledge to manipulate and ultimately visualise 11 – 4 on a Rekenrek.

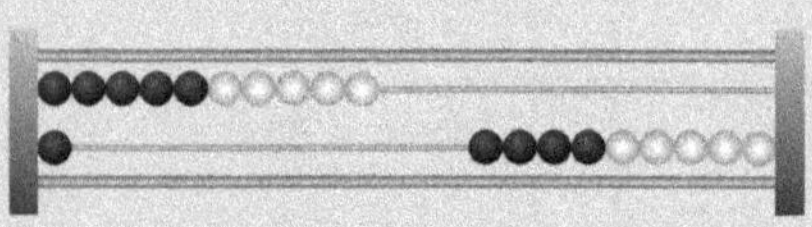

11 is 10 and 1

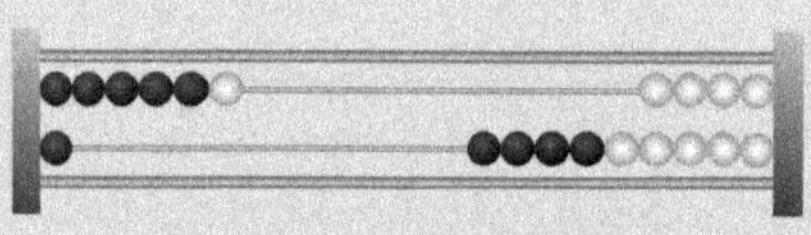

4 is 1 less than 5. Take 4 beads away and leave 1 behind. 6 on the top and 1 on the bottom makes 7

or

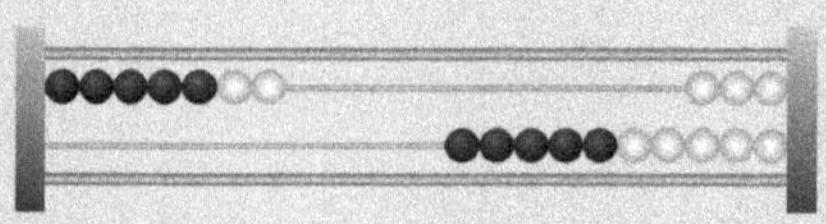

Take away 1 on the bottom and 3 on the top to make 4. I see 5 and 2, which makes 7

The commutative nature of addition, introduced informally at Early Level through activities such as 'Finger Flash', is further developed. Understanding commutativity is important as it halves the number of addition facts required to be remembered. Pair-wise patterns are extended, to include double 6 through to double 10, and serve as a meaningful introduction to ten plus facts. For example, by making double 8 on a Rekenrek pupils can clearly see that 8 + 8 (8 on the top; 8 on the bottom) is the same as 10 + 6 (10 black; 6 white).

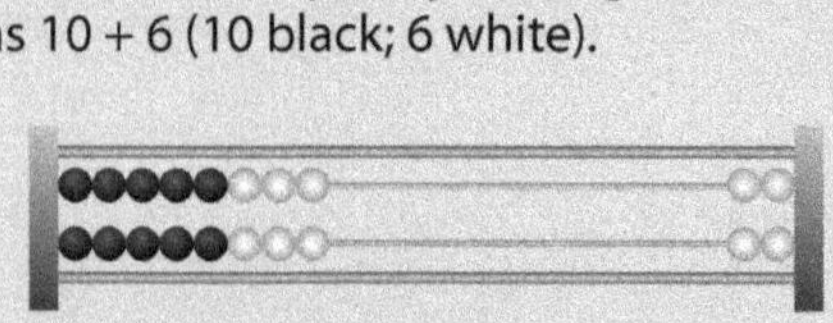

Counting on and back in ones, to add and subtract on graduated number lines, is also extended to include numbers within the range 0–20. Screening activities within this number range support pupils as they progress from using 'count all' to more efficient 'count on' strategies.

Central to the development of number sense is the ability to connect mathematical ideas and see the relationships between the four operations. Through many and varied opportunities to explore number properties, pupils come to realise that whilst addition is commutative, subtraction is not. It is important that pupils experience the full range of problem types, i.e. start, change and result unknown, combine and compare (see Units 3.11 – 3.15). They should also be encouraged to represent word problems in multiple ways (for example, with concrete materials, pictures, diagrams such as the number line and bar model, words and symbols) hence developing their understanding of the inverse relationship. In Book 1A this is achieved through a focus on 'part-part-whole'.

Resources

- 1–6 spot dice
- 20-bead string per pupil
- Blank ten frames
- Blank double ten frames
- Cuisenaire rods
- Double-sided counters
- Empty opaque box
- Everyday objects for counting; (for example, straws, buttons, counters, blocks)
- Interlocking cubes
- Number line from 0–20 per pupil
- Opaque paper or plastic cups
- Opaque paper or card for screening activities
- Pack of 0–10 digit cards
- Sets of number fact cards

Key vocabulary

- **Addition**
- **Bead string**
- **Difference**
- **Digit**
- **Double**
- **Double ten frame**
- **Equal**
- **Number bonds**
- **Number line**
- **Number sentence**
- **Partition**
- **Rekenrek**
- **Subitise**
- **Subtraction**
- **Sum**
- **Think Board**

Misconceptions

Potential misconception	Addressing the misconception
Units 3.8, 3.9 and 3.10 Pupils may use the number line incorrectly, counting numerals instead of jumps. For example, for 8 + 3 the child points to the numerals 8, 9 and 10 so thinks the answer is 10 because he/she has pointed to three numbers.	Make a 0–20 number line on the floor and have the child physically jump from one number to the next. Once pupils are confident in counting their own jumps, draw a graduated number line on a large piece of paper and have them 'jump' a cut out character along it. Progress to 'jumping' from one number to the next with their finger.
Units 3.9 and 3.10 Pupils may be unable to partition quantities to ten and so rely on counting forward and backwards by ones.	Provide lots of subitising and partitioning practice with ten frames to help pupils visualise different combinations of the same number. For example: 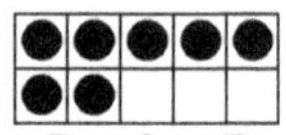 5 + 2 = 7 What can you see? How many dots on the top? How many on the bottom? How many dots altogether? 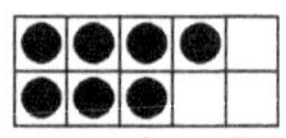 4 + 3 = 7 6 + 1 = 7 2 + 2 + 2 + 1 = 7
Units 3.11 and 3.12 Pupils may not trust counting on or counting back as a reliable strategy and so may have difficulty with missing addend and missing subtrahend tasks.	Pupils should be permitted to combine and separate visible collections of objects for as long as required. Once they are confident in counting on from the first addend to solve a missing sum question (for example 7 + 4 = ?) where both collections are visible, either addend can be 'screened' with a clear cover, progressing to a translucent cover before being fully screened with an opaque cover. **'What' add four equals eleven? Seven add 'what' equals eleven?** Similarly, once pupils are confident in counting back to find the difference (for example 11 – 4 = ?) some objects can be placed inside a clear box, where they can still be seen, before being fully screened. **Eleven take away 'what' equals four? Eleven take away 'what' equals seven?**
Units 3.13 and 3.14 Pupils may be unable to connect how they solved a problem to an appropriate number sentence.	Provide pupils with lots of opportunities to represent and solve problems with concrete materials and drawings. Start with questions where movement is inferred (for example, objects being given and taken or appearing and disappearing) and allow the child to role play the action. Progress to combine problems (for example, Unit 3.13, questions 3 and 4) where no action is inferred. In each case model connecting each step of the process to the appropriate mathematical symbol, representing the unknown with an empty box.

Potential misconception	Addressing the misconception
Unit 3.15 Pupils may be unable to connect what they know about addition and subtraction with problems that require them to compare two quantities.	Provide simple missing difference word problems in which there is an inferred action. For example: *There are 13 people on the ground floor of the store. Four people go upstairs. How many are on the ground floor now?* Ask pupils to model the situation with concrete objects and/or pictures. **How did you show the people in the story? How did you show what happened?** Encourage pupils to explain their thinking. For example: • *I put out 13 counters for the people then took 4 away because they went upstairs.* • *I drew 13 stick people and crossed 4 out to show they weren't there anymore.* **What is the difference between the 13 people who were downstairs and the number of people that are there now? How many more were there at the start? How many fewer people are there now?** Record pupils' explanations on a flipchart or whiteboard and write a number sentence to match what they say, i.e. 13 – 9 = [4]. Make the link with addition by telling the pupils that the those who went upstairs came back down. Ask them to show this with objects or as a picture. **There were nine people on the ground floor. Four more joined them. How many are there now?** 9 + [4] = 13. Once pupils are confident with problems similar to those above, introduce examples where the 'action' is less obvious (see examples on page 71 of the Pupil Book). Introduce matching as a useful way to compare two quantities.

Teaching ideas

Unit 3.1 Addition bonds to 10

- Ask pupils to work in pairs. Give each pair a collection of 10 objects (for example, beads, buttons, counters, cubes). Ask them to find and record as many different combinations of 10 as they can. **How many different ways can you find?** List pupils' ideas on a flipchart or whiteboard. Focus discussion on pairs of related facts. **Is 6 + 4 the same as 4 + 6?** Give one pupil 6 blue cubes and another 4 yellow cubes. **Amman has 6 cubes and Finlay has 4 cubes, how many cubes altogether? If they swap so that Finlay has 6 and Amman has 4 will there still be 10 cubes? Why?** Record 6 + 4 = 4 + 6 on the flipchart or whiteboard. Ask pupils to review the original list and record any other pairs of facts that they spot on a mini whiteboard. If appropriate, extend to sets of three numbers; for example: **Is 3 + 2 + 5 the same as 2 + 3 + 5?**
- Ask pupils to work with the person sitting opposite them. Each pair will need up to 10 double-sided counters. Call out a number between 0–10 (for example, 8). Pupils agree how many of each colour they will use to give a total of 8 counters. **How have you made 8? What is the same and what is different about what you and your partner can see?** Draw out how both see the same total (8) but arranged in different ways. For example, Isla sees 1 red counter on her left and 7 yellow counters on her right and writes 1 + 7 = 8, whereas Nuria sees 7 yellow counters on her left and 1 red counter on her right and writes 7 + 1 = 8. Ask pupils what they notice about the double facts, e.g. 4 + 4. **Do you and your partner see 8 in the same way or in different ways? Will your write the same number sentence or different number sentences? Can you think of other addition facts where this is the case?**

- If appropriate, extend the above activity by providing each pair of pupils with interlocking cubes of three different colours. Ask pupils to partition the set into three groups and record what they each see as a number sentence. **Which parts of your number sentences are the same and which are different?**
- Pupils work in pairs. Each pair will need a set of number fact cards. The cards are spread out face-up on the table. Pupil A selects two cards with equivalent totals and says the total (for example, *five plus two equals 7 and three plus four equals 7*). Pupil B must find a third card to complete the 'hat trick' (for example, *I choose four plus three to complete the hat trick*). The three cards are set to one side. Players swap roles. The game continues until no more 'hat tricks' are possible. **How many hat tricks did you find? Is there more than one hat trick with the same total? Are there any cards left over? If so, which bundle could they be added to?**

Unit 3.2 Fact families within 10

- Show pupils a stick of 8 interlocking cubes; 5 of one colour and 3 of another. **How many cubes?** Tell pupils that the whole stick of cubes is worth 8. ***How many (green) cubes?*** *The green part is worth 5.* ***How many (red) cubes?*** *The red part is worth 3.* Ask pupils to write the corresponding number sentence (5 + 3 = 8) on a mini whiteboard and 'show you'. Rotate the whole stick of cubes through 180°. **What can you see now?** Focus discussion on the position of the (red) part and the (green) part. Ask pupils to write a number sentence to match what they see underneath the first number sentence written on their mini whiteboards. **If I take away the green part, what will be left?** Invite pupils to write a number sentence to match the action performed. **If I take away the red part, what will be left?** Invite pupils to write a number sentence to match the action performed. **Compare what you have written with a partner, have you both written the same *number fact family?***

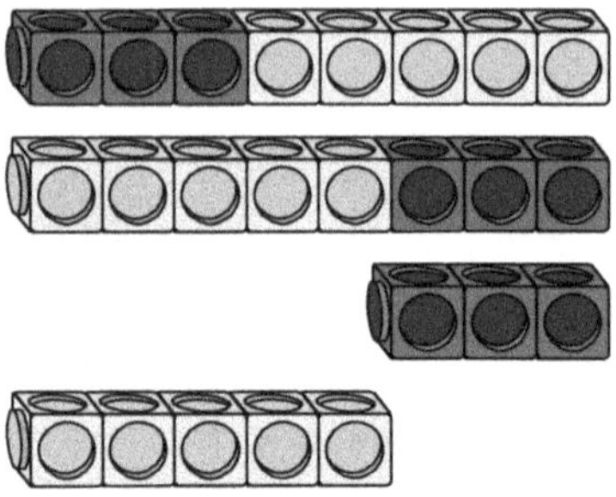

3 + 5 = 8

5 + 3 = 8

8 − 5 = 3

8 − 3 = 5

- Display a domino. **How many spots on the left? How many spots on the right? How many spots altogether?** Flip the domino through 180°. **How many spots on the left? How many spots on the right? How many spots altogether?** Cover the spots on the left. **How many spots altogether? How many can you see? How many are hiding?** Cover the spots on the right. **How many spots altogether? How many can you see? How many are hiding?** Challenge pupils to write a fact family about the domino. Focus discussion on the two additions, the two subtractions and the relationship between the additions and subtractions. Include doubles. **How many number facts in the fact family this time?**

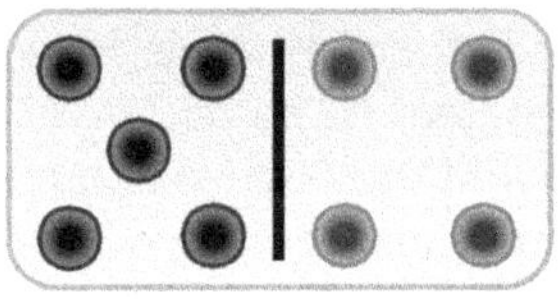

5 + 4 = 9
4 + 5 = 9
9 − 4 = 5
9 − 5 = 4

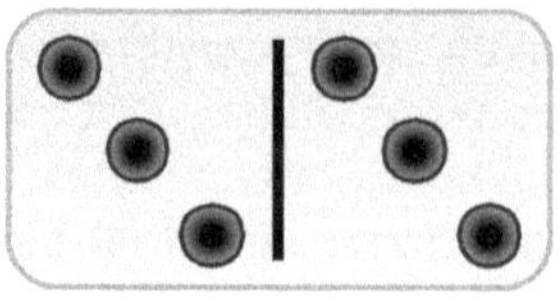

3 + 3 = 6
6 − 3 = 3

- Repeat the above activity for strips of ten dots of two contrasting colours. Discourage counting by ones. **If there are ten dots altogether, how many are red? How do you know?**

- Tell pupils that you have a picture in your head of a stick of 10 cubes. Some of the cubes are yellow and the rest are blue. **If the yellow part is 8 cubes long, how many cubes long is the blue part?** Repeat for other combinations to 10.
- Discuss the 'Let's Learn' section on page 40 of the Pupil Book. Focus the discussion on part-part-whole. Give each pupil a blank ten frame and a set of 10 double-sided counters. Pupils arrange their counters on their ten frame in any way they wish then swap ten frames with a partner. **Can you write a fact family for your partner's ten frame?**

Unit 3.3 Doubles to 20

- Pupils work in pairs. Give each pair a collection of objects (for example, 5 counters/blocks/buttons/pencils/straws) and ask them to double it. **What does it mean to double a number? How did you work out double 5?** Repeat for other amounts from 6 to 10.
- Show the number 12 as a pair-wise pattern on a Rekenrek and have pupils subitise the amount. **How many beads? How do you know? What do you see?** Encourage responses such as 'ten and two', '6 + 6', 'two sixes', 'double six'. **What is double six? Double what makes 12?** Repeat for other even totals from 12 to 20.

- Challenge pupils to use their Rekenrek and their knowledge of doubles to work out other number facts. **How can we use the fact that double six is twelve (6 + 6 = 12) to work out the answer to 7 + 6 or 6 + 5? Etc.**
- Challenge pupils to use their knowledge of doubles and/or concrete materials to work out 'double doubles'; (for example, double 2 is 4 and double 4 is 8). **How many groups of 2? How many groups of 4?** Repeat for other single-digit numbers.

Unit 3.4 Ten plus facts

- Pupils work in pairs. Give each pair a collection of between 10 and 19 objects (for example, counters/blocks/buttons/pencils/straws) and have them count to find how many. Next, ask each pair to separate out ten of their objects to make a bundle of ten and some more. **How many altogether (14)? Ten and how many more make (14)?** Record on a flipchart or whiteboard 10 + 4 = 14. Repeat for other collections of objects. Draw pupils' attention to what is written on the flipchart or whiteboard. **What do you notice?** Tell pupils that in the teens numbers (i.e. 11–19) the 1 represents one group of ten. **What about the number ten itself? What do you think the digits mean? How about the number 20?**
- Flash a series of double ten frames (one full ten frame and the other showing the numbers 1–9). **How many dots? What did you see?** Encourage responses such as *'I saw ten and seven more'.* **You didn't have time to count all of the dots, how did you know there were (17)? How did you work it out?**

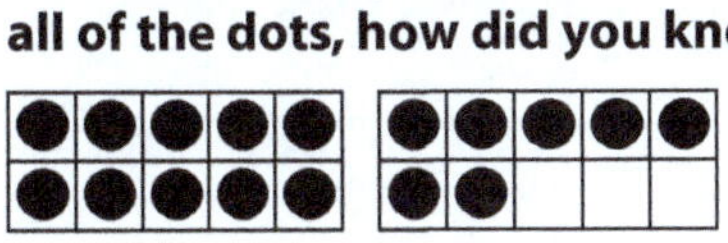

- Flash the number 15 on a Rekenrek. **How many beads? What did you see? Who saw 10 on the top and 5 on the bottom? Who saw 10 red and 5 white? Does it matter that we saw different things? Why is that?** Ask pupils to write a number sentence to match what they saw. Repeat for other numbers within the range 10–20.

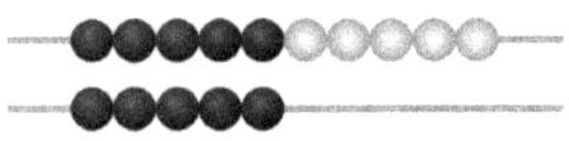

- Ask pupils to show you 10 + 8 on a bead string. **How many red beads? How many white beads? How many beads altogether? How did you count out the ten/eight beads? Did you have to count them one at a time? Why not?** Next ask the pupils to use their bead string to show you 8 + 10? **Are there still 18 beads altogether? What is the same and what is different?**

Unit 3.5 Five plus facts

- Write the calculation 5 + 7 = on a flipchart or whiteboard. Ask pupils to discuss the calculation in pairs and come up with a possible answer. Invite pairs to share their strategy with the class. **Did everyone get the same answer? If not, what might have happened? How did you work it out? What did you use? What did you do/see/draw?** Discuss the merits of each strategy.
- Give each pair two blank ten frames and a set of double-sided counters. Tell pupils that Isla thinks the answer to five plus seven is eleven. **How could you use your ten frames and counters to convince Isla that she is wrong?** Invite pairs to share their ideas with the class and discuss the merits of each. Display two ten frames showing the addends 5 and 7 (Figure 1). Model moving five counters from the second ten frame to the first ten frame to make a ten plus fact (Figure 2). **Does this make it easier to see how many altogether? Why is that?** Encourage responses such as '5 + 7 is the same as 10 + 2 so the answer is 12'. Repeat for other five plus facts. Encourage pupils to predict how many counters will need to be moved over each time and justify their decision. Increase the challenge by asking pupils to visualise both ten frames and the movement of the counters, then check using the concrete materials.

Figure 1

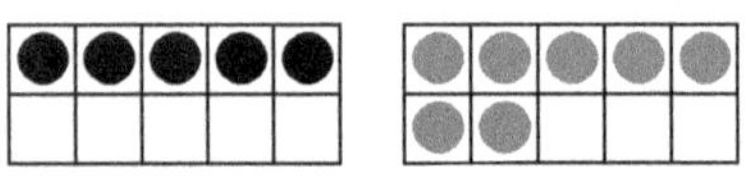

Figure 2

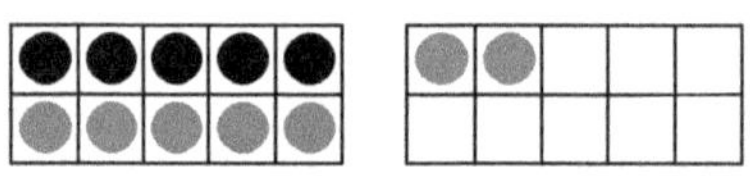

- Pose a series of result unknown addition word problems. For example: *Amman puts 5 biscuits on one plate and 8 biscuits on another plate. How many biscuits are there?* Invite pupils to write a number sentence to match the problem on their mini whiteboards then use or visualise ten frames and counters to work out the answer. **How did you work it out? Is there more than one way? Did anyone do 8 plus 5? Why?** Encourage responses that focus on five as a reference point and ten plus facts. For example: '*I know that 8 is 5 and 3. 5 plus 5 equals 10 and 3 more makes 13.*'

Unit 3.6 Addition bonds to 20

- Ask pupils to make the addition 9 + 6 on a Rekenrek by pushing 9 beads over on the top row and 6 on the bottom row (Figure 3). If Rekenreks are unavailable these can be substituted with blank double ten frames and counters. **How many beads/counters altogether? How did you see sixteen?** Encourage responses that show evidence of partitioning rather than counting by ones. For example: *'I saw 10 + 4 + 1. Ten plus four makes fourteen and one more makes fifteen', 'I saw 10 + 2 + 3. I know that 2 + 3 = 5. Ten plus five makes fifteen.'* Show pupils how we can swap one bead on the bottom row for one on the top row to show 10 + 5 more clearly (Figure 4). Record 9 + 6 is the same as 10 + 5 so 9 + 6 = 15.

  Figure 3

  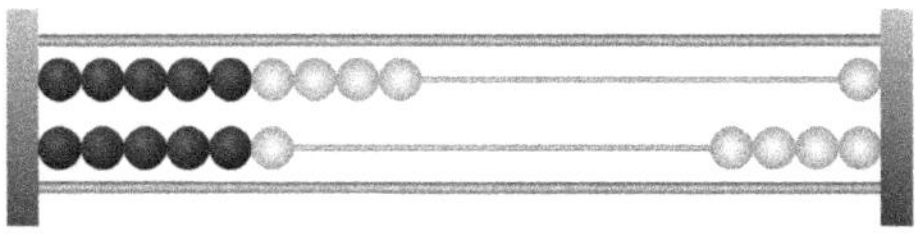

  Figure 4

  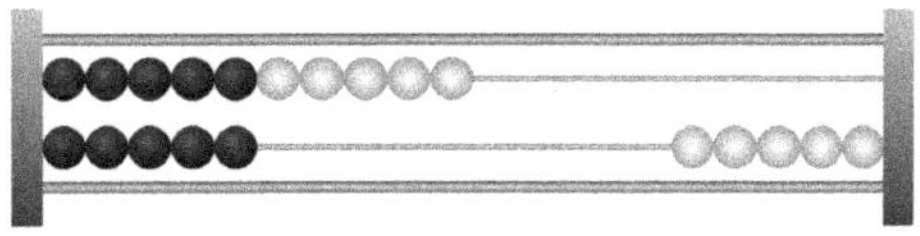

  Repeat for different additions where one addend is 9.

- Repeat the above activity for additions where one addend is 8 and it is necessary to swap two beads/counters. For example, 8 on the top and 4 on the bottom (8 + 4) becomes 10 on the top and 2 on the bottom (10 + 2); 6 on the top and 8 on the bottom (6 + 8) becomes 4 on the top and 10 on the bottom (4 + 10).
- Challenge pupils to use a Rekenrek or double ten frame to calculate the answer to 4 + 7. **How did you work it out?**
- Pupils work in pairs or small groups. Give each pair/group a collection of 11–20 objects and two sheets of paper or card. They should agree on what the objects/paper will represent (for example, the objects might represent animals and the sheets of paper fields). **How many different ways can you find to put your (animals) into two (fields)?** Ask them to record each combination as an addition number sentence. **How many different ways did you find? How can you be sure that you have found them all?** Encourage pupils to work systematically and look for patterns. They should keep their completed lists as these will be required for Unit 3.7.

Unit 3.7 Subtraction within 20

- Discuss the 'Let's Learn' section on page 50 of the Pupil Book. **Why do you think Isla decided to partition 7 into 2 and 5?** Give each pupil a blank double ten frame and 12 counters and ask them to represent the calculation 12 – 7 = 5. Encourage removal of the 7 counters in two stages, i.e. subtract two counters to leave ten, then another five counters to leave five remaining.

  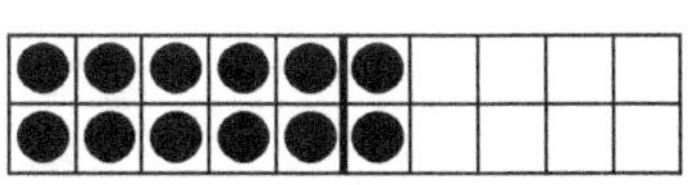

  12

  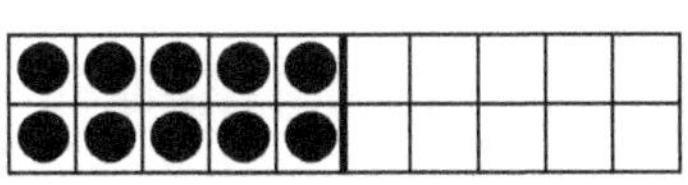

  subtract 2 leaves 10

  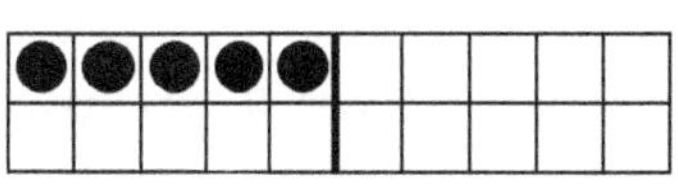

  subtract 5 leaves 5

  Repeat for other subtractions where the minuend is within the range 11–20 and both the subtrahend and difference are less than 10. **How many are we taking away? How should we partition this number? Why?** Encourage the use of 5 and 10 as reference points. For example, 15 – 8 (partition 8 into 5 and 3); 11 – 4 (partition 4 into 1 and 3); 12 – 9 (partition 9 into 2 and 7).

- Pupils work in pairs or small groups. Give each pair/group a collection of between 11–20 objects. They should be given the same number of objects as they were given for the final activity listed in Unit 3.6. Ask pupils to remove some of the objects and record the corresponding subtraction number sentence; for example, 14 – 6 = 8. **How many different ways can you find? Have you found them all? How can you be sure?** Encourage pupils to look for patterns. **How can we use the subtraction fact 7 – 4 = 3 to work out the answer to 17 – 4? Etc.** Return the list of addition bonds created in Unit 3.7 to each group and challenge them to find pairs of number sentences containing the same three numbers; for example, 8 + 6 = 14 and 14 – 8 = 6. **What do you notice?** Challenge pupils to use concrete objects to prove that each pair of number sentences is true.

Unit 3.8 Counting on and counting back

- You will need a set of flashcards with the words: *plus, minus, add, take away, equals* and *subtract* on them. Show the cards one at a time, saying the word out loud. Pupils must draw the corresponding symbol (+, – or =) on a mini whiteboard and 'show you'. Alternatively, ask pupils to write each symbol on a piece of paper and hold up the correct symbol as they hear the corresponding word within the context of a story.
- Refer to the 'Let's Learn' section on page 52 of the Pupil Book. Tell pupils that the frog is calculating the answer to 9 + 3 but he is unsure whether or not he is correct. Ask pupils to use concrete materials of their choice to check the frog's answer. **Is he correct? Why did the frog start at 9? Does starting at 9 and counting on give the same answer as starting at one and counting all of the objects?** Challenge pupils to explain why this works. Encourage responses such as '*He has already jumped on all of the stones up to the ninth stone: 1, 2, 3, 4, 5, 6, 7, 8, 9*', '*He's made 9 jumps already, so he only has to make 3 more jumps*'. Similarly, ask pupils to use concrete materials to prove that the ladybird is correct.
- Peg images of stones and/or leaves with the numerals 0–20 on them onto a washing line. Write an addition on a flipchart or whiteboard; for example, 8 + 4. Model starting on zero and taking 8 jumps then adding 4 more jumps with your finger. **Eight jumps add four jumps makes how many jumps altogether? Will I get the same answer if I start on eight and take four jumps? Why is that?** Write the addition 4 + 8 on a flipchart or whiteboard. **Will I get the same answer? How can we check? Is it easier to start on 8 and take 4 jumps, or start on 4 and take 8 jumps? Would this work for subtraction? Why not? How can we use our washing line to work out the answer to 15 – 9?** Repeat for other calculations within the range 0–20.
- Present additions with one addend within the range 1–4 and subtractions where the subtrahend is within the range 1–4. Ask pupils to find the answers by closing their eyes and picture counting on and back on a washing line/number track in their heads.

Unit 3.9 Adding two one-digit numbers using a number line

- Introduce a 0–20 number line. Tell pupils that Nuria thinks the answer to nine plus eight is sixteen. **How could we use the number line to convince Nuria that she is wrong? What mistake has Nuria made?** Emphasise that when using a number line to add and subtract we must remember to count the *jumps*.

- Show pupils two ten frames, each with between 3 and 9 dots. Ask them to write an addition to match what they see; for example, the ten frames below would generate the addition 7 + 6.

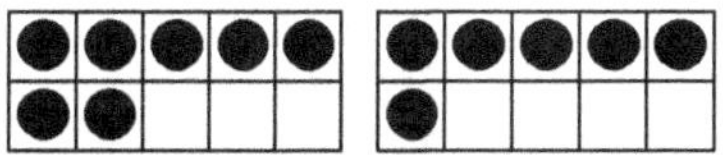

How many dots altogether? How did you count them? What did you see? Ask pupils to use a number line to calculate 7 + 6. **What number will you start on? How many jumps will you take? Does counting on give the same answer as starting at zero and counting every jump? Would you get the same answer if you started on six and took seven jumps? Why? Could you use the count on strategy with ten frames? How would you do that?**

- Discuss the 'Let's Learn' section on page 56 of the Pupil Book. **What is the same and what is different about the girls' strategies? How has Nuria partitioned 6? Whose strategy do you prefer? Why?** Pose addition and subtraction problems within the number range 0–20 and have pupils use a number line to solve them. Encourage the use of commutativity and partitioning. **How did you work it out? Which number did you start with? Why? Did you partition the second number? If so, how did you partition it? Why did you do that?**
- Pupils work in pairs. Challenge pairs to use a number line to find all the combinations of a number within the range 11–20. Swap with another pair. **Have they found all the different ways? How do you know?**

Unit 3.10 Subtracting using a number line

- Discuss the 'Let's Learn' section on page 58 of the Pupil Book. **What is the same and what is different about the boys' strategies? How has Finlay partitioned 7? Why do you think he has done that?**
- Display a 0–20 number line. Write a subtraction on a flipchart or whiteboard where the minuend is within the range 11–20 and the subtrahend is less than 10. When solved, the difference should also be less than 10. For example: 11 – 7 or 16 – 8 but not 15 – 4 or 19 – 6. **Can you use a number line to work out the answer?** Invite pupils to share strategies and solutions. **How did you work it out? Why did you do it that way?** Encourage partitioning of the subtrahend rather than counting by ones.
- Pupils work in pairs or small groups. Write a single-digit number on a flipchart or whiteboard and challenge pupils to write as many subtractions as they can with the chosen number as the answer. For example: the number 7 could lead to the subtractions 10 – 3, 12 – 5, 14 – 7, etc. **How many subtractions did you find? How did you work them out?** Discuss strategies, patterns and relationships; for example, *'I noticed that 14 – 7 = 7 because 7 + 7 = 14'.*

Unit 3.11 Missing addend

- Count out a set of 15 objects; for example, blocks or counters. Partition the set and screen one subset.

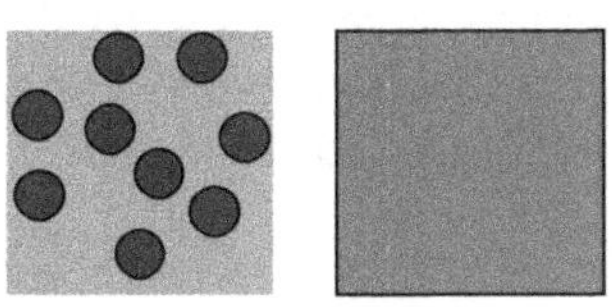

Tell pupils that there are 15 counters altogether. **How many counters can you see?** Write 9 + [ ] = 15 on a flipchart or whiteboard and say: **'Nine plus something makes 15'. How many counters are hiding under the piece of card? How did you work it out?** Write 6 in the empty box and ask pupils to read the completed number sentence aloud with you. Repeat for other amounts between 11–20. Alternate between screening the first and second subset but keep the missing addend within the range 1–6. For example, the above image could be swapped round to form the calculation [ ] + 9 = 15. Increase the challenge by modelling the situation with objects and a screen and asking pupils to generate the missing number sentence themselves.

- Pupils work in pairs. Give each pair a complete set of Cuisenaire rods. If pupils are new to these materials, show them the white rod, tell them it has a value of 1 then challenge them to work out the value of the red, light green, pink, yellow, dark green, black, brown, blue and orange rods. Write a missing addend number sentence on a flipchart or whiteboard; for example, 5 + [ ] = 12. Challenge pupils to use Cuisenaire rods to solve the problem. **How did you work out the missing number? Which rod(s) did you choose? Why did you do it that way? Who did it a different way? Did everyone get the same answer?** Repeat for different missing addend calculations. Possible solutions for 5 + [ ] = 12 are shown below.

5	+1	+1	+1	+1	+1	+1	+1

5	+5	+1	+1

5	+5	+2

- Have pupils play 'Fish' in pairs. Each pair/trio needs a set of numeral cards with the numbers 0–20. A target number within the range 11–20 is chosen (for example, 14). Each player is dealt five cards. The remaining cards are spread out face down on the table. Players try to make combinations for the chosen number. For example, if Player 1 has the number 6 and the chosen number is 14, they ask Player 2, 'Do you have the number 8?' If their opponent has the required digit card, he/she must hand it over. If not, Player 1 turns over a card on the table. If the required number is revealed, Player 1 keeps the card and takes another turn. If not, it is Player 2's turn. The game ends when no more combinations can be made. The player with the most cards at the end of the game is the winner.

Unit 3.12 Missing subtrahend

- Ask pupils to solve the problem at the bottom of page 63 of the Pupil Book. **How many cubes are in the box? How did you work it out?** Model writing a number sentence to match the pupil's thinking. For example, *Jenny thought '11 cubes take away some cubes leaves 9 cubes'.* 11 – [ ] = 9. *Ben thought '9 cubes on the table and some cubes in the box makes 11 cubes altogether'.* 9 + [ ] = 11. Discuss Isla and Amman's solutions at the top of page 64 of the Pupil Book. **Who counted back like Isla? Who counted on like Amman? Did anyone do it a different way?**
- Act out different missing subtrahend situations. For example: invite twelve pupils to come to the front of the room. Ask the others to close their eyes whilst six pupils hide behind a screen. **Open your eyes. How many people are there now? How many were there? How many people are hiding?** Ask pupils to find the answer using a method of their choice, e.g. by visualising the action, using concrete materials to represent the people and the action, by drawing or by counting on and back on a number line. Invite pupils to share how they solved the problem and model the appropriate number sentence on a flipchart or whiteboard: 12 – [6] = 6 or 6 + [6] = 12. **Who solved the problem by counting back? Who solved it by counting on?**

- Present a combine problem in which one of the parts is unknown; for example, *'Amman has 13 toy vehicles. 6 of them are lorries and the rest are cars. How many cars does Amman have?'* Ask pupils to solve the problem using a method of their choice, e.g. by drawing the vehicles or by representing them with concrete materials. Invite pupils to write a number sentence to show how they solved the problem and share it with the class. Write all of the different ways on a flipchart or whiteboard. For example, $13 = 6 + \boxed{7}$; $6 + \boxed{7} = 13$; $13 - 6 = \boxed{7}$. **Look at the number sentences. What is the same and what is different? Are they all correct? Why can different number sentences tell the same story?** Focus discussion on 'part-part-whole', i.e. we know there are 13 toy vehicles in the *whole* set. Part of the set is made up of lorries and the rest are cars. Knowing how many lorries there are helps us to work out the number of cars.

Unit 3.13 Representing and solving word problems (1)

- Make simple bar models out of card. In the example shown, the top bar represents the whole and the bottom bar represents the parts. Show the bar model with either the whole or one of the parts missing and ask pupils to work out the missing value. **The whole is missing, what is its value? What number is written on the missing part? How do you know?** Pupils who are not yet confident with addition bonds to 20 should be permitted to use concrete materials of their choice to solve the problem. Those who are confident in recalling number bonds to 20 could be asked to use concrete materials to prove they are correct.

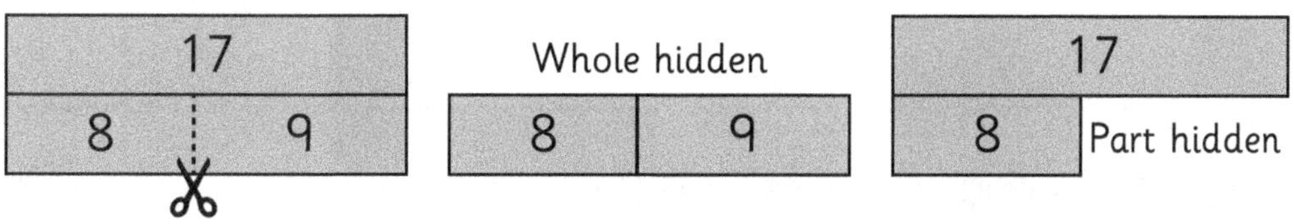

- Challenge pupils to use concrete materials (for example, ten frames, bead string, Cuisenaire rods) to represent a word problem, write the appropriate number sentence, then solve it. For example: *Finlay puts 7 fruity biscuits and 6 chocolate biscuits on a plate. How many biscuits are there?* **Did you add or subtract? Why? What was it about the problem that told you it was an addition/subtraction?**
- Challenge pupils to use a number line to solve word problems then write a number sentence to match how they solved it. For example: *Nuria had 14 football stickers. She gave 5 to her brother. How many stickers does she have now?* **Is it possible to solve this problem by counting on or counting back? How did you solve it? What number sentence did you write? How many stickers did Nuria give to her brother? Is this number the whole or one of the parts?**
- Help pupils connect the mathematical symbols and operations with real-life situations by presenting an addition or subtraction within the number range 0–20 (for example, 6 + 8 or 20 – 10) and asking them to tell or write their own word problem to match it. **Tell or give your word problem to a partner; can they solve it?**

Unit 3.14 Representing and solving word problems (2)

- Ask pupils to work together to mentally solve number problems as they arise in the classroom. For example: *There are 16 boys in our class. Six are going home for lunch, how many are staying in school?* **Can you write a number sentence to match what you did in your head? What helped you decide whether to add or subtract?**
- Discuss the Think Board in the 'Let's Learn' section on page 68 of the Pupil Book. **How has Isla thought about this problem? Why has she drawn arrows on some of the cakes? Why hasn't she written the numbers 1 to 9 beside the green cubes? Why has she added 1 then 6 on the number line? How else could she have solved the problem?**
- Group pupils into fours. Give each group a large sheet of paper on which there is a Think Board with the following headings: number sentence, picture, objects, number line. Display a non-standard (i.e. start unknown or change unknown) problem and read it aloud to the class. For example: *Amman had some sweets. He gave Isla 7 and kept 7 for himself. How many sweets did Amman start off with?* Tell pupils that you would like them to work together to create a Think Board for this problem and solve it. **Will you count on or will you count back? Which part of the Think Board will each person do? How will you decide?** Compare completed Think Boards. **What is the same and what is different? Which symbols did you use (+, –, =)?**
- Provide blank A4-sized Think Boards with the same four section headings. Have pupils work in pairs or individually to create a Think Board for one or more of the word problems in the 'Let's Practise' section on page 69 of the Pupil Book.

Unit 3.15 Representing and solving word problems (3)

- Present two different-sized groups of objects; for example, 12 blue blocks and 9 yellow blocks. **Which group has more? How can we work out how many more blue blocks there are?** Demonstrate how one-to-one matching makes it easier to see which group has more. Focus on the yellow blocks. **What would we need to do to make the number of yellow blocks the same as the number of blue blocks?** Focus on the blue blocks. **What would we need to do to make the number of blue blocks the same as the number of yellow blocks? Which action shows addition and which action shows subtraction?** Introduce the word difference when talking about the way in which the sets were compared, i.e. the difference between 12 and 9 is 3. Repeat for different sets of objects. Include questions about how many less/fewer.
- Discuss the 'Let's Learn' section on page 70 of the Pupil Book. Draw pupils' attention to the objects and bar model. **What do you notice? How has 'matching' helped Finlay to work out the numbers he needs for his bar model and where the numbers should go?** Challenge pupils to create bar models to represent the problems presented above and/or to represent different word problems.
- Tell pupils there are 13 bottles and 8 straws. If necessary, write '13 bottles and 8 straws' on a flipchart or whiteboard, show pictures of 13 bottles and a bundle of 8 straws, or display actual objects. **Isla wants to put one straw in each bottle, does she have enough? How many bottles won't have a straw? How do you know?** Ask pupils to represent the problem as a drawing and solve it. **How did you work it out?** Challenge pupils to create a bar model and write one addition and one subtraction to match what they did. Repeat for other word problems that require pupils to compare two quantities and find the difference between them.

Number - addition and subtraction 1B

Section overview

Textbook 1B units	Review units	Prior learning	Benchmarks/ Es&Os
Unit 3.1 Compatible numbers: pairs to ten	**1A** Units 3.1, 3.2, 3.3, 3.4 and 3.11	• Recall all number bonds to 10. • Recall ten plus facts to 20. • Recall doubles to 20. • Solve missing addend problems (range 0–20).	**MNU 1-03a** • Uses correct mathematical vocabulary when discussing the four operations including subtract, add, sum of, total, multiply, produce, divide and shared equally. • Demonstrates understanding of the commutative law; for example, $6 + 3 = 3 + 6$ or $2 \times 4 = 4 \times 2$. • Solves addition and subtraction problems with three-digit whole numbers.
Unit 3.2 Doubles and near doubles	**1A** Unit 3.3	• Recall all doubles up to $10 + 10 = 20$.	**MNU 1-03a** • Uses correct mathematical vocabulary when discussing the four operations including subtract, add, sum of, total, multiply, produce, divide and shared equally. • Demonstrates understanding of the commutative law; for example, $6 + 3 = 3 + 6$ or $2 \times 4 = 4 \times 2$. • Solves addition and subtraction problems with three-digit whole numbers.

Unit 3.3 Fact families	**1A** Units 3.1, 3.2, 3.6, 3.7, 3.11 and 3.12	• Recall number bonds within 10. • Create fact families within 10. • Use, draw or visualise double ten frames/0–20 bead string/ 20 bead rack to work out addition and subtraction facts within the range 0–20. • Solve missing addend and missing subtrahend problems involving screened collections.	**MNU 1-03a** • Uses correct mathematical vocabulary when discussing the four operations including subtract, add, sum of, total, multiply, produce, divide and shared equally. • Demonstrates understanding of the commutative law; for example, $6 + 3 = 3 + 6$ or $2 \times 4 = 4 \times 2$. • Solves addition and subtraction problems with three-digit whole numbers.
Unit 3.4 Complements to the next multiple of 10	**1A** Unit 2.2 and Units 3.8, 3.9 and 3.10 **1B** Unit 2.11	• Partition 2-digit numbers in standard ways; for example, $67 = 60 + 7$; $24 = 20 + 4$; $51 = 50 + 1$. • Appreciate that addition is commutative. • Recall the decade number sequence forwards and backwards. • Count forwards and backwards on a number line to add and subtract.	**MNU 1-03a** • Uses correct mathematical vocabulary when discussing the four operations including subtract, add, sum of, total, multiply, produce, divide and shared equally. • Demonstrates understanding of the commutative law; for example, $6 + 3 = 3 + 6$ or $2 \times 4 = 4 \times 2$. • Solves addition and subtraction problems with three-digit whole numbers.

Unit 3.5 Adding 0, 1 and 10	**Early – B** Unit 1.14 **1A** Units 2.2 and 2.9 Unit 3.11 and Unit 11.1 **1B** Unit 2.11 and Units 3.3 and 3.4	• Appreciate that zero means there is none of a particular quantity. • Partition 2-digit numbers in standard ways; for example, 67 = 60 + 7; 24 = 20 + 4; 51 = 50 + 1. • Appreciate that addition is commutative. • Count forwards and backwards in tens both on and off the decade. • Appreciate the part–whole relationship between addition and subtraction.	**MNU 1-03a** • Uses correct mathematical vocabulary when discussing the four operations including subtract, add, sum of, total, multiply, produce, divide and shared equally. • Demonstrates understanding of the commutative law; for example, 6 + 3 = 3 + 6 or 2 × 4 = 4 × 2. • Solves addition and subtraction problems with three-digit whole numbers. • Adds and subtracts multiples of 10 or 100 to or from any whole number to 1000.
Unit 3.6 Subtracting 0, 1 and 10	**Early – B** Unit 1.14 **1A** Units 2.2 and 2.9 Units 3.11 and 3.12 Unit 11.1 **1B** Unit 2.11	• Appreciate that zero means there is none of a particular quantity. • Partition 2-digit numbers in standard ways; for example, 67 = 60 + 7; 24 = 20 + 4; 51 = 50 + 1. • Appreciate that addition is commutative but subtraction is not. • Count forwards and backwards in tens both on and off the decade. • Appreciate the part–whole relationship between addition and subtraction.	**MNU 1-03a** • Uses correct mathematical vocabulary when discussing the four operations including subtract, add, sum of, total, multiply, produce, divide and shared equally. • Solves addition and subtraction problems with three-digit whole numbers. • Adds and subtracts multiples of 10 or 100 to or from any whole number to 1000.

Unit 3.7 Adding and subtracting single and double-digit numbers	**1A** Unit 2.9 Units 3.1, 3.2, 3.11 and 3.12 Unit 11.1	• Recall number bonds within 10. • Count forwards and backwards in tens off the decade. • Understand that addition is commutative but subtraction is not. • Solve missing addend and missing subtrahend problems involving screened collections.	**MNU 1-03a** • Uses correct mathematical vocabulary when discussing the four operations including subtract, add, sum of, total, multiply, produce, divide and shared equally. • Demonstrates understanding of the commutative law; for example, 6 + 3 = 3 + 6 or 2 × 4 = 4 × 2. • Solves addition and subtraction problems with three-digit whole numbers.
Unit 3.8 Adding and subtracting multiples of 10 to and from two-digit numbers	**1A** Unit 2.9 Units 3.9, 3.10, 3.11 and 3.12 **1B** Units 2.7, 2.8 and 2.11	• Partition 2-digit numbers in standard ways; for example, 67 = 60 + 7; 24 = 20 + 4; 51 = 50 + 1. • Count forwards and backwards in tens, both on and off the decade. • Use a jump strategy on a number line to add and subtract. • Understand that addition is commutative but subtraction is not. • Solve missing addend and missing subtrahend problems involving screened collections.	**MNU 1-03a** • Uses correct mathematical vocabulary when discussing the four operations including subtract, add, sum of, total, multiply, produce, divide and shared equally. • Demonstrates understanding of the commutative law; for example, 6 + 3 = 3 + 6 or 2 × 4 = 4 × 2. • Solves addition and subtraction problems with three-digit whole numbers. • Adds and subtracts multiples of 10 or 100 to or from any whole number to 1000.

Unit 3.9 Partitioning through 10	**1A** Units 3.1, 3.2, 3.5, 3.11 and 3.12 and Unit 11.1 **1B** Unit 2.11 and Units 3.4, 3.5 and 3.6	• Use known facts to partition numbers within the range 3–10 in different ways. • Partition 2-digit whole numbers in standard ways; for example, 67 = 60 + 7; 24 = 20 + 4; 51 = 50 + 1. • Count on and back to the next multiple of ten. • Appreciate that the equals sign symbolises balance in a number sentence. • Count on and count back to solve missing addend and missing subtrahend problems.	**MNU 1-03a** • Uses correct mathematical vocabulary when discussing the four operations including subtract, add, sum of, total, multiply, produce, divide and shared equally. • Solves addition and subtraction problems with three-digit whole numbers.
Unit 3.10 Adding two-digit numbers	**1A** Units 2.9, 2.11 and 2.12 and Units 4.3, 4.4 and 4.5 **1B** Units 2.9 and 2.11 and Unit 3.4	• Partition 2-digit whole numbers in standard ways; for example, 67 = 60 + 7; 24 = 20 + 4; 51 = 50 + 1. • Skip count forwards in twos and fives. • Count forwards in tens both on and off the decade. • Count in tens and ones to find a total. • Count on to the next multiple of ten.	**MNU 1-03a** • Uses correct mathematical vocabulary when discussing the four operations including subtract, add, sum of, total, multiply, produce, divide and shared equally. • Solves addition and subtraction problems with three-digit whole numbers. • Adds and subtracts multiples of 10 or 100 to or from any whole number to 1000.
Unit 3.11 Subtracting two-digit numbers	**1A** Units 2.9 and 2.12 and Units 4.3, 4.4 and 4.5 **1B** Units 2.9 and 2.11 and Unit 3.4	• Partition 2-digit whole numbers in standard ways; for example, 67 = 60 + 7; 24 = 20 + 4; 51 = 50 + 1. • Skip count backwards in twos and fives. • Count backwards in tens both on and off the decade. • Count back to the next multiple of ten.	**MNU 1-03a** • Uses correct mathematical vocabulary when discussing the four operations including subtract, add, sum of, total, multiply, produce, divide and shared equally. • Solves addition and subtraction problems with three-digit whole numbers. • Adds and subtracts multiples of 10 or 100 to or from any whole number to 1000.

Unit 3.12 Inverse relationships	**1A** Units 3.1, 3.2, 3.11 and 3.12 and Unit 11.1 **1B** Units 3.1, 3.3, 3.5, 3.6, 3.8, 3.9, 3.10 and 3.11	• Use an empty number line to add and subtract. • Appreciate that addition is commutative but subtraction is not. • Appreciate that the equals sign symbolises balance in a number sentence. • Solve missing addend and missing subtrahend problems involving screened collections. • Use a bar model to generate families of related addition and subtraction facts. • Identify the missing whole or part on a bar model.	**MNU 1-03a** • Uses correct mathematical vocabulary when discussing the four operations including subtract, add, sum of, total, multiply, produce, divide and shared equally. • Demonstrates understanding of the commutative law; for example, $6 + 3 = 3 + 6$ or $2 \times 4 = 4 \times 2$. • Solves addition and subtraction problems with three-digit whole numbers.
Unit 3.13 Strategies for solving number puzzles	**1A** Units 3.4 and 3.5 **1B** Units 3.1, 3.2 and 3.12	• Add a string of numbers by looking for pairs that make ten. • Use doubles and near doubles to add two numbers within the range 0–20. • Use 5 and 10 as reference points when adding within the range 0–20. • Appreciate that addition is commutative but subtraction is not. • Count on and count back to solve addition and subtraction problems.	**MNU 1-03a** • Uses correct mathematical vocabulary when discussing the four operations including subtract, add, sum of, total, multiply, produce, divide and shared equally. • Demonstrates understanding of the commutative law; for example, $6 + 3 = 3 + 6$ or $2 \times 4 = 4 \times 2$. • Solves addition and subtraction problems with three-digit whole numbers.
Unit 3.14 Representing and solving word problems (1)	**1A** Units 3.11, 3.12, 3.13, 3.14 and 3.15 **1B** 3.12 and 3.13	• Represent and solve start, change and result unknown addition and subtraction word problems (within the number range 0–20) using objects and/or pictures, and write the corresponding number sentence. • Represent simple comparison problems with concrete materials, pictures or diagrams (bar model) and solve them. • Appreciate that the same word problem can be represented and solved in different ways.	**MNU 1-03a** • Solves addition and subtraction problems with three-digit whole numbers. • Solves two-step problems.

Unit 3.15 Representing and solving word problems (2)	**1A** Units 3.11, 3.12, 3.13, 3.14 and 3.15 **1B** Units 3.12 and 3.13	• Represent and solve start, change and result unknown addition and subtraction word problems (within the number range 0–20) using objects and/or pictures, and write the corresponding number sentence. • Represent simple comparison problems with concrete materials, pictures or diagrams (bar model) and solve them. • Appreciate that the same word problem can be represented and solved in different ways.	**MNU 1-03a** • Solves addition and subtraction problems with three-digit whole numbers. • Solves two-step problems.

Conceptual context

In Book 1B there is a continuing focus on mental agility. Strategies are extended to include the use of near doubles, compatible numbers and other known facts to generate new facts. There is a strong emphasis on the use of place value partitioning and the empty number line is introduced as a helpful way by which pupils can keep track of their thinking when adding and subtracting two-digit numbers. Effective use of the empty number line is of course dependent on pupils' conceptual understanding of place value and their ability to count forwards and backwards in tens and ones, from any starting number. Building on this, counting in multiples of 10 is introduced as a more efficient way to add or subtract larger numbers. The recurring patterns in our number system are continually highlighted.

Although 'count on and back in ones to add and subtract' is an Early Level benchmark, many children will be well into First Level before they truly trust counting on and back from an addend, or the subtrahend, as a reliable strategy. Whilst the use of prompts such as 'hold the biggest number in your head and count on' can serve as useful 'brain training' it is the ability to solve missing addend and missing subtrahend tasks that is the true indicator of a 'count on' pupil. Through opportunities to solve missing addend and missing difference tasks, by counting on and back on an empty number line, pupils will develop their growing understanding of the inverse relationships between addition and subtraction.

Also central to pupils' growing understanding of the inverse relationship is the ability the think 'part-part-whole', i.e. to know and understand that a whole quantity can be split into parts. Through opportunities to create families of related addition and subtraction facts, supported by bar modelling (see Units 3.3, 3.14 and 3.15), pupils come to realise that, if the whole is missing, addition is the correct choice of operation; if one of the parts is missing then subtraction is required. The ability to solve missing minuend tasks; for example, $\square - 36 = 28$ provides a good indication as to whether or not a pupil fully understands the inverse relationship. This idea is introduced in Book 1B and further developed in Book 1C.

The full range of problem types (i.e. start, change and result unknown, combine and compare) is again emphasised with lots of opportunities to represent the same problem in multiple ways, such as concrete materials, pictures, diagrams (e.g. the number line and bar model), words and symbols. Linking with the focus on the inverse relationship, compare problems are given particular emphasis.

Resources

- 100 bead strings
- Bar model template
- Base 10 blocks
- Blank function machines
- Blank graduated numbered lines (10 graduations – spaced)
- Concrete materials; for example, beads, counters, etc.
- Cuisenaire rods
- Double-sided counters
- Empty number lines
- Full ten frames
- Hundred squares
- Interlocking cubes
- Opaque paper or card for screening activities
- Pack of 0–20 digit cards
- Pair-wise ten frames
- Partially completed ten frames
- Rekenrek
- Set of dice
- Straws bundled in tens and single straws
- Think Board templates (see Pupil Book pages 76 and 78)

Key vocabulary

- **Addition**
- **Bar model**
- **Bead string**
- **Commutative**
- **Difference**
- **Digit**
- **Double**
- **Empty number line**
- **Equal**
- **Jump strategy**
- **Method**
- **Near double**
- **Number bonds**
- **Number line**
- **Number sentence**
- **Partition**
- **Split strategy**
- **Strategy**
- **Subtraction**
- **Sum**

Misconceptions

Potential misconception	Addressing the misconception
Unit 3.2 Pupils may have difficulty recalling doubles facts.	Help pupils to visualise doubles patterns using pair-wise ten frames or a Rekenrek.
Unit 3.3 Pupils may be unable to recall number bonds to 20, and/or not yet fully understand that, for example, one unit of eight is equivalent to eight units of one. The pupil therefore has difficulty using materials such as Cuisenaire rods and bar models where the individual ones that make up each unit are not visible.	Ask pupils to represent part-part-whole situations using interlocking cubes in two different colours, one colour to represent each 'part' (see 'Let's Learn' on page 44 of the Pupil Book). Once pupils are confident with the above model, ask them to represent part-part-whole situations with interlocking cubes of three different colours, then use their model to generate a family of four related facts. For example: 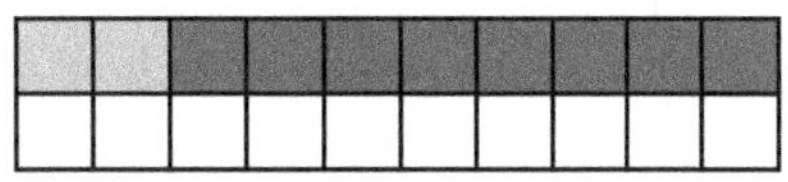 $2 + 8 = 10$ $8 + 2 = 10$ $10 - 2 = 8$ $10 - 5 = 2$ Focus discussion on the value of each part (for example 2 pale grey cubes and 8 dark grey cubes equal 10 white cubes), and on the relationship between addition and subtraction.
Units 3.3, 3.6 and 3.15 Pupils may not yet fully understand the inverse relationship between addition and subtraction and so have difficulty solving missing minuend calculations; for example, ☐ – 10 = 38.	Present missing minuend word problems involving small, easily visualised quantities. For example: *Amman has eaten 9 sweets and has 4 left. How many sweets did Amman have to start with?* Have pupils act out the problem with concrete materials or pictures. Encourage pupils to articulate the problem and connect their thinking to a number sentence; for example, *'some sweets take away 9 sweets leaves 4 sweets'* ☐ – 9 = 4. Provide lots of opportunities for pupils to investigate missing minuend tasks with concrete materials in this way. Start with small numbers and progress to numbers in the range 0–99.
Units 3.8, 3.9, 3.10 and 3.11 Pupils may struggle to partition quantities mentally and solely depend on taking jumps of ten and one only when using an empty number line.	Provide lots of practice in: • subitising and partitioning, quantities up to and including ten, on ten frames. • reciting number word sequences in 2s, 5s, etc. (see Book 1A, Units 2.12, 4.3 and 4.5. Also Book 1B, Units 2.9 and 4.1).
Unit 3.12, 3.13, 3.14 and 3.15 Pupils may be able to count on and back to solve addition and subtraction problems without fully understanding how these strategies are related.	Provide pupils with lots of opportunities to model counting on and counting back situations with small quantities of concrete materials and write number sentences to match. For example: 9 black cubes and 6 cubes makes 15 cubes altogether. 9 + [6] = 15 15 cubes take away the 9 black cubes leaves 6 white cubes. 15 – 9 = [6] Once pupils are confident with the above idea, provide opportunities to invert number sentences by playing the following game in pairs. Pupil A secretly enters a number into his or her calculator. Both pupils agree on a number to be added (for example, 8). Pupil A adds 8 to the 'secret number' and shows the result to Pupil B. Pupil B must work out the original number by performing a subtraction. For example, if the answer is 17, Pupil B must enter 17 – 8 to return to the starting number.

Teaching ideas

Unit 3.1 Compatible numbers: pairs to 10

- Write 6 + 3 + 4 on a flipchart or whiteboard. Ask pupils to find the sum and 'show you' on a mini whiteboard. **How did you work it out?** Discuss Finlay's strategy in the 'Let's Learn' section on page 40 of the Pupil Book. **Why do you think Finlay decided to add the 6 and 4 first? What if the calculation had said 4 + 3 + 6 or 3 + 4 + 6? Would Finlay have got the same answer or a different answer? Why is that?** Have pupils work in pairs to prove their theory with concrete materials.
- Write a set of similar calculations on a flipchart or whiteboard; for example, 2 + 7 + 8; 7 + 4 + 3; 1 + 9 + 6; 6 + 5 + 4. (Note that each sum is less than or equal to 20). Ask pupils to find each total using number buddies to 10. **Which pair of numbers will you add together first? Why?**
- Extend the above activity to include examples that involve adding four single-digit numbers, for example, 4 + 2 + 2 + 6; 3 + 5 + 7+ 5; 9 + 3 + 2 + 1. (Note that the sum is less than or equal to 20). **How many number buddy pairs can you see? Which pair of numbers will you add together first? Does the order matter? How could you check your answer?** Increase the challenge by including missing addend questions; for example, 8 + 2 + ☐ + 7 = 18.
- Pupils play in pairs. Give each pair three dice. Pupils take turns to roll the dice. Both players add the three numbers together independently, record their answer on a mini whiteboard then compare strategies and solutions. **Did you both get the same answer? If not, what might have happened? Explain your strategy to your partner, did you do it the same way or a different way? Were you able to add two numbers together to make ten? What else helped?** Extend to using four dice.

Unit 3.2 Doubles and near doubles

- Revise double facts up to 10 + 10. Call out questions and ask pupils to 'show you' on a mini whiteboard. **What is double five/eight plus eight/double ten/three add three? Etc.**
- Make a double fact on a Rekenrek or double ten frame. Screen one row. **I have made the number 12, 18, etc. How many beads/dots are hidden? How do you know?** Encourage responses such as 'six add six makes twelve', 'double 9 is 18'.
- Show a near double on a Rekenrek or double ten frame (for example, 8 + 7).

  What can you see? Where is the double? Encourage responses such as 'I can see double seven and one more', 'I can see fourteen plus one', 'It's just the same as 8 + 7', 'It's the same as 10 + 5, that's 15'. Repeat for other near doubles.
- Write a near double fact on a flipchart or whiteboard (for example, 6 + 7). Challenge pupils to work out the answer by picturing the near double in their heads. **Who saw 6 + 6 in their heads? How did you use this double fact to work out 6 + 7? Did anyone see 7 + 7 in their heads? How did you use this double fact to work out 6 + 7? Why do both strategies work? Can you explain?** Ask pupils to use a Rekenrek or double ten frame to prove that 6 + 7 can be thought of as double 6 plus 1 or double 7 minus 1. **Which way do you prefer? Why?**

Unit 3.3 Fact families

- Discuss the 'Let's Learn' section on page 44 of the Pupil Book. Focus the discussion on 'part-part-whole', i.e. blue part + green part = whole row of cubes; green part + blue part = whole row of cubes; whole row of cubes – green part = blue part; whole row of cubes – blue part = green part.
- Pupils work in pairs. Give each pair a number between 11 and 20. Ask them to choose two colours and count out the required number of interlocking cubes, some of one colour and some of another colour. For example, if the quantity selected is 13 they may count out 6 red cubes and 7 yellow cubes; 9 brown cubes and 4 blue cubes; 5 orange cubes and 8 pink cubes, etc. Pairs use their cubes to make and record a Fact Family. **How many different Fact Families are there for the number 13? Can you think of any others? Can we write them without using cubes? How many different number facts can be made when we have equal amounts of yellow and orange cubes?**
- If available, ask pupils to use Cuisenaire rods to illustrate a number fact such as 9 + 8 = 17. **How did you make 17?** Encourage the use of 10 as a base, i.e. 17 = 10 + 7 so 9 + 8 = 10 + 7. **How many different addition and subtraction number sentences can you make about your model?** Focus on Fact Families. **If I know that 9 + 8 = 17, what else do I know?** 8 + 9 = 17; 17 – 8 = 9; 17 – 9 = 8.
- Display a bar model similar to the one shown below. Cover up the numbers on the parts. **What numbers could the parts represent? Why is the missing number on the first part unlikely to be one? Could the missing number on the second part be one? What makes you say that?** Reveal the hidden numbers. Challenge pupils to write two additions and two subtractions to match the bar model.

11	
8	3

- Display a set of partially completed bar models (one part or whole unknown). **What number is missing? How do you know? Could it be ___? Why not?** Have pupils recreate and complete the bar model then write a family of four related facts about it. Encourage pupils to consider the relative size of the parts when drawing their own bar models.

Unit 3.4 Complements to the next multiple of 10

- Draw a blank graduated number line on a flipchart or whiteboard. Indicate the first point on the scale (far left).

If this is 85 where is 90? Record 85 + 5 = 90. Repeat for other two-digit numbers, asking pupils to indicate where the next multiple of ten would be in each case. Indicate the last point on the scale (far right). **If this is 77 where is 70?** Record 77 – 7 = 70. Repeat for other two-digit numbers, asking pupils to indicate where the next multiple of ten would be. Focus discussion on the number of jumps required. Draw pupils' attention to the number sentences recorded. **What do you notice?** Focus discussion on addition bonds to 10 and tens and ones.

- Discuss the 'Let's Learn' section on pages 47–48 of the Pupil Book. **What do you notice? How else could Amman and Finlay work out the answers?** Model pupils' ideas on number lines. For example: *Amman could have counted on in twos.*

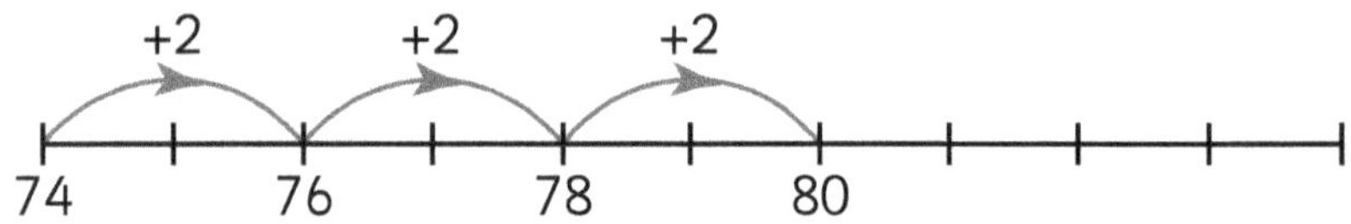

Finlay could have counted back three to get to 35. Thirty-five take away five makes thirty.

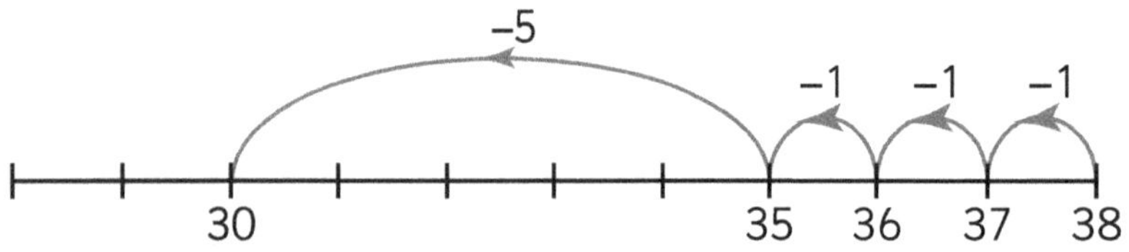

- Give each pupil a blank graduated number line. Write missing addend calculations on a flipchart or whiteboard (for example 34 + ☐ = 40). Ask pupils to work out the answers on their number line and 'show you'. **What number will you write down first? Why? Will you count on or count back? Why?** Repeat for missing subtrahend calculations (for example, 96 – ☐ = 90). **What number will you write down first this time? Why? Will you count on or count back? Why?** Ask pupils to explain their number lines to the class. **How did you do it? Who did it a different way?**
- Challenge pupils to use known facts and place value or visualise the number line in their heads, keeping track on their fingers if necessary, to solve missing addend and missing subtrahend problems such as the following: **Start at 67, what do we need to subtract to reach 60? Start at 32, what do we need to add to reach 40? How do you know?**

Unit 3.5 Adding 0, 1 and 10

- Discuss the 'Let's Learn' section on pages 50–51 in the Pupil Book. **How many jumps of ten has Finlay made? Why did he do that? Why did Nuria turn the numbers round to make the addition say 62 + 10 = ? Whose method do you prefer? Why?**
- Ask pupils to picture a hundred square in their heads to solve missing sum problems such as 47 + 10 = ☐; 74 + 10 = ☐; 52 + 10 = ☐. Discuss what happens to a number when we add 10, 1 or 0. Make links with movements on a hundred square, i.e. moving down a row is the same as adding ten/counting forwards in tens; moving forwards one place along a row is the same as adding one/number after; when we add zero the total remains the same.
- Call out a range of missing sum or missing addend additions and ask pupils to 'show you' the answers on a mini whiteboard. In each example, one of the addends should be 0, 1 or 10. For example: **What does 87 add 10 make? Seventy-six add what makes seventy-seven? How do you know? How did you work it out? Did you see anything in your head?**

- Extend the above activity to include examples where one addend and/or the sum is greater than 100. For example: 96 + 10 = □; 265 + 1 = □; 0 + □ = 572.
- Challenge pupils to use what they know about adding 10 and 1 to add 11 to a two-digit number.
- Draw a simple Function Machine on a flipchart or whiteboard. Tell pupils that the machine adds ten to each number that is entered. **If I put the number 122 into the machine, what number will come out? If the number 450 comes out, what number went in? Did you count on or did you count back? Why?**
- Link the action of counting on and counting back in the above activity to a number line. For example:

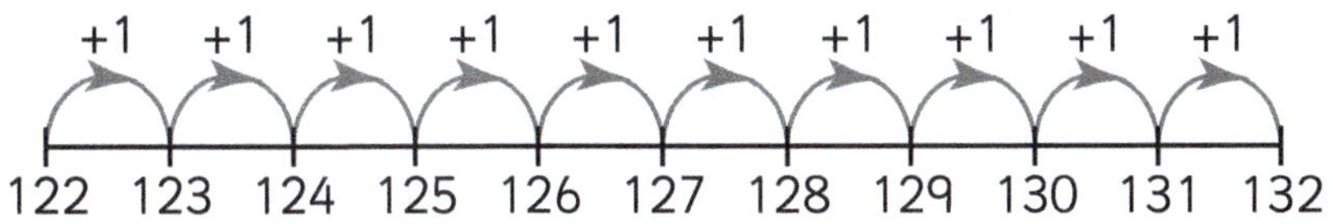

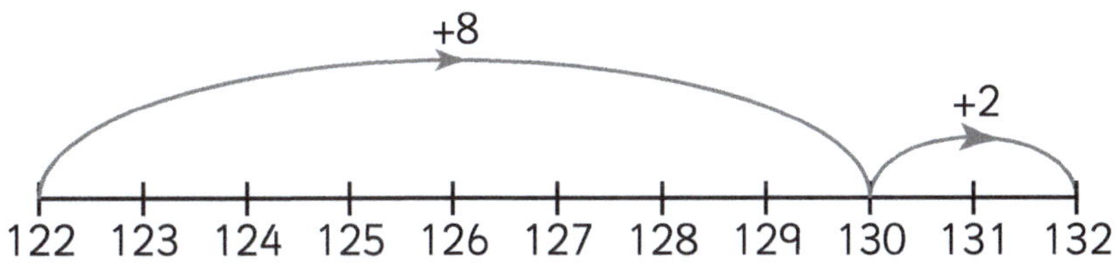

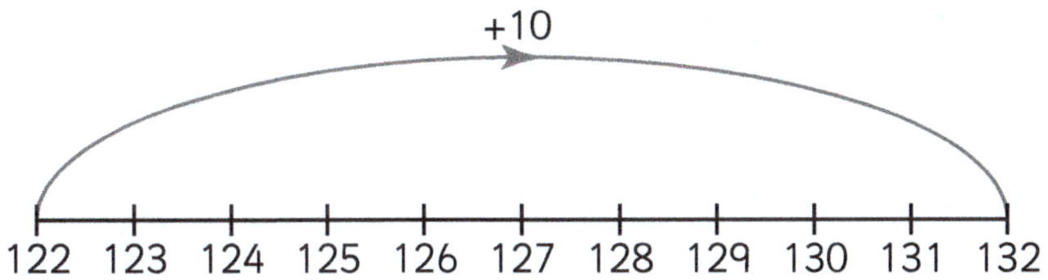

Discuss the merits of each method shown. **Which way do you prefer? Why? What would happen if we started at 132 and counted back?**

Unit 3.6 Subtracting 0, 1 and 10

- Discuss the 'Let's Learn' section on pages 53–54 of the Pupil Book. **Look at Isla's number line. How has she subtracted 10? Why do you think she did that?** Discuss the absence of marks to represent the numbers in-between 62 and 60, and in-between 60 and 52, and introduce the term 'empty number line'. **How has Amman found the answer? Whose method do you prefer? Why?**
- Ask pupils to picture a hundred square in their heads to solve missing difference problems such as 88 – 10 = □; 93 – 10 = □; 66 – 10 = □. Discuss what happens to a number when we subtract 10, 1 or 0. Make links with movement on the hundred square, i.e. moving up a row is the same as subtracting ten/counting back in tens; moving backwards one place along a row is the same as subtracting one/number before; when we subtract zero the number does not change.
- Call out a range of missing difference or missing subtrahend subtractions and ask pupils to 'show you' the answers on a mini whiteboard. In each example, the subtrahend should be 0, 1 or 10. For example: **'What' take**

away ten makes sixty-nine? What is ninety-one minus one? How do you know? How did you work it out? Did you see anything in your head?

- Extend the above activity to include examples where the minuend and/or difference is greater than 100; for example, 106 – 10 = ☐; 265 – 1 = ☐; 708 – ☐ = 708.
- Challenge pupils to use what they know about subtracting 10 and 1 to subtract 11 from a two-digit number.
- Draw a simple Function Machine on a flipchart or whiteboard. Tell pupils that the machine subtracts ten from each number that is entered. **If I put the number 378 into the machine, what number will come out? If the number 710 comes out, what number went in? Did you count on or count back? Why?**
- Link the action of counting on and counting back in the above activity to a number line. For example:

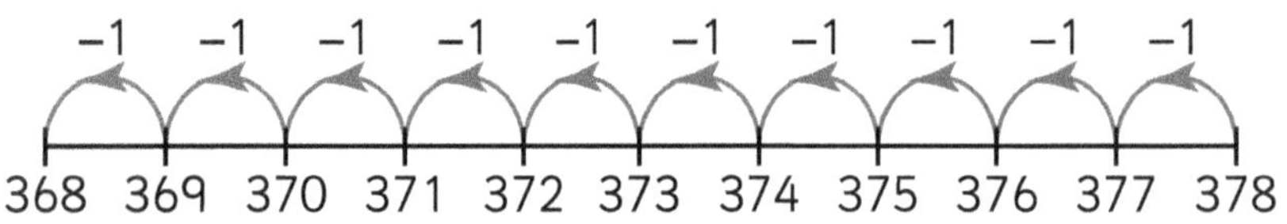

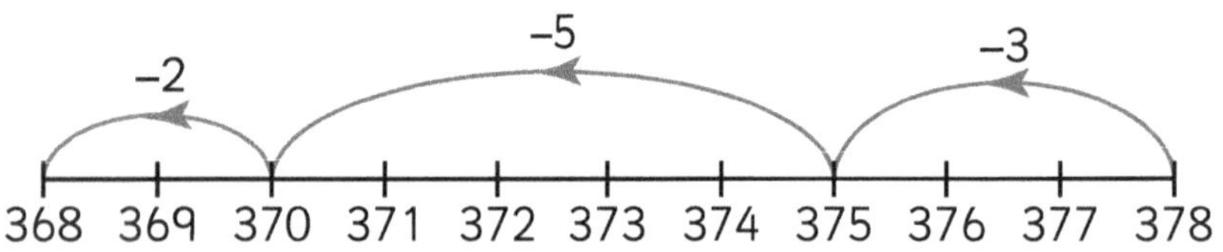

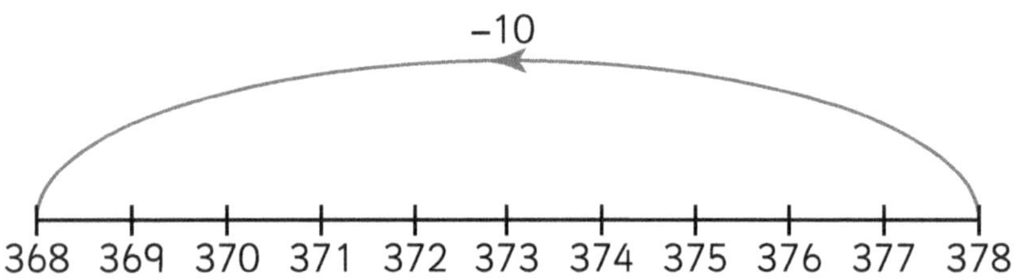

Discuss the merits of each method. **What is the same and what is different? Which way do you prefer? Why? What would happen if we started at 368 and counted forwards?** If appropriate, model how the second and third examples would look on an empty number line, i.e.

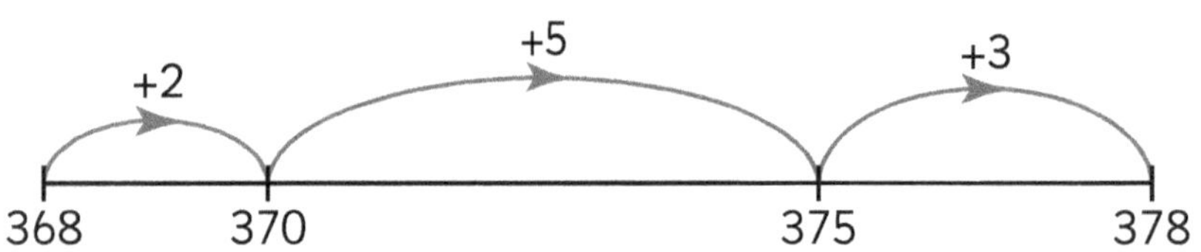

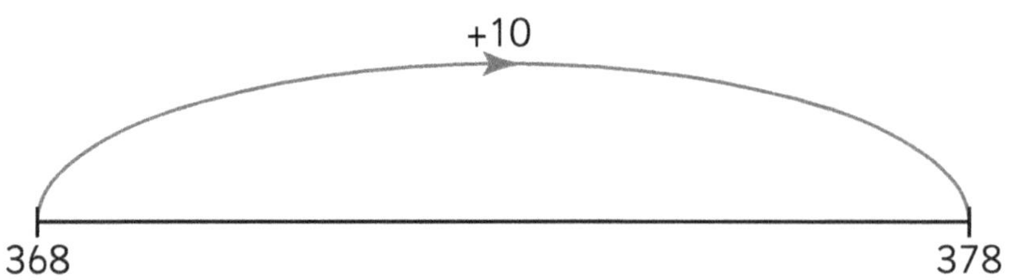

Unit 3.7 Adding and subtracting single- and double-digit numbers

- Discuss the 'Let's Learn' section on pages 56–57 of the Pupil Book. Challenge pupils to extend each pattern. **How far can you go?**
- Pupils work in pairs. Give each pair an addition or subtraction fact and have them generate at least twenty related facts. For example, they might be given 5 + 2 = 7 and come up with 65 + 2 = 67, 205 + 2 = 207, 825 + 2 = 827, etc. Challenge pupils to represent the number sentences produced on number lines.
- Highlight mathematical relationships by having pupils generate families of four related facts. **What is 22 + 4? How did you work it out? If 22 + 4 = 26 what does 4 + 22 make?** Write 22 + 4 = 26 and 4 + 22 = 26 on a flipchart or whiteboard. Challenge pupils to complete the Fact Family by writing two different subtractions using the same three numbers. **How do you know that you are correct?** Ask pupils to prove the accuracy of their answers using concrete materials (for example, ten frames, straws or base 10 blocks).
- Write a range of missing sum, addend, difference or subtrahend number sentences on a flipchart or whiteboard. For example, 4 + 65 = ☐; 81 + ☐ = 85; 37 – 3 = ☐ ; 99 – ☐ = 92. Ask pupils to 'show you' the answer on a mini whiteboard. **What number fact did you use to help you work out the missing number?**

Unit 3.8 Adding and subtracting multiples of 10 to and from two-digit numbers

- Recap on the learning focus of Unit 3.7. **If 2 + 6 = 8, what is 52 + 6? If 7 – 3 = 4, what is 77 – 3? How does knowing that 2 + 6 = 8 help you to add 20 and 60? What is 20 + 60? How does knowing that 7 – 3 = 4 help you to subtract 40 from 70? What is 70 – 40?** Ask pupils to predict the answer, record it on a mini whiteboard then check by counting in tens with concrete materials or on a number line. Repeat for different examples.
- Repeat the above activity for examples where the sum or minuend is a three-digit multiple of 10; for example, 40 + 70; 120 – 60. **What makes these questions more challenging? What known fact can you use to help you?**
- Discuss the 'Let's Learn' section on pages 59–60 of the Pupil Book. **Why has Isla taken three jumps of ten? How many tens has she added? How many tens has Nuria subtracted? Why has she done that?** Present similar calculations on a flipchart or whiteboard, i.e. examples that require the pupils to add or subtract a multiple of ten to or from a two-digit number. Ask pupils to draw an empty number line, count in tens to work out the answer and 'show you'. **Did everyone get the same answer? How many tens did you add/subtract? Which digit changes and which digit stays the same? Why is that?** Repeat for different examples. Note that in questions 3 and 4, pupils could be asked to record the answers as number sentences (for example, 27 + 50 = 77; 86 – 40 = 46).
- Discuss examples such as 72 – 70. **Is the zero needed in the answer? Do 02 and 2 mean the same thing or something different?**

Unit 3.9 Partitioning through 10

- Discuss the 'Let's Learn' section on page 62 of the Pupil Book. **How many other ways are there to partition the numbers 9 and 7? Why do you think Isla chose to partition 9 into 2 and 7? Why do you think Nuria chose to partition 7 into 3 and 4?** Focus the discussion around counting on and back to the next multiple of 10. **How else could the girls have used a number line to calculate 78 + 9 and 63 – 7? How would you have worked it out?**
- Display a calculation such as 47 + 8 = ☐ on a flipchart or whiteboard. Draw a line alongside it. Model using an empty number line to find the answer. **How can I use an empty number line to help me find the answer to this question? Will I count on or back? Why? What number will I start with? Where should I write this number? How big will my first jump be? What number will that take me to? I have already added 3, how much more do I need to add so that I add 8 altogether? What is fifty add five? What is the answer to 47 + 8? How do you know?** Repeat for different additions of the same type and subtraction examples such as 93 – 7 = ☐.
- Pose questions similar to those presented in the unit, i.e. two-digit number plus or minus a single-digit number. Examples should require the pupil to cross a decade. Ask pupils to draw empty number lines to work out the answers. **Compare number lines with a partner. Did you both work it out the same way? What is the same and what is different?** Invite pupils to share their method with the class. Encourage them to justify their method. For example: *'I added three to get me to 50 because it's easy to add on to a tens number', 'I wasn't sure how to partition 8 so I counted on in ones.'*
- Repeat all of the above for missing addend additions and missing subtrahend subtractions. For example: 82 = 75 + ☐; 47 + ☐ = 54; 31 – ☐ = 22; 78 = 86 – ☐.

Unit 3.10 Adding two-digit numbers

- Discuss the 'Let's Learn' section on page 65 of the Pupil Book. **What is the same and what is different about the boys' methods?** Point out that both boys have taken the same five jumps but in a different order. **Is it possible to add 28 and 36 in fewer than five jumps? How would you do it?** Take suggestions from the pupils, modelling each suggestion on an empty number line. For example, *'I would do 28 add 30 is 58. Then I would add 2 to make 60, then add 4 to make 64'.*

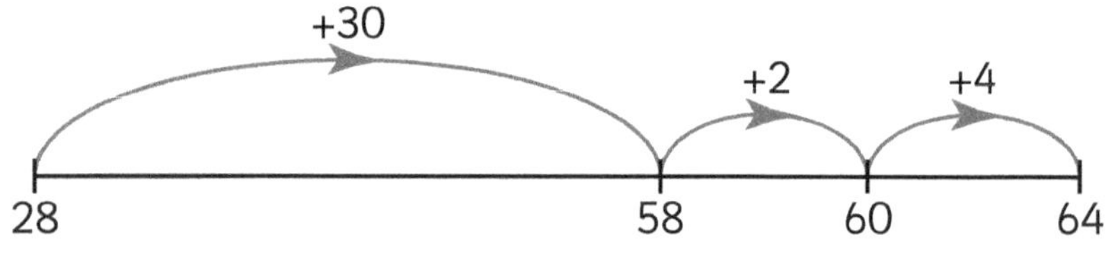

Challenge pupils to explain why their method works; for example, *'I added 30 + 2 + 4, so that's 36 added altogether'.*

- Pose a range of two-digit additions and ask pupils to draw empty number lines to work out the answers. **Compare number lines with a partner, did you both work it out the same way? What is the same and what is different?** Invite pupils to share their method with the class.
- Pupils work in pairs. Pupil A tells their partner a two-digit addition and challenges him or her to draw an empty number line to model the calculation. Likewise, Pupil B poses a question for Pupil A. Each pupil shares their number line with the question setter and tells them the answer. **Can you see how your partner worked it out? Is their method clear? Do you agree that this is the correct answer? If not, what has gone wrong?**

- Ask pupils to show how they would use concrete materials grouped in tens and ones (for example, straws, ten frames, base 10 blocks) to calculate 54 + 32. Demonstrate partitioning both addends into tens and ones. *Add the tens first. 50 + 30 = 80. Next, add the ones. 4 + 2 = 6. 80 + 6 = 86 so 54 + 32 = 86.* Challenge pupils to use place value partitioning (supported by concrete materials if necessary) to add a range of two-digit numbers where the sum is 100 or less.
- Challenge pupils to use place value partitioning to add two-digit numbers mentally, supported by jottings. For example, 27 + 57 could be thought of as (20 + 50) + (7 + 7). Twenty plus fifty is seventy (jot down 70). Seven plus seven is fourteen (jot down 14). 70 + 14 = 84 so 27 + 57 = 84.

Unit 3.11 Subtracting two-digit numbers

- Discuss the 'Let's Learn' section on page 68 of the Pupil Book. **What is the same and what is different about the girls' methods?** Point out that both girls have taken the same four jumps but in a different order. **Is it possible to subtract 35 from 63 in fewer than four jumps? How would you do it?** Take suggestions from the pupils, modelling each suggestion on an empty number line. For example: *'I would do 63 take away 20 is 43. Then I would take away 3 to get to 40. I've taken 23 away so far so I need to take away another 5'.*

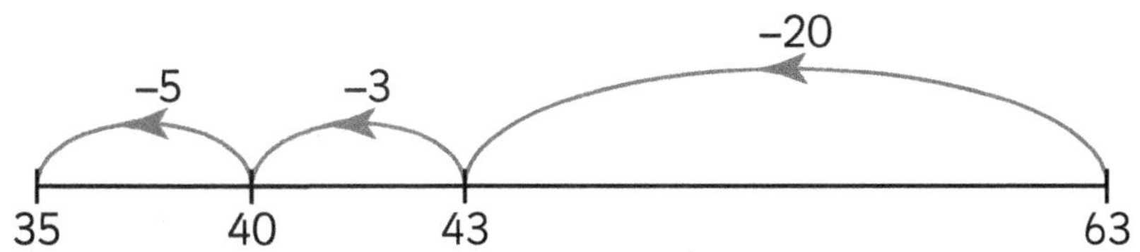

Challenge pupils to explain why their method works; for example, *'I needed to take away 28. 20 + 3 + 5 makes 28'.*

- Pose a range of two-digit subtractions and ask pupils to draw empty number lines to work out the answers. **Compare number lines with a partner, did you both work it out the same way? What is the same and what is different?** Invite pupils to share their method with the class.
- Pupils work in pairs. Pupil A tells their partner a two-digit subtraction and challenges him or her to draw an empty number line to model the calculation. Likewise, Pupil B poses a question for Pupil A. Each pupil shares their number line with the question setter and tells them the answer. **Can you see how your partner worked it out? Is their method clear? Do you agree that this is the correct answer? If not, what has gone wrong?**
- Ask pupils to show how they would use concrete materials grouped in tens and ones (for example, straws, ten frames, base 10 blocks) to calculate 76 – 52. Demonstrate subtracting the tens then the ones. *70 – 50 = 20 and 6 – 2 = 4. 20 and 4 makes 24 so 76 – 52 = 24.* Challenge pupils to use place value partitioning (supported by concrete materials if necessary) to subtract from a range of two-digit numbers. Care should be taken to ensure that no exchanging of material is necessary at this stage.
- Pose a question, such as 83 – 27, and ask pupils to find the answer by drawing an empty number line. Ensure everyone agrees on the answer. Next, ask pupils to make the number 83 with straws or base 10 blocks and partition it into 80 and 3. **What will we subtract from 80? Why? What do we need to subtract from 3? Can we do this at the moment? Why not?** Invite pupils to suggest possible solutions. Use this example and others to draw pupils' attention to the limitations of the split strategy for subtraction.
- Pose further two-digit subtraction questions. Ask pupils to find the answers by jumping along an empty number line, or by using or visualising base ten materials. **How did you work it out? What strategy did you choose? Why did you choose it?**

Unit 3.12 Inverse relationships

- Make the number fifty-seven with base 10 material or straw bundles. **How many tens? How many ones? How many straws/blocks altogether?** Ask pupils to close their eyes while you remove and screen fifteen, i.e. 1 ten and 5 ones. **How many blocks are hidden? How do you know?** Model linking the concrete representation to a number sentence; for example, '*I had 57. I took 15 away and then there were 42*'. 57 – 15 = 42. Model combining both collections again and write 42 + 15 = 57. Repeat for other two-digit numbers. Ask pupils to write the corresponding subtraction and addition on a mini whiteboard as they observe your actions.
- Show two pieces of paper or string (for example, one the same length as 31 blocks of equal size/31 centimetres long; and another the same length as 24 blocks of equal size/24 centimetres long). Tell the class the length of each. **How could we find the difference between the two lengths?** Ask all pupils to draw an empty number line on a mini whiteboard. Ask one half of the class to find the difference between 31 and 24 by counting back, and the other half by counting on. **Did everyone get the same answer? Why does both counting back and counting on work?** Ask pupils to write a number sentence to match how they solved the problem. Write 31 – 24 = 7 and 24 + 7 = 31 on a flipchart or whiteboard.
- Represent these Fact Families as bar models. Challenge pupils to come up with one other addition and one other subtraction to make a family of four related facts. Repeat for different pairs of two-digit numbers. Focus discussion on the parts and the whole. **Which number tells you the whole in an addition/subtraction? Which numbers represent the parts in an addition/subtraction?**

Unit 3.13 Strategies for solving number puzzles

- Discuss the 'Let's Learn' section on pages 74–75 of the Pupil Book. **How would you calculate the answer to 5 + 4 + 6? Would you use one of the strategies shown or would you do it a different way?**
- Ask pupils to use interlocking cubes, ten frames, base ten blocks, Cuisenaire rods or a number line to prove that 17 + 3 = 20. **If I know that 17 + 3 = 20, what else do I know?** Focus discussion on the relationships between addition and subtraction.
- Display calculations such as 9 + 3 + 5 = ☐; ☐ + 3 + 5 = 17; 9 + ☐ + 5 = 17; 9 + 3 + ☐ = 17 and ask pupils to 'show you' the answers on a mini whiteboard. **How did you work out the missing number?**
- Practise recall of number bonds to 20 by playing Bingo. Give each pupil a rectangular piece of paper and have them fold it to make an eight-box grid. Ask pupils to choose eight numbers between 0 and 20 and write one in each box. Call out or hold up addition or subtraction facts within 20. Pupils cross off the answers on their grid. The first pupil to cross off all eight numbers on their grid is the winner.
- Ask pupils to make a poster about their favourite number between 0 and 20, showing what they know about it. For example: '*My favourite number is 16. It is double five plus six; 1 ten and 6 ones; 20 – 4*,' etc.

Unit 3.14 Representing and solving word problems (1)

- Display a comparison-type problem on a flipchart or whiteboard. For example: *'There are 28 sweets in a jar. 12 are fruit flavoured and the rest are toffees. How many toffees are there?'.* Ask pupils to represent the problem using concrete materials and to solve it. **Can you write an addition number sentence to match this problem? Can you write a subtraction number sentence to match this problem? Which number sentence best shows the way that you worked out the answer? Is one way easier than the other? Why is that?**
- Discuss the 'Let's Learn' example on page 76 of the Pupil Book. Arrange pupils in pairs or trios. Write a different comparison problem on a piece of paper. Distribute a copy to each pair/trio and have them stick it down in the top left-hand corner of a Think Board that has been drawn on a large sheet of paper. Ask pupils to work together to represent the problem as a picture, bar model and number sentence then solve it. Compare completed Think Boards. **What is the same and what is different? Can you think of another way to represent and solve this problem?**
- Display two different word problems (one change and one combine) on a flipchart or whiteboard. The problems should contain the same two numbers. For example: *'There were 16 children in the playground. Some more came. Now there are 35. How many more children came?'* and *'There are 35 children in playground. 16 are boys and the rest are girls. How many girls are there?'* Ask pupils to write a number sentence for each problem and choose how they will represent and solve them, i.e. concrete materials, pictures, bar model, empty number line. **What is the same and what is different about the two problems? What made you think of them as addition/subtraction?**

Unit 3.15 Representing and solving word problems (2)

- Display two groups of objects (for example, 41 blue blocks and 24 red blocks) and ask pupils to estimate which group has more. **How could we use an empty number line to work out how many more blue blocks there are?** Draw empty number lines on a flipchart or whiteboard and use these to model pupils' thinking. **What should I do to the smaller number to make it match the bigger number? What should I do to the bigger number to make it match the smaller number? Which movement shows addition and which shows subtraction?** Link movements with the appropriate number sentence; for example, 24 + [17] = 41; 41 – 24 = [17]. Repeat for other 'how many more?' and 'how many fewer' type problems that involve different quantities. Ask pupils to solve the problem using an empty number line, then write a number sentence that mirrors how they thought about it.
- Ask pupils to represent the following word problem with objects or a picture. *Isla's mum is running a marathon. She has already run 27 kilometres and has 15 kilometres still to go. How far is the race?* **Is this an addition or subtraction problem? How do you know?** Next, ask pupils to draw a bar model to represent the problem. **What are we being asked to work out? Is that the whole or one of the parts? Do you still think it is an addition/subtraction problem? What makes you say that? If 27 and 15 are the parts, how do we find the whole?** Ask pupils to find the solution, using a method of their choice. Repeat for different word problems that involve two-digit numbers. Ensure all problem types are included.

Number - addition and subtraction 1C

Section overview

Textbook 1C units	Review units	Prior learning	Benchmarks/Es&Os
Unit 3.1 Adding and subtracting a one-digit number to and from a three-digit number	**1B** Units 2.4, 2.5, 2.6, 2.7 and 2.8 Units 3.2, 3.3 and 3.7	• Recognise the patterns in the way we say, read and write three-digit numbers. • Recall addition and subtraction facts within the range 0–20. • Count forwards and backwards in tens and hundreds. • Add and subtract 0–9 to/from a two-digit number.	**MNU 1-02a** • Counts forwards and backwards in 2s, 5s, 10s, 100s. **MNU 1-03a** • Uses correct mathematical vocabulary when discussing the four operations including subtract, add, sum of, total, multiply, produce, divide and shared equally. • Solves addition and subtraction problems with three-digit whole numbers.
Unit 3.2 Adding and subtracting 10 and 100	**1B** Units 2.7, 2.8 and 2.10 Units 3.5 and 3.6 **1C** Unit 2.7	• Count in hundreds, tens and ones to find the value of a model created with base 10 blocks. • Partition three-digit numbers in standard ways; for example, 567 = 500 + 60 + 7. • Count forwards and backwards in tens and hundreds from a three-digit number. • Identify the number 10/100 more/less than a three-digit number. • Add and subtract 10 to/from a two-digit number.	**MNU 1-02a** • Identifies the value of each digit in a whole number with three digits, for example, 867 = 800 + 60 + 7. **MNU 1-03a** • Uses correct mathematical vocabulary when discussing the four operations including subtract, add, sum of, total, multiply, produce, divide and shared equally. • Solves addition and subtraction problems with three-digit whole numbers. • Adds and subtracts multiples of 10 or 100 to or from any whole number to 1000. • Applies knowledge of inverse operations (addition and subtraction; multiplication and division).

Unit 3.3 Adding and subtracting multiples of 10 and 100	**1B** Unit 2.10 Unit 3.8 **1C** Units 2.4 and 2.5	• Represent three-digit numbers with base 10 blocks and place value houses. • Count forwards and backwards in 20s and 50s. • Use an empty number line to add and subtract. • Add and subtract multiples of 10 to and from two-digit numbers.	**MNU 1-02a** • Identifies the value of each digit in a whole number with three digits; for example, 867 = 800 + 60 + 7. **MNU 1-03a** • Uses correct mathematical vocabulary when discussing the four operations including subtract, add, sum of, total, multiply, produce, divide and shared equally. • Solves addition and subtraction problems with three-digit whole numbers. • Adds and subtracts multiples of 10 or 100 to or from any whole number to 1000. • Applies knowledge of inverse operations (addition and subtraction; multiplication and division).
Unit 3.4 Number bonds to 100	**1B** Unit 2.11 Units 3.1, 3.3 and 3.4	• Recall complements to 10 and 20 (part-part-whole). • Partition two-digit numbers in standard ways; for example, 45 = 40 + 5. • Count on and back from a two-digit number to the next multiple of 10.	**MNU 1-03a** • Uses correct mathematical vocabulary when discussing the four operations including subtract, add, sum of, total, multiply, produce, divide and shared equally. • Demonstrates understanding of the commutative law; for example, $6 + 3 = 3 + 6$ or $2 \times 4 = 4 \times 2$. • Applies knowledge of inverse operations (addition and subtraction; multiplication and division).
Unit 3.5 Doubling and halving	**1A** Unit 5.6 **1B** Unit 2.11 Unit 3.2 Units 4.6 and 4.7	• Find half of a quantity by sharing a set of objects equally. • Find half of a quantity within the range 0–20 by dividing by 2. • Recall double facts from 1 + 1 to 10 + 10. • Understand that the value of a digit is determined by its place.	**MNU 1-02a** • Demonstrates understanding of zero as a place holder in whole numbers to 1000. **MNU 1-03a** • Uses multiplication and division facts to solve problems within the number range 0 to 1000. • Uses correct mathematical vocabulary when discussing the four operations including subtract, add, sum of, total, multiply, produce, divide and shared equally. • Applies knowledge of inverse operations (addition and subtraction; multiplication and division).

Unit 3.6 Adding a string of numbers	**1A** Unit 2.2 Unit 4.4 **1B** Units 3.1, 3.4 and 3.8	• Identify the multiples of 10 within the range 0–100. • Recall complements to 10. • Count on and back from a two-digit number to the next multiple of 10. • Add and subtract multiples of 10 to and from two-digit numbers.	**MNU 1-03a** • Uses correct mathematical vocabulary when discussing the four operations including subtract, add, sum of, total, multiply, produce, divide and shared equally. • Demonstrates understanding of the commutative law; for example, $6 + 3 = 3 + 6$ or $2 \times 4 = 4 \times 2$. • Adds and subtracts multiples of 10 or 100 to or from any whole number to 1000.
Unit 3.7 Adding and subtracting 8 or 9 using round and adjust	**1B** Units 1.1 and 1.2 Units 3.5 and 3.6	• Round two-digit numbers to the nearest ten. • Add and subtract 10 to and from a two-digit number.	**MNU 1-03a** • Uses correct mathematical vocabulary when discussing the four operations including subtract, add, sum of, total, multiply, produce, divide and shared equally. • Adds and subtracts multiples of 10 or 100 to or from any whole number to 1000.
Unit 3.8 Solving number problems	**1B** Units 3.2, 3.3, 3.9, 3.12 and 3.13 **1C** Units 3.4, 3.5 and 3.7	• Recall number bonds within the range 0–20. • Double and halve two-digit numbers. • Use place value partitioning to add and subtract two-digit numbers. • Add 8 or 9 using round and adjust. • Identify number bonds to 100. • Choose between counting on and counting back to solve a missing addend or missing subtrahend problem.	**MNU 1-03a** • Uses correct mathematical vocabulary when discussing the four operations including subtract, add, sum of, total, multiply, produce, divide and shared equally. • Demonstrates understanding of the commutative law; for example, $6 + 3 = 3 + 6$ or $2 \times 4 = 4 \times 2$. • Solves addition and subtraction problems with three-digit whole numbers. • Adds and subtracts multiples of 10 or 100 to or from any whole number to 1000. • Applies knowledge of inverse operations (addition and subtraction; multiplication and division).
Unit 3.9 Solving word problems	**1B** Units 3.12, 3.14 and 3.15	• Choose between counting on and counting back to solve a missing addend or missing subtrahend problem within the number range 0–99. • Represent *start, change and result unknown* addition and subtraction word problems (within the number range 0–99); select the appropriate operation and solve them using concrete materials. • Draw a bar model to represent and solve comparison problems (part-part-whole) within an appropriate number range. • Appreciate that the same word problem can be represented and solved in different ways.	**MNU 1-03a** • Uses correct mathematical vocabulary when discussing the four operations including subtract, add, sum of, total, multiply, produce, divide and shared equally. • Demonstrates understanding of the commutative law; for example, $6 + 3 = 3 + 6$ or $2 \times 4 = 4 \times 2$. • Solves addition and subtraction problems with three-digit whole numbers. • Adds and subtracts multiples of 10 or 100 to or from any whole number to 1000. • Applies knowledge of inverse operations (addition and subtraction; multiplication and division).

Unit 3.10 Adding two- and three-digit numbers	**1B** Units 3.9 and 3.10 **1C** Units 2.7 and 2.8 Units 3.4 and 3.7	• Use an empty number line to add two-digit numbers (jump strategy). • Use place value partitioning and jottings to add two-digit numbers (split strategy).	**MNU 1-03a** • Uses correct mathematical vocabulary when discussing the four operations including subtract, add, sum of, total, multiply, produce, divide and shared equally. • Demonstrates understanding of the commutative law; for example, $6 + 3 = 3 + 6$ or $2 \times 4 = 4 \times 2$. • Solves addition and subtraction problems with three-digit whole numbers. • Adds and subtracts multiples of 10 or 100 to or from any whole number to 1000.
Unit 3.11 Subtracting two-digit numbers from three-digit numbers	**1B** Units 3.9 and 3.11 **1C** Units 2.7 and 2.8	• Use an empty number line to subtract two-digit numbers. • Know when it is appropriate to use partitioning to subtract one two-digit number from another.	**MNU 1-02a** • Identifies the value of each digit in a whole number with three digits; for example, $867 = 800 + 60 + 7$. **MNU 1-03a** • Uses correct mathematical vocabulary when discussing the four operations including subtract, add, sum of, total, multiply, produce, divide and shared equally. • Solves addition and subtraction problems with three-digit whole numbers. • Adds and subtracts multiples of 10 or 100 to or from any whole number to 1000.
Unit 3.12 Adding three-digit numbers	**1B** Units 3.9 and 3.12 **1C** Units 2.7 and 2.8 Units 3.4, 3.7 and 3.10	• Partition numbers in standard and non-standard ways. • Choose between counting on and counting back to solve a missing addend problem. • Use place value understanding and round and adjust to simplify an addition. • Use an empty number line to add two-and three-digit numbers.	**MNU 1-02a** • Identifies the value of each digit in a whole number with three digits; for example, $867 = 800 + 60 + 7$. • Uses correct mathematical vocabulary when discussing the four operations including subtract, add, sum of, total, multiply, produce, divide and shared equally. **MNU 1-03a** • Demonstrates understanding of the commutative law; for example, $6 + 3 = 3 + 6$ or $2 \times 4 = 4 \times 2$. • Solves addition and subtraction problems with three-digit whole numbers. • Adds and subtracts multiples of 10 or 100 to or from any whole number to 1000.

Unit 3.13 Subtracting three-digit numbers	**1B** Unit 3.9 **1C** Units 2.7 and 2.8 Unit 3.11	• Partition numbers in standard and non-standard ways. • Understand that addition is commutative but subtraction is not. • Understand why a split strategy works for some subtractions but not for others. • Use an empty number line to subtract a two-digit number from a three-digit number.	**MNU 1-02a** • Identifies the value of each digit in a whole number with three digits; for example, 867 = 800 + 60 + 7. **MNU 1-03a** • Uses correct mathematical vocabulary when discussing the four operations including subtract, add, sum of, total, multiply, produce, divide and shared equally. • Solves addition and subtraction problems with three-digit whole numbers. • Adds and subtracts multiples of 10 or 100 to or from any whole number to 1000.
Unit 3.14 Representing and solving word problems	**1B** Units 3.14 and 3.15 **1C** Unit 3.9	• Understand the inverse relationship and so can choose between addition and subtraction to solve word problems. • Represent a range of addition and subtraction word problems (number range 0–999) and choose a suitable strategy to solve them. • Appreciate that the same word problem can be represented and solved in different ways.	**MNU 1-03a** • Uses correct mathematical vocabulary when discussing the four operations including subtract, add, sum of, total, multiply, produce, divide and shared equally. • Demonstrates understanding of the commutative law; for example, $6 + 3 = 3 + 6$ or $2 \times 4 = 4 \times 2$. • Solves addition and subtraction problems with three-digit whole numbers. • Adds and subtracts multiples of 10 or 100 to or from any whole number to 1000. • Applies knowledge of inverse operations (addition and subtraction; multiplication and division).
Unit 3.15 Two-step word problems	**1B** Units 3.14 and 3.15 **1C** Units 3.9 and 3.14	• Understand the inverse relationship and so can choose between addition and subtraction to solve word problems. • Represent a range of addition and subtraction word problems (number range 0–999) and choose a suitable strategy to solve them. • Appreciate that the same word problem can be represented and solved in different ways.	**MNU 1-03a** • Uses correct mathematical vocabulary when discussing the four operations including subtract, add, sum of, total, multiply, produce, divide and shared equally. • Demonstrates understanding of the commutative law; for example, $6 + 3 = 3 + 6$ or $2 \times 4 = 4 \times 2$. • Solves addition and subtraction problems with three-digit whole numbers. • Adds and subtracts multiples of 10 or 100 to or from any whole number to 1000. • Applies knowledge of inverse operations (addition and subtraction; multiplication and division). • Solves two-step problems.

Conceptual context

Book 1C sees a continuing focus on the development of sound mental agility and algebraic reasoning skills. Mental strategies introduced in earlier books (i.e. use known facts and place value, doubles and near doubles, compatible numbers, commutativity, partitioning and counting on and back) are consolidated and extended to include the strategies of halving and round and adjust. Conceptual place value understanding *underpins* a pupil's ability to use these strategies effectively. Pupils with sound conceptual place value understanding will be able to use and combine mental strategies, supported by the empty number line and/or informal jottings where necessary, to add and subtract two- and three-digit numbers without having to perform standard written algorithms. Such formal written methods are introduced in the Second Level textbooks, *after* pupils understand base-ten, as a more efficient way to deal with additions and subtractions that are too tricky to calculate mentally. Indeed, it is essential that we refrain from introducing standard written algorithms before this stage because to do so may hamper the development of sound number sense. From Unit 3.12 onwards, pupils are introduced to the idea that the same calculation can be written both horizontally and vertically, and that *all* strategies can be applied to either setting, hence paving the way for the introduction of semi-formal and formal written methods later in the series.

Pupils are again provided with opportunities to represent and solve the full range of problem types (i.e. start, change and result unknown, combine and compare problems) in multiple ways, and there is a continued focus on the development of part–whole thinking, i.e. splitting numbers into two or more parts. The bar model supports this development by helping pupils visualise addition and subtraction problems as part–whole situations. Linking with the idea that the whole can be made up of more than two parts, two-step word problems are introduced, i.e. problems that require the pupil to first add then subtract, or vice-versa. Missing minuend tasks gain prominence and align with pupils' growing understanding of subtraction as the inverse of addition. The realisation that a missing minuend subtraction can be solved by adding provides a good indication that this understanding has been fully acquired. Some pupils will reach this stage earlier than others. Until they do, it is important that we allow them to represent and solve such problems in ways that make sense to them, thereby nurturing their ability to reason algebraically.

Resources

- 100 bead strings
- Base 10 blocks
- Bar model template
- Empty number lines
- Hundred square
- Mini whiteboards
- Place value arrow cards (HTO)
- Place value counters
- Place value houses
- Set of four dice displaying the following numbers: Dice A – 10, 20, 30, 40, 50, 60; Dice B – 40, 50, 60, 70, 80, 90; Dice C – 0, 1, 2, 3, 4, 5; Dice D – 6, 7, 8 ,9, 1, 0
- Sets of 1–9 digit cards
- Squared paper
- Think Board template

Key vocabulary

- **Addition**
- **Bar model**
- **Calculate**
- **Difference**
- **Digit**
- **Double**
- **Empty number line**
- **Jottings**
- **Method**
- **Number bonds**
- **Number line**
- **Number sentence**
- **Partition**
- **Place value**
- **Strategy**
- **Subtraction**
- **Sum**

Misconceptions

Potential misconception	Addressing the misconception
Units 3.1, 3.10 and 3.12 Pupils may think they will get a different answer if they swap the numbers around in an addition (i.e. may believe that 7 + 146 will give a different answer to 146 + 7) and so always attempt to count on from the first addend.	Demonstrate the commutative nature of addition with concrete materials. For example, represent the numbers 7 and 146 with base 10 blocks. Lay 7 on the left and 146 on the right. Ask the pupil to count in hundreds, tens and ones to find the total. Swap the representations over and ask them to count again. Record 7 + 146 = 153 and 146 + 7 = 153. Point out that 7 + 146 means the same as 146 + 7.
Units 3.11 and 3.13 Pupils may understand that the addends of an addition are interchangeable but wrongly assume this rule also applies to subtraction; for example, they may try to solve 358 – 74 by partitioning both numbers (split strategy) and get an incorrect answer of 324 (thinks 50 – 70 = 20 because 70 – 50 = 20).	Use concrete materials to demonstrate why addition is commutative but subtraction is not. For example, ask the pupil to make the number 354 with place value counters to show why, if there are only 5 tens counters, we are unable to remove 7 tens counters. NB: exchanging 1 hundred for 10 tens and 1 ten for 10 ones is introduced in Book 2A prior to the introduction of standard written methods.
Units 3.3, 3.4, 3.9, 3.10, 3.11, 3.12 and 3.13 Pupils may struggle to partition quantities mentally and solely depend on taking jumps of one hundred, ten and one when using an empty number line.	Provide lots of practice in reciting number word sequences in 2s, 3s, 5s, multiples of 10 and multiples of 100 from different starting numbers.
Units 3.8, 3.9 and 3.14 Pupils may be unsure of the inverse relationship and so be unable to choose between addition and subtraction, counting on and counting back, to solve missing addend/ subtrahend/minuend calculations.	Provide opportunities to investigate part-part-whole situations with screened concrete materials where the individual ones that make up each part can be counted. For example: Represent the number 56 with base 10 blocks. Ask the pupil to close their eyes while you screen 6 blocks. **How many blocks were there? How many can you see now? How many did I hide?** Record 56 – □ = 50. Return the 6 blocks to the table: 50 + □ = 56. Repeat, but this time remove then return 50 (5 tens). 56 – □ = 6; 6 + □ = 56. Tell the pupil that you have some tens and ones in a box but don't tell them how many. Remove 50 (5 tens) and lay them on the table. **There are 6 ones left in the box.** □ – 50 = 6. Return the 50 straws to the box. 6 + 50 = □. Extend to include to three-digit numbers, using materials grouped in hundreds, tens and ones. Finally, link the above idea to bar models where the individual ones that make up each quantity are not visible. Model writing number sentences to match the situation.
Units 3.9, 3.14 and 3.15 Pupils may be able to solve a word problem using concrete materials and/or a number line but do not consider how their actions relate to the operations and so have difficulty writing an appropriate number sentence to show what they did.	Encourage pupils to interpret the word problem and link how they think about it to a number sentence *before* attempting to solve it. For example: *Finlay's grandpa has some chickens and 158 sheep. There are 188 animals altogether. How many chickens are there?* May be interpreted as □ + 158 = 188 or 188 – □ = 158.

Teaching ideas

Unit 3.1 Adding and subtracting a one-digit number to and from a three-digit number

- Tell pupils that the children are playing a game of Number Bond Bingo. Amman has covered all of the numbers on his board, except the number fourteen. The teacher calls out '8 add 7'. Amman crosses off the number 14 and cries 'Bingo!' **Has Amman won the game? Why not? If Amman can't remember the answer to 8 + 7, how could he work it out?** Encourage responses such as *Double 7 then add 1 more; Double 8 then take 1 away; Take 2 from the 7 and add it to the 8 to make 10 + 5.* Repeat for other addition and subtraction facts within the range 0–20. **What advice would you give someone who had forgotten…?**
- Play your own class game of Number Bond Bingo. Ask each pupil to fold a rectangular piece of paper to make eight boxes. They should write a different number between 0–20 in each box. Call out additions and subtractions with a sum or difference within this range. The first player to cross off all eight numbers on their grid is the winner.
- Tell pupils that Finlay's teacher has asked him to work out the answer to 8 + 122. He is trying to count on from eight but keeps losing his place. **What advice would you give Finlay? How would you work out 8 + 122?**
- Tell pupils that Isla knows lots of addition facts but sometimes finds it hard to remember subtraction facts. **How could Isla use addition to help her work out 18 – 9?** Repeat for other subtraction facts.
- Ask pupils to picture a hundred square in their heads. **What number is three to the right of 91? What number is 4 to the left of 68? How can we use the fact that 91 + 3 = 94 to work out 591 + 3; 191 + 3; 791 + 3? How can we use the fact that 68 – 4 = 64 to work out 268 – 4; 968 – 4; 668 – 4?** Ask similar questions about different two-digit numbers.

Unit 3.2 Adding and subtracting 10 and 100

- Ask pupils to picture a hundred square in their heads. **What number is below 75? How do you know? What number is above 32? How do you know? How can we use the fact that 75 + 10 = 85 to work out 175 + 10; 575 + 10; 975 + 10? How can we use the fact that 32 – 10 = 22 to work out 432 – 10; 832 – 10; 132 – 10?** Ask similar questions about different two- and three-digit numbers.
- Challenge pupils to work together to create a giant number square with 1–100 along the top, 101–901 down the left-hand side and 100–1000 down the right-hand side. **What number will go below 434/807/540, etc? How much bigger is this number? What would 173/651/370 plus 100 be? What number is above 434/807/540, etc? How much smaller is this number? What would 173/651/370 minus 100 be?** Remove the number square and ask pupils to picture it in their heads in order to answer similar questions. Ask pupils to check their answers using base 10 blocks.
- Display partially completed grids similar to those below and challenge pupils to fill in the missing numbers. **Compare completed grids with a partner, have you both completed the grids in the same way?** Ask pupils to work in pairs to generate as many addition and subtraction facts as they can using the numbers in the grid and the numbers 1, 10 and 100.

245		
		347
	446	

510			513	
520				
		532		
	541			

Unit 3.3 Adding and subtracting multiples of 10 and 100

- Display a set of calculations similar to the following: 80 + 70; 200 – 50; 70 + 70; 90 + 60; 30 + 120; 180 – 30; 190 – 40. **Which is the odd one out and why? Can you think of more than one reason for your answer?** Repeat for different sets of calculations. Ask pupils to write their own set of additions and/or subtractions and challenge a partner to identify the odd one out. **Do you both agree on which number is the odd one out? If not, can you both be right?**
- Display a three-digit number on a place value house and ask pupils to represent it with base 10 blocks or place value counters.

H	T	O
5	3	5

  What number have you made? How could we change the model so that it represents the number 935/335? Encourage responses such as 'add 400' and 'subtract 200'. **Can you write a number sentence to show what we did?** Record 535 + 400 = 935 and 535 – 200 = 335 on a flipchart or whiteboard. **What do you notice? Can you draw a place value house to represent the new number? Which digits stay the same? Which digit changes? Can you explain this?** Focus discussion on adding and subtracting hundreds. Repeat for adding and subtracting multiples of 10 to and from three-digit numbers (for example, 714 + 50; 664 – 20). Care should be taken to avoid examples where it is necessary to exchange tens for a hundred at this stage.

- Write a range of missing addend and missing subtrahend questions on a flipchart or whiteboard. For example: □ + 245 = 345; 956 + □ = 976; 711 – □ = 211; 583 – □ = 573. **Which digit has changed? How has it changed? How does this help you to work out the missing number?**
- Tell pupils that Nuria is trying to work out the answer to 251 – 80 in her head. She thinks the answer might be 231 but she is unsure. Ask pupils to discuss Nuria's thinking in pairs or small groups then use base 10 blocks or place value counters to test their ideas. **Where did Nuria go wrong?** Ask pupils to find the correct answer to 251 – 80 by drawing an empty number line. **Did everyone work it out in the same way? How did you do it? Why did you choose that method?**
- Display a set of additions and subtractions on a flipchart or whiteboard. One addend in each addition should be a multiple of 10 or 100. The subtrahend in each subtraction should also be a multiple of 10 or 100. Ask pupils to work in pairs to arrange the calculations into two groups: those that are easily solved mentally and those that are best solved using an empty number line. Compare completed lists. **Why did you put that addition in the 'empty number line list'?** Etc.

Unit 3.4 Number bonds to 100

- Provide each pupil with some 10 × 10 grids or ask them to draw their own 10 × 10 grids on squared paper. Call out a two-digit number (for example, 62). Ask pupils to partition their grid into two parts so that one of the parts has 62 small squares in it. **How many squares in the other part? How many squares altogether?** Ask pupils to write an addition number sentence to represent their grid, i.e. 62 + 38 = 100. **What if I had called out the number 38? How many squares in the other part now?** Record 38 + 62 = 100. **We have the start of a Fact Family, can you write two subtractions to complete the family?** Record 100 – 38 = 62 and 100 – 62 = 38.

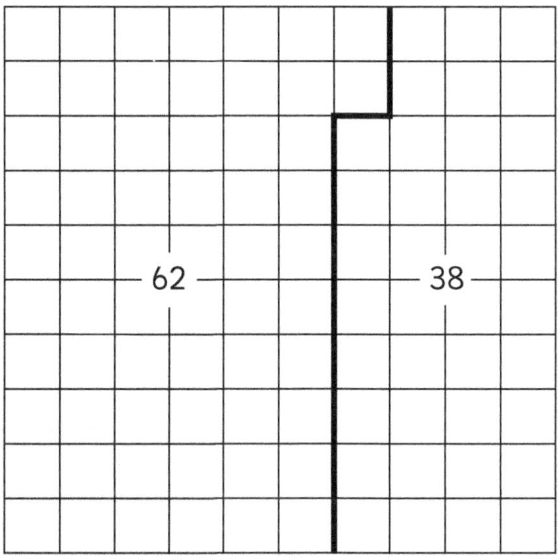

62 + 38 = 100

38 + 62 = 100

100 – 38 = 62

100 – 62 = 38

Call out different two-digit numbers. Ask pupils to partition a 100 square grid to find each complement to 100. Ask them to use the completed grid to generate a family of four related facts.

- Discuss the 'Let's Learn' section on pages 41–42 of the Pupil Book. Display part-unknown bar models similar to those shown below.

100	
51	?

100	
87	?

100	
38	?

Ask pupils to find the missing part in each case using a method of their choice. **How did you work it out?** Complete the bar models displayed and ask the pupils to compare the parts in each. **What do you notice? What do the tens total each time? What do the ones total each time?**

- Present a word problem such as the following: *Nuria has counted out 75 straws so far. Her teacher asked her to get 132. How many more straws does Nuria need?* Encourage pupils to look for pairs of numbers that total 100 to help them solve the problem. For example, *75 + 25 = 100. 25 + 32 = 57 so Nuria needs 57 more straws.* **How did you work it out? Why did you do it that way? Which pair of numbers add to 100?**

Unit 3.5 Doubling and halving

- Introduce the 'Let's Learn' section on pages 44–45 of the Pupil Book. Arrange the pupils into groups of four. Allocate one character (i.e. Finlay, Nuria, Amman and Isla) to each group member. Challenge pupils to use concrete materials, drawings or diagrams to prove that the character allocated to them is correct. Invite pupils to explain their representations to the class. Compare different representations of the same character's solution. **What is the same and what is different?**
- Have pupils use known facts and place value to double or half multiples of 10 and 100 and 'show you' the answers on a mini whiteboard. **What double fact did you use to help you each time?** Highlight and discuss the inverse relationship. For example: **If double 90 is 180, what is half of 180? If half of 600 is 300, what is double 300?**
- Have pupils use place value partitioning to double a range of two-digit numbers and 'show you' on a mini whiteboard. Jottings may help them keep track of their thinking. For example: **What is double 96?** The pupil thinks *double 90 is 180 (jot down 180) and double 6 is 12 (jot down 12). 180 + 12 = 192. The answer is 192.* **Which double facts did you use to help you?**
- Have pupils use place value partitioning to half a range of two- and three-digit numbers and 'show you' on a mini whiteboard. Jottings may help them keep track of their thinking. For example: **What is half of 410?** The pupil thinks *half of 400 is 200 (jot down 200). Half of 10 is 5 (jot down 5). 200 and 5 makes 205. The answer is 205.* **Which number facts did you use to help you?** Focus discussion on the inverse relationship (for example, if we know that double 200 is 400 we can use this to work out half of 400).

Unit 3.6 Adding a string of numbers

- Ask pupils to look at the 'Let's Learn' section on pages 46–47 of the Pupil Book. Model thinking about the calculation and using jottings for the first example, i.e. **Which two numbers did Amman add together first? Why did he do that?** *So, 6 plus 4 makes ten and 20 plus 30 makes 50 (jot down 10 + 50). That's 60 so far. Add on 11. The answer is 71 (write down Answer 71).* Emphasise how jottings can help us keep track of our thinking. **How else could we find the answer to 24 + 11 + 36? What would you do?** Encourage pupils to use and describe mental strategies, supported by jottings where necessary. For example, a pupil might say *24 plus 11 makes 35. I jotted that number down, then I added 30 and jotted down 65. 65 plus 5 makes 70, add one makes 71. The answer is 71.*
- Write 40 + 17 + 53 + 4 on a flipchart or whiteboard. Ask pupils to look at Amman's jottings at the top of page 47 of the Pupil Book. **Which two numbers has Amman added together first this time? How do you know?** Focus discussion on the commutative nature of addition and the advantages of looking for and using multiples of 10.
- Display the digit cards 1–7. Invite pupils to use the cards to make three 2-digit numbers and one single-digit number (for example: 71, 23, 64 and 5) and write them on a flipchart or whiteboard. Tell them that they are going to find the sum of these numbers. **Can you see any numbers that add to give a multiple of 10? What if we were to add 5 to one of the 2-digit numbers?** Encourage pupils to consider adding 5 to 71 to make 76. Jot down 76 and discard these digit cards. **Which number can be added to 76 to give a multiple of 10?** Jot down 70 + 60 = 130 and 6 + 4 = 10. Discard the digit cards for 64 and jot down 140. **Our total is 140 so far, what number do we still need to add? What is 140 + 23?** Write down the answer (163). Ask pupils to check the solution by adding the original four numbers on a calculator. Have pupils work in pairs to make a different set of numbers using the digit cards 1–7 and find the total. **What numbers did you make? How did you add them? Why did you decide to add the numbers in that order?** Challenge pupils to explain their jottings.

Unit 3.7 Adding and subtracting 8 or 9 using round and adjust

- Show pupils a hundred square. **What is 48 + 9 / 62 – 9 / 36 + 8 / 73 – 8, etc.?** Record completed number sentences on a flipchart or whiteboard. **How did you work it out?** Focus discussion on adding / subtracting 10 then compensating. Challenge pupils to explain why this strategy works. Connect this idea to the empty number line by discussing the examples in the 'Let's Learn' section on page 48 of the Pupil Book. Ask pupils to draw empty number lines to prove that 48 + 9 = 57; 62 – 9 = 53; 36 + 8 = 44; 73 – 8 = 65.
- Call out a range of questions where the pupil is required to add/subtract 8 or 9 to/from a two- or three-digit number. Ask pupils to work out the answers and 'show you' on a mini whiteboard. They may choose to visualise a number grid or draw an empty number line. **Did everyone get the same answer? How did you work it out? Did you always use the same strategy? If not, what helped you decide which strategy to use?**
- Display a mixed set of calculations on a flipchart or whiteboard, some of which are incorrect. For example: 59 + 9 = 68; 77 + 8 = 86; 64 + 8 = 72; 36 + 9 = 81; 55 – 8 = 47; 41 – 8 = 29; 83 – 9 = 74. Tell pupils that Isla has been adding and subtracting 8 and 9 but she has made some mistakes. Pupils should work in pairs to identify which answers are correct and which are wrong. **What has Isla done wrong? Can you spot her mistake? What should the answer be?**
- Write some missing addend and missing subtrahend questions on a flipchart or whiteboard. For example: 57 + □ = 66; □ + 34 = 42; 81 – □ = 73; 31 – □ = 22. Tell the pupils that the missing number is either 8 or 9. **Which do you think it is most likely to be? What makes you say that?** Encourage pupils to focus on the ones digits in the known addend and sum, or minuend and difference, then test their predictions by drawing number lines.
- Write some missing minuend questions on a flipchart or whiteboard. For example: □ – 9 = 16; □ – 8 = 65 and challenge pupils to work in pairs to find the missing numbers. **How will you work it out? Would it help to draw a bar model?** Focus discussion on 'part-part-whole'.

Unit 3.8 Solving number problems

- Write a range of two-digit additions (sum unknown) and subtractions (difference unknown) on a flipchart or whiteboard. Ask pupils to work out each answer and 'show you' on a mini whiteboard. **Did everyone get the same answer? How did you work it out?** Record the different methods for each example on the flipchart / whiteboard. Discuss similarities and differences between them. **Which methods involve using known facts / place value / doubling or halving / partitioning / looking for multiples of 10 or 100 /counting on or back? Which way do you find easiest? Why?**
- Write a range of three-digit + or – one-digit problems on a flipchart or whiteboard. For example: 213 + 9 = □; 597 + □ = 605; 782 – 6 = □; 302 – □ = 295. Ask pupils to solve each problem by picturing a number line in their heads. **What did you say to yourself each time? Would jottings have helped?**
- Write two-digit missing addend problems on a flipchart or whiteboard. Model finding the unknown number by counting on in tens on a hundred square. For example: 36 + □ = 74. Put your finger on 36. Ask pupils to count in tens with you as you count 46, 56, 66, 76. **How many tens have we added (4)? What number is this (40)? Can the answer be 40? Why not? How can we get back to 74 (–2)? What is the missing number?** Model solving missing subtrahend problems such as 93 – □ = 68 by counting back in tens on a hundred square and compensating.
- Write simple missing minuend problems on a flipchart or whiteboard. The minuend should be a three-digit number. For example: □ – 600 = 34. **What is missing, is it the whole or one of the parts? How might a bar model help you to work out the missing number?** Ask pupils to draw a bar model to represent the calculation and solve it. **Can you write an addition number sentence about the bar model?**

Unit 3.9 Solving word problems

- Discuss the 'Let's Learn' section on pages 54–55 of the Pupil Book. **Which method do you prefer? Why?** Present different word problems that require pupils to compare two quantities, such as those shown below. Ensure examples involve calculations that pupils can do mentally.
    - o *Isla's sunflower measures 135 cm. Nuria's measures 120 cm. How much shorter is Nuria's sunflower?*
    - o *Mr Smith orders 160 books for the school library. The books arrive in two boxes. There are 90 books in the first box he opens. How many books are in the second box?*
    - o *There are 224 pupils in the playground and 100 fewer in the dining hall. How many pupils are in the dining hall?*

  Ask pupils to write a number sentence that shows how they solved each problem. **Who thought of the problem as an addition? Who thought of it as a subtraction?** Ask pupils to draw a bar model to represent each problem and write three more number sentences (one addition and two subtractions or vice-versa) to complete families of four related facts.
- Following on from the previous activity, ask pupils to choose one of the problems to represent on an empty number line. **Which numbers represent the parts and which number represents the whole? Did you jump forwards or backwards along the number line to solve the problem? Which operation is represented by jumping forwards/backwards?**
- Repeat the above activity but have pupils visualise jumping along the number line in their heads. **What is the difference between the two numbers in the problem? Did you count on or did you count back? What number did you jump to first? Then what did you do?** For example, in the first problem the pupil might say *I counted on from 120. I took one jump of ten to reach 130 then I took a jump of five to get to 135. 10 + 5 = 15 so the difference between 135 and 120 is 15.* Repeat for similar word problems.

Unit 3.10 Adding two- and three-digit numbers

- Discus the 'Let's Learn' section on page 56 of the Pupil Book. **Why do you think both children chose to partition 83 rather than 675? How would you use a number line to solve this problem?** Draw pupils' ideas on a flipchart or whiteboard. **Is it always easier to add the tens first, then the ones?** Display similar additions on a flipchart or whiteboard; for example, 788 + 57; 63 + 279. Ask pupils to work out the answers by drawing number lines. **Which number did you keep whole? Which number did you partition? How did you partition it? How many jumps did you take? Why?**
- Tell pupils that Finlay and Isla are calculating 253 + 36 in their heads. Finlay said *263, 273, 283, 289.* Isla jotted down 200, 80, 9. Ask pupils to discuss this with a partner. **Can you work out what Finlay and Isla were thinking? What strategies do you think they used? How are their strategies the same, how are they different? Whose strategy would you use to calculate: 633 + 22; 458 + 76, etc.?**
- Keep mental addition skills sharp by playing 'Target 150'. Pupils work in pairs or small groups. Each pair/group needs four dice with the following numbers on their faces:

  Dice A – 10, 20, 30, 40, 50, 60

  Dice B – 40, 50, 60, 70, 80, 90

  Dice C – 0, 1, 2, 3, 4, 5

  Dice D – 6, 7, 8 ,9 ,1, 0

  Pupils take turns to roll all four dice and add the numbers together. The pupil with the answer closest to 150 wins the round. The overall winner is the player who has won most rounds after an agreed period of time or number of rounds.

Unit 3.11 Subtracting two-digit numbers from three-digit numbers

- Discus the 'Let's Learn' section on pages 58–59 of the Pupil Book. **How have Amman and Isla solved 753 – 77? What is the same and what is different about their number lines? How would you use a number line to solve this problem? How have Finlay and Nuria solved 959 – 34? Would this strategy work for 753 – 77?** Pupils should be challenged to justify and prove their answer. Display similar subtractions on a flipchart or whiteboard (for example: 894 – 71; 302 – 37). Ask pupils to solve each problem using either of the strategies shown. **Which strategy did you use? Why did you choose it?**
- Tell pupils that Amman and Finlay are calculating 996 – 42 in their heads. Amman said *986, 976, 966, 956, 954.* Finlay jotted down 900, 50, 4. Ask pupils to discuss this with a partner. **Can you work out what Amman and Finlay were thinking? What strategies do you think they used? How are their strategies the same, how are they different? Whose strategy would you use to calculate: 851 – 76; 583 – 21, etc.?**
- Keep mental calculation skills sharp by playing a modified version of 'Target Number'. You will need a set of place value arrow cards (HTO). Pupils work in small teams. Place all arrow cards face down on a table. Ask pupils to randomly select a hundreds card, a tens card and a ones card. The number generated becomes the target number. For example, if the numbers 600, 40 and 3 are selected, 643 becomes the target number. Teams have 5 minutes to generate as many additions and subtractions as they can which have the target number as the answer. After 'time up' teams take turns to call out one of the number sentences they have written down. The teacher records each number sentence on a flipchart or whiteboard, grouping them according to specific strategies and highlighting any emerging patterns (for example, the patterns created by repeatedly subtracting ones, tens or hundreds). Teams earn one point for each number sentence called out that no other team has written. The first team to identify five unique answers wins the game. **How well did you work as a team? How did you organise yourselves to maximise your time? What strategy did you use to try to win the game? If we were to play the game again, what would you keep/change?**

Unit 3.12 Adding three-digit numbers

- Present the same three-digit addition in horizontal and vertical format. For example:

  166 + 538 =

  ```
    166
  + 538
  _____
  _____
  ```

  What do you notice?

  Tell pupils that, just as the same calculation can be solved in different ways, the same calculation can be set down in different ways: horizontally and vertically. **Where have you seen these words before? What do they mean? Which calculation is written horizontally/vertically?** Ask pupils to draw a number line to help them solve 166 + 538. Compare and contrast methods and solutions. Model recording the answer in both formats. Highlight how, when using the vertical layout, it is important to align the hundreds, tens and ones. **How is the equals sign represented in the vertical layout?** Repeat for different three-digit additions. Ask pupils to record their answers in the new vertical layout and 'show you' on a mini whiteboard.
- Write a three-digit addition (for example, 216 + 672) *vertically* on a flipchart or whiteboard. Ask pupils to represent each addend with base 10 blocks then add them. For example:

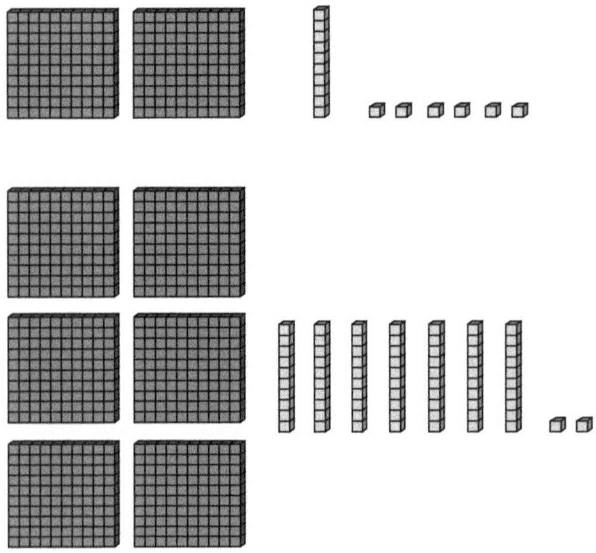

200 + 10 + 6

600 + 70 + 2

800 + 80 + 8

What is 800 + 80 + 8? So, what does 216 + 672 equal? Invite pupils to count in hundreds, tens and ones to check the total. Repeat for different three-digit additions. Include examples where the number of tens and/or ones is equal to or greater than 10. For example: 340 + 472 = 700 + 110 + 2; 138 + 259 = 300 + 80 + 17; 563 + 187 = 600 + 140 + 10.

- Display calculations such as 435 + 199; 104 + 599; 198 + 230; 300 + 598. Challenge pupils to use what they know about adding 8 and 9 to make these calculations as straightforward as possible. **How did you add the numbers? Why did you do that?**

Unit 3.13 Subtracting three-digit numbers

- Present the same three-digit subtraction in horizontal and vertical format. Tell pupils that, just as additions can be presented both horizontally and vertically, so can subtractions. Ask pupils to draw a number line to help them solve 643 – 128. Compare and contrast methods and solutions. Ask pupils to write the calculation and solution in vertical format on a mini whiteboard and 'show you'. Remind pupils that, when using the vertical layout, it is important to line up the hundreds, tens and ones correctly. Repeat for different 3-digit subtractions.
- Write 876 – 124 on a flipchart or whiteboard. Ask pupils to mentally partition both numbers according to their place values, i.e. 800 + 70 + 6 and 100 + 20 + 4. **What is 800 minus 100, 70 minus 20, 6 minus 4?** Jot down the numbers that the pupils tell you, i.e. 700; 50; 2. **So, what is 876 – 124?** Invite pupils to check the answer by setting out and removing place value counters.
- Return to the calculation 643 – 128. Ask pupils to represent the number 643 with place value counters, i.e.

Point out that we have 600 + 40 + 3. We need to subtract 100 + 20 + 8. **Why is this tricky? Can we subtract 100?** Remove a 100 counter and jot down 500. **Can we subtract 20?** Remove two 10s counters and jot down 20. **How could we subtract 8?** Repeat for 537 – 261; 798 – 563; 642 – 475. **Is it better to partition one number only and draw any empty number line for this calculation, or is it better to partition both numbers? What makes you say that?**

- Display a range of three-digit subtractions on a flipchart or whiteboard. Ask pupils to identify which would be better solved by jumping along a number line and which could easily be solved by partitioning both numbers according to their place values. **Do we all agree? Is there another way?** Ask pupils to find the solutions using their preferred method.
- Display calculations such as 500 – 199; 674 – 299; 300 – 98; 517 – 298. Challenge pupils to use what they know about subtracting 8 and 9 to make these calculations as straightforward as possible. **How did you do it?**

Unit 3.14 Representing and solving word problems

- Pupils work in pairs. Give each pair a Think Board like the one below and ask them to work together to complete it.

Word Problem A train is on a journey of 700 kilometres. It has got 285 kilometres to go. How far has it already travelled?	**Bar model**
Number Line	**Number sentence**

Answer (centre box)

Discuss Amman and Finlay's Think Board (see the 'Let's Learn' section on pages 66–67 of the Pupil Book). **Compare your Think Board with Amman and Finlay's, what is the same and what is different? Who has written an addition number sentence, i.e. 285 + □ = 700? Who has written a subtraction like Amman and Finlay? Why does both addition and subtraction work for this problem?**

- Present pupils with a range of word problems. Ask them to work together in pairs or small groups to sort the problems into those that can thought of as addition only, subtraction only or either addition or subtraction. For example:

  There are 54 children in one bus and 48 children in another bus. How many children went on the school trip?

  Primary 4 baked 126 cakes for the School Fayre. They sold 116 of them. How many cakes didn't sell?

  Nuria's dad travelled 237 kilometres over the weekend. If he travelled 185 kilometres on Saturday, how far did he travel on Sunday?

  Isla has been saving her pocket money. She spent £53 whilst on holiday. When she got home she had £18 left. How much money did Isla have to begin with?

  What helped you decide which group the problem belonged to? Why can 'missing number' additions (e.g. 185 + □ = 237) be solved by subtracting? Why can 'missing number' subtractions e.g. □ – 53 = 18) be solved by adding? Focus discussion on the whole and the parts.

- Ask pupils to work in pairs to write a word problem for a given number sentence. **Swap problems with another pair. Does their problem match the number sentence?**

Unit 3.15 Two-step word problems

- Discuss the 'Let's Learn' section on pages 69–70 of the Pupil Book. **Why is addition the correct choice of operation for Step 1? How else could we work out how much money Amman still needs? How would you have solved this problem?**
- Present pupils with a range of two-step word problems. Ask them to work together in pairs to paraphrase the problem and identify the steps required. For example:

  A supermarket sells 900 pieces of fruit in a week. 279 were oranges, 197 were pears and the rest were apples. How many apples were sold?

  Step 1: Add 279 and 197 to work out how many oranges and pears there are altogether.

  Step 2: Count on from the answer up to 900 or subtract the answer from 900.

- Ask the class to help you represent the same set of word problems as bar models. For example, the problem above can be represented with the following bar model.

900		
279	197	?

  Which number in the problem represents the whole? How do you know? How does our bar model help you decide which calculations to do? Which operations will you use? Which strategies will you choose? Ask pairs to work together to find the solutions.

Number – multiplication and division 1A

Section overview

Textbook 1A units	Review units	Prior learning	Benchmarks/Es&Os
Unit 4.1 Making equal groups	**1A** Unit 2.1	• I can count forwards to at least twenty. • I can form and count a collection of up to twenty items. • I know number names and symbols up to at least twenty.	**MNU 1-03a** • Counts forwards and backwards in 2s, 5s, 10s and 100s. • Applies strategies to determine multiplication facts; for example, repeated addition, grouping, arrays and multiplication facts.
Unit 4.2 Using arrays	**1A** Unit 2.1 Unit 4.1	• I can count forwards to at least twenty. • I can form equal-sized groups. • I know number names and symbols up to at least twenty.	**MNU 1-03a** • Counts forwards and backwards in 2s, 5s, 10s and 100s. • Applies strategies to determine multiplication facts; for example, repeated addition, grouping, arrays and multiplication facts.
Unit 4.3 Skip counting in twos	**1A** Unit 2.1	• I can count forwards to at least thirty. • I can count backwards from twenty. • I know number names and symbols up to at least thirty.	**MNU 1-03a** • Counts forwards and backwards in 2s, 5s, 10s and 100s. • Applies strategies to determine multiplication facts; for example, repeated addition, grouping, arrays and multiplication facts.
Unit 4.4 Skip counting in tens	**1A** Units 2.5 and 2.7	• I can count forwards to one hundred. • I can count backwards from one hundred. • I know number names and symbols up to one hundred.	**MNU 1-03a** • Counts forwards and backwards in 2s, 5s, 10s and 100s. • Applies strategies to determine multiplication facts; for example, repeated addition, grouping, arrays and multiplication facts.
Unit 4.5 Skip counting in fives	**1A** Units 2.5 and 2.7	• I can count forwards to one hundred. • I can count backwards from one hundred. • I know number names and symbols up to one hundred.	**MNU 1-03a** • Counts forwards and backwards in 2s, 5s, 10s and 100s. • Applies strategies to determine multiplication facts; for example, repeated addition, grouping, arrays and multiplication facts.
Unit 4.6 Multiplying using skip counting	**1A** Units 2.5 and 2.7 Unit 4.1	• I can count forwards to one hundred. • I know number names and symbols up to one hundred. • I can form equal-sized groups.	**MNU 1-03a** • Counts forwards and backwards in 2s, 5s, 10s and 100s. • Applies strategies to determine multiplication facts; for example, repeated addition, grouping, arrays and multiplication facts.
Unit 4.7 Sharing equally	**1A** Units 2.5 and 2.7 Unit 4.1	• I can count forwards to one hundred. • I can count backwards from one hundred. • I can form equal groups. • I can skip count in twos, fives and tens.	**MNU 1-03a** • Counts forwards and backwards in 2s, 5s, 10s and 100s. • Applies strategies to determine division facts; for example, repeated subtraction, equal groups, sharing equally, arrays and multiplication facts.
Unit 4.8 Grouping	**1A** Units 2.5 and 2.7 Units 4.1, 4.3, 4.4 and 4.5	• I can count forwards to one hundred. • I can count backwards from one hundred. • I can form equal groups. • I can skip count in twos, fives and tens.	**MNU 1-03a** • Counts forwards and backwards in 2s, 5s, 10s and 100s. • Applies strategies to determine division facts; for example, repeated subtraction, equal groups, sharing equally, arrays and multiplication facts.

Conceptual context

In beginning the topic of multiplication and division, pupils first need to explore the concept of equal groups. This requires a wide range of experiences of organising concrete materials into equal groups, with pupils building a strong understanding that this means each group has the same amount of objects. A range of different materials should be used (for example, counters, teddies, and cubes of various colours and sizes). It is important at this stage that pupils can physically move and sort groups themselves, and that they are given enough experience with concrete materials to feel fully secure with this concept before moving on.

Next, arrays are introduced as a way of representing equal groups in the form of rows and columns. This vocabulary should be introduced and used consistently at this stage, as this is provides a useful way for pupils to think about and describe multiplication problems. Pupils can now begin to count, using concrete materials, the number in an array; it will be important to assess knowledge of counting sequences and numeral names and symbols to ensure the number range does not move beyond pupils' understanding.

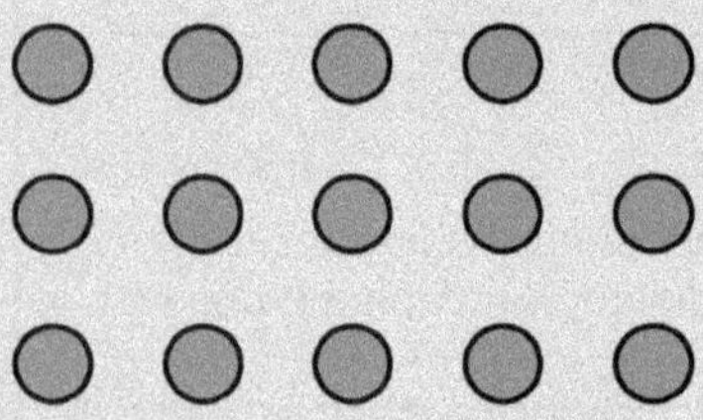

As pupils become familiar with equal groups and arrays, skip counting can be introduced. Pupils now need to understand that we can 'skip' past certain numbers to only count given multiples. Counting in twos is a useful place to start skip counting, as pupils can clearly see that we skip over one number each time, e.g. 2, 4, 6, etc. Ensure pupils have as much experience as they need with tools such as number lines before expecting them to skip count without them – they will need lots of practice, repetition and visual support and need to build the idea of being able to form mental images of number lines in the right order. Removing materials before pupils are ready can affect their emerging number sense, as well as their confidence. Pupils should explore skip counting in even numbers and odd numbers, before moving on to counting in 10s and 5s as their confidence grows. Placing a coloured peg on each number counted on a number line (e.g. 2, 4, 6, 8, etc.), washing lines with pegged numeral cards or even pupils holding up numeral cards are all useful visual resources to help to develop skip counting. Body percussion, such as clapping or tapping can also be fun and useful ways to skip count.

Pupils can then begin to apply skip counting to count equal groups. Using arrays, pupils can make and describe equal groups; they can then begin to skip count to work out how many there are altogether, moving on from counting each one.

For instance, to work out 4 groups of 2 we could make an array to show the problem:

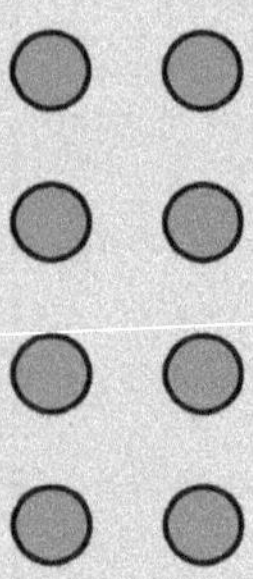

We can then model skip counting each row at a time to solve the problem, here 2 … 4 … 6 … 8 altogether.

A number line could also be used for this type of problem; one big enough to fit a counter onto each number is very useful here:

Allowing the pupils to physically move one row at a time onto the number line is a very effective way of promoting the understanding that we are adding equal groups together.

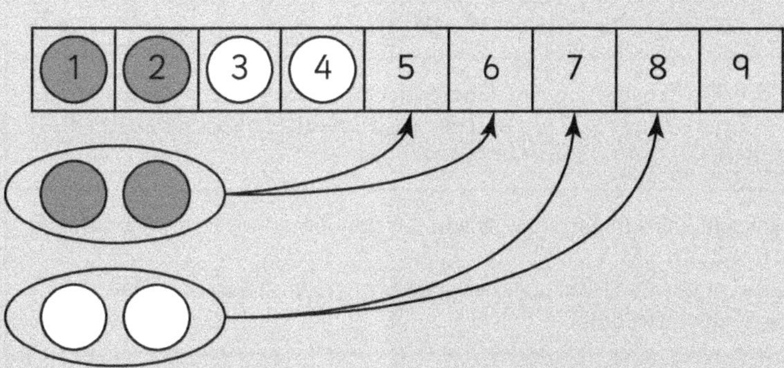

Pupils should have lots of practice using a range of arrays to skip count, although it is best to stick to skip counting sequences that they are familiar with, such as 2, 3, 5 and 10 at this stage.

When exploring division it is crucial that pupils understand that this can involve sharing equally or forming equal groups. They need ample opportunities to explore both of these concepts through a range of experiences linked to real life. Pupils usually have a strong sense of what is fair when sharing and enjoy exploring sharing one-by-one to solve problems (materials that they are familiar with sharing such as pencils, pens and toys are useful materials here) and they should be encouraged to share them equally onto or into objects such as paper plates, cups or bowls. They also need to have experience of problems where we sort objects into equal groups then count the number of groups made. For example, we need to put 5 pencils in each pot. We have 20 pencils – how many pots will we need? It is important that pupils have understanding of both sharing and grouping problems before moving on.

We have also introduced the symbols for multiplication and division in this unit. Pupils should be able to show understanding of these when reading and writing them and solving problems, and be able to clearly explain the multiplication symbol as 'equal groups or sets of' and the division symbol as 'shared equally' or 'grouped equally'.

Resources

- Arrays
- Bead strings
- Counters
- Counting objects, such as teddies, elephants, dinosaurs
- Cubes
- Dot cards
- Hundred squares
- Number lines

Key vocabulary

- **Array**
- **Divide**
- **Grouping**
- **Multiply**
- **Repeated addition**
- **Repeated subtraction**
- **Sharing**
- **Skip counting**
- **Times**

Misconceptions

Potential misconception	Addressing the misconception
Unit 4.1 Pupils may have a lack of understanding of what equal means.	Ensure lots of experience making equal groups with concrete materials and opportunities to share and discuss with other pupils what equal means.
Unit 4.2 Pupils may experience confusion with the terms row and column.	Physically point to each row as you say the name, and vice versa with each column. Ensure pupils have lots of experience both making and describing arrays with each other.
Units 4.3, 4.4 and 4.5 Pupils may have difficulties with skip counting.	Do not remove visual materials, such as number lines, before pupils are ready. Try using body percussion so that pupils develop an understanding of each number they are skipping.
Unit 4.6 Pupils may have a lack of understanding of skip counting, which results in pupils counting one-by-one to solve problems.	Review understanding of the skip counting sequence needed to solve the problem and go back to materials if needed. Check that the problem involves a skip counting sequence the pupils have had experience with.
Units 4.7 and 4.8 Pupils may have difficulties sharing or grouping equally.	Make sure that pupils have access to concrete materials at this stage.

Teaching ideas

Unit 4.1 Making equal groups

- Give pupils a range of different materials to work with, such as cars, teddies, dinosaurs. Ask them to count you out 12 dinosaurs of any colour. **Now can you sort them into equal groups of 2?** Here are 10 teddies. **Can you sort them into groups of 5? How many groups do you have? How do you know each group is the same?**
- Give a wide range of opportunities for pupils to form and describe equal groups using a range of different materials.

Unit 4.2 Using arrays

- Put out 5 red counters, 5 green counters and 5 blue counters. Model moving them into an array. Explain that you have made an array. **An array is where we organise the equal groups into a grid. We call these rows (point to each row). We call these columns. (Point to each column.) How many rows? How many columns? How many counters altogether?**
- Repeat for a wide range of different examples, reinforcing the vocabulary used. The pupils can create posters of the arrays that they make. As the collection builds up they can look to make connections and identify commutative pairs, e.g. 3 × 5 is the same as 5 × 3 but rotated (see Unit 4.6).

Unit 4.3 Skip counting in twos

- Use a washing line with numeral cards to 20 pegged up in the correct order. Explain that when we skip count we are going to skip over the ones and just count the twos. Point to each number as we say it. **Two, four, six … twenty. Now try saying the ones very quietly and the twos very loudly. Now try saying the ones inside our head and the twos out loud. Now try turning the odd numbers back to front and only saying the twos. Finally try turning round all the numbers and see if we can remember to only say the twos!** (Go back to visible numbers if this is tricky.)

Unit 4.4 Skip counting in tens

- Use a number line to 100 and place pegs on all the decade numbers. Explain that we are going to count in tens, so we only say the decade numbers. **What do all the decade numbers have in common?** Point to the pegs as the pupils say the numbers forwards and then backwards. Check pronunciation of 'ty' numbers so pupils do not get confused with 'teen' numbers. Try starting at different numbers, e.g. start from 30 and stop at 90, start from 70 and count down to 40 in tens.
- Try one half of the class saying the first number and the other half saying the next skip counter number to add some fun.

Unit 4.5 Skip counting in fives

- Use body percussion to count in fives; for example, clap knee, knee, shoulder, shoulder, head. **We only say the fives when we clap our head**. Ask pupils to come up with their own ideas for counting in fives using body percussion. Count forwards and backwards, starting from different numbers. **What patterns do you notice?**

Unit 4.6 Multiplying using skip counting

- Make an array showing 3 rows of 2. **What can you see? This array has 3 rows of 2.** Model skip counting to work out how many altogether … 2 … 4 … 6. Model recording this problem as

  $3 \times 2 = 6$. Explain that the × symbol means 'equal groups of'. **We can skip count to work out how many.**
- Repeat with a wide range of examples of arrays that involve skip counting sequences they are familiar with. Ask them to write a multiplication sentence using the symbol to record their thinking. Ensure pupils are clear about the meaning of the multiply '×' symbol by asking them to read their multiplication sentences and explain what they mean.

Unit 4.7 Sharing equally

- Give a problem such as: **Isla has 8 pens and shares them with Amman, Nuria and Finlay. How many will they each get?** Ask pupils to count out 8 pens. Now get a paper plate or a pot for each of the children in the problem. **Let's share them out equally**. Ask a pupil to share out the pens one-by-one in each pot. **How many do they each get?**
- Give another problem and deliberately model sharing unequally, e.g. give 5 pens to one pupil and 1 to another. Ask if this is equal sharing. **Why not?** Establish that equal sharing means that everyone needs to get the same amount.
- Repeat with a wide range of examples for pupils to share materials equally and record the results. Introduce the division symbol '÷' and explain that in this case it means 'shared equally'.

Unit 4.8 Grouping

- Pose a problem such as: **Isla has made 15 biscuits and puts 5 on each plate. How many plates will she need?** Ask pupils to count out 15 counters. Now get paper plates. Ask pupils to put 5 on each plate. **How many plates do we have?**

  Give another problem and deliberately model putting unequal groups on each plate. Ask if we have made equal groups. Why not? Establish that to divide we need to make equal groups
- Repeat with a wide range of examples for pupils to group materials equally and record the results. Introduce the division symbol '÷' and explain that in this case it means 'grouped equally'.
- Ensure that pupils understand we can use either sharing or grouping to solve division problems. Present the pupils with a range of problems to solve to practise using the correct vocabulary and symbols.

Number - multiplication and division 1B

Section overview

Textbook 1B units	Review units	Prior learning	Benchmarks/Es&Os
Unit 4.1 Multiplying by skip counting	**1A** Units 2.5 and 2.7 Units 4.3, 4.4, 4.5 and 4.6	• I can count forwards and backwards to numbers up to 100. • I know the number names and symbols for numbers up to 100. • I can skip count in twos, fives and tens. • I understand that I can use skip counting to solve multiplication problems.	**MNU 1-03a** • Counts forwards and backwards in 2s, 5s, 10s and 100s. • Demonstrates understanding of the commutative law; for example, $6 + 3 = 3 + 6$ or $2 \times 4 = 4 \times 2$. • Applies strategies to determine multiplication facts; for example, repeated addition, grouping, arrays and multiplication facts.
Unit 4.2 Understanding multiplication as repeated addition	**1A** Units 2.5 and 2.7 Units 4.2, 4.3, 4.4 and 4.5	• I can count forwards and backwards to numbers up to 100. • I know the number names and symbols for numbers up to 100. • I can skip count in twos, fives and tens. • I can make and draw arrays to represent equal groups of objects.	**MNU 1-03a** • Counts forwards and backwards in 2s, 5s, 10s and 100s. • Demonstrates understanding of the commutative law; for example, $6 + 3 = 3 + 6$ or $2 \times 4 = 4 \times 2$. • Applies strategies to determine multiplication facts; for example, repeated addition, grouping, arrays and multiplication facts.
Unit 4.3 Arrays	**1A** Units 2.5 and 2.7 Units 4.2, 4.3, 4.4 and 4.5	• I can count forwards and backwards to numbers up to 100. • I know the number names and symbols for numbers up to 100. • I can skip count in twos, fives and tens. • I can make and draw arrays to represent equal groups of objects.	**MNU 1-03a** • Counts forwards and backwards in 2s, 5s, 10s and 100s. • Demonstrates understanding of the commutative law; for example, $6 + 3 = 3 + 6$ or $2 \times 4 = 4 \times 2$. • Applies strategies to determine multiplication facts; for example, repeated addition, grouping, arrays and multiplication facts.
Unit 4.4 Repeated addition	**1A** Units 2.5 and 2.7 Units 4.3, 4.4, 4.5 and 4.6	• I can count forwards and backwards to numbers up to 100. • I know the number names and symbols for numbers up to 100. • I can skip count in twos, fives and tens. • I understand that multiplication is the same as repeated addition.	**MNU 1-03a** • Counts forwards and backwards in 2s, 5s, 10s and 100s. • Demonstrates understanding of the commutative law; for example, $6 + 3 = 3 + 6$ or $2 \times 4 = 4 \times 2$. • Applies strategies to determine multiplication facts; for example, repeated addition, grouping, arrays and multiplication facts.

Unit 4.5 Multiplying using known facts	**1A** Units 2.5, 2.7 and 2.11 Units 4.3, 4.4 and 4.5	• I can count forwards and backwards to numbers up to 100. • I know the number names and symbols for numbers up to 100. • I can skip count in twos, fives and tens. • I know doubles to 20. • I know how many tens in decade numbers.	**MNU 1-03a** • Demonstrates understanding of the commutative law; for example, $6 + 3 = 3 + 6$ or $2 \times 4 = 4 \times 2$. • Applies strategies to determine multiplication facts; for example, repeated addition, grouping, arrays and multiplication facts. • Uses multiplication and division facts to solve problems within the number range 0 to 1000.
Unit 4.6 Dividing by sharing	**1A** Units 2.5 and 2.7 Units 4.3, 4.4, 4.5 and 4.7	• I can count forwards and backwards to numbers up to 100. • I know the number names and symbols for numbers up to 100. • I can skip count in twos, fives and tens. • I can share objects equally.	**MNU 1-03a** • Counts forwards and backwards in 2s, 5s, 10s and 100s. • Applies strategies to determine multiplication facts; for example, repeated addition, grouping, arrays and multiplication facts.
Unit 4.7 Dividing by grouping	**1A** Units 2.5 and 2.7 Units 4.3, 4.4, 4.5 and 4.8	• I can count forwards and backwards to numbers up to 100. • I know the number names and symbols for numbers up to 100. • I can skip count in twos, fives and tens. • I can form equal groups.	**MNU 1-03a** • Counts forwards and backwards in 2s, 5s, 10s and 100s. • Applies strategies to determine multiplication facts; for example, repeated addition, grouping, arrays and multiplication facts.
Unit 4.8 Multiplying by ten	**1A** Units 2.5, 2.7 and 2.11 Units 4.3, 4.4 and 4.5	• I can count forwards and backwards to numbers up to 100. • I know the number names and symbols for numbers up to 100. • I can skip count in twos, fives and tens. • I know how many tens and ones in numbers up to 100.	**MNU 1-03a** • Multiplies and divides whole numbers by 10 and 100 (whole number answers only).
Unit 4.9 Dividing by ten	**1A** Units 2.5, 2.7 and 2.11 Units 4.3, 4.4 and 4.5	• I can count forwards and backwards to numbers up to 100. • I know the number names and symbols for numbers up to 100. • I can skip count in twos, fives and tens. • I know how many tens and ones in numbers up to 100.	**MNU 1-03a** • Multiplies and divides whole numbers by 10 and 100 (whole number answers only).

Conceptual context

Pupils at this stage should have a sound understanding of multiplication as repeated equal groups and understand division within either a sharing or grouping context. We will now extend skip counting sequence into threes, using materials such as bead strings and hundred squares to allow pupils to explore the more complex patterns of threes. As we move on, we need pupils to develop an understanding of multiplication as repeated addition, beginning to record multiplication problems as both addition and multiplication problems, e.g. $5 + 5 + 5 = 15$ and $3 \times 5 = 15$.

Pupils require a strong understanding of arrays as a way of representing multiplication problems, and now explore writing multiplication sentences for given arrays, using skip counting to work out the answer.

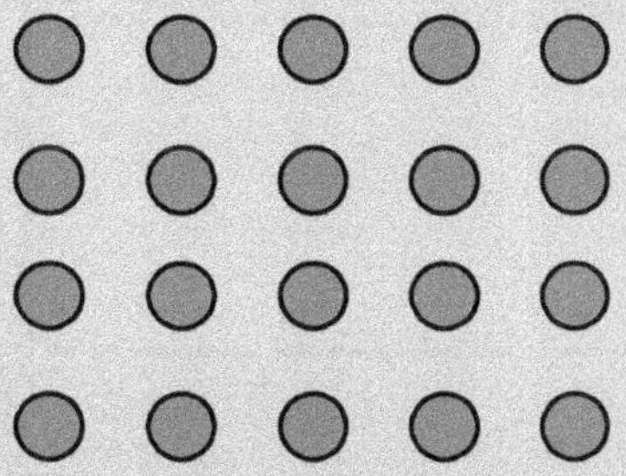

For instance, using the above array pupils can record the multiplication sentence as 4×5, and skip count in 5s to work out the answer as 20.

We further extend understanding of multiplication as repeated addition to encourage pupils to begin to use facts they know to solve problems, rather than relying solely on skip counting. For instance, if solving the problem 3×4 pupils might now begin to recognise that they know the double fact for 4 is 8. They then can just add one more group of 4 to get the answer, $8 + 4 = 12$. We can promote this idea of deriving new facts from existing facts we know from the use of visual materials such as arrays, and lots of opportunities for pupils to share different ways of solving problems with each other. This can be further extended by exploring connections between facts such as doubles and multiplication facts for 2, and groups of 10 within decade numbers and multiplication facts for 10. As pupils are given a range of different experiences solving multiplication problems they will make links between their existing and new knowledge, allowing them to develop confidence in themselves as problem solvers rather than worrying or memorising facts by rote.

Division is now extended within both sharing and grouping contexts, and pupils are encouraged to write division sentences to record problems. They are now beginning to relate skip counting to grouping problems, and use this strategy to work out how many equal groups.

Concrete materials such as cubes or bundles of sticks can be used to explore patterns when multiplying and dividing by 10. Pupils need a strong knowledge of place value to 100 at this stage and understand that when we multiply by 10, the number gets 10 times bigger, and when we divide by 10 the number gets 10 times smaller. Place value grids are a useful way for pupils to explore how the digits move one place to the left or right accordingly.

Resources

- Abacus
- Arrays
- Bead strings
- Counters
- Counting objects, such as teddies, elephants, dinosaurs.
- Cubes
- Dot cards
- Hundred squares
- Number lines
- Place value materials
- Place value grids

Key vocabulary

- **Array**
- **Divide**
- **Grouping**
- **Multiply**
- **Repeated addition**
- **Repeated subtraction**
- **Sharing**
- **Skip counting**
- **Times**

Misconceptions

Potential misconception	Addressing the misconception
Units 4.1, 4.2 and 4.3 Pupils may have a lack of understanding of skip counting resulting in pupils counting one-by-one to solve problems.	Review understanding of the skip counting sequence needed to solve the problem and go back to materials if needed. Check that the problem involves a skip counting sequence they have had experience with.
Units 4.4 and 4.5 Pupils may have difficulties when concrete materials are removed, resulting in errors of understanding where pupils add instead of multiply, such as $4 \times 2 = 6$.	Review understanding of multiplication as joining of equal groups, and ask pupils to make arrays to show multiplication problems so they have a visual representation of the concept.
Units 4.6 and 4.7 Pupils may have difficulties sharing or grouping equally.	Encourage pupils to use concrete materials or draw pictures when sharing or making groups until they have developed confidence with this concept. Check understanding of skip counting sequences being used.
Units 4.7 and 4.8 Pupils may have a lack of understanding that numbers get 10 times bigger when multiplied by 10 and 10 times smaller when divided by 10.	Use concrete materials such as cubes when multiplying by 10 to show number gets 10 times bigger. Use materials, such as sticks, which can be bundled into groups of 10 when dividing to show number gets 10 times smaller.

Teaching ideas

Unit 4.1 Multiplying by skip counting

- Use a 100 bead string and model moving multiples of 3 as you skip count. Ask pupils what patterns they see. Try giving pupils a hundred square and asking them to explore the patterns of 3. **What do you notice?** Put counters on each multiple of 3 up to 30. Ask them to predict if a number will continue the sequence, e.g. **Do you think 36 will be in the pattern? What about 41? 50?** Allow them to continue the pattern to 100.
- Use body percussion to count in threes, such as knee, knee, clap. Encourage them to say the first two numbers very quietly and the third number in a loud voice.
- Using a 100 square, the pupils can colour in different skip counting sequences to explore the patterns they make.

1	2	3	4	5	6	7	8	9	10
11	12	13	14	15	16	17	18	19	20
21	22	23	24	25	26	27	28	29	30
31	32	33	34	35	36	37	38	39	40
41	42	43	44	45	46	47	48	49	50
51	52	53	54	55	56	57	58	59	60
61	62	63	64	65	66	67	68	69	70
71	72	73	74	75	76	77	78	79	80
81	82	83	84	85	86	87	88	89	90
91	92	93	94	95	96	97	98	99	100

Unit 4.2 Understanding multiplication as repeated addition

- Make an array showing 4 rows of 3. Ask the pupils all the different ways you could record this problem. Model writing 3+3+3+3 and 'double 3 + double 3' as well as 4 × 3. Ensure pupils can understand that these are different ways to write the same problem. Ask them why we might write it as a multiplication sentence rather than an addition sentence. Look for answers such as the time it might take to write a long multiplication problem using repeated addition. Give a wide range of different examples to ensure pupils are confident in writing problems as both addition and multiplication problems.
- The pupils can create a poster to explain the different ways to show how they calculate multiplication (repeated addition) problems.

Unit 4.3 Arrays

- Make an array showing 5 rows of 3. Ask the pupils to write a multiplication sentence for this array (5 × 3). **How would we solve this problem?** Model skip counting in threes to work out the answer … 3 … 6 … 9 … 12 … 15. Give a wide range of different arrays for the pupil to record and work out. Check they are able to use skip counting to solve the problems (make sure you are giving them problems that involve skip counting sequences they have had experience working with).
- The pupils can create posters of the arrays that they make. As the collection builds up they can look to make connections and identify commutative pairs (for example, 3 × 5 is the same as 5 × 3 but rotated).

Unit 4.4 Repeated addition

- Give pupils a problem, such as 3 × 5. Ask them about the different ways they could solve this. Look for answers such as skip counting. If a pupil tells you that they know double 5 is 10 then just add 5 more to get 15, and tell them this is a fantastic way to solve the problem! Or model this to the pupils yourself using an array to illustrate. Explain that now we are confident multiplying, we are beginning to know lots of facts that can help us. **We can use these facts to help us to solve problems.** Add another row of 5 your array. **How many now? We can just add one more group of 5 to 15 to get the answer. What about one more group? What multiplication sentence do we have now?**

Unit 4.5 Multiplying using known facts

- Explain that we already know a lot of facts about multiplication that can help us. Discuss doubles and show a double fact (for example, double 3). **What do you notice? Double 3 is the same as 3 × 2. If we know our double facts then we also know our multiplication facts for 2. Use an abacus to show 5 groups of 10. How many? How do you know?** Link knowledge of groups of 10 in decade numbers to multiplication facts for 10.
- Create a set of cards with doubles on them, 2 + 2, 3 + 3, etc. Challenge the pupils to flash the cards in pairs and see if they can recall the solution. You can create a set of cards for 2s, 5s and 10s as appropriate.

Unit 4.6 Dividing by sharing

- Give a problem such as, *I have 8 marbles and I want to share them with someone* (pick a pupil). **How many will we each get? Can you make a prediction?** Lay out the 8 marbles and share 1 each. **How many are left now? There are 6 left. Share out 1 more each. How many do we each have now? How many are left? Does anyone want to change their prediction?** Carry on like this, encouraging pupils to predict at each stage until they are all shared out. Record answer using a division sentence: 8 ÷ 2 = 4.
- Repeat with a wide range of examples, using concrete materials, and encourage prediction at each stage.

Unit 4.7 Dividing by grouping

- Give a problem such as, *I have 18 pencils and I want to put 3 in each pot. How many will pots will we need?* Ask: **Can you make a prediction?** Lay out the 18 pencils and put 3 in one pot. **How many are left now?** There are 15 left. Put another 3 in another pot. How many pots now? How many are left? **Does anyone want to change their prediction?** Carry on like this, encouraging pupils to predict at each stage until they are all grouped. Record the answer using a division sentence: $18 \div 3 = 6$.
- Repeat with a wide range of examples, using concrete materials, and encourage prediction at each stage.

Unit 4.8 Multiplying by 10

- Lay out 6 rows of 10 cubes or dot strips. **How many altogether?** Record problem as $6 \times 10 = 60$. Repeat with 4 rows of 10, then 5 rows of 10. **What do you notice?** Explain that, when we multiply by 10 the number gets 10 times bigger. Use a place value grid to model what happens to each digit. Explain that the ones digit moves to the tens column and we use zero as a place holder. Repeat with lots of examples using materials.

Unit 4.9 Dividing by 10

- Lay out 30 loose sticks or straws. Ask the pupils to group them into tens because we are going to divide by 10. **How many groups of 10?** Record as a division sentence: $30 \div 10 = 3$.
- Repeat with 40 sticks. **What do you notice?** Explain that when we divide by 10, the number gets 10 times smaller. Use a place value grid to show what happens to each digit. The tens digit moves to the ones column. Repeat with lots of examples using materials.

Number - multiplication and division 1C

Section overview

Textbook 1C units	Review units	Prior learning	Benchmarks/Es&Os
Unit 4.1 Dividing by skip counting	**1B** Units 2.5 and 2.6 Units 4.1, 4.2 and 4.4	• I can count forwards and backwards to numbers up to 1000. • I know the number names and symbols for numbers up to 1000. • I can skip count in twos, threes, fives and tens. • I understand that I can use skip counting to solve multiplication problems.	**MNU 1-03a** • Counts forwards and backwards in 2s, 5s, 10s and 100s. • Applies strategies to determine division facts; for example, repeated subtraction, equal groups, sharing equally, arrays and multiplication facts.
Unit 4.2 Dividing with remainders	**1B** Units 2.5 and 2.6 Units 4.1, 4.2 and 4.4	• I can count forwards and backwards to numbers up to 1000. • I know the number names and symbols for numbers up to 1000. • I can skip count in twos, threes, fives and tens. • I understand that I can use skip counting to solve multiplication and division problems.	**MNU 1-03a** • Counts forwards and backwards in 2s, 5s, 10s and 100s. • Applies strategies to determine division facts; for example, repeated subtraction, equal groups, sharing equally, arrays and multiplication facts.
Unit 4.3 Solving multiplication problems	**1B** Units 2.5, 2.6 and 2.11 Units 4.1, 4.2, 4.4 and 4.5	• I can count forwards and backwards to numbers up to 1000. • I know the number names and symbols for numbers up to 1000. • I can skip count in twos, threes, fives and tens. • I know doubles to 20. • I know how many tens in decade numbers.	**MNU 1-03a** • Applies strategies to determine multiplication facts; for example, repeated addition, grouping, arrays and multiplication facts. • Uses multiplication and division facts to solve problems within the number range 0 to 1000.
Unit 4.4 Multiplying by 100	**1B** Units 2.5, 2.6 and 2.11 Units 4.1. 4.2, 4.4 and 4.8	• I can count forwards and backwards to numbers up to 1000. • I know the number names and symbols for numbers up to 1000. • I can skip count in twos, threes, fives and tens. • I know the value of each digit in 3-digit numbers.	**MNU 1-03a** • Multiplies and divides whole numbers by 10 and 100 (whole number answers only).
Unit 4.5 Dividing by 100	**1B** Units 2.5, 2.6 and 2.11 Units 4.1. 4.2, 4.4 and 4.9	• I can count forwards and backwards to numbers up to 1000. • I know the number names and symbols for numbers up to 1000. • I can skip count in twos, threes, fives and tens. • I know the value of each digit in 3-digit numbers.	**MNU 1-03a** • Multiplies and divides whole numbers by 10 and 100 (whole number answers only).

Unit 4.6 Linking multiplication and division	**1B** Units 2.5 and 2.6 Units 4.1. 4.2, 4.4 and 4.5	• I can count forwards and backwards to numbers up to 1000. • I know the number names and symbols for numbers up to 1000. • I can skip count in twos, threes, fives and tens. • I can use facts I know to solve multiplication problems.	**MNU 1-03a** • Applies knowledge of inverse operations (addition and subtraction; multiplication and division). • Applies knowledge of inverse operations (addition and subtraction; multiplication and division).
Unit 4.7 Recalling multiplication and division facts for 2, 5 and 10	**1B** Units 2.5 and 2.6 Units 4.1, 4.2, 4.4 and 4.5	• I can count forwards and backwards to numbers up to 1000. • I know the number names and symbols for numbers up to 1000. • I can skip count in twos, threes, fives and tens. • I know doubles and halves to 20. • I know how many tens in decade numbers.	**MNU 1-03a** • Applies strategies to determine multiplication facts; for example, repeated addition, grouping, arrays and multiplication facts. • Uses multiplication and division facts to solve problems within the number range 0 to 1000.
Unit 4.8 Multiplying and dividing using known facts	**1B** Units 2.5, 2.6 and 2.11 Units 4.8 and 4.9	• I can count forwards and backwards to numbers up to 1000. • I know the number names and symbols for numbers up to 1000. • I know what happens to each digit in a number when I multiply or divide by 10 or 100. • I know multiplication and division facts for 2, 5 and 10. • I know the value of each digit in numbers up to 1000.	**MNU 1-03a** • Applies strategies to determine multiplication facts; for example, repeated addition, grouping, arrays and multiplication facts. • Applies strategies to determine division facts; for example, repeated subtraction, equal groups, sharing equally, arrays and multiplication facts. • Uses multiplication and division facts to solve problems within the number range 0 to 1000.
Unit 4.9 Solving number problems	**1B** Unit 2.11 Unit 3.1 Units 4.4, 4.5, 4.6 and 4.7	• I can solve multiplication and division problems using facts I know. • I can solve addition and subtraction problems using a range of strategies. • I know multiplication division facts for 2, 5 and 10. • I know the value of each digit in numbers up to 1000.	**MNU 1-03a** • Applies strategies to determine multiplication facts; for example, repeated addition, grouping, arrays and multiplication facts. • Applies strategies to determine division facts; for example, repeated subtraction, equal groups, sharing equally, arrays and multiplication facts. • Uses multiplication and division facts to solve problems within the number range 0 to 1000. • Solves two-step problems.

Conceptual context

Pupils should now have a strong grasp of the concepts of multiplication and division, understanding multiplication as repeated addition, and be able to use strategies such as skip counting or use known facts to solve problems. Pupils should understand division as both sharing and grouping and be able to record multiplication and division sentences.

We will now extend understanding of division to repeated subtraction and pupils will be able to skip count forwards or backwards to solve problems in both sharing and grouping contexts. A sharing context involves splitting a collection equally between a given number; for example, 15 cakes shared between 5 people – how many do they each get? A grouping context involves placing objects into equal groups; for example, putting 15 cakes into boxes containing 5 each – how many boxes do we need? We will begin to explore remainders and how we record them when working out problems.

Pupils will explore new strategies to solve multiplication problems, using existing knowledge as well as skip counting. Pupils should be encouraged to use facts they know such as doubles, and multiplication facts (for example, a pupil might work 4×5 as double 5 + double 5 or might know $3 \times 5 = 15$ and add 5 more). Pupils should be encouraged to model and share strategies with each other and to record different ways of working out the same problem.

We build on the understanding of multiplying and dividing by 10 and extend this to 100. Place value materials or money can be used as a material so that pupils understand that we when we multiply by 100 the number gets 100 times bigger, and that when we divide by 100 the number gets 100 times smaller. It is important that pupils are given lots of opportunities to explore what happens to the digits using materials and place value grids. At this stage it is also a prerequisite that pupils have a strong understanding of place value up to 4-digit numbers.

The inverse relationship between multiplication and division is explored in Unit 4.6. Pupils should understand that multiplication is the opposite action of division and vice versa, and begin to see the connections between multiplication and division.

As we move on now, pupils should be beginning to develop recall of multiplication and division facts the more they use them. In particular we focus on recalling multiplication facts for 2, 5 and 10, drawing on the connections we have explored with doubles, groups of ten and skip counting patterns. Pupils should have lots of opportunities planned for practising these facts on a regular basis throughout their learning, and to discuss how they can use the facts they learn to help them solve problems. Games are an ideal way for pupils to practise and learn facts in a fun way, and resources such as playing cards, dice and dominoes are all very effective.

As their knowledge grows, we extend pupils' thinking to use known facts to solve problems involving 2- and 3-digit numbers. Pupils are encouraged to use their recall of facts, as well as what they have learned about multiplying and dividing by 10 and 100 to solve problems such as 3×20 or $90 \div 3$.

Finally, pupils learn to solve problems that involve more than one operation. Pupils need to read and interpret a problem, and to think about which processes they will need to use to solve it effectively and record how they work out each step.

Resources

- Arrays
- Bead strings
- Counters
- Counting objects, such as teddies, elephants, dinosaurs.
- Cubes
- Dice
- Dominoes
- Dot cards
- Hundred squares
- Number lines
- Place value grids
- Place value materials
- Playing cards
- Think Boards

Key vocabulary

- **Array**
- **Commutative properties**
- **Divide**
- **Dividend**
- **Divisor**
- **Factor**
- **Grouping**
- **Inverse properties**
- **Multiple**
- **Multiplicand**
- **Multiplier**
- **Multiply**
- **Product**
- **Quotient**
- **Repeated addition**
- **Repeated subtraction**
- **Sharing**
- **Skip counting**
- **Times**

Misconceptions

Potential misconception	Addressing the misconception
Units 4.4 and 4.5 Pupils may lack an understanding that numbers get 100 times bigger when they are mvultiplied by 100, and 100 times smaller when they are divided by 100.	Use concrete materials, such as hundred squares or base 10 blocks, when multiplying by 100 to show that a number gets 100 times bigger. Use materials such as base 10 blocks that can be bundled into groups of 100 when dividing to show number gets 100 times smaller.
Unit 4.6 Pupils may be confused with the inverse relationship between multiplication and division, e.g. $3 \times 4 = 12$, so $3 \div 4 = 12$.	Use arrays to explore the relationship between multiplication and division. Record multiplication and division sentences using the materials so that children can develop an understanding of multiplication as the opposite action of division.
Units 4.7 and 4.8 Pupils may have a rote understanding of 'times tables' in order, without an understanding of each fact as a number of equal groups. Pupils may have to recite all the memorised multiplication facts before they arrive at the answer required, e.g. 6×5 is '5 … 10 … 15 … 20 … 25 … 30'.	Explore visual representations of each fact using arrays, dot cards or squared paper. Link with repeated addition so pupil is clear what each fact represents.
Unit 4.9 Pupils may misinterpret correct operation to solve problem.	Ensure pupils have a wide range of opportunities to explore, share and discuss word problems and interpret the correct operation to solve the problem.

Teaching ideas

Unit 4.1 Dividing by skip counting

- Draw or use a large number line to 20. Explain that we are going to work out $20 \div 5$ by jumping backwards. Model beginning at 20 and jumping back to 15, then 10, then 5, then 0.

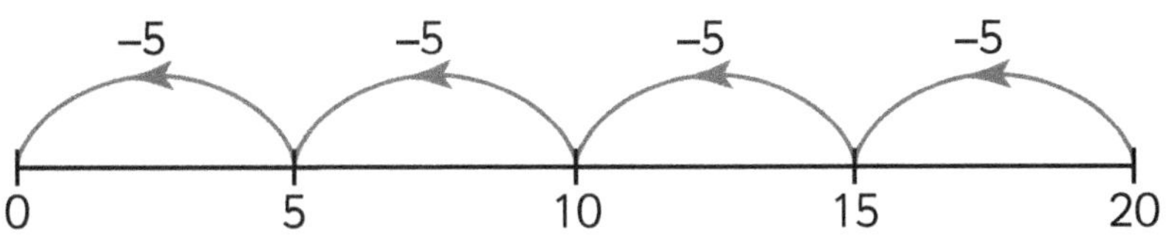

How many jumps? There are 4 jumps backwards. Would it be the same if we started at 0 and jumped forwards? Model jumping 4 groups of 5 forwards to 20.

Record as division sentence: $\mathbf{20 \div 5 = 4}$.

Explain that we can skip count forwards or backwards to work out division problems. Repeat with a wide range of examples using number lines. Look for pupils who have learned multiplication facts and have instant recall. Where they do, can they use this learned fact to work out the next multiplication fact?

Unit 4.2 Dividing with remainders

- Give a problem such as: *I have made 7 brownies and I want to share them between 3 people*. Use playdough to make 7 brownies and share them between three plates. **What do you notice? There is one left over**. Explain that in life this very often happens so we need to know how to record these leftovers. Write the division sentence as $7 \div 3 = 2$ remainder 1, and explain that we often shorten this to r1. Ask pupils if they can think of examples in life when they might get remainders. Explore a range of examples for pupils to solve and record.
- Show the following problem as a bar model: *I have 26 apples to share between 4 children*. As you build up the bottom bar, ask the pupils to tell you the skip counting sequence. Can the pupils predict there will be some left over? The bottom bar can be filled in with counters or numbers depending on the level of understanding of the pupils. Remember to give the solution in context as well as an equation; $26 \div 4 = 6$ r2. Each child will get 6 apples and there will be two left over. Repeat using the bar model for similar examples.

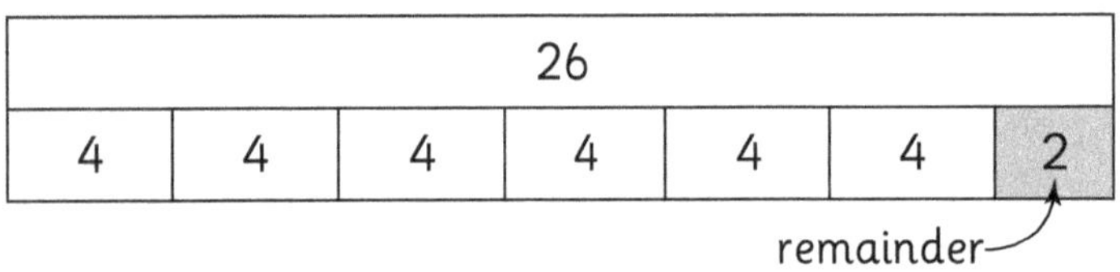

Unit 4.3 Solving multiplication problems

- Make an array to show 6×5. Ask pupils to write the multiplication sentence and to share different ways they could solve this problem. Look for strategies such as skip counting, commutative property (5×6) and beginning to use facts they know. Model ideas if they do not come up, such as double 5, double 5 and double 5; or if you know a fact such as $5 \times 5 = 25$ then just adding 1 more group of 5 to get 30. Explore a range of problems and record all the different ways pupils solve them using facts they know. Pupils could be encouraged to make a floor book or a poster that illustrates all the different ways they are finding to solve multiplication problems.

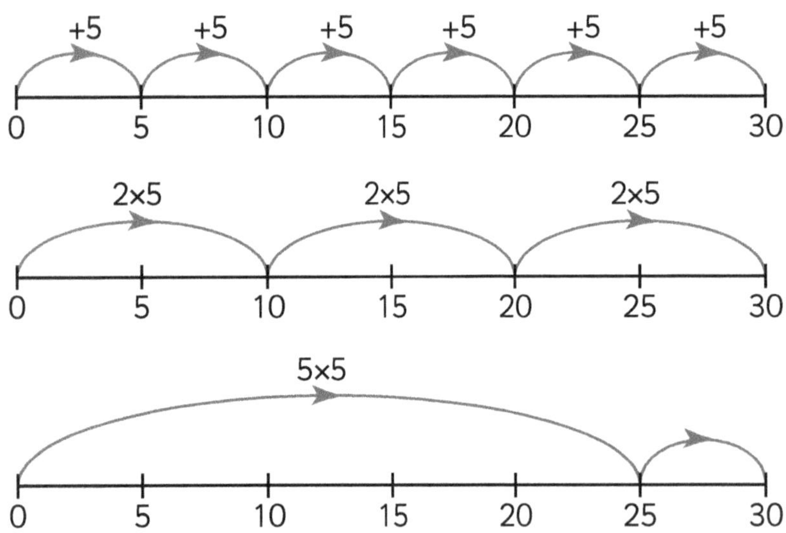

Unit 4.4 Multiplying by 100

- Lay out 3 small hundred squares or base 10 blocks. Ask the pupils how they can work out 3 × 100. Look for understanding that when we multiply by 100, the number gets 100 times bigger. Repeat with 5 × 100. Show with a place value grid how the digits move two places to the left and we use zero as a place holder.

HUNDREDS	TENS	ONES
		3
3	0	0

× 100

- Look for children saying 'add zeros' and repeat the calculation with materials. Show the pupils on the place value house that zeros act as place holders.
- Note that similar activities can be used to explore any number multiplied by 10 or 100.

Unit 4.5 Dividing by 100

- Draw a grid showing 10 rows of 10. **How many? This is a giant bar of chocolate with one hundred squares. If we divide it between 10 people, how many pieces will they each get?** You could cut the grid into strips of 10 to prove this. **What about if 100 people all got a piece? How many would they get?** Model that 100 ÷ 100 = 1. Show on a place value grid that when we divide by 100 the number gets 100 times smaller. Repeat with a wide range of examples.
- Provide the pupils with squared paper, blocks or similar so that they can act out dividing the hundreds into smaller parts. Check the pupils can record the calculation using the division symbol and also give a full answer where a context question is used.

Unit 4.6 Linking multiplication and division

- Make an array that shows 3 rows of 4. Ask the pupils to write a multiplication sentence to show this problem. 3 × 4 = 12. Now move each row of the array slightly apart from each other. Explain that we also know that 12 grouped into 3 equals 4. We know this because we can see there are 3 rows of 4. When we multiply we add equal groups, but when we divide we start with all the groups together then split them back into equal groups. Move the array so pupils can see that multiplication is the opposite of division. Explain that we call this an inverse relationship – multiplying is the reverse of division. Repeat with a wide range of examples and allow pupils to physically move the arrays to make the connection that they are opposite actions and reverse each other.

- Make an array showing 8 × 5 but cover up the array. Uncover one row of 5. Pose the question: **Finlay has 40 chews to give away. The chew sweets come in packets of 8. How many packets does Finlay have?** Show the problem both as a multiplication and a division: ____ × 8 = 40

  40 ÷ 8 = ____. Ask the pupils to solve the problem and to record their various strategies (they can use materials if they need to). Discuss the different strategies. Pose a second question: **Nuria has 18 cakes to give away to 6 children. How many cakes do the children get each?** Again, ask the pupils to solve the problem and share their strategies. Challenge the pupils to record the problem as a multiplication and a division.

Unit 4.7 Recalling multiplication and division facts for 2, 5 and 10

- Discuss ways that we know multiplication facts already; connect doubles and halves with multiplication and division facts for 2 and connect groups of 10 in decade numbers with multiplication and division facts for 10. Discuss with pupils how we can use what we know about 10s to help up with 5s (for example, use an abacus to show that if we know 4 tens are 40 and double 5 is ten, then we know there are 8 fives in 40).
- Use multiplication triangles to practise recalling missing facts, e.g. if a triangle has 2, 5 and 10 on each corner, encourage the pupils to cover one corner and ask each other questions like, 10 ÷ 'what' = 5?

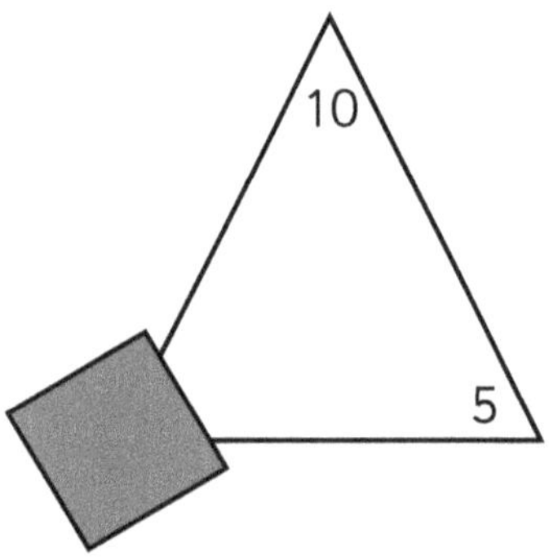

Unit 4.8 Multiplying and dividing using known facts

- Review what we have learned about multiplying and dividing by 10 and 100. Explain that we can use this, along with other facts we know, to solve problems with bigger numbers. For example: **If we are working on 2 × 300, what facts do we know that would help us?** Look for answers such as double 3 or 2 × 3 = 6. We can use this fact and multiply it by 100 to get our answer of 600. Show the calculations on a place value house to reinforce using zeros as place holders.
- **What fact do we know that would help us with 4 × 50?** Look for knowledge such as 4 × 5 = 20 or double 5 is 10 add 10 is 20. Then we multiply this by 10 to get our answer.
- Repeat with a wide range of examples, linking known facts with multiplying and dividing by 10 and 100.

Unit 4.9 Solving number problems

- Explain that when we are solving problems, the first step is to decide what operation we need to use to work out the correct answer. Sometimes when we are solving problems we need to use more than one operation. For example: **Amman and Finlay go shopping. Amman buys 3 books at £24 each and Finlay buys 2 books that cost £11 each. How much have they spent altogether?**

  What do we need to work out first? Look for answers that show understanding that we need to use multiplication to work out how much they each spent first. Record each step as you work it out. Amman spend £72 and Finlay spent £22. **What do we need to work out next?** Look for understanding that we need to use addition now to add both amounts together. Record your answer as an addition sentence and also answer the problem in the context it is given.

- Repeat with a wide range of examples involving different combinations of two of addition, subtraction, multiplication or division operations. Encourage pupils to record each step and share the different strategies that they use.

- Try using Think Boards to explore different ways to record problems.

Word problem

Finlay has £16 in the bank. He gets a job and earns £5 each week. How much does he have altogether when he has worked for 9 weeks?

Bar model

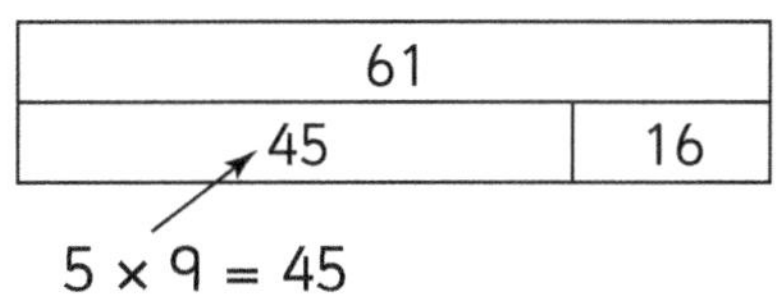

Empty number line

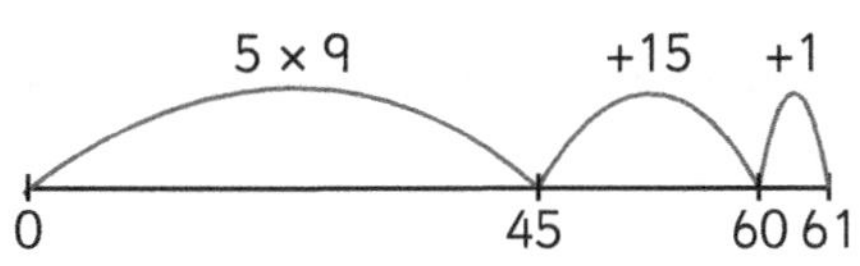

Calculations

$5 \times 9 = 45$

$45 + 16 = 45 + 10 + 5 + 1$

$= 61$

5 Fractions, decimal fractions and percentages

Fractions, decimal fractions and percentages 1A

Section overview

Textbook 1A units	Review units	Prior learning	Benchmarks/Es&Os
Unit 5.1 Make and identify halves	**Early** Units 4.4 and 4.5 **1A** Units 4.1 and 4.7	• I can make equal groups. • I can share equally.	**MNU 1-07a** • Explains what a fraction is using concrete materials, pictorial representations and appropriate mathematical vocabulary.
Unit 5.2 Make and identify quarters	**Early** Units 4.4 and 4.5 **1A** Units 4.1 and 4.7 Unit 5.1	• I can make equal groups. • I can share equally. • I can make and identify halves.	**MNU 1-07a** • Explains what a fraction is using concrete materials, pictorial representations and appropriate mathematical vocabulary.
Unit 5.3 Counting in halves and quarters	**1A** Unit 5.1 and 5.2	• I can make and identify halves and quarters. • I can count forwards and backwards on a number line.	**MNU 1-07a** • Explains what a fraction is using concrete materials, pictorial representations and appropriate mathematical vocabulary.
Unit 5.4 Sharing and grouping equally	**Early** Units 4.3 and 4.4 **1A** Units 4.1 and 4.7	• I can make equal groups. • I can share equally.	**MNU 1-07b** • Uses known multiplication and division facts and other strategies to find unit fractions of whole numbers; for example, $\frac{1}{2}$ or $\frac{2}{4}$.
Unit 5.5 Finding equivalent fractions	**1A** Unit 5.1 and 5.2	• I can make and identify halves. • I can make and identify quarters.	**MNU 1-07c** • Uses pictorial representations and other models to demonstrate understanding of simple equivalent fractions; for example, $\frac{1}{2} = \frac{2}{4} = \frac{3}{6}$.
Unit 5.6 Share equally	**Early** Units 4.3 and 4.4 **1A** Units 4.1 and 4.7 Units 5.1 and 5.2	• I can make equal groups. • I can share equally. • I can make and identify halves and quarters.	**MNU 1-07b** • Explains what a fraction is using concrete materials, pictorial representations and appropriate mathematical vocabulary.

Conceptual context

Fractions can be an area of maths in which misconceptions are plentiful and those developed at the early stages can have a profound impact as skills and concepts become progressively more challenging. Many of these misconceptions can be avoided if we develop a deep, conceptual understanding of fractions and fractional reasoning through the use of concrete and pictorial representations at all levels of maths. Units 5.1 and 5.2 focus on developing pupils' ability to make and identify halves and quarters. Equivalence is key to developing an understanding of fractions at all levels and these units introduce this concept from the outset, e.g. 'I can make quarters accurately by making halves and halving them'. This understanding is one of the foundations upon which a deep understanding of fractions can be built. Another key conceptual building block we want to establish is that equal fractions only need to be equal in size and do not need to be equal in shape. It is therefore important that pupils are given plenty of practical experience to make halves and quarters in different ways and set in different contexts.

Unit 5.3 develops pupils' ability to count in fractions. Once again, by developing this in context, i.e. 'let's count the half slices of cakes' rather than 'let's count in halves', we can support a deeper understanding that will in turn support pupils' ability to solve problems that require them to add, subtract, multiply and divide fractions. Units 5.4 and 5.6 aim to support pupils' ability to understand the intrinsic links between fractions and division i.e. 'When we share or divide something into two equal parts, we are halving it'.

Resources

- A4 or A5 paper
- Base 10 materials
- Card
- Counting stick
- Modelling clay (to represent cookies, chocolate bars, etc.)
- Resource sheet 5: Fraction wall
- Resource sheet 5A: Fraction cards

Key vocabulary

- **Equal shares**
- **Equivalent**
- **Group**
- **Half**
- **Quarter**
- **Whole**

Misconceptions

Potential misconception	Addressing the misconception
Units 5.1 and 5.2 Pupils may fail to understand that when we half or quarter something it must be split into *equal* parts.	Represent fractions using concrete materials and visuals. Provide opportunities for pupils to make and identify fractions in many different contexts. Encourage pupils to justify why they think something is a half or quarter.
Units 5.1 and 5.2 Pupils may think that 'equal parts' means the parts need to be the same shape rather than simply the same size.	Provide opportunities for pupils to make and identify halves and quarters that are different shapes (see the activities outlined in Units 5.1 and 5.2 below).
Units 5.1, 5.2, 5.3, 5.4, 5.5 and 5.6 Pupils may consider fraction names to be absolute labels, rather than relational labels.	Give answers (or count in fractions) that relate to the whole amount set in context, i.e. *one quarter of the bar* or *half of the pizza* rather than just *one quarter* or *one half.*
Units 5.1, 5.2, 5.3, 5.4, 5.5 and 5.6 Pupils consider fractions written numerically, e.g. $\frac{1}{2}$, as 2 whole numbers rather than a single relational entity.	Avoid fractional notation until pupils have a firm grasp of fractions through extensive exploration using concrete materials and pictorial representations. Note that when fractional notation is eventually introduced, it should not replace concrete and pictorial representations but rather be taught as an additional way of representing fractions. The ability to visualise fractions will support deep understanding at the highest levels of maths.

Potential misconception	Addressing the misconception
Unit 5.4 Pupils may think that, for example, two quarters of something is more than one half because there are two parts compared to one part.	• Represent equivalents using concrete materials and visuals. • Provide opportunities for pupils to make quarters by halving and halving again.
Unit 5.3 Pupils fail to understand that we can have any number of equal parts. For example, when counting in halves we do not stop when we reach two halves; we can continue without limit.	• Provide regular opportunities for pupils to count fractions, providing concrete and / or pictorial representations (see the activities outlined in Unit 5.3).

Teaching ideas

Unit 5.1 Make and identify halves

- Draw or display the following diagram and ask pupils to discuss the following statement:

True or false: I have split the chocolate bar into two parts. I have made halves.

Encourage pupils to justify their responses, e.g. *'We think the chocolate bar has been split in half because there are two parts'* or *'We think the chocolate bar has not been split in half because the parts are not equal in size'.*

Discuss the fact that in order to make halves, the chocolate bar must be cut into **two equal parts.**

- Use a square piece of paper to represent a sandwich and demonstrate making halves by folding and cutting it as follows:

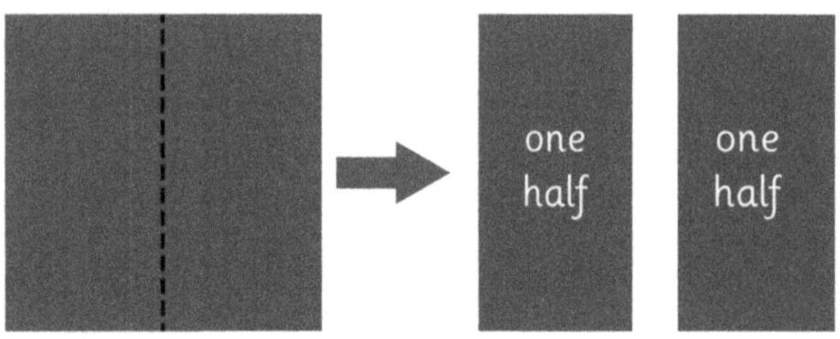

Ask pupils: **How many parts have I made?** *Two*; **Are the parts equal?** *Yes*; **What fraction of the sandwich is each part?** *Half a sandwich.*

Give one half sandwich to a pupil (Pupil A) and ask them to hold it up at the front of the class. Take another 'sandwich', explain that it is exactly the same as the first sandwich and this time fold and cut it as follows:

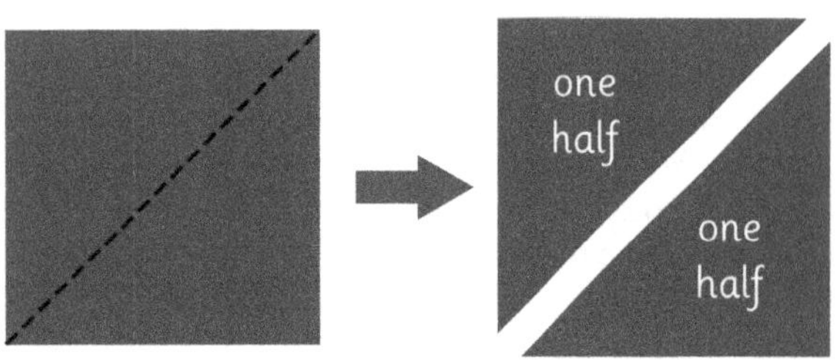

Ask pupils, **How many parts have I made?** *Two*; **Are the parts equal?** *Yes*; **What fraction of the sandwich is each part?** *Half a sandwich*.

Give one half sandwich to a second pupil (Pupil B) and ask them to hold it up at the front of the class. Ask the class to discuss which portion of sandwich they would rather have (Pupil A or B) and justify their choice.

NB: Pupils could communicate their choice using signals; for example, Pupil A: Hands on head, Pupil B: Fold arms, either sandwich: Finger on nose.

Pupils may justify by saying *'I would prefer Pupil A's half because it is bigger'* or *'I would prefer Pupil B's half because it is bigger'*. Note that their justifications are the same despite making different choices.

- Ask pupils again, **What fraction of a sandwich does each pupil have?** *Half a sandwich*.

  Explain to the pupils that you can prove that both pupils' portions are exactly the same size. Take Pupil B's portion (triangular portion) and fold it as follows:

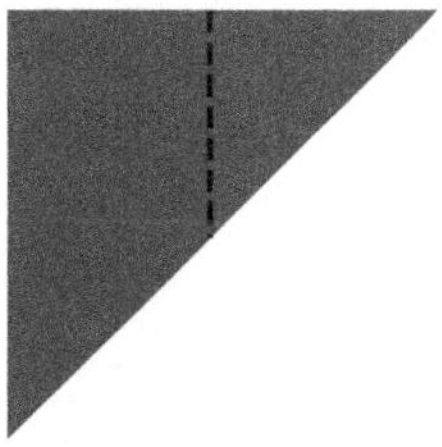

  Cut along the line to create two parts:

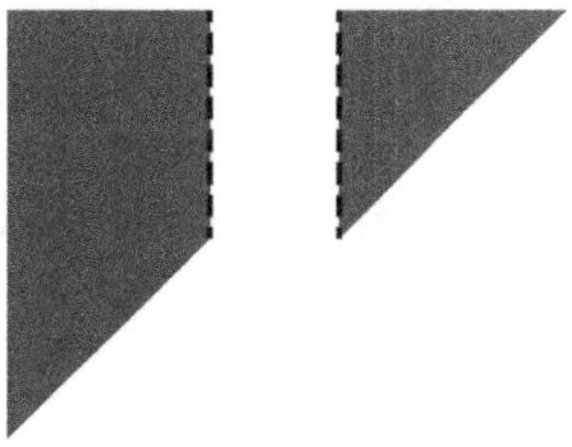

  Reposition the parts to make a portion exactly the same size and shape as Pupil A:

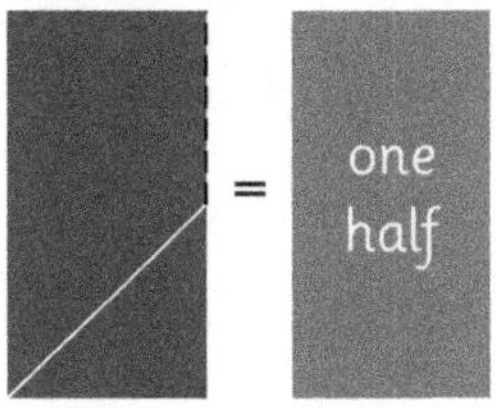

  Explain that **halves must be the same size**; however, **they do not need to be the same shape**.

- Provide pupils with paper shapes: squares, rectangles, triangles, circles, etc.

  Challenge them to make halves by folding and cutting. Can they make different halves with any of the shapes?

Unit 5.2 Make and identify quarters

- Draw or display the following diagram and ask pupils to discuss the following statement:

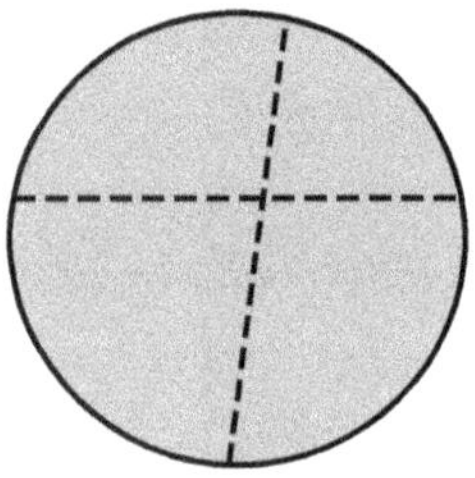

True or false: I have split the pizza into four parts. I have made quarters.

Encourage pupils to justify their responses, e.g. *'We think the pizza has been split into quarters because there are four parts'* or *'We think the pizza has not been split into quarters because the parts are not equal in size'.*

Discuss the fact that in order to make **quarters**, the pizza must be cut into **four equal parts**.

- Use a rectangular piece of paper and demonstrate making quarters by folding and cutting it as follows:

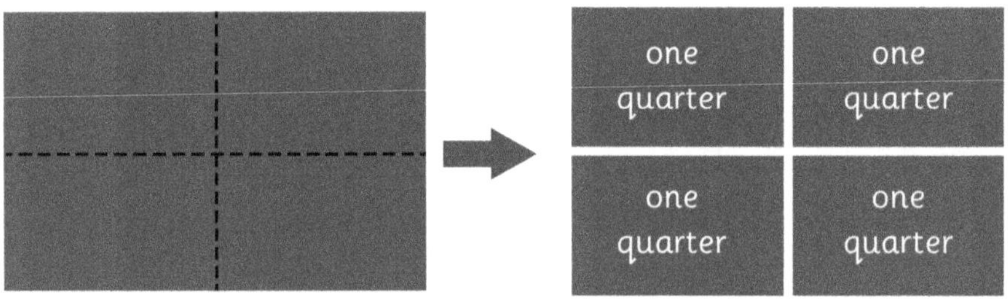

Ask pupils: **How many parts have I made?** *Four*; **Are the parts equal?** *Yes*; **What fraction of the whole piece of paper is each part?** *One quarter of the paper.*

Give one quarter to a pupil (Pupil A) and ask them to hold it up at the front of the class.

Take another piece of paper and this time fold and cut it as follows:

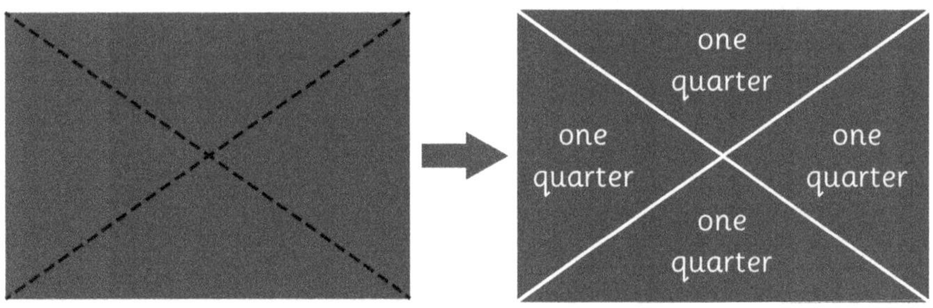

Ask pupils: **How many parts have I made?** *Four*. **Are the parts equal?** *Yes*. **What fraction of the whole piece is each part?** *One quarter of the paper.*

Give pupil B and C the following quarters:

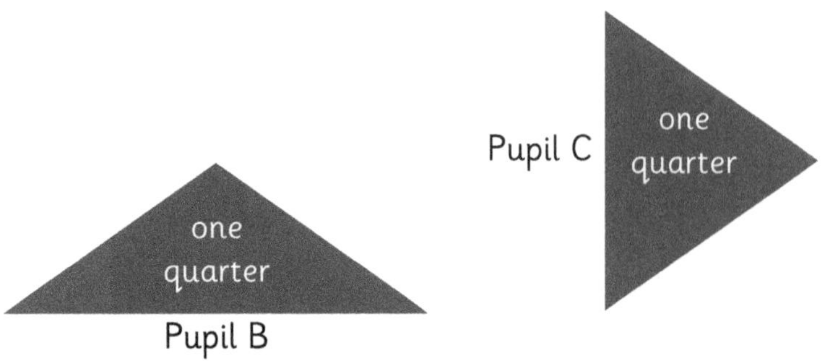

Ask the class to compare the size of each quarter and justify their responses.
Ask pupils again: **What fraction of the paper does each pupil have?** *One quarter of the paper.*
Explain to the pupils that you can prove that all three pupils' portions are exactly the same size.
Fold and cut Pupil B's quarter as follows:

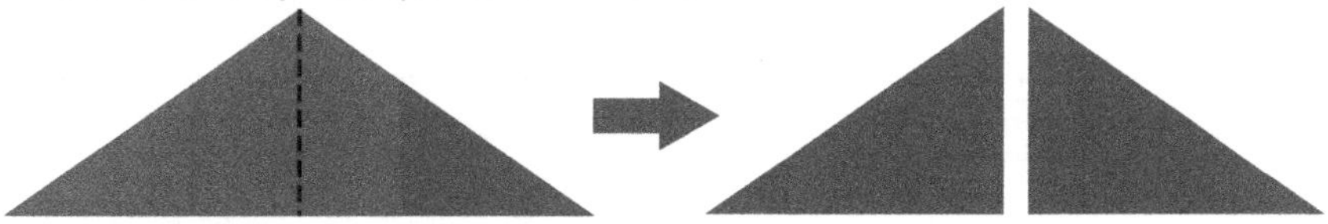

Reposition the parts to make a portion exactly the same size and shape as Pupil A:

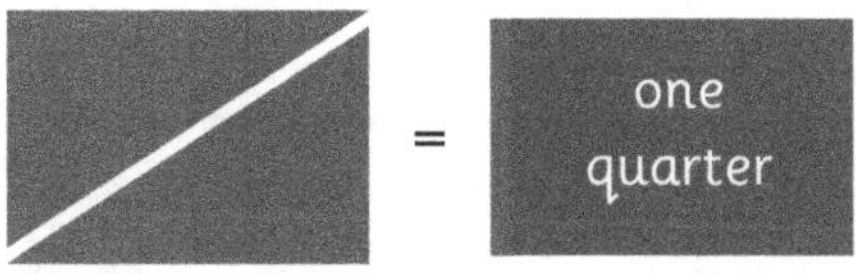

Fold and cut Pupil C's quarter as follows:

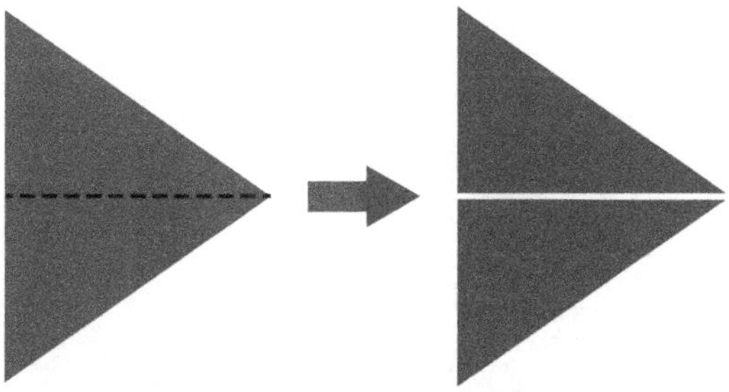

Reposition the parts to make a portion exactly the same size and shape as Pupil A:

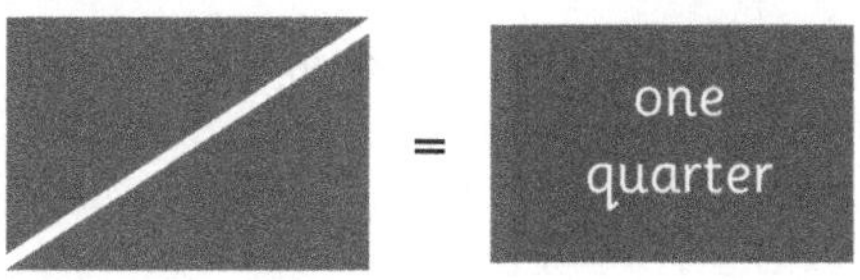

Explain that **quarters must be the same size**; however, **they do not need to be the same shape**.

- Provide pupils with paper squares.

  Challenge them to make quarters by folding and cutting. Can they make different quarters by folding in different ways?

Unit 5.3 Counting in halves and quarters

- When counting in halves or quarters (or any fraction) it is important that it is done in context in order that pupils don't simply see fractions as a numerical value but rather as an equal part of something real to them.
  Provide different contexts for pupils to count in halves (for example, half glasses of water, half chocolate bars, half sandwiches, etc.).
  Let's try counting on in half glasses of water:

Display the halves as you count and encourage the pupils to count with you; for example, *one half glass, two half glasses, three half glasses, etc.*

- **Let's try counting back from ten half glasses**:
  Display ten half glasses and remove one at a time as you count back: *ten half glasses, nine half glasses, eight half glasses, etc.*
  Repeat the activity but this time introduce a counting stick to demonstrate counting on and back in halves.
  Repeat above activities for quarters.

Unit 5.4 Sharing and grouping equally

- Draw or display the following:

  True or False

  Finlay has shared his sweets with his friends.

Encourage pupils to justify their decisions. For example, *'Yes, Finlay has shared his sweets because he has given some to Isla and Nuria'* or *'No, Finlay has not shared his sweets because they do not each have the same amount'.*
Discuss the fact that Finlay HAS shared his sweets (because he has given some sweets to the girls) but he HAS NOT shared his sweets fairly (because they do not each have the same amount of sweets).
Ask pupils: **What could we do so that the sweets are shared fairly?** *Finlay could give one of his sweets to Isla so that all three children have two sweets.*

- Set up tables with a set of items to be shared out and bowls or plates to be shared between, for example,
  - o Ten pieces of fruit between 2 bowls
  - o 9 cookies between 3 bowls
  - o 15 pencils between 5 bowls
  - o 13 bars of chocolate between 4 bowls

Challenge pupils to share out the items and determine how many there should be in each bowl.
Ask questions, such as: **Can all the items be shared out equally between the bowls?**
Note: Pupils may come up with different responses to the chocolate bars example. Some pupils may correctly argue that they CANNOT be shared equally because there is one bar left over. Other pupils may correctly argue that they CAN be shared out equally because the spare chocolate bar can be split into four parts.
This provides an excellent opportunity to investigate examples that have a 'remainder'. The context should determine what to do with any remainder. In this example, the chocolate bar can be cut into quarters (or they may decide to leave one bar spare). If it was 13 pencils that needed to be shared between the 4 bowls then it would make no sense to cut one into quarters; pupils therefore may decide to leave it as a spare. Avoid setting division questions like $13 \div 4 =$ _____ and expecting an answer of *3 remainder 1*. Instead, set a sharing or grouping problem and challenge the pupils to justify what to do with the 'remainder'.
For example, *13 people need to order taxis (4 seats) to the airport. How many taxis are needed?* In this example, the context determines that the extra person also needs a taxi, so the answer would be *four taxis*.

Unit 5.5 Finding equivalent fractions

- Practise counting forwards and backwards in halves and quarters using materials or visuals (See Teaching Ideas: Unit 5.3).
  Show pupils, for example, a cookie and ask: **Would you prefer to have one half or two quarters of the cookie?**

  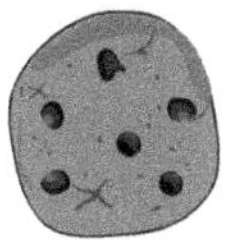

  Encourage pupils to discuss their thoughts with each other and justify their choice.
  Demonstrate that half of the cookie is exactly the same size as two quarters. There is no difference in how much of the cookie they would get:

  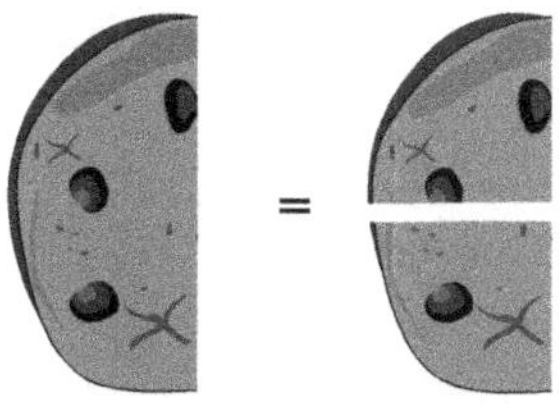

  One half cookie   Two quarter cookies

- Provide pupils with equal-sized sheets of paper (e.g. A4) and challenge them to make halves with one sheet and quarters with another. Instruct them to label each part correctly, i.e. write *'one half'* on both halves and *'one quarter'* on all four quarters.

  Some pupils may have problems making quarters. They may:

  - make four folds resulting in them creating five parts
  - attempt to make quarters without making halves first, resulting in uneven parts.

  Compare their results and discuss whether or not they have successfully created halves and quarters.

- Model how to make halves by ensuring that the paper is folded precisely so that both parts are exactly the same size (otherwise, they are not halves).

  Model how to make quarters precisely by halving the sheet of paper and then halving again.

  Discuss the fact that quarters can be made easily if we half and half again and that one half is exactly the same as two quarters. We can say that one half is equal to two quarters or one half is equivalent to two quarters.

- Provide pupils with a range of fraction cards (see Resource sheet 5A: Fraction cards): 3 halves, 1 whole and one half, 6 quarters, 4 halves, 2 wholes, 8 quarters, 5 halves, 2 wholes and 2 quarters, 10 quarters, etc. and challenge them to find their 'equivalent' partners. **What fraction do you have? Who has the same size as you?** Etc.
  Challenge pupils to make a display of equivalent fractions using halves and quarters of cakes, cookies, oranges, etc.

Unit 5.6 Share equally

- Unit 5.6 consolidates the understanding developed in Unit 5.4 by linking the concept of finding a fraction of a value to that of division.
  Provide pupils with A4 paper and make halves and quarters as outlined in Teaching Ideas: Unit 5.5, Finding equivalent fractions. These can be used as 'sharing boards' for the following activities and textbook questions. Alternatively, pupils can be provided with the following:

one half	one half

- Explain that the bar represents a whole cake and that it has been cut into two equal slices. **What fraction is each slice?**
- Organise pupils into pairs and provide them with 3 sets of coloured counters to represent decorations:
  - o Eight chocolate buttons
  - o Ten dolly mixture
  - o Twelve gummy bears

  Challenge pupils to decorate the cake fairly. Ask questions, such as: **How many chocolate buttons should there be on each half of the cake?** *Four chocolate buttons.* **What fraction of the chocolate buttons are on each slice?** *One half of the chocolate buttons.* **What is half of eight chocolate buttons?** *Four chocolate buttons.*
- Explain to the pupils that this bar represents a whole class:

one quarter	one quarter	one quarter	one quarter

  Ask questions, such as **How many groups are there in the class?** *Four groups.* **What can you tell me about each group?** *They are all the same size.* **What fraction of the whole class is each group?** *One quarter of the class.* Explain to the class that you have some resources that you want to share fairly between the groups. Challenge pupils to share out the following:
  - o Eight rubbers
  - o Twelve rulers
  - o Nine packs of post-its

  Challenge pupils to share the resources fairly. Ask questions, such as **How many rubbers should each group get?** *Two rubbers.* **What fraction of the rubbers should each group get?** *One quarter of the rubbers.* **What is one quarter of eight rubbers?** *Two rubbers.*
  The post-its example challenges pupils to share out an unequal number of items. Some pupils may correctly deduce that we can't find a quarter of nine packets of post-its because there will be one packet spare. Other pupils may correctly deduce that the spare packet can be divided into four equal parts so that each group receives two and a quarter packets.

Fractions, decimal fractions and percentages 1B

Section overview

Textbook 1B units	Review units	Prior learning	Benchmarks/Es&Os
Unit 5.1 Making and naming equal parts	**1A** Units 5.1 and 5.2	• I can make and identify halves. • I can make and identify quarters.	**MNU 1-07a** • Explains what a fraction is using concrete materials, pictorial representations and appropriate mathematical vocabulary.
Unit 5.2 Identifying equal parts	**1B** Unit 5.1	• I can make and name equal parts.	**MNU 1-07a** • Explains what a fraction is using concrete materials, pictorial representations and appropriate mathematical vocabulary.
Unit 5.3 Naming fractions	**1B** Units 5.1 and 5.2	• I can make and name equal parts. • I can identify equal parts.	**MNU 1-07a** • Uses the correct notation for common fractions to tenths; for example, $\frac{1}{2}$, $\frac{2}{3}$ and $\frac{5}{8}$.
Unit 5.4 Counting fractions	**1A** Units 2.4 and 2.5 **1B** Units 5.1 and 5.2	• I can identify forward number sequences on a number line. • I can make and name equal parts. • I can identify equal parts.	**MNU 1-07a** • Compares the size of fractions and places simple fractions in order on a number line.
Unit 5.5 Comparing fractions	**1B** Unit 5.1	• I can make and name equal parts.	**MNU 1-07a** • Compares the size of fractions and places simple fractions in order on a number line.
Unit 5.6 Equivalent fractions	**1A** Unit 5.5 **1B** Units 5.1 and 5.5	• I can find equivalent fractions (halves and quarters). • I can make and name equal parts. • I can compare fractions.	**MNU 1-07c** • Uses pictorial representations and other models to demonstrate understanding of simple equivalent fractions; for example, $\frac{1}{2} = \frac{2}{4} = \frac{3}{6}$.
Unit 5.7 Counting in fractions	**1B** Units 5.3 and 5.4	• I can name fractions. • I can count fractions on a number line.	**MNU 1-07a** • Compares the size of fractions and places simple fractions in order on a number line.
Unit 5.8 Finding part of a set	**1A** Units 5.4 and 5.6	• I can share and group equally (halves, thirds and quarters).	**MNU 1-07a** • Uses known multiplication and division facts and other strategies to find unit fractions of whole numbers; for example, $\frac{1}{2}$ or $\frac{1}{4}$.

Conceptual context

Perhaps the most significant contributory factor to pupils developing difficulty with fractions is our impulse to move to the abstract too soon. Although fractional notation is introduced in this book (Unit 5.3, Naming fractions), we should be cautious of how and when we use it, as notation can be the cause of much confusion. You will note that throughout this and the preceding books, fractions are predominately written in words rather than numerically and always represented visually. *Two thirds of a chocolate bar* is much easier to interpret and visualise than $\frac{2}{3}$ *of a chocolate bar* (quite often read as 'two over three of a chocolate bar'). It is vital that pupils are given plenty of experience of making, identifying and naming fractions using concrete materials and pictorial representations (Units 5.1 and 5.2) before fractional notation is introduced. Once introduced, fractional notation should simply be seen as one way in which fractions can be represented (not the only way!). This will support conceptual understanding throughout second level and beyond. For example, a pupil presented with the (poorly written) question: *What is* $5 \times \frac{3}{4}$ *?* may be forgiven for multiplying both the numerator and denominator by five and producing an incorrect answer of $\frac{15}{20}$. The same pupil presented with the question: *Five people each have three quarters of a pizza. How much pizza do they have altogether?* and either given or able to produce visual representations, will have a much better understanding of why we get an answer of fifteen quarters (and that the quarter pizzas don't somehow magically turn into twentieths).

The chapter also consolidates and extends the understanding developed in Book 1A, Counting in halves and quarters, by counting in thirds, fifths, sixths, etc. Once again, this understanding is developed by using concrete materials in conjunction with the counting stick. These should support pupils' ability to place fractions on the number line in the challenge questions.

Pupils will be supported to compare fractions visually. The activities outlined in the Teaching Ideas encourage children to make fractions (using bars) and compare them visually. Some pupils may be able to make this comparison without the need to draw the bars as they may understand that quarters are larger than twelfths; therefore, three of these larger parts (quarters) must be greater than three of the smaller parts (twelfths).

It is important to develop pupils' understanding of equivalence by making connections between fractions when physically making them. For example, when making quarters, we half and half the halves; when making sixths, we can make thirds and half them. This approach forms a far deeper understanding of equivalence than relying on a 'rule' such as *Whatever you do to the top, you do to the bottom*. Pupils may be able to find equivalents this way without having any idea why they are doing it.

Unit 5.7 extends on the learning developed in Unit 5.4 by applying understanding of equivalence. We can count one half, two halves, three halves, four halves, etc. but we can also use the equivalent whole numbers, i.e. one half, ONE, two halves, TWO, etc. Once again, the counting stick should be complimented by using visuals (e.g. fraction cards) to embed this understanding.

Finally, Unit 5.8 demonstrates how pupils' understanding of fractions, developed through bar modelling, can be applied to finding a fraction of a value. These visual representations remain consistent throughout as we build up pupils' skills and understanding of fractions.

Resources

- A4 or A5 paper
- Base 10 materials
- Card
- Counting stick
- Resource sheet 5A: Fraction cards
- Modelling clay (to represent cookies, chocolate bars, etc)
- Resource sheet 5E: Fraction wall

Key vocabulary

- **Compare**
- **Eighth**
- **Equal shares**
- **Equivalent**
- **Fifth**
- **Fraction**
- **Fractional notation**
- **Group**
- **Half**
- **Quarter**
- **Seventh**
- **Share**
- **Sixth**
- **Tenth**
- **Third**
- **Twelfth**
- **Whole**

Misconceptions

Potential misconception	Addressing the misconception
Units 5.1 and 5.2 Pupils may fail to understand that when we half or quarter something it must be split into *equal* parts.	Represent fractions using concrete materials and visuals. Provide opportunities for pupils to make and identify fractions in many different contexts. Encourage pupils to justify why they think something is a half or quarter.
Units 5.1 and 5.2 Pupils may fail to take account of the different sizes of parts when naming fractions, such as the darker part in the following diagram: 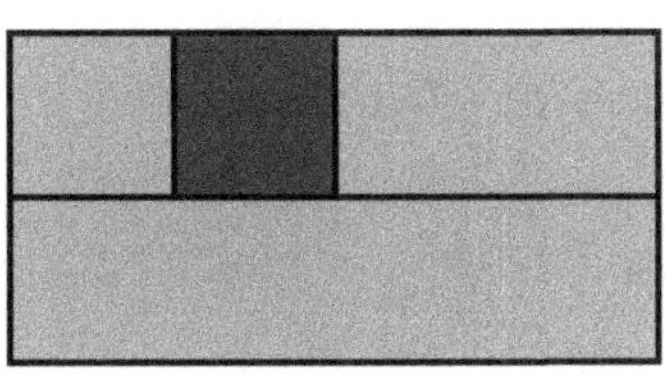	Provide opportunities for pupils to make and identify fractions by folding paper shapes.

Potential misconception	Addressing the misconception
Units 5.3, 5.4, 5.6 and 5.7 Pupils may consider fractions written numerically, e.g. $\frac{1}{2}$, as 2 whole numbers rather than a single relational entity. They struggle to interpret fractions when written numerically, which impacts their ability to solve, for example, a fraction of an amount.	Avoid fractional notation until pupils have a firm grasp of fractions through extensive exploration using concrete materials and pictorial representations. Note: when fractional notation is eventually introduced it should not replace concrete and pictorial representations but rather be taught as an additional way of representing fractions. The ability to visualise fractions will support deep understanding at the highest levels of maths. Continue to represent fractions in words even after fractional notation is introduced. Note: the diagrams of fraction cards throughout the books display fractions written in both fractional notation and words.
Units 5.1 to 5.8 Pupils may consider fraction names to be absolute labels rather than relational labels.	Give answers that relate to the whole amount, e.g. *one quarter of the bar* or *two thirds of the pizza* rather than just *one quarter* or *two thirds.*
Unit 5.6 Pupils think that, for example, four eighths of something is more than two quarters because there are four parts compared to two parts.	Represent equivalents using concrete materials and visuals. Provide opportunities for pupils to make fractions by making appropriate links; for example, make sixths by making thirds and halving them.
Units 5.4 and 5.7 Pupils may fail to understand that we can have any number of equal parts, i.e. when counting in halves we do not stop when we reach two halves; we can continue without limit.	Provide regular opportunities for pupils to count fractions, providing concrete and / or pictorial representations (see the activities outlined in Unit 5.3).

Teaching ideas

Unit 5.1 Making and naming equal parts

- Draw or display the following:

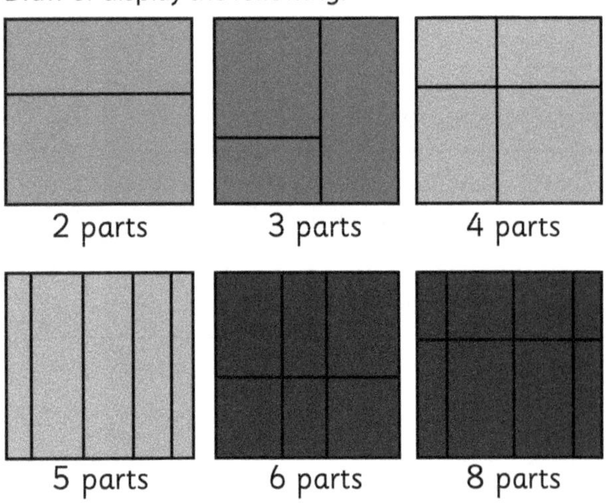

Ask pupils to discuss the following statement and justify their responses: **Agree or disagree – The squares have been split into parts. We can give these fractions names.**

Through discussion, ascertain from the pupils that we are unable to name these parts as fractions (halves, thirds, etc.) because the parts are not equal in size.

- Provide each pupil with 5 sheets of A4 paper (it may be useful to provide different colours to differentiate between each fraction).

- Display the following challenge:

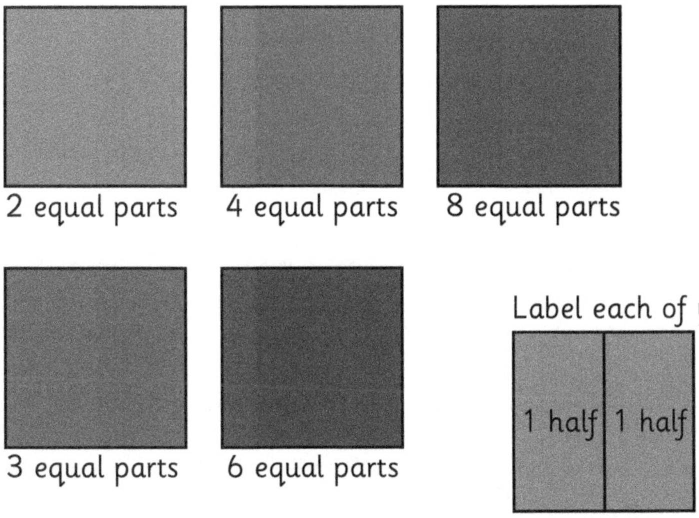

Ask pupils to check and compare their results. Ask questions, such as: **Are all of the parts equal? Has anyone made quarters that look different?** (i.e. by folding the paper in different ways) **Which fractions were easiest to make? Which fractions can we use to help us make other fractions?** Etc.

Through discussion, ascertain that halves, quarters and eighths are the easiest to make (quarters – half and half again; eighths – make quarters and then half them). Thirds are trickier to make because we can't use halves to help us and need to rely on judgement (see Book 2C, Teaching Guide, Unit 6.2 for a more accurate strategy for making thirds). Once we have made thirds, we can make sixths easily by halving the thirds.

Unit 5.2 Identifying equal parts

- Organise pupils into pairs / groups and provide them with A4 blank paper.

  Display the following challenge (see Resource sheet 5B: Chilli challenge):

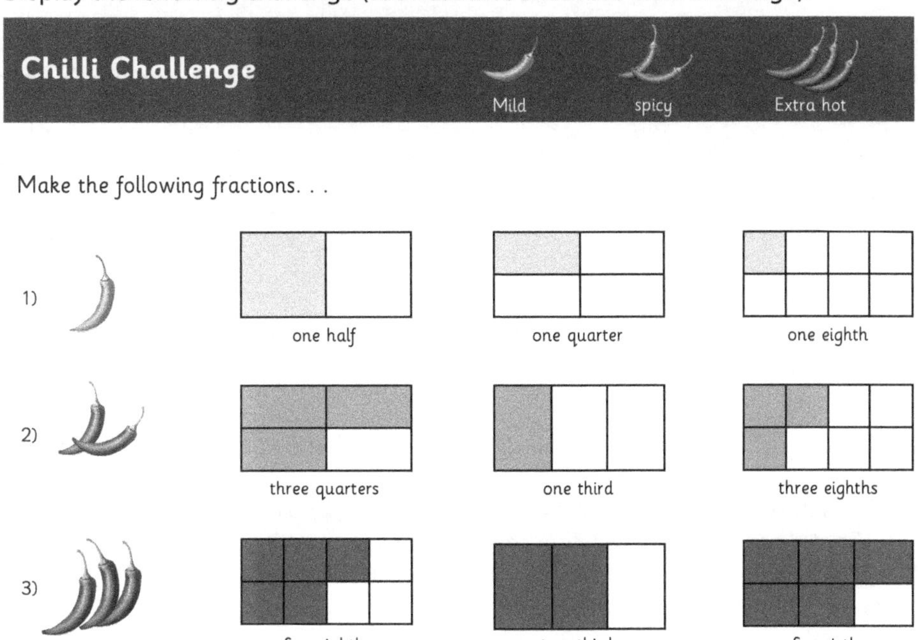

When attempting, for example, to make three quarters, some pupils may fold the paper into three parts and therefore incorrectly make thirds. It is important when making fractions that pupils write the name of each part before cutting out the parts needed.

- The following success criteria should be developed for making the fractions:
  - Fold into equal parts
  - Label each part
  - Cut out the parts we need

When making quarters, we must start by folding the paper into four equal parts. We can then label each part 'one quarter'. Now we can cut out the number of quarters we need (in this example we need to cut out three of these parts). This should also avoid pupils falling into the trap of looking at the three parts they have cut out and incorrectly deducing that they have three thirds.

Compare and review the pupils' attempts. Ascertain, through discussion, the links between the different levels of challenge. For example, when attempting to make one quarter as part of the mild challenge, they have also completed part of the 'spicy challenge', i.e. three quarters (hopefully this hasn't ended up in the bin!). Pupils who attempted the three fractions in the spicy challenge will therefore have made six of the fractions altogether: three quarters and one quarter, one third and two thirds, three eighths and five eighths.

- When attempting 'Let's Practise' Question 3, pupils are challenged to create fractions using bars. When attempting to draw, for example, three eighths, some pupils may draw the bar and attempt to split the bar into eight parts by starting at one end and drawing seven vertical lines which may result in very unequal parts:

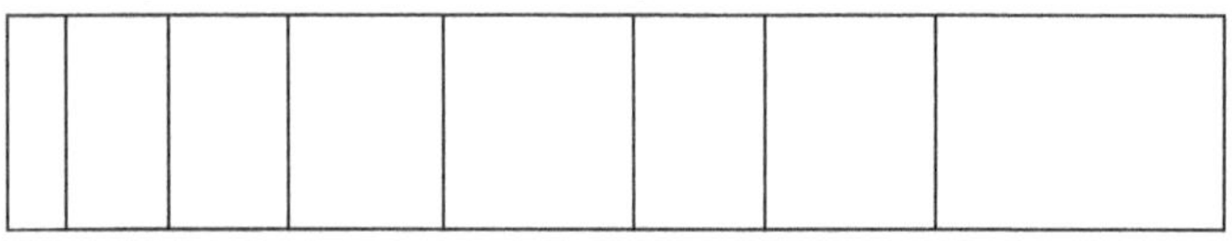

- Refer the pupils to the practical activity of making eighths in the previous unit. This was achieved by halving, halving and halving again. This logic can be applied when splitting the bar in order to achieve more accurate eighths, i.e. draw a vertical line down the middle, then in the middle of each half, then in the middle of each quarter:

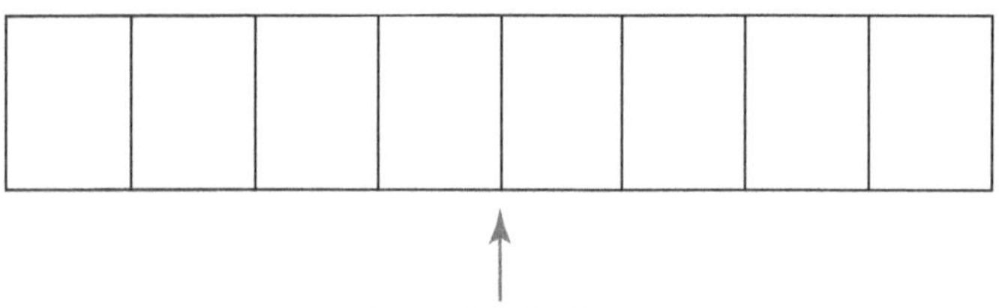

Unit 5.3 Naming fractions

- Revisit or review the activities conducted in the previous two units (5.1, Making and naming equal parts and 5.2, Identifying equal parts). It is vital that pupils have a firm understanding of these concepts prior to introducing fractional notation.
- Display various visual representations of one half (for example, show images of half a pizza, half a football pitch, half an apple, etc.).
  Ask pupils to identify each of the pictures, i.e. *one half of a pizza / football pitch / apple.*
  Ask pupils questions, such as: **What does 'half' tell us?** *That the whole has been split into two equal parts.* **How do we know these are halves?** *Because we would need another part of the same size to make a whole.* **What does 'one' tell us?** *That we are interested in (or have) one out of these two parts.*

Elicit through discussion that: **We can think of one half as one out of two equal parts that make up the whole. So, one half of a pizza is one out of two equal parts that make up the whole pizza.**
We can write this in words: one *out of* two equal parts.
We can also represent this numerically: $\frac{1}{2}$
The 2 tells us how many parts make up the whole and therefore tells us the name of the fraction: half (or halves). The 1 tells us how many parts we are interested in (or have): we are interested in 1 of the halves.

- Organise pupils into groups and provide them with piles of fraction cards (halves, thirds, quarters, fifths and sixths).

  Roll a dice to generate a digit for the denominator and write this on the board, e.g. '/3'.
  Roll the dice again to generate a digit for the numerator and write this in correct position, e.g. roll a 4 so display $\frac{4}{3}$.
  Challenge the pupils to represent the fraction using the fraction cards, i.e. each group should lay out four thirds.
  Repeat with different examples.
  Provide each group with a dice and instruct them to challenge each other to make and display fractions correctly.

- Display various visual representations of fractions for pupils (see Resource sheet 5C: Fraction bars).

  Challenge pupils to write each fraction in words and fractional notation, i.e. three quarters = three out of four equal parts = $\frac{3}{4}$.

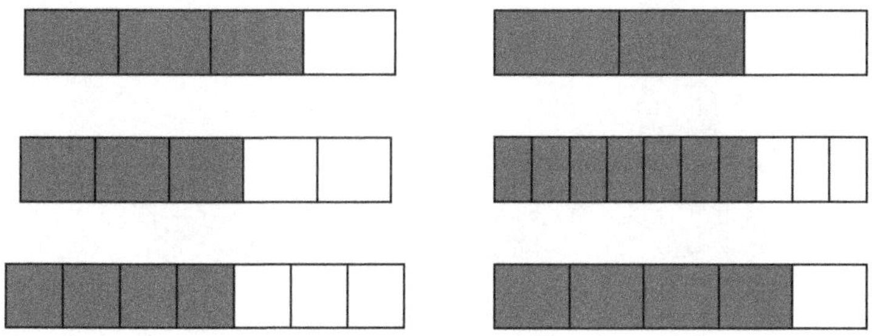

Unit 5.4 Counting fractions

- Count on and back in halves and quarters using slides (showing number lines and pizza portions) referred to in Teaching Guide 1A: Unit 5.3, Counting in halves and quarters.
- Provide pupils with stacks of fraction cards, e.g. 5 thirds, 4 sixths, 7 eighths, 12 tenths, etc.

  Challenge pupils to count out how many of each fraction there are and represent this on a number line (or counting stick) by drawing jumps:

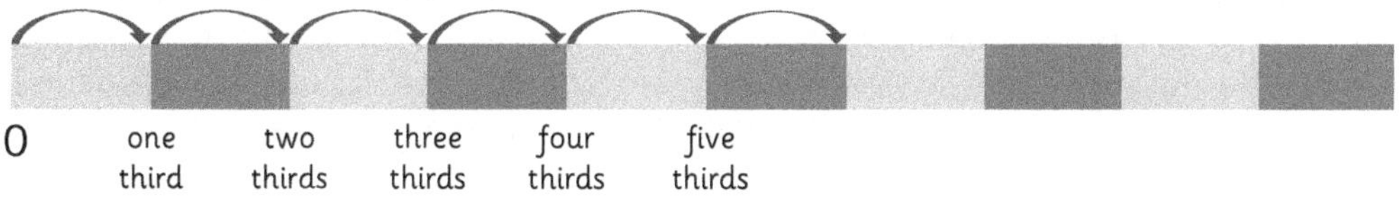

- Attach fraction cards, back to front, on a counting stick so that they are hidden (zero, one third, two thirds, three thirds, etc.)
  Show pupils the counting stick and explain that you are going to count on from zero in thirds (turn over the zero). Challenge pupils to count on in thirds, turning over each card as they count:

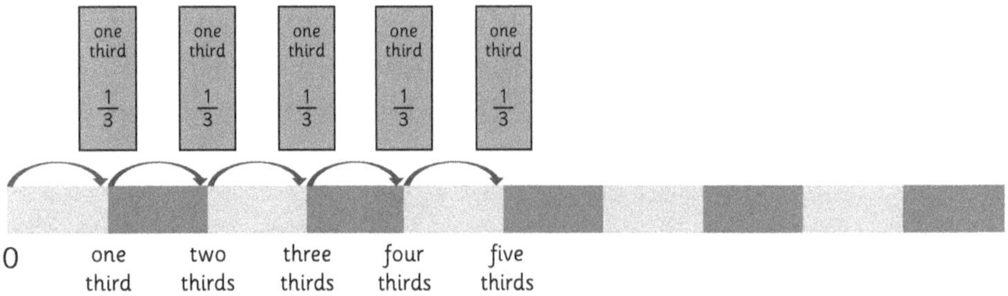

  Hide the values again and practise counting back in thirds.
  Repeat counting on and back with other sets of fraction card e.g. fifths, sixths, eighths, etc.
  Note that when changing the value of the jumps (e.g. from thirds to fifths), demonstrate 'wiping clean' the counting stick to show that you are resetting the values.
  Hide the values again and this time turn over a random card (for example, four thirds). Ask questions, such as: **If this is four thirds, what value will be next (or before)? What value will be two jumps after?** Etc.

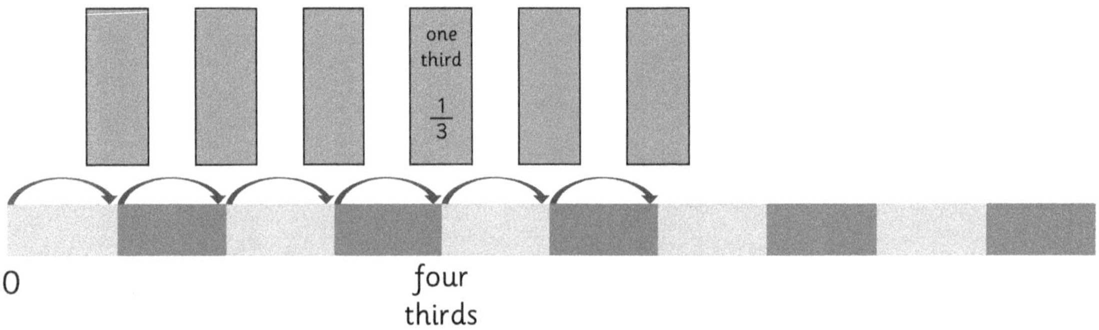

  Repeat using different sets of fraction cards (remembering to 'wipe clean' the counting stick).

Unit 5.5 Comparing fractions

- Write or say the following statement: **I would rather have one tenth than one fifth of a bar of chocolate.**
  Ask pupils to discuss whether they agree or disagree with this statement and to justify their responses. NB: Some pupils may consider one tenth to be larger because ten is larger than five.
  Challenge pupils to represent both portions visually. Ask questions, such as: **How do we make fifths?** *By splitting the bar into five equal parts.* **How do we make tenths?** *By splitting the bar into ten equal parts.* **Which portions are larger?** *Fifths.* NB: It is important that when representing each portion, the size of the whole bar is the same for each. Draw the following bars (or ask a pupil to demonstrate) so that a direct comparison can be made:

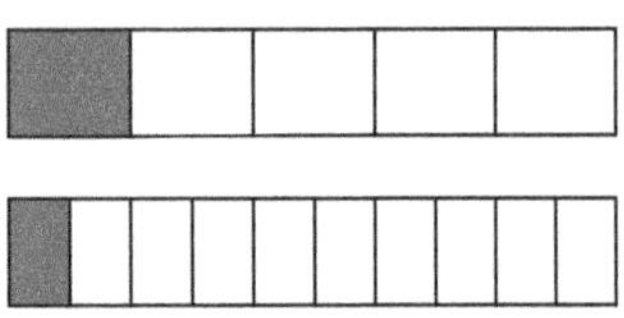

- At this point you may wish to discuss the following: **True, false, sometimes: one fifth of a bar of chocolate is always bigger than one tenth?** By drawing chocolate bars of different sizes, we can demonstrate that this is only sometimes true. In this example, one fifth of the small bar of chocolate is actually smaller than one tenth of the larger bar:

  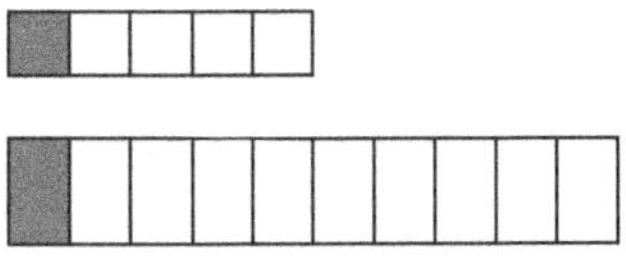

  The concept of comparing fractions of different sized wholes is explored in Book 1C: Comparing fractions.
- Repeat the above activity using a comparison between three quarters and three eighths. i.e. comparing fractions with the same numerator.
- Repeat the above activity using three quarters and two thirds. i.e. both the numerators and denominators are different. By aligning the bar models one on top of the other, as demonstrated below, we can make a direct comparison between the two visually (comparison by equivalence is explored in Book 2B: Comparing and ordering fractions).

  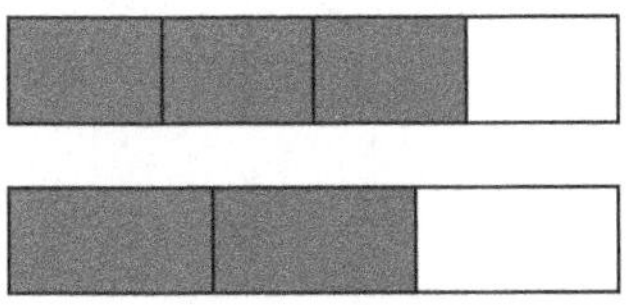
- Provide pupils with fraction cards and challenge them to compare the following
  - o One third and one sixth
  - o One eighth and one twelfth
  - o Three sixths and three twelfths
  - o Five tenths and five eighths
  - o One quarter and two sixths
  - o Five twelfths and three fifths
  - o Etc.

Unit 5.6 Equivalent fractions

- Practise counting forwards and backwards in various fractions using materials or visuals (see Teaching Ideas: Unit 5.4, Counting fractions).
- Organise pupils into groups and provide them with a selection of fraction cards including halves, thirds, quarters, fifths, sixths, eighths, tenths and twelfths.
  Display one half and challenge pupils to use the fraction cards to make an equivalent fraction. Award points to each group for the number of cards they use, e.g. 2 quarters = 2 points; 3 sixths = 3 points; 4 eighths = 4 points; etc. Award bonus points if groups are able to make more than one equivalent fraction.
- Repeat using different fractions:
  - o One quarter
  - o One third

- o Three quarters
- o Two thirds
- o Three fifths
- o Etc.

Note that pupils may create an equivalent fraction using a combination of different fraction cards (for example, one half could be made using one quarter and two eighths). Encourage pupils to check their solutions by comparing them to the original fraction.

- Provide pupils with equal-sized pieces of paper. Demonstrate making one half by folding a piece of paper equally, writing 'one half' on each part and then cutting (or folding) the paper in order to display one of the halves.
  Challenge pupils to create fractions that are equivalent to one half. Compare pupils' results and ask questions, such as: **How can we make sure that we create fractions equivalent to one half?** Demonstrate that equivalents can be found by folding the paper in half to begin with and then folding the halves into equal parts. For example, two equal parts makes quarters (two quarters); three equal parts makes sixths (three sixths); four equal parts makes eighths (four eighths), etc.
  Challenge pupils to make fractions equivalent to:
  - o One quarter
  - o Three quarters
  - o Two thirds
  - o Etc.

Unit 5.7 Counting in fractions

- This unit consolidates and extends the learning developed in Unit 5.4, Counting fractions. As such, the activities outlined in the teaching guides should be revisited; however, this time our intention is to make the link between counting solely in fractions (one half, two halves, three halves, four halves, etc.) to counting in fractions and wholes (one half, one, one and a half, two, etc.). When counting in fractions, ask questions, such as: **What are two halves the same as? What are six thirds the same as? Etc.**

  Draw or display the following counting stick:

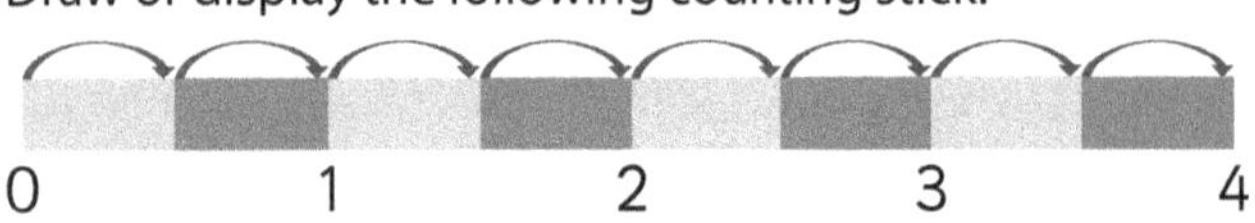

  Ask questions, such as: **How many jumps are there between each whole number?** *Two*. **What must be the value of each jump?** *One half*. Fill in the missing jumps as follows:

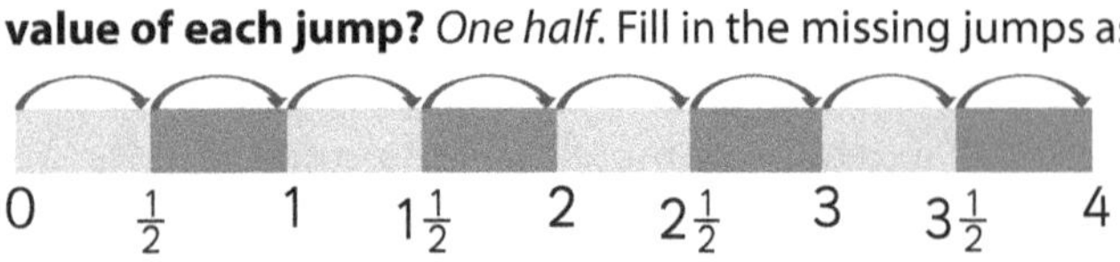

- Repeat for the following counting sticks:

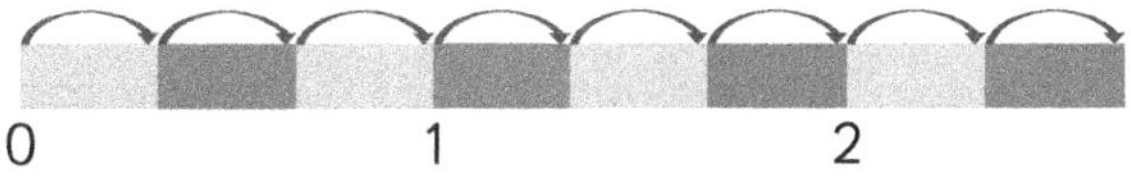

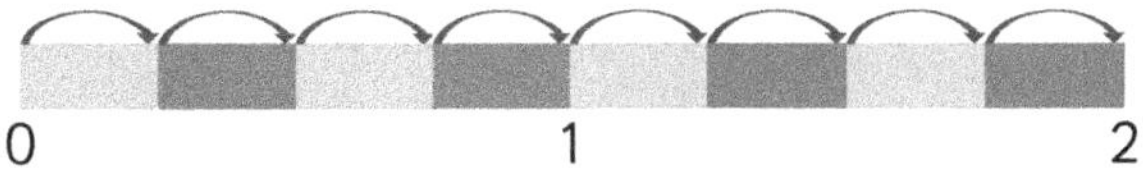

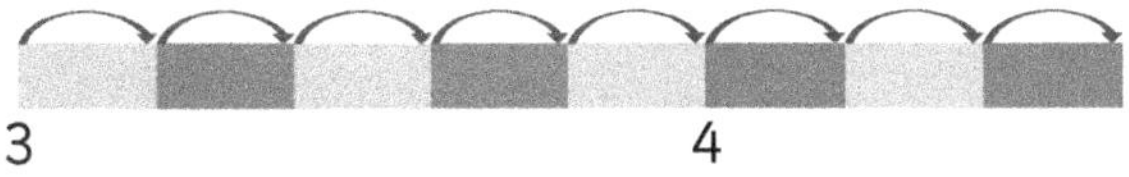

- Challenge pupils to draw number lines that count on from:
    - o Zero to three in jumps of one fifth
    - o Four to six in jumps of one third
    - o One and a half to four in jumps of one quarter
    - o Etc.

Unit 5.8 Finding part of a set

- Unit 5.8 consolidates the understanding developed in Book 1A, Unit 5.6 by extending the range of fractions beyond halves and quarters.
- Provide pupils with fraction sharing boards (or challenge pupils to make them) for the following fractions:
    - o Halves
    - o Quarters
    - o Eighths
    - o Thirds
    - o Sixths

  See Resource sheet 5D: Fraction sharing boards.

one sixth	one sixth	one sixth	one sixth	one sixth	one sixth

- Repeat the activities described in Book 1A, Teaching Guide, Unit 5.6 using different fraction boards (eighths, thirds or **sixths**):
    - o Explain that the bar represents a whole cake and that it has been cut into equal slices. **What fraction is each slice?**
    - o Organise pupils into pairs and provide them with three sets of coloured counters to represent decorations:
        - ■ Twelve chocolate buttons
        - ■ Eighteen dolly mixture
        - ■ Twenty-four gummy bears

- o Challenge pupils to decorate the cake fairly. Ask questions, such as: **How many chocolate buttons should there be on each slice of the cake?** *Two chocolate buttons.* **What fraction of the chocolate buttons are on each slice?** *One sixth of the chocolate buttons.* **What is one sixth of twelve chocolate buttons?** *Two chocolate buttons.*

- Ensure that pairs of pupils have a full set of fraction sharing boards (listed above) and enough counters.
  Ask questions, such as
  - o **What is one third of nine pencils?**
  - o **What is one eighth of sixteen sweets?**
  - o **What is one sixth of £30?**
  - o **Etc.**

  Explain to the pupils that they must show you the answers using the boards and counters (rather than writing or shouting out the answer). This could be done by firstly sharing out the counters equally on the fraction board:

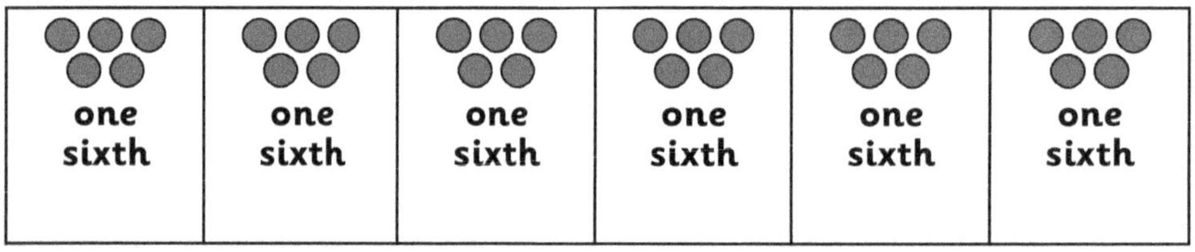

then hiding the parts we are not interested in:

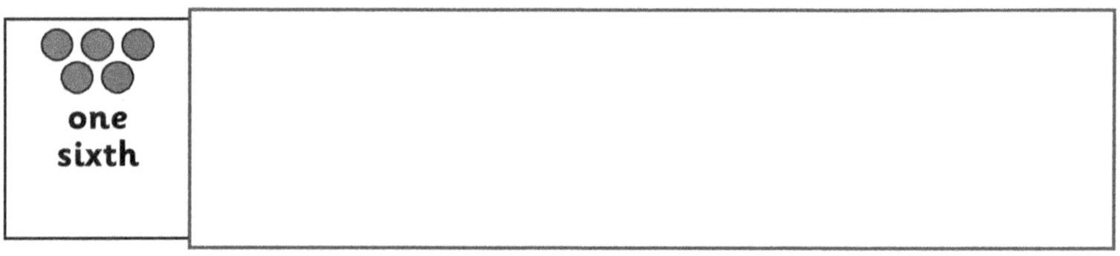

Fractions, decimal fractions and percentages 1C

Section overview

Textbook 1C units	Review units	Prior learning	Benchmarks/Es&Os
Unit 5.1 Finding part of a set (multiple parts)	**1A** Units 5.4 and 5.6 **1B** Unit 5.8	• I can share and group equally. • I can find part of a set (one part).	**MNU 1-07b** • Uses known multiplication and division facts and other strategies to find unit fractions of whole numbers; for example, $\frac{1}{2}$ or $\frac{1}{4}$.
Unit 5.2 Making a whole	**1B** Units 5.1, 5.5 and 5.6	• I can make and name equal parts. • I can compare fractions. • I can find equivalent fractions.	**MTH 1-07c** • Uses pictorial representations and other models to demonstrate understanding of simple equivalent fractions, for example, $\frac{1}{2} = \frac{2}{4} = \frac{3}{6}$.
Unit 5.3 Ordering fractions	**1B** Unit 5.5	• I can compare fractions.	**MNU 1-07a** • Compares the size of fractions and places simple fractions in order on a number line.
Unit 5.4 Adding and subtracting fractions	**1B** Unit 5.4	• I can count fractions.	**MNU 1-07a** • Explains what a fraction is using concrete materials, pictorial representations and appropriate mathematical vocabulary.
Unit 5.5 Creating equivalent fractions	**1A** Unit 5.6 **1B** Units 5.5 and 5.6	• I can share equally. • I can compare fractions. • I can identify equivalent fractions.	**MNU 1-07c** • Uses pictorial representations and other models to demonstrate understanding of simple equivalent fractions; for example, $\frac{1}{2} = \frac{2}{4} = \frac{3}{6}$.
Unit 5.6 Comparing fractions	**1B** Unit 5.5 **1C** Unit 5.2	• I can compare fractions (relative to the same whole). • I can make a whole. • I understand that the size of a fraction is dependant on the size of the whole.	**MNU 1-07a** • Compares the size of fractions and places simple fractions in order on a number line.
Unit 5.7 Find a fraction of an amount	**1B** Units 5.3 and 5.8 **1C** Unit 5.1	• I can name fractions. • I can find part of a set (one part). • I can find part of a set (multiple sets).	**MNU 1-07b** • Uses known multiplication and division facts and other strategies to find unit fractions of whole numbers; for example, $\frac{1}{2}$ or $\frac{1}{4}$.
Unit 5.8 Sharing one whole	**1A** Units 5.4 and 5.6 **1C** Units 5.2 and 5.5	• I can share and group equally. • I can make a whole. • I can create equivalent fractions.	**MNU 1-07b** • Uses known multiplication and division facts and other strategies to find unit fractions of whole numbers; for example, $\frac{1}{2}$ or $\frac{1}{4}$.

Conceptual context

Unit 5.1 consolidates the understanding developed in Book 1B, Unit 5.8 by extending the number of parts we are interested in (i.e. rather than simply finding one quarter of the children in a class, we might want to find three quarters). The challenge question requires pupils to solve inverse fraction problems (i.e. rather than knowing the whole amount and finding, for example, three quarters of the whole, pupils are given the value of equivalent to three quarters and challenged to find the value of the whole).

Unit 5.2 explores the concept of making one whole and develops pupils' understanding of fractions through *iteration* (i.e. *I understand that this is one third because three lots of it makes one whole*). It also challenges pupils' understanding of equivalence through their ability to make the whole using more than one fraction type (for example, using one half and two quarters). This unit links directly to Unit 5.8 where pupils' ability to share one whole further develops their understanding of fractions through *partitioning* (i.e. *I understand that this is one third because I have split the whole into three equal parts*).

Units 5.3 and 5.4 aim to develop the ability to compare fractions relative to the *same whole* and *different wholes*, respectively. It is important that pupils gain an appreciation that the size of a fraction is determined entirely by the size of the whole it relates to. We cannot conclusively compare the abstract terms $\frac{1}{2}$ and $\frac{1}{3}$ by saying that $\frac{1}{2}$ is bigger than $\frac{1}{3}$ without being told what they specifically relate to (i.e. one third of the money in your pocket could very well be greater than half of the money in mine).

Unit 5.4 introduces addition and subtraction of fractions, which can be a difficult concept to understand when introduced using fractional notation. This can lead to pupils relying on an abstract process they don't really understand and cause them to mistakenly add both numerators and denominators, e.g. $\frac{1}{4} + \frac{3}{4} = \frac{4}{8}$. This common misconception can be addressed by introducing addition and subtraction within a context and using visual representations.

Unit 5.5 develops pupils' ability to create equivalent fractions. This is key to the development of fractional understanding and it is vital that pupils have a deep understanding of equivalence because it links to many of the concepts across fractions, decimals and percentages.

Unit 5.7 consolidates the understanding developed in Unit 5.1 by introducing the more abstract process of dividing by the denominator and multiplying by the numerator. It is vital that this strategy does not replace the skills developed previously. It is simply an alternative strategy that should only be introduced and applied when pupils have a deep conceptual understanding of the former, visual strategy. It should be used with caution going forward as this abstract process can often act as a barrier to pupils' understanding and mask a lack of understanding because the assumption is made that *if they can do it, they understand it*.

Resources

- A4 or A5 paper
- Card
- Counters
- Place value counters
- Printable fraction wall
- Resource sheet 5A: Fraction cards
- Resource sheet 5E: Fraction wall

Key vocabulary

- **Compare**
- **Denominator**
- **Equivalent**
- **Fractional notation**
- **Numerator**

Misconceptions

Potential misconception	Addressing the misconception
Units 5.1 and 5.7 Pupils may be confused by whether to multiply or divide by the numerator and denominator when finding a fraction of a set.	• Avoid the use of fractional notation when setting problems. • Use fraction boards and bar models to represent the problem visually.
Units 5.3 and 5.6 Pupils may think, for example, that $\frac{1}{3}$ is bigger than $\frac{1}{2}$ of an object or amount.	• Avoid use of the word 'over' when naming fractions. • Use fraction cards and bar models to represent fractions visually.
Unit 5.4 Pupils may add (or subtract) fractions by adding the numerators together and the denominators together e.g. they think $\frac{1}{2}$ plus $\frac{1}{2} = \frac{2}{4}$.	• Use concrete materials, fraction cards, etc. when adding or subtracting fractions. • Avoid fractional notation when adding or subtracting fractions. • Use bar models to represent addition / subtraction of fractions visually.
Unit 5.5 Pupils may regard equivalence as process where you have to 'multiply the numerator and denominator by the same number'. They fail to understand that the size of the portion remains constant.	• Use paper, modelling clay, fraction cards, etc. to create equivalent fractions and represent these visually using bar models.
Unit 5.6 Pupils may think, for example, that one half is always bigger than one quarter because they fail to understand that these are not discrete numbers and that their size is fully dependent on the 'whole' to which they relate. Therefore, the fractions do not necessarily have to relate to the same whole.	• Provide opportunities for pupils to create and compare fractions relating to different sized 'wholes', both using concrete materials and visual representations.

Teaching ideas

Unit 5.1 Finding part of a set

- Organise pupils into pairs or groups and provide them with strips of paper or card.

  Challenge pupils to make the following fractions (see activity outlined in Book 1B: Unit 5.2, Identifying equal parts, only this time instruct pupils to colour the relevant parts rather than cut them out):
  - Three quarters
  - Two thirds
  - Four fifths
  - Five eighths
- The context of decorating a cake could be used (or any other appropriate context). Choose one of the fraction bars to work with (for example, quarters).

- Explain that the bar represents a whole cake, pizza, etc. and that it has been cut into equal slices. **What fraction is each slice?**
- Organise pupils into pairs and provide them with 3 sets of coloured counters to represent decorations:
  - Twelve chocolate buttons
  - Sixteen dolly mixtures
  - Twenty gummy bears
- Challenge pupils to decorate the cake fairly. Ask questions, such as: **How many chocolate buttons should there be on each slice of the cake?** *Three chocolate buttons.* **What fraction of the chocolate buttons are on each slice?** *One quarter of the chocolate buttons.* **What is one quarter of twelve chocolate buttons?** *Three chocolate buttons.*

Explain to the pupils that they can get three slices of the cake. Ask questions, such as: **What fraction of the cake will you get?** *Three quarters of the cake.* **How many chocolate buttons / dolly mixtures / gummy bears should you get?** *Nine chocolate buttons / twelve dolly mixtures / fifteen gummy bears.* **What fraction of the chocolate buttons / dolly mixtures / gummy bears is this?** *Three quarters.* **What is three quarters of twelve / sixteen / twenty?** *Nine / twelve / fifteen.*

Repeat with alternative fraction examples identified above.

Ask questions, such as:

- **What is two thirds of twelve children?**
- **What is five eighths of twenty-four sweets?**
- **What is four fifths of £35?**

Explain to the pupils that they must show you the answers using the boards and counters. This could be done by firstly sharing out the counters equally on the fraction board:

one quarter	one quarter	one quarter	one quarter

Then hiding the parts we are not interested in:

one quarter	one quarter	one quarter	

Unit 5.2 Making a whole

- Organise pupils into pairs and provide them with a selection of fraction cards (see photocopy resource) including halves, thirds, quarters, fifths, sixths, eighths, tenths and twelfths (or a fraction wall cut into strips).

  Display one half and challenge pupils to use the fraction cards to make one whole. Award points to each group for the type of fraction cards they use, e.g. Same type of fraction (i.e. one half) = 1 point; Different type of fraction, e.g. 2 quarters, 3 sixths, 4 eighths, etc. = 2 points; Combination of different fraction cards, e.g. 1 quarter and 2 eighths or 1 third and 1 sixth = 3 points.

Repeat using different fractions:

- One quarter
- One third
- Three quarters
- Two thirds
- Three fifths

- Demonstrate the following 2-player game (each player will need one of each fraction cut from Resource sheet 5E: Fraction wall:
  - Place the 'one whole' strip in the middle:

  - Each player takes turns to play one of their fraction strips.
  - The goal of the game is to be the player who completes one whole or force your opponent to go over one whole.
  - For example, player 1 starts by playing a third:

  - Player 2 plays a half:

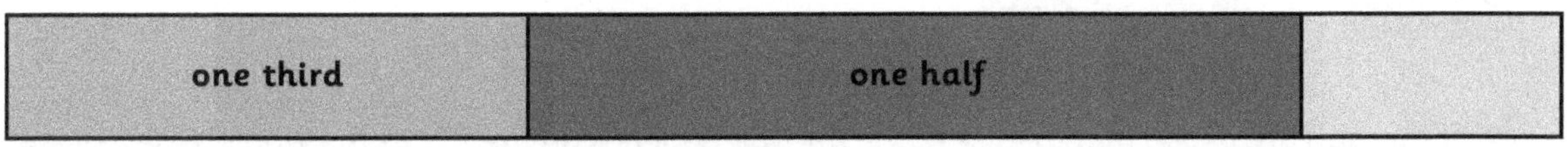

  - Player 1 plays a sixth to complete the whole and win:

  - Player 2 starts by playing a quarter:

  - Player 1 plays a third:

  - Player 2 plays a fifth:

- Player 1 plays a sixth:

- Player 2 is forced to play a twelfth which takes them over the 'whole' and loses:

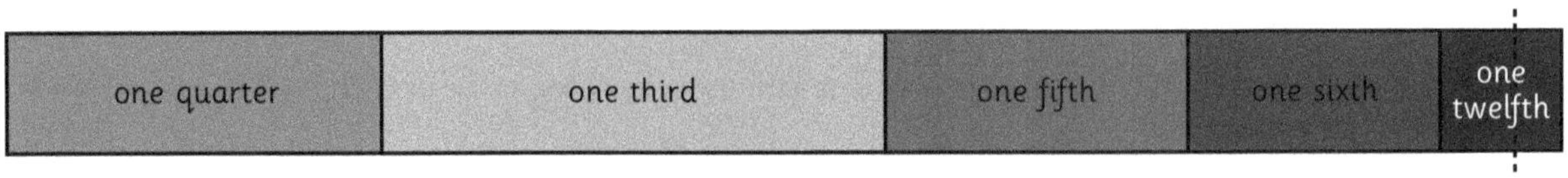

Unit 5.3 Ordering fractions

- Display the following statement: **One half is larger than one quarter: Sometimes, always or never true.**

  Ask pupils to discuss their thoughts and justify their responses.

- Show pupils the following images and ask: **Which is larger, one half of the small bar of chocolate or one quarter of the large bar?**

  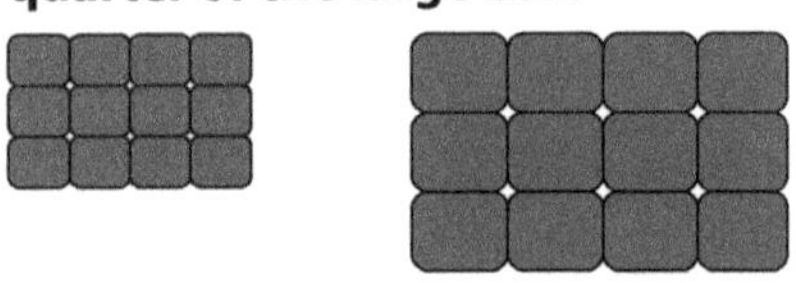

  Elicit through discussion that the size of the fraction depends on the size of the whole. One half is always larger than one quarter if they relate to the same whole. Sometimes one quarter can be larger than one half if the wholes in question are of different sizes.

- Explain that we will be comparing fractions that relate to the same whole.

  Write the following fractions on the board: one quarter, one twelfth, one eighth, one sixth, one third and one half.

  Organise pupils into pairs or groups and challenge them to write the fractions in order of size from smallest to largest.

  Provide the pupils with equal-sized pieces of paper and challenge them to make each of the fractions. The same success criteria should be used as in the activity outlined in Book 1B, Unit 5.2, i.e.

  - Fold into equal parts
  - Label each part
  - Cut out the parts we need

  Once the pupils have made each unit fraction, ask them to order them from smallest to largest and compare this to their original response. Ask questions, such as: **Has your order changed? Why do you think this is? Which would be smaller: one twentieth or one hundredth?** Etc.

  Note that pupils may struggle to make thirds, sixths and twelfths accurately. The activity outlined in Book 2C, Unit 6.2 can be adapted for first level and used to enable pupils to make accurate comparisons.

- Write the following fractions on the board: three quarters, five twelfths, three fifths and four eighths.

  Challenge pupils to write the fractions in order from smallest to largest.

Provide pupils with a fraction wall and challenge them to cut out each of the above fractions. Once again, ask pupils to order these from smallest to largest.

Note that pupils may have originally thought that, for example, five twelfths is larger than three quarters because five is larger than three. Elicit through discussion that the size of the parts is different (i.e. twelfths and quarters) so it is difficult to determine which is larger until we compare them visually.

Unit 5.4 Adding and subtracting fractions

- Display the following: $\frac{1}{4} + \frac{1}{4} = \frac{2}{8}$, True or False?

  Ask pupils to discuss and justify their responses.

  Display the following:

  Elicit through discussion reasons that people may incorrectly think that the original statement was true, i.e. they may simply add the numerators and denominators together. The visual representation of this statement helps us see that this can't possibly be the case.

  Ask: **How can we change this number story to make it true?** *One quarter pizza + one quarter pizza = two quarters of a pizza* (or one half of a pizza if we apply our understanding of equivalence).

- Organise pupils into pairs and provide them with fraction cards (see Resource sheet 5A: Fraction cards).

  Display the following problem: **Finlay has three quarters of a bar of chocolate and Amman also has three quarters of a bar of chocolate. How much do they have altogether?**

  Challenge pupils to *solve it* using the fraction cards and to *prove it* by drawing pictures to represent the problem. Challenge pupils to see how many different ways they could express the total chocolate (i.e. six quarters, one whole and two quarters, one whole and a half, three halves, etc.)

  Repeat with different fraction types, for example:

  - Five thirds and two thirds
  - Three eighths and six eighths
  - Two tenths and eight tenths

- Display the following problem: **Isla has five half apples and she eats three of the halves. How much does she have left?**

  Once again, challenge pupils to *solve it* using the fraction cards and to *prove it* by drawing pictures to represent the problem.

  Repeat with different fraction types, for example:

  - Eight thirds take away four thirds
  - Seven sixths take away two sixths
  - Eleven twelfths take away five twelfths

Unit 5.5 Creating equivalent fractions

- Provide pupils with equal-sized strips of paper.

  Challenge pupils to make halves. Ask questions, such as: **How do we know we have made halves accurately?** *They should match up exactly when folded into two parts.*

  Challenge pupils to fold their halves into two equal parts. Ask questions, such as: **What have we made now?** *Quarters.* **How many quarters can we make with our two halves?** *Four.* **What is one half the same as?** *Two quarters.* **How do we know we have made quarters accurately?** *They should match up exactly when folded.*

  Challenge pupils to use the other strips to make halves. Repeat the above activity with each strip but challenge them to fold each set of halves into:

  - Three equal parts (to make sixths)
  - Four equal parts (to make eighths)
  - Five equal parts (to make tenths)

  Ensure that pupils check their accuracy by folding to make sure that they have made equal parts each time. Note that it will be much trickier to make sixths and tenths than quarters and eighths because they cannot rely on halving each time.

- Question 2 requires pupils to find equivalents to thirds. Repeat the above activity but by folding the strips into three equal parts to begin with. It may be useful to make the initial thirds using the activity outlined in Book 2C, Unit 6.2 to ensure greater accuracy.
- The challenge question requires pupils to find equivalents to multipart fractions, e.g. two thirds. Repeat the activities above; encourage pupils to identify two of the thirds by colouring them before finding any equivalents. This will allow them to identify equivalents visually.

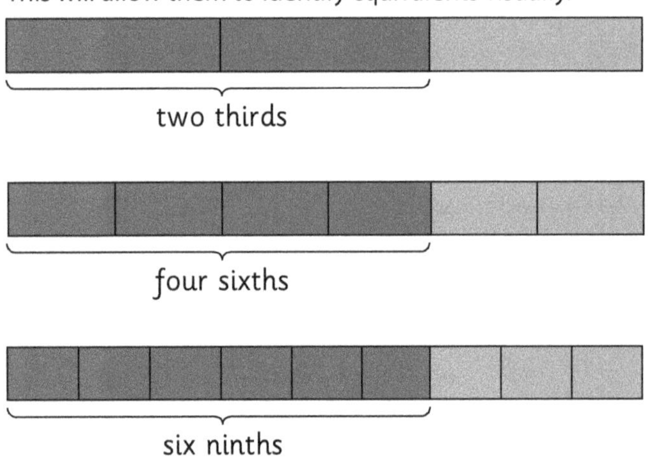

Unit 5.6 Comparing fractions

- Repeat the activity outlined in Unit 5.3, i.e.
  - Display the following statement: **One half is larger than one quarter: Sometimes, always or never true.**
  - Ask pupils to discuss their thoughts and justify their responses.

- Show pupils the following images and ask: **Which is larger, one half of the small bar of chocolate or one quarter of the large bar?**

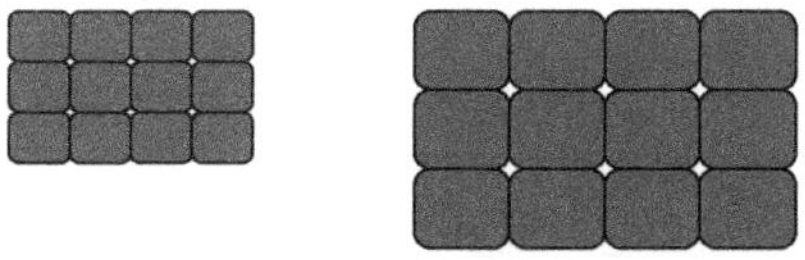

- Elicit through discussion that the size of the fraction depends on the size of the whole. One half is always larger than one quarter if they relate to the same whole. Sometimes one quarter can be larger than one half if the wholes in question are of different sizes.

- Organise pupils into pairs and challenge them to draw diagrams (or use appropriate materials) to prove the following:
  - One half is only sometimes bigger than one third
  - One quarter is only sometimes bigger than one eighth
  - Two thirds is only sometimes bigger than two sixths
- You may wish pupils to make a display that demonstrates this understanding (i.e. that the size of a fraction is entirely dependant on the size of the 'whole' it relates to). We can only make the assumption that $\frac{1}{2} > \frac{1}{3}$ if we contextualise the fractions by stating what they relate to (for example, one half of the glass of orange juice is greater than one third of the glass of orange juice).

Unit 5.7 Finding a fraction of an amount

- Display the following bar model:

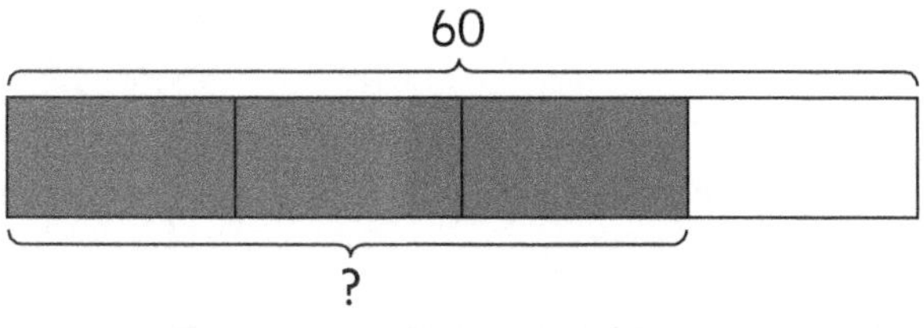

Ask pupils questions, such as: **What question does this bar represent?** *What is three quarters of sixty?* **How could we work this out?** *We could share out sixty equally between the four parts, then add up three of the parts.*

- Challenge pupils to come up with problems that this bar might represent. For example:
  - I had £60. I spent three quarters of it on a pair of trainers. How much were the trainers?
  - Three quarters of the children at a football club are boys. How many boys are in the club if there are 60 children altogether.
  - Etc.

Ask pupils to discuss what is actually happening when we solve a problem like this. Elicit through discussion that when we share out the whole amount equally between the parts we are *dividing*.

- Draw the following to reflect on this (place value counters or base ten materials could be used to consolidate the idea of partitioning the 60 into chunks to manage the division more efficiently):

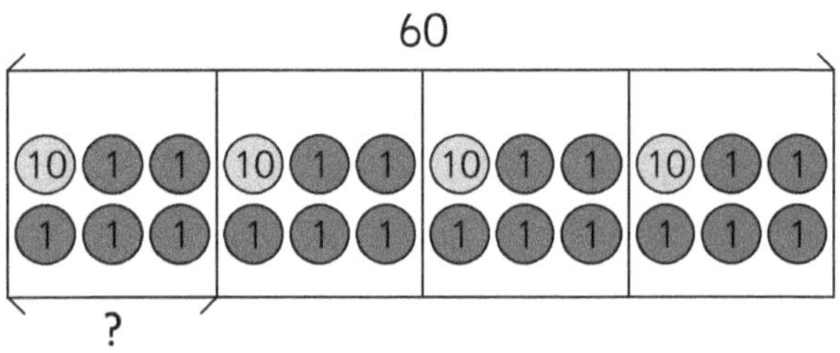

$60 \div 4 = 15$

Then, when we add up the parts we are interested in we are actually *multiplying* the amount in one part by the number of parts:

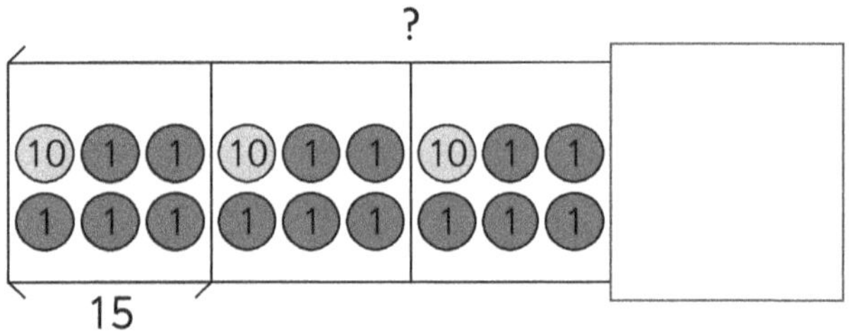

$15 \times 3 = 45$

Therefore, when we are asked to solve $\frac{3}{4}$ of 60, we are actually dividing by the number of equal parts that make up the whole (denominator) and multiplying the result by the number of parts we are interested in (numerator):

$\frac{3}{4}$ of 60: $60 \div 4 = 15$

$15 \times 3 = 45$

Note that the same result will be achieved by reversing this process (i.e. multiplying by the numerator and dividing by the denominator). However, this is more abstract again as this process doesn't fit with the narrative when solving a problem such as finding three quarters of £60 because the 60 represents the whole. It makes no sense to multiply the whole amount of money by three to get £180 then dividing by four to get £45 because at no point in the problem would there actually be £180.

- Draw various bar models to represent examples of finding a fraction of a value. For example:
    - Two thirds of 32
    - Three fifths of 45
    - Seven eighths of 160
    - Etc.
- Challenge pupils to make up problems for each of the bars and solve both visually and using the abstract calculation.

Unit 5.8 Sharing one whole

- Organise pupils into groups of two, three, four, five, six, etc. and provide them with paper strips.

  Challenge them to make equal shares for everyone in their group, i.e. each person in the group of three has to make thirds to be shared with their partners (it may help to provide different colours for each pupil in one group so that their attempts can be easily identified).

  Ask questions, such as: **What fractions have you made? How many *thirds* make one whole?**

- Demonstrate the following activity with a pupil (you will need fraction cards or strips and two pieces of paper / card):
  - Ask pupil to close their eyes
  - Select a set of fraction cards, e.g. sixths:

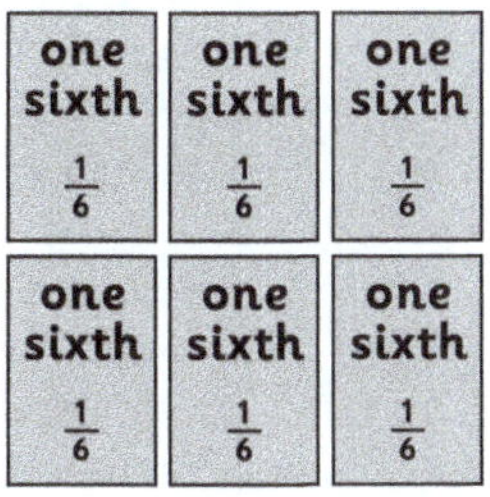

  - Hide some of the cards and display the remainder:

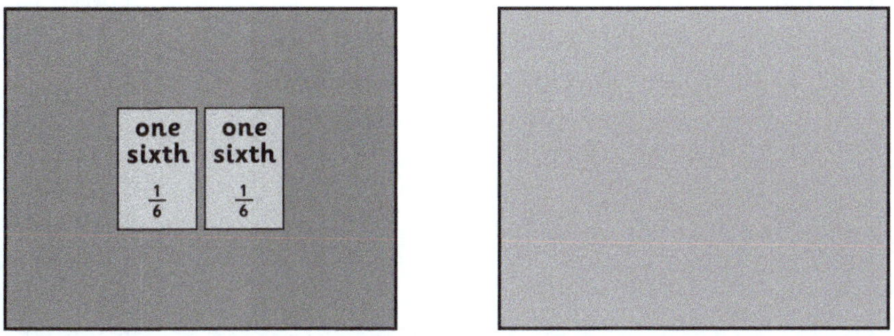

  - Challenge the pupil to work out what you have hidden (this could be differentiated by turning the cards over so that the pupil has to work out what cards have been selected in the first place).
- Organise pupils into pairs and provide them with fraction cards (enough of each fraction to make one whole with each set, i.e. four quarters, etc.) and two pieces of paper / card.

  Instruct pupils to take turns to work out the hidden fraction (selecting different fraction cards each time).

  Challenge pupils to make one whole using two or more different fractions (see the activity outlined in Unit 5.2). For example:

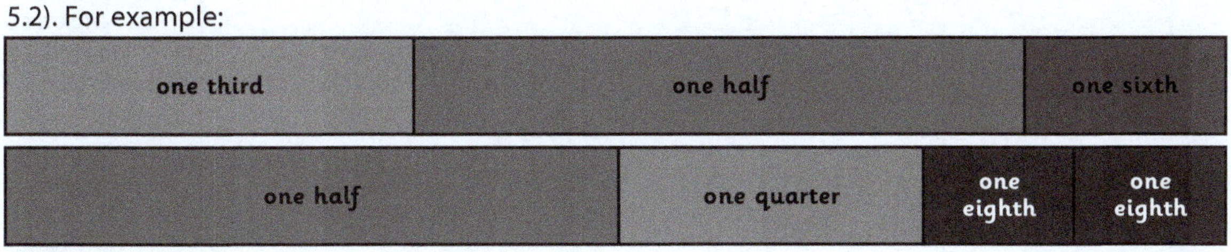

  Repeat the demonstration and pupil activity above, only this time using combinations of fractions that make one whole, for example:

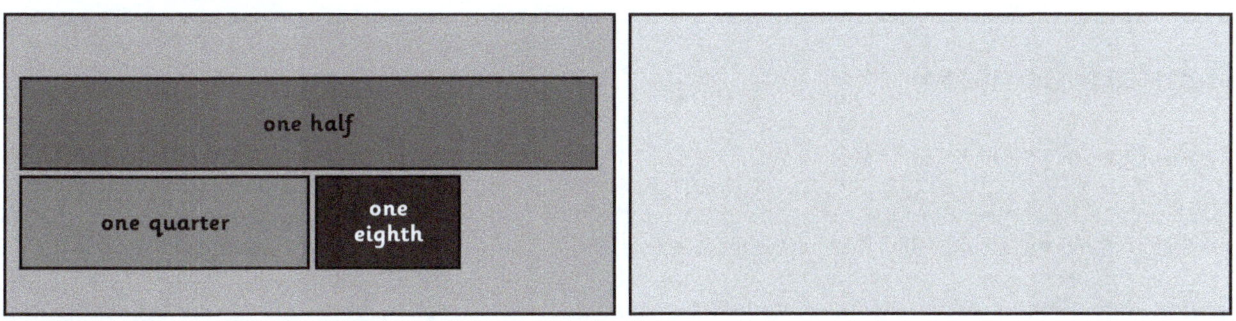

Money 1A

Section overview

Textbook 1A units	Review units	Prior learning	Benchmarks/ Es&Os
Unit 6.1 Making amounts	**1A** Unit 1.1 Units 2.2, 2.4, 2.5, 2.9, 2.10, 2.11 and 2.12	• I can identify coins up to 20p. • I can add and subtract within 20. • I can pay for items up to 10p with the exact amount.	**MNU 1-09b** • Identifies and uses all coins and notes to £20 and explores different ways of making the same total.
Unit 6.2 Adding amounts	**1A** Units 3.1 to 3.6	• I can identify coins up to 20p. • I can add and subtract within 20. • I can pay for items up to 10p with the exact amount.	**MNU 1-09a** **MNU 1-09b** • Identifies and uses all coins and notes to £20 and explores different ways of making the same total. • Uses a variety of coin and note combinations to pay for items and give change within £10.
Unit 6.3 Calculating change	**1A** Units 3.7 to 3.15	• I can identify coins up to 20p. • I can add and subtract within 20. • I can pay for items up to 10p with the exact amount.	**MNU 1-09a** **MNU 1-09b** • Identifies and uses all coins and notes to £20 and explores different ways of making the same total. • Uses a variety of coin and note combinations to pay for items and give change within £10.

Conceptual context

Financial education in schools is the best way to help pupils to build their knowledge and understand how to manage their personal finances later in life. The first part of this is being able to recognise coins and notes and to apply what is already known about calculation in the context of money. The idea of 'part and whole' is key to enabling pupils to understand how to calculate total costs and change; this being a skill first met when pupils explore number bonds within 10 and 20.

As well as providing a basis for future learning, early financial education can also be of benefit to primary school pupils in the shorter term. Young people are encountering money earlier and earlier in life; for example, when they have their first mobile phone or perhaps use an adult's debit card to purchase items online.

Although the trend is towards an increasingly cashless society, the proliferation of new technology allows children access to money in many ways and they need to be financially aware and understand the value of our currency. It is an important life skill to be able to budget effectively and personal finance learning needs to start from an early age. This is essential in ensuring that children can build up their money knowledge and skills as they progress through school.

Pupils need to understand the 'many-to-one' correspondence as each coin has a different value based on the number of pennies it is worth. For young pupils, used to counting on 'ones', the challenge is to see that one coin can be worth 'two' or 'five' or 'ten'. For this reason, the skills of skip counting and the links to early multiplication facts are important when learning about the value of coins.

When pupils are working with coins and notes, place value understanding is very important. The context of money is often the first place that pupils begin to calculate with numbers to 2 decimal places. Using the equivalence fact 'for every £1, there are 100 pennies' is only possible if pupils are fluent with multiplication and division by 100 and understand how multiples of 10 relate to our base 10 number system.

Resources

- Bronze and silver crayons for coin rubbing
- Cards with different amounts of money written on them for pupils to make up using coins
- Counting objects (such as counters) to help with adding three sums together initially
- Number lines (0–20)
- Plastic coins to aid with calculation and comparing
- Real-life coins as examples so that pupils can feel them and see the difference
- Real-life purse and wallet
- Role-play shop (so that pupils can buy items and work out change)
- Small items such as toys with price tags attached

Key vocabulary

- **Amount**
- **Coin**
- **Exact (money)**
- **Highest**
- **Least**
- **Less than**
- **Lowest**
- **Money**
- **More than**
- **Most**
- **Pence (p)**
- **Penny (p)**
- **Total**
- **Value (of a coin)**

Misconceptions

Potential misconception	Addressing the misconception
Units 6.1, 6.2 and 6.3 Pupils may see each coin as worth 'one'.	Show lots of pennies and compare with the 2p, 5p, 10p and 20p. Model how one item can be worth more using base ten materials and number rods (where one rod can be worth 10). Make up different amounts of money (2p, 5p, 10p and 20p) by counting out pennies, then exchange for the other coins. Revisit Textbook 1A, Unit 2.2 for counting in tens and using one jump on a number line to count for ten.

Potential misconception	Addressing the misconception
Units 6.1, 6.2 and 6.3 Pupils may think that the addition of three amounts of money must be done 'in order'.	Revisit Textbook 1A, Units 3.13–3.15 to consolidate addition in contexts.
Unit 6.3 Pupils may think that counting-on when giving change is addition and not subtraction.	Show pupils bar models to emphasise the part–whole relationships within 20. We can count on from one part to find the other part. Show how the same answer is obtained when counting back and discuss when it is easier to count-on (when the subtrahend and the minuend are far apart, i.e. a large difference) and when it is easier to count-back (when the difference is small).

Teaching ideas

Unit 6.1 Making amounts

- Show pupils real-life 1p, 2p, 5p, 10p and 20p coins. If appropriate, let pupils handle real coins so that they can feel the difference in weight.

  Ask: **What are we looking at today?** *Coins, money* **What is the same and what is different about the coins we are looking at?** Pupils discuss and explain the difference in size, colour and (possibly) value. They might notice that some are 'brown' and some are 'silver'.

  Explain that the silver ones have a higher value and show the different values of the coins.

  Ask pupils to draw around the coins and name their value.

  Ask pupils to do some 'coin rubbing' by placing each coin under a piece of paper and colouring over the paper with a crayon (this can be done with a bronze or silver crayon if available).

  Explain that different combinations of coins can be used to make different amounts of money.

  Model making up different amounts of money (within 20p) by counting out pennies, then exchange for the other coins.

  Discuss the different ways that you could make 10p using coins.

  Can you think of a way to use 10 coins, 2 coins, 1 coin, 5 coins that are all the same? *10 × 1p coins, 2 × 5p coins, 1 × 10p coin, 5 × 2p coins.* **Can you think of a way to use 4 coins, with some being different?** *5p, 2p, 2p, 1p.* Give pupils plastic coins and cards with different amounts written on them. The pupils can then explore how to make the amounts on the cards. As the pupils are making the amounts, ask: **Can you make that amount a different way?**

  Ask pupils to record what they have found in their jotters and discuss drawing around the coins and writing the value in 'p'. Pupils should record their work as a picture, by drawing around the coins, and as a number sentence showing pence. For example: 2p + 2p + 1p = 5p

  Give pupils a 0–20 number line and ask them to show how they worked out their amounts of coins using counting-on.

- Show a bar model for 10p as the whole and ask pupils to suggest different parts, e.g.

10p			
5p	1p	2p	2p

(the coins could be drawn in if necessary)
Show this as jumps on a number line, counting on from 5p.

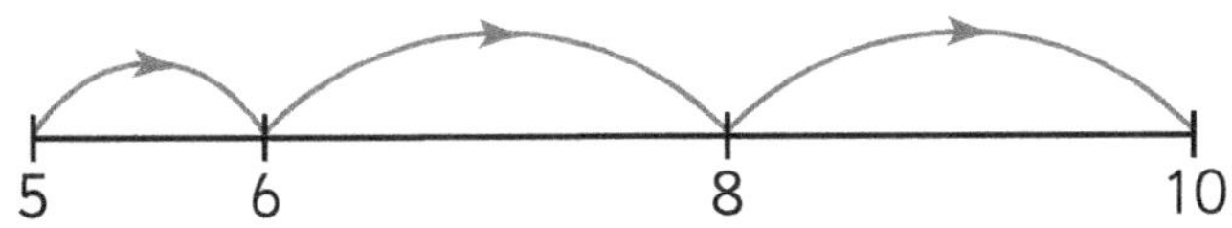

- Show the pupils some small items with prices attached, such as toys or food items from a role-play shop. Ask pupils to find different ways to pay the shopkeeper.
- Put some money (up to 20p) in a purse or wallet. Tell the pupils how much in total is in the purse and ask which coins might be inside.

Unit 6.2 Adding amounts

- Review number bonds to 20 and show as different bar models (0 + 20, 1 + 19 and so on). This will show pupils that addition is commutative and will help when choosing how to add more than two sums together.
- Ask pupils how they might add three numbers together using counting objects. Give pupils 20 counters and ask them to put into three groups of any size. Pupils count and record how many there are in each pile. Model how to record a calculation, agreeing that there are 20 counters in total, e.g. 3 + 7 + 10 = 20. Pupils should then record some different ways that they can get a total of 20 using three amounts and agree that they can do this in any order and still have 20 counters, e.g. 4 + 5 + 11 is the same as 5 + 11 + 4.
- Show pupils three small items with prices attached, such as toys or food items from a role-play shop. Ask pupils how much they will need to pay in total. Model counting-on on a number line as one strategy for adding three numbers. Notice that the number of jumps is the same as the number of sums of money to be added.
- Revise the language of 'most, 'least', 'fewest', etc. Show pupils a card with 18p written on it. Ask them to find ways to make 18p using the fewest number of coins (10p, 5p, 2p, 1p) and the largest number of coins (18 pennies). Discuss strategies for finding the fewest by finding the largest possible value coin first, then the next largest and so on. Notice that the greatest number of coins will always be pennies.

Unit 6.3 Calculating change

- Review number bonds to 20 and show as different bar models (20–0, 20–1 and so on). Use the same bar models as used for the addition section (Unit 6.2) and ensure that pupils can see the part–whole relationship. This will help to consolidate the understanding that addition and subtraction are inverses of each other and help pupils see why you can count-on to work out change (because this is counter-intuitive and we often teach pupils to count-back for early subtraction).
- Show pupils a small item with a price attached (say, 3p) and look in the purse to discover that there is only a 10p coin in there. Ask pupils what we should do. Model counting-on on the number line to find the amount of change we should receive. Show 3 and 7 as parts of the whole 10 on a bar model. Discuss counting on in ones and show counting on in ones to the next multiple of 5 and then jumping 5, so 3 + 1 + 1 = 5 and then 5 + 5 = 10.
- Give pupils a 20p coin each (or picture card with 20p on) and then a range of cards with different prices written on. Ask them to use a number line and count on to find out how much change is needed.
- Challenge pupils to buy two or three items from the role-play shop (total under 20p) and work out how much change they will get from 20p. Ask them to record each step using a number line, a number sentence and a bar model, as appropriate.

Money 1B

Section overview

Textbook 1B units	Review units	Prior learning	Benchmarks/Es&Os
Unit 6.1 Making and recording amounts	**1A** Units 3.6, 3.7, 3.8 **1B** Units 2.1, 2.2, 2.3, 2.11, 3.1 and 3.3	• I can identify coins up to £2. • I can make amounts up to 20p using a range of coins, including finding the most efficient way to pay. • I can add up amounts within 20p. • I can calculate change within 20p.	**MNU 1-09b** • Identifies and uses all coins and notes to £20 and explores different ways of making the same total. • Records amounts accurately in different ways using the correct notation; for example, 149p = £1·49 and 7p = £0·07.
Unit 6.2 Adding amounts	**1B** Units 2.4 to 2.7, 2.9, 2.10 and 2.11 Units 3.5 to 3.10	• I can add and subtract within 100. • I can add amounts and give change up to 20p. • I can recognise coins and notes to £10. • I can find the most efficient coins to make an amount. • I know that amounts can be represented as pounds and pence, or as pence (£1 and 49p = £149p).	**MNU 1-09a** **MNU 1-09b** • Identifies and uses all coins and notes to £20 and explores different ways of making the same total. • Uses a variety of coin and note combinations to pay for items and give change within £10.
Unit 6.3 Calculating change	**1B** Units 2.8 to 2.11 Units 3.4, 3.7, 3.8, 3.11, 3.12 and 3.14	• I can add and subtract within 100 • I can add amounts and give change up to 20p. • I can recognise coins and notes to £10. • I can find the most efficient coins to make an amount. • I know that amounts can be represented as pounds and pence, or as pence (£1 and 49p = £149p).	**MNU 1-09a** **MNU 1-09b** • Identifies and uses all coins and notes to £20 and explores different ways of making the same total. • Uses a variety of coin and note combinations to pay for items and give change within £10. • Applies mental agility number skills to calculate the total spent in a shopping situation and is able to calculate change.

Conceptual context

Financial education in schools is the best way to help pupils build their knowledge and to understand how to manage their personal finances later in life. The first part of this is being able to recognise coins and notes and to apply what is already known about calculation in the context of money. The idea of 'part and whole' is key to enabling pupils to understand how to calculate total costs and change; this being a skill first met when pupils explore number bonds within 10, 20 and 100.

As well as providing a basis for future learning, early financial education can also be of benefit to primary school pupils in the shorter term. Young people are encountering money earlier and earlier in life; for example, when they have their first mobile phone or perhaps use an adult's debit card to purchase items online.

Although the trend is towards an increasingly cashless society, the proliferation of new technology allows children access to money in many ways and they need to be financially aware and understand the value of our currency. It is an important life skill to be able to budget effectively and personal finance learning needs to start from an early age. This is essential in ensuring that children can build up their money knowledge and skills as they progress through school.

Pupils need to understand the 'many-to-one' correspondence as each coin and note has a different value based on the number of pennies it is worth. For young pupils, used to counting on 'ones', the challenge is to see that one coin can be worth 'two' or 'five' or 'ten'. For this reason, the skills of skip counting and the links to early multiplication facts are important when learning about the value of notes and coins.

When pupils are working with coins and notes, place value understanding is very important. The context of money is often the first place that pupils begin to calculate with numbers to two decimal places. Using the equivalence fact 'for every £1, there are 100 pennies' is only possible if pupils are fluent with multiplication and division by 100 and understand how multiples of 10 relate to our base 10 number system.

Resources

- 100 square showing pennies in each cell (100p = £1) laminated so that pupils can write on them.
- Number lines (0–100 in 10s, 0–200 in 10s, and 0–1000 in 100s)
- Plastic coins and notes to aid with calculation and comparing
- Real-life coins and notes as examples so that pupils can feel them and see the difference
- Real-life purse and wallet
- Role-play shop such as a café or pet shop with items priced
- Small items such as toys with price tags attached

Key vocabulary

- **Amount**
- **Change**
- **Coin**
- **Cost**
- **Count on**
- **Exact (money)**
- **Highest**
- **Least**
- **Less than**
- **Lowest**
- **Money**
- **More than**
- **Most**
- **Penny (p)**
- **Pence (p)**
- **Pound (£)**
- **Total**
- **Value (of a coin)**

Misconceptions

Potential misconception	Addressing the misconception
Units 6.1, 6.2 and 6.3 Pupils may confuse £1 and 1p, as they are both worth 'one'.	Show pupils the two coins and ask them to notice what is the same and what is different. Ask pupils to collect 100 pennies and exchange for £1.
Units 6.1, 6.2 and 6.3 Pupils may think that a £5 note is not worth as much as a £1 coin or a £2 coin due to the weight and look of the coins.	Remind pupils that 100p is the same as £1 and use the 100 squares with pennies on to make the £5 note and the £2 coin to show that the note is worth more.

Teaching ideas

Unit 6.1 Making and recording amounts

- Review comparison language (smallest, least, most, largest) and ask pupils to make 15p using the least amount of coins and the most amount of coins possible. Discuss strategies for finding the least by finding the largest possible value coin first, then the next largest and so on. Notice that the greatest number of coins will always be pennies.
- Revisit number bonds to 100 (Textbook 1A, Units 2.5 and 2.9). Show a 100 square and ask pupils to put one penny in every square. When this is full, explain that this is equivalent to one pound (£1) or two 50ps. Make sure all pupils know that 50 + 50 = 100. Ask pupils how many pennies would be needed for two 100 squares and agree that £2 is the same as 200p. Show this as a practical resource.

  Remove 10 pennies from one of the 100 squares and ask how much money is left. Agree 190p and this is the same as £1·90. Introduce how to record money in pounds and pence.
- Give pupils two laminated 100 squares showing 100 pennies and some cards showing different amounts of money between £1 and £2. Ask pupils to cross off the pennies not needed and write down the money in £ and p and in pennies (such as £1·37 = 137p).
- Introduce amounts greater than £2 and use the 100 squares if required. Show the pupils a card saying £5·60 and ask how we can make this using the least amount of coins. Remind pupils of the strategy of finding the largest possible value coin first, then the next largest and so on. Ask them if they would like to find the most amount of coins and agree that this would be 560 pennies, too many to count out.
- Show money on bar models as pennies and as £ and p so that pupils can see how to partition amounts and see the parts and the whole. For example, £5·60 can be shown as £1 + £1 + £1 + £1 + £1 + 50p + 10p. Introduce the £2 coin and show the same bar model with £2 + £2 + £1 + 50p + 10p.

  Agree that this is still the same as 560 pennies.

  Introduce the £5 note and discuss why this is not a coin. Explain that there is a £5 coin but it is very large, because of its large value and would be difficult to store in your wallet or purse. It is mostly commemorative and is rarely seen in circulation. We use notes for larger sums of money.

Unit 6.2 Adding amounts

- Remind pupils about adding three amounts of money using a number line and showing on a bar model.
  For example: Show a bar model for 16p as the whole and ask pupils to suggest different parts, e.g.

16p		
10p	5p	1p

  (the coins could be drawn in if necessary)

  Show this as jumps on a number line, counting on from 10p.

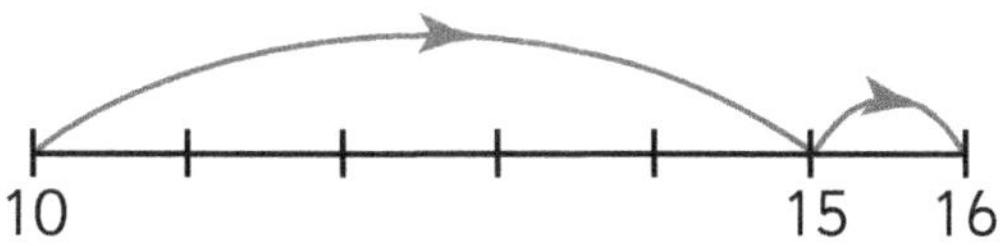

- Give the pupils a collection of coins and ask them to find out in pairs how much money there is in total. Share the different ways that pupils found their totals and agree that counting in ones is not helpful for large amounts. Counting-on on a number line can be useful but encourage pupils to think about larger jumps that equal the value of coins (so adding £1 is the same as a jump of 100).
- Give pupils two items, priced to a total in the range 2–50p and a card with 50p drawn on (or a 50p coin); for example, a ball for 34p and a pencil for 7p. Ask them to work out how much money will be left after buying the two items. Repeat with other combinations and discuss strategies for adding amounts of money and counting-on to find change. Repeat with items up to 75p.
- Give the pupils £1 and four priced items that sum to more than £1. Ask them, in pairs, if they have enough money. Then ask them which combinations of items can be afforded and how much money will be left over.

Unit 6.3 Calculating change

- Revisit subtraction strategies for two-digit and three-digit numbers (up to 200). Use strategies learned in Textbook 1A, Units 3.7, 3.8, 3.10 and 3.12. Model part–whole relationships on a bar model and link to partitioning into hundreds, tens and ones and partitioning in other ways. Revisit counting on and counting back. Discuss when each strategy and representation might be useful.
- Explain to pupils that it is best to count on when working out change. Show an example on a number line and ask a pupil to count out the coins as the teacher is jumping on the number line. For example, if the cost is 33p and we need change from 50p, we start at the price (33p) on the number line and then count out 2p (to the nearest 5p), then 5p (to the nearest 10p) and then the final 10p.

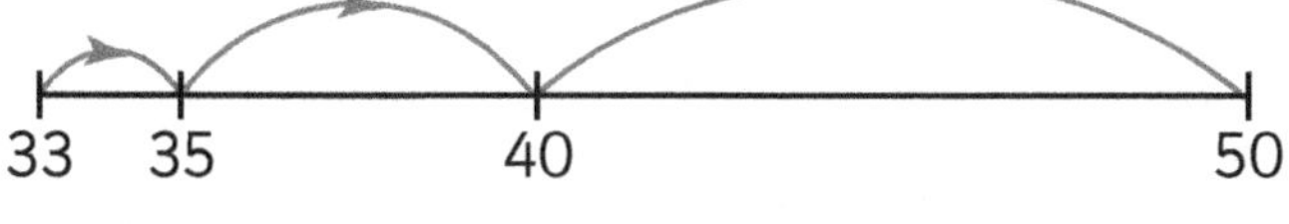

  Say **33, 35, 40, 50**. Ask pupils to count on to give change to 50p using different amounts of money (this could be on cards that pupils pick randomly) and ask them to show the jumps on the number line.
- Remind pupils that £1 is the same as 100p and £2 is the same as 200p. Repeat the above exercise with one cost. For example, if the cost is £1·72 and we need change from £2, we say '£1·72, £1·73, £1·75, £1·80, £2' whilst drawing jumps from 172 + 1, +2, +5, +20 to get to 200.
- Use the role-play shop or cards with different priced items on them. Ask the pupils to work in pairs to purchase two or three items and record on a number line how they count on to find the change.

Money 1C

Section overview

Textbook 1C units	Review units	Prior learning	Benchmarks/Es&Os
Unit 6.1 Recording amounts	**1B** Units 4.8 and 4.9 **1C** Units 2.1 to 2.8 Units 4.4 and 4.5	• I can identify amounts up to £10. • I can record amounts up to £10 using pence or £ and p. • I know that £ and p or pence are equivalent.	**MNU 1-09b** • Identifies and uses all coins and notes to £20 and explores different ways of making the same total. • Records amounts accurately in different ways using the correct notation; for example, 149p = £1·49 and 7p = £0·07.
Unit 6.2 Adding amounts	**1C** Units 3.1 to 3.4, 3.6, 3.10 and 3.12 Units 4.4 and 4.5	• I can add amounts up to £1. • I can find the most efficient coins to pay. • I can record amounts in £ and p or in decimal notation.	**MNU 1-09a** **MNU 1-09b** • Identifies and uses all coins and notes to £20 and explores different ways of making the same total. • Records amounts accurately in different ways using the correct notation; for example, 149p = £1·49 and 7p = £0·07. • Uses a variety of coin and note combinations to pay for items and give change within £10. • Demonstrates awareness of how goods can be paid for using cards and digital technology.
Unit 6.3 Calculating change	**1C** Units 3.1 to 3.4, 3.11 and 3.13 Units 4.4 and 4.5	• I can add and subtract within 1000. • I can add amounts and give change up to £1. • I can recognise coins and notes to £20. • I can find the most efficient coins to make an amount. • I know that amounts can be represented as pounds and pence or in digital notation.	**MNU 1-09a** **MNU 1-09b** • Identifies and uses all coins and notes to £20 and explores different ways of making the same total. • Records amounts accurately in different ways using the correct notation; for example, 149p = £1·49 and 7p = £0·07. • Uses a variety of coin and note combinations to pay for items and give change within £10. • Applies mental agility number skills to calculate the total spent in a shopping situation and is able to calculate change.

Conceptual context

Financial education in schools is the best way to help pupils build their knowledge and to understand how to manage their personal finances later in life. The first part of this is being able to recognise coins and notes and to apply what is already known about calculation in the context of money. The idea of 'part and whole' is key to enabling pupils to understand how to calculate total costs and change; this being a skill first met when pupils explore number bonds within 10, 20 and 100.

As well as providing a basis for future learning, early financial education can also be of benefit to primary school pupils in the shorter term. Young people are encountering money earlier and earlier in life. For example, when they have their first mobile phone or perhaps use an adult's debit card to purchase items online.

Although the trend is towards an increasingly cashless society, the proliferation of new technology allows children access to money in many ways and they need to be financially aware and understand the value of our currency. It is an important life skill to be able to budget effectively and personal finance learning needs to start from an early age. This is essential in ensuring that children can build up their money knowledge and skills as they progress through school.

Pupils need to understand the 'many-to-one' correspondence as each coin and note has a different value based on the number of pennies it is worth. For young pupils, used to counting on 'ones', the challenge is to see that one coin can be worth 'two' or 'five' or 'ten'. For this reason, the skills of skip counting and the links to early multiplication facts are important when learning about the value of notes and coins.

When pupils are working with coins and notes, place value understanding is very important. The context of money is often the first place that pupils begin to calculate with numbers to 2 decimal places. Using the equivalence fact 'for every £1, there are 100 pennies' is only possible if pupils are fluent with multiplication and division by 100 and understand how multiples of 10 relate to our base 10 number system.

Resources

- 100 square showing pennies in each cell (100p = £1)
- Cards to represent debit and gift cards for role play
- Cards with different monetary amounts on, including £.p and pence only
- Dual number line showing 0–100 (p) and 0–1 (£) so that pupils see that 67p = £0·67
- Number lines (0–100 in 10s, 0–200 in 10s, and 0–1000 in 100s)
- Place value chart for pounds and pence (i.e. hundreds, tens, ones, decimal point, tenths, hundredths). Label the left-hand side as £ and the right-hand side as 'p'.
- Plastic coins and notes to aid with calculation and comparing
- Real-life coins and notes as examples so that pupils can feel them and see the difference
- Real-life debit and gift cards to show pupils
- Real-life menus for well-known food outlets (or teacher-created versions)
- Real-life catalogues for well-known local retail shops (such as clothes shops, DIY stores, etc.)
- Real-life purse and wallet
- Small items such as stationery, with price tags attached

Key vocabulary

- **Amount**
- **Bank transfer**
- **Cash**
- **Change**
- **Checkout**
- **Coin**
- **Cost**
- **Count on**
- **Debit card**
- **Decimal (notation)**
- **Exact (money)**
- **Gift card (money)**
- **Highest**
- **Least**
- **Less than**
- **Lowest**
- **Money**
- **More than**
- **Most**
- **Penny (p)**
- **Pence (p)**
- **Pound (£)**
- **PayPal**
- **Total**
- **Value (of a coin)**

Misconceptions

Potential misconception	Addressing the misconception
Units 6.1, 6.2 and 6.3 Pupils may make incorrect use of decimal notation for amounts such as three pounds and five pence.	Ask pupils how many pennies is the same as three pounds and five pence. Agree that this is three hundred and five. Write '305'. Remind pupils that the pounds go before the decimal point and the pence go after, giving £3·05. Link this to 305 and agree that this is not the same as 350, so we cannot write £3·5 for 305 pence.
Units 6.1, 6.2 and 6.3 Pupils may make incorrect use of decimal notation for money greater than 100 pence.	If pupils record 750p as £0·750, remind pupils that the pounds go before the decimal point and the pence go after, giving £7·50 and not 75 pence. If necessary, make the amount of money using pound coins and smaller coins and use a place value chart to place the coins in columns.

Teaching ideas

Unit 6.1 Recording amounts

- Remind pupils about the different denominations of coins and notes and ensure that all pupils know that £1 is the same as 100 pence.
- Count up and back in 100s from any number, integer and decimal.
- Choose any number on the number line and ask pupils to identify 100 more and 100 less.
- Ask pupils to make different amounts of £ and pence using the least number of notes and coins, reminding them of the strategy of starting with the largest denomination. For example, £7·11: start with a £5 note, leaving £2·11. Then use a £2 coin, leaving 11 pence. Then select a 10p coin and a 1p coin. Ask pupils for the largest amount of coins or notes that can be used to make £7·11 and agree 711 pennies. Show £7·11 on a place value chart with £1 coins and then swap them for a £5 note and a £2 coin.
- Model how to record different amounts of money using decimal notation. Make sure that pupils know that 50p is always recorded as £0·50 and not £0·5, since this is different to normal decimal 'rules'. Draw pupils' attention to amounts such as £1 and 7p, ask them to say how many pennies this represents (they can use the pennies 100 square to remind them if necessary). Ensure all pupils can see that 107 pence is recorded as £1·07 and show this on a dual number line (see resources list).

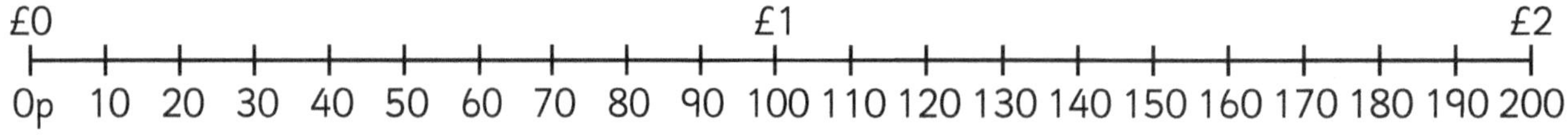

Give pupils a 'place value for money' chart and some different amounts of money in both £.p and in pence only. Ask them to represent the amounts on the Money Place Value chart and then to order them from least value to highest value (and vice versa). Include some that are the same value. For example 605p, £6·50, 65p £5·60, 650p.

£			•	p	
Hundreds	Tens (£10 = 1000p)	Ones (£1 = 100p)	•	tenths	hundredths
			•		
			•		

Unit 6.2 Adding amounts

- Ask pupils to work out how many pennies are the same as £10. Show pupils a 0–1000 number line and ask them to add £3·54 to £4·20 by converting to pence and counting on (345 + 420). Label each multiple of 100 as £1. Pupils should now be using an 'empty' number line as the numbers increase.
- Show pupils different debit and gift cards. Use the role-play area or teacher-created gift cards to make purchases and work out how much is left on the card. Model a bank account with a starting balance and use the role-play area or teacher-created debit cards to make purchases and work out how much is left in the bank account.
- Explain that some people use services such as 'PayPal'. PayPal is a service that enables you to pay, send money, and accept payments quickly and easily without putting your card number in all the time when purchasing online.
- Give pupils a 'place value for money' chart and ask them to record (using coins) two amounts such as £3·42 and £1·33 (i.e. no carrying). Model adding £3·42 to £1·33 and discuss how many pennies we have in total (75p) plus £4, so £4·75. If appropriate, model column addition with carrying as a 'greater depth' activity.
- Use an empty number line labelled zero to £5. Ask pupils to add two amounts that total less than £5 (say, £3·25 and £1·03) by counting-on in sensible jumps on the number line; discuss different strategies such as adding the pounds first or adding the pence first. Now ask pupils to add two amounts that total more than £5 (say, £3·25 and £3·80). Ask them how much more is needed if we have £5 on a gift card (or in a bank account). Model extending the number line and counting on to find the total, then counting-on from £5 to find how much is needed.
- Give pupils a gift card for a budget clothes shop with a limit, say £5, and a teacher-created list of items for sale. Ask them to decide what they can afford without going over £5. How much is left over?
- Give pupils a bank account with £10 as the starting balance. Give pupils a teacher-created price list of items in a gift shop. Ask pupils to decide what they could buy without going over £10. Remind them that they can buy the same thing more than once (so three pencils, for example). How much is left over?

Unit 6.3 Calculating change

- Review subtraction of three-digit numbers where the subtrahend is a multiple of 100. For example, 300 – 182. Discuss different strategies such as counting on or back on a number line, partitioning into 100 and 80 and 2, thinking about 300 is the whole and 182 is one part. Remind pupils that when calculating change, we usually count on.

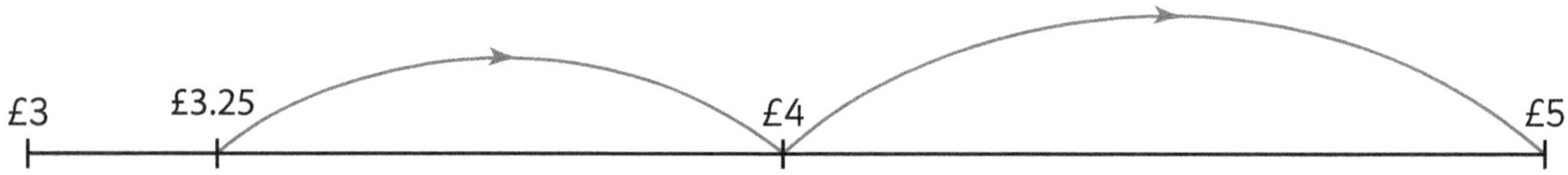

- Model using the empty number line to count on to find change. For example, if I spend £3·25 and I pay with a £5 note, the number line will start at £3·25, then a jump of +75p, then a jump of +£1 to get to £5. This gives me change of £1·75. Ask pupils to use the empty number line to find different amounts of change from £5 using counting on. Discuss differently sized jumps that pupils choose and agree which ones work well and which are inefficient. For example, we don't want to count up in 10ps if I spend 35p and pay with a £5 note, but pupils will need to see this modelled to recognise how long it takes.
- Introduce the £10 note and the £20 note. Give pupils cards with different amounts on to spend and ask them to use the empty number line and counting on to work out change from £10 and £20.
- Give pupils a real-life restaurant menu, or a catalogue for a well-known store such as a DIY, clothing or homeware store. Give them a budget of £20 and ask them to buy three items so that they spend less than £20. Ask pupils to calculate the change they will receive. Ask pupils to get as close as possible to £20 without going over. Ask pupils to spend more than £20 and then calculate how much more money they need to pay for their items.
- Use the role-play area to practise purchasing items and giving change to £20.
- Ask pupils to plan a day out to an attraction or film near them with a given budget of £50. Increase the budget so that they can take a friend and ask pupils to calculate total cost and money left over.
- Go online to a well-known supermarket and ask pupils to purchase food for a birthday party for 8 people. Give them a budget, say £50, and ask for total cost and amount of change.
- Make cakes for a charity cake sale. Pupils sell the cakes during break-time and record each sale with total cost of each purchase and change given. They will need a small float to allow them to give change, so should be able to pay back the float before giving the charity any proceeds!

Time 1A

Section overview

Textbook 1A units	Review units	Prior learning	Benchmarks/Es&Os
Unit 7.1 Days of the week	**Early – B** Unit 6.1	• I know how many days are in a week. • I can name and order the days of the week. • I can use appropriate vocabulary to sequence and order time – before, after.	**MNU 1-10b** • Orders the months of the year and relates these to the appropriate seasons.
Unit 7.2 Measuring time	**Early – B** Units 6.3 to 6.6	• I know that some activities take more time than others. • I can use appropriate time vocabulary to sequence events – morning, afternoon, evening… • I can recognise simple timing devices – clock, stopwatch and sand timer. • I understand that time can be measured and recognise basic units of time – seconds, minutes and hours.	**MNU 1-10a** **MNU 1-10b** **MNU 1-10c** • Tells the time using half past, quarter past and quarter to using analogue and digital 12-hour clocks. • Records 12-hour times using am and pm and is able to identify 24-hour notation; for example, on a mobile phone or computer. • Records the date in a variety of ways, using words and numbers. • Uses and interprets a variety of calendars and 12-hour timetables to plan key events. • Knows the number of seconds in a minute, minutes in an hour, hours in a day, days in each month, weeks and days in a year. • Orders the months of the year and relates these to the appropriate seasons. • Selects and uses appropriate timers for specific purposes.

Unit 7.3 Read o'clock and half past	Early – B Units 6.3 to 6.6	• I can identify an analogue clock. • I can identify the minute hand and the hour hand. • I understand the terms o'clock and half past.	**MNU 1-10a** • Tells the time using half past, quarter past and quarter to using analogue and digital 12-hour clocks. • Records 12-hour times using am and pm and is able to identify 24-hour notation; for example, on a mobile phone or computer. • Records the date in a variety of ways, using words and numbers. • Uses and interprets a variety of calendars and 12-hour timetables to plan key events. • Knows the number of seconds in a minute, minutes in an hour, hours in a day, days in each month, weeks and days in a year. • Orders the months of the year and relates these to the appropriate seasons. • Selects and uses appropriate timers for specific purposes.
Unit 7.4 Change o'clock and half past from analogue to digital	**Early – B** Units 6.3 to 6.6	• I understand the terms o'clock and half past. • I recognise the difference between analogue and digital. • I know the difference between the hour hand and the minute hand.	**MNU 1-10a** **MNU 1-10b** • Tells the time using half past, quarter past and quarter to using analogue and digital 12-hour clocks. • Records 12-hour times using am and pm and is able to identify 24-hour notation; for example, on a mobile phone or computer. • Knows the number of seconds in a minute, minutes in an hour, hours in a day, days in each month, weeks and days in a year. • Orders the months of the year and relates these to the appropriate seasons. • Selects and uses appropriate timers for specific purposes.

Conceptual context

As pupils learn about time, they will explore:

1. Days, weeks, months – when things happen
2. The duration of an event – the passing of time
3. Telling the time

Before starting this chapter, pupils will know the days of the week, simple time durations and be able to make links to their everyday routine. They will also be starting to use a calendar and/or a timetable to track events and develop the concept of passing time by measuring the length of time it takes for familiar tasks. To help pupils grasp the concept of time, incorporate vocabulary like morning, noon, afternoon, evening and night times into your general discussion. Let the pupils know when activities occur during specific times of the day: 'you eat breakfast in the morning' or 'you go to bed at night', to assist in learning these periods of time.

As pupils develop their understanding of time they will start to learn about duration and telling the time informally through their interactions with other people both in and out of school. Pupils need to understand the concept of duration for time periods; once pupils have the necessary number skills, they can begin to tell the time using the hour. They should be exposed to and use a range of displays to show and record time to strengthen the links.

To develop the concept of duration, students can make water timers, use pendulums, or count 'the number of claps' as non-standard measurement of time. Once students can measure and talk about time through non-standard units of time, they are ready to learn to use standard units of time. At this point we can use vocabulary such as minute and hour. The pupils should also start to read the time from analogue and digital clocks. Again, opportunities to develop these concepts can come from the student's own experiences. They could be using different ways of measuring the length of the same events and need to agree on a format to become consistent in their measurements. There could be discussion about the accuracy and importance of measuring time, such as being on time to class.

It is likely that students will be able to read time to the nearest hour before understanding the concept of time units because of their early exposure to adult conversation and encouragement. Pupils should start to record their answers on their own clock faces (using concrete materials) by drawing clock faces, as digital time and written in words.

Once students can identify the hour with confidence, you can reinforce the concept of duration through timing activities. Pupils will have experience of various timing devices such as: analogue clocks, digital clocks, watches, sand timers, simple sun dials and stopwatches. Practical activities can be used to introduce the concept of speed with obvious links to Science, Health and Wellbeing and P.E.

Resources

- Analogue and digital clock faces (see Resource sheet 7G)
- Analogue clock faces (see Resource sheet 7E)
- Blank timetable (see Resource sheet 7C)
- Blue and red crayons/coloured pencils
- Clock face (see Resource sheet 7D)
- Days of the week cards (see Resource sheet 7A)
- Digital clock faces (see Resource sheet 7F)
- Individual whiteboards and whiteboard pens
- Paper fasteners – to attach hands onto the clock face
- Sand timers
- Scissors
- Stopwatches
- Subject post-its (see Resource sheet 7B)

Key vocabulary

- **Analogue**
- **Device**
- **Digital**
- **Durations**
- **Estimate**
- **Interval**
- **Least**
- **Most**
- **Quarter**
- **Timetable**

Misconceptions

Potential misconception	Addressing the misconception
Units 7.1, 7.2, 7.3 and 7.4 Pupils might confuse the minute hand and the hour hand.	Using an analogue clock, ensure that pupils are aware that the short hand points to the hour and the longer hand points to the minute.
Units 7.1, 7.2, 7.3 and 7.4 Pupils might not be confident about the direction that the clock hands rotate around the clock face.	Using an analogue clock, explain that the hands move in a clockwise direction, which means that they move towards the left-hand side, down and around the face of the clock.
Units 7.1, 7.2, 7.3 and 7.4 Pupils may think that time can only be measured using a clock and in seconds, minutes and hours.	Through questioning and quality discussion, ensure that pupils are familiar with the many different **instruments of measure** that are used: clock, watch, stopwatch, sundial, calendar, diary, etc. Also, ensure that pupils are familiar with the different **units of measure** that are used: milliseconds, seconds, minutes, hours, days, weeks, years, decades, etc.

Teaching ideas

Unit 7.1 Days of the week

- Ask pupils to name the days of the week.
- Ask pupils to tell you what day it is today – how do they know?
- Ask pupils what day it will be tomorrow – how do they know?
- You can continue with this discussion until you are confident pupils have an understanding of the days of the week and their relationship to one another.
- Put pupils into pairs and give each pair the days of the week cards (Resource sheet 7A).
- Ask them to order the days of the week (this could be from the current day or from Sunday depending on their understanding), hold up the day before Tuesday, the day after Saturday…
- Give pupils Resource sheet 7B and ask them to put them into an order. Once they have ordered their post-its, ask them to explain why they have placed them in the way they have…

  What is *first* – why?

  What do you have *next* – can you explain this?

  What do you have *after* break/lunch?
- Once you have established that pupils have an idea of how their day is structured, give them a copy of Resource sheet 7C – blank timetable, and ask them to fill in what they will be doing today.
- Depending on their understanding, you can ask pupils to complete the rest of the timetable.

Unit 7.2 Measuring time

- Ask pupils to explain what they think 'estimate' means and discuss their understanding.
- Now, ask pupils to give you examples of units of time they might use to measure an activity.
- Record their answers on the board –

  Minutes

  Hours

  Seconds

  Days

  Weeks

  Depending on the order pupils give you these in, you could then ask them to order them from smallest to largest unit.
- For each of the appropriate units of time you get from the pupils, ask them to give you an example of an activity that they would be able to measure with it and note them on the board against the appropriate unit.
- Use questioning to establish their understanding. **Why would you use this unit of time and not __________? How many minutes/hours do you think this activity would take? Is there any other unit of time that would be more appropriate?**
- Next, ask pupils if they can give you examples of timing devices that they would use for the units of time they have already given you.
- As above, use questioning to explore their understanding: **Why would you use this device? How does this device measure time? Is there any other device that would be more appropriate? Why?**

Unit 7.3 Read o'clock and half past

- Give each pupil a copy of the Clock Face Resource sheet 7D and ask them to cut out the the face and the two hands at the bottom.
- Ask pupils: **Why are there two hands? What do you notice about the two hands? Which hand is for minutes and which is for the hour?**
- Get pupils to colour the hour hand in blue and the minute hand red.
- Give pupils each a paper fastener and help them to attach their hands to the clock face.
- Ask pupils if they know how to show *o'clock* on their clock face. Discuss which hand they would use and where it would be pointing.
- Ask them to show you a variety of *o'clock* times to establish their understanding.
- Ask pupils if they know how to show *half past* on their clock face. Discuss which hand they would use and where it would be pointing.
- Ask them to show you a variety of *half past* times to establish their understanding.

Unit 7.4 Change o'clock and half past to analogue and digital

- Ask pupils if they know the difference between an analogue clock and a digital clock. **What are the differences? How do you know? Do they both show the same time? How do you know?**
- Show pupils a picture of a digital clock or an actual digital clock showing an o'clock time and ask them what they see. Ask them if they can tell you what digits tell us that it is *o'clock*, encourage them to identify the two zeroes on the right-hand side as representing the minutes and therefore the *o'clock* time.
- Now, show pupils a picture of a digital clock showing a half past time and ask them what they see.
- Ask them if they can tell you what digits tell us that it is o'clock, encourage them to identify the *'30'* on the right-hand side as representing the minutes and therefore the half past time.
- Use the blank analogue and digital clock faces on the resources sheets to allow pupils to practise recording both o'clock and half past times in digital and analogue.

Time 1B

Section overview

Textbook 1B units	Review units	Prior learning	Benchmarks/Es&Os
Unit 7.1 Time word problems	**1A** Units 7.1, 7.2, 7.3 and 7.4	• I know basic time facts including days of the week and months of the year. • I can recognise different ways to record and measure time. • I can use appropriate vocabulary to sequence and order time – before, during, after, etc.	**MNU 1-10a** **MNU 1-10b** **MNU 1-10c** • Tells the time using half past, quarter past and quarter to using analogue and digital 12-hour clocks. • Records 12-hour times using am and pm and is able to identify 24-hour notation; for example, on a mobile phone or computer. • Records the date in a variety of ways, using words and numbers. • Uses and interprets a variety of calendars and 12-hour timetables to plan key events. • Knows the number of seconds in a minute, minutes in an hour, hours in a day, days in each month, weeks and days in a year. • Orders the months of the year and relates these to the appropriate seasons. • Selects and uses appropriate timers for specific purposes.
Unit 7.2 Finding durations	**1A** Unit 7.2	• I know basic time facts including days or the week and months of the year. • I can recognise basic units of time – hours, minutes. • I can use appropriate vocabulary to sequence and order time – before, after, etc.	**MNU 1-10c** • Tells the time using half past, quarter past and quarter to using analogue and digital 12-hour clocks. • Records the date in a variety of ways, using words and numbers. • Uses and interprets a variety of calendars and 12-hour timetables to plan key events. • Knows the number of seconds in a minute, minutes in an hour, hours in a day, days in each month, weeks and days in a year. • Orders the months of the year and relates these to the appropriate seasons. • Selects and uses appropriate timers for specific purposes.

Unit 7.3 Recording time	**1A** Units 7.2 and 7.3	• I understand simple time durations. • I can recognise different ways of recording time. • I can use appropriate vocabulary to discuss periods of time.	**MNU 1-10a** **MNU 1-10b** **MNU 1-10c** • Records 12-hour times using am and pm and is able to identify 24-hour notation; for example, on a mobile phone or computer. • Records the date in a variety of ways, using words and numbers. • Knows the number of seconds in a minute, minutes in an hour, hours in a day, days in each month, weeks and days in a year. • Selects and uses appropriate timers for specific purposes.
Unit 7.4 Telling the time	**1A** Units 7.1, 7.2, 7.3 and 7.4	• I can read o'clock on analogue and digital clocks. • I can recognise half past on analogue and digital clocks. • I can recognise basic time vocabulary – o'clock, half past, analogue and digital.	**MNU 1-10a** **MNU 1-10b** **MNU 1-10c** • Tells the time using half past, quarter past and quarter to using analogue and digital 12-hour clocks. • Records 12-hour times using am and pm and is able to identify 24-hour notation; for example, on a mobile phone or computer. • Records the date in a variety of ways, using words and numbers. • Uses and interprets a variety of calendars and 12-hour timetables to plan key events. • Knows the number of seconds in a minute, minutes in an hour, hours in a day, days in each month, weeks and days in a year. • Orders the months of the year and relates these to the appropriate seasons. • Selects and uses appropriate timers for specific purposes.

Unit 7.5 Five-minute intervals	**1A** Units 7.3 and 7.4	• I can read o'clock, half past and quarter to on analogue and digital clocks. • I can recognise basic time vocabulary – o'clock, half past, analogue, digital, quarter past and quarter to. • I understand that time is based on jumps of 5 minutes.	**MNU 1-10a** **MNU 1-10b** **MNU 1-10c** • Tells the time using half past, quarter past and quarter to using analogue and digital 12-hour clocks. • Records 12-hour times using am and pm and is able to identify 24-hour notation; for example, on a mobile phone or computer. • Records the date in a variety of ways, using words and numbers. • Uses and interprets a variety of calendars and 12-hour timetables to plan key events. • Knows the number of seconds in a minute, minutes in an hour, hours in a day, days in each month, weeks and days in a year. • Orders the months of the year and relates these to the appropriate seasons. • Selects and uses appropriate timers for specific purposes.

Conceptual context

This section will continue to develop pupils' knowledge of the concept of time by exploring duration, telling the time and speed/distance/time calculations. To support this, reinforce vocabulary like morning, noon, afternoon, evening, and night times into your general discussion. Let the pupils know when activities occur during specific times of the day: 'you come to school in the morning' or 'you go to bed at night', to assist in learning these periods of time. Discuss the difference between *recorded time*, which is the time at which an event takes place and *time intervals*, which is the length of time an activity lasts for and is measured in units. When using an analogue clock, make it clear that the hands go around the face twice in one day and allow time to discuss the different types of watches and clocks that pupils may use.

Ensure that pupils know that, unlike other areas of measurement, time is not metric and the units of measure are different (60 seconds in a minute, 60 minutes in an hour, 24 hours in 1 day), which can make calculating time intervals using subtraction tricky. Encourage dialogue with pupils about the different instruments that can be used to measure time, including some less conventional methods. This will highlight the depth of understanding pupils have about the concept of time.

When reading and writing times, use a variety of terms to reinforce the relationships for pupils, e.g. 15 minutes past 3, quarter past 3, three fifteen, to ensure they recognise that it is the same time. Encourage pupils to name and correctly use different instruments of measure to calculate time so they are exposed to as many different experiences as possible.

Resources

- Analogue and digital clock faces (see Resource sheet 7G)
- Analogue clock faces (see Resource sheet 7E)
- Blank timetable (see Resource sheet 7C)
- Blue and red crayons/coloured pencils
- Clock face (see Resource sheet 7D)
- Days of the week cards (see Resource sheet 7A)
- Digital clock faces (see Resource sheet 7F)
- Individual whiteboards and whiteboard pens
- Paper fasteners – to attach hands onto the clock face
- Sand timers
- Scissors
- Stopwatches
- Subject post-its (see Resource sheet 7B)

Key vocabulary

- **Analogue**
- **Device**
- **Digital**
- **Durations**
- **Estimate**
- **Interval**
- **Least**
- **Most**
- **Quarter**
- **Timetable**

Misconceptions

Potential misconception	Addressing the misconception
Units 7.1, 7.2, 7.3 and 7.4 Pupils might confuse the minute hand and the hour hand.	Using an analogue clock, ensure that pupils are aware that the short hand points to the hour and the longer hand points to the minute.
Units 7.1, 7.2, 7.3 and 7.4 Pupils might not be confident about the direction that the clock hands rotate around the clock face.	Using an analogue clock, explain that the hands move in a clockwise direction, which means that they move towards the left-hand side, down and around the face of the clock.
Units 7.1, 7.2, 7.3 and 7.4 Pupils may think that time can only be measured using a clock and in seconds, minutes and hours.	Through questioning and quality discussion, ensure that pupils are familiar with the many different **instruments of measure** that are used: clock, watch, stopwatch, sundial, calendar, diary, clapping hands, sand timer… Also, ensure that pupils are familiar with the different **units of measure** that are used: milliseconds, seconds, minutes, hours, days, weeks, years, decades, etc.

Teaching ideas

Unit 7.1 Time word problems

- Give pupils an A3 piece of paper and in groups of 3 or 4 ask them to generate as many time facts as they can. Explain that there are no right or wrong answers at this stage, we are just gathering information about what we already 'think' about time.
- Allow pupils to share their thinking with each other either by carousel learning, moving the paper around the groups or by giving each group the opportunity to stand and share their ideas with the rest of the class.
- Pick out examples from all groups that you can use to build a fact file on the board:

  60 seconds = 1 minute

  60 minutes = 1 hour

  24 hours = 1 day

  7 days = 1 week

  12 months = 1 year
- Ask pupils to turn to their shoulder partner and find out when they were born. Now, ask them to use this information to tell you who from each pair is the oldest. How do they know this? What information have they used to work this out? You are looking for them to mention the date or month they were born and the difference between these two dates – they don't need to be accurate to the days but display an understanding of the difference in time and the implications this will have on the age of each pupil.
- Write the following question on the board: Isla has two brothers. They are 24 months younger than her. If she is 9, what age are they?
- Ask them to write their answer on a whiteboard. Encourage them to use the time facts that you have already recorded on the board: 12 months = 1 year.
- Discuss with pupils their answers and ask them to explain how they worked it out.

Unit 7.2 Finding durations

- Ask pupils to tell you what a duration of time is.
- Ask them to give you examples of time durations. Refer back to the time facts that you generated in the previous unit.
- Write the following questions on the board: 1 hour = ______________? 1 day = ______________? 60 minutes = ____________? 1 week = ______________?
- Ask pupils to fill in the missing information on their whiteboards, pointing out that they may have more than one answer for each.

  Some possible answers:

  1 hour = 60 minutes or $2 \times \frac{1}{2}$ hours

  1 day = 24 hours or 2×12 hours

  60 minutes = 1 hour

  1 week = 7 days or 168 hours
- Ask pupils to calculate how long they spend at school. This may vary depending on the structure of your school day, but you are looking for them to recognise if they start at 9am and finish at 3pm they will spend 6 hours at school each day. You can extend this by asking how long will this be per week that they spend at school?

Unit 7.3 Recording time

- Ask pupils how long they think it would take them to write their name ten times. How do they know this? How will they measure this? How will they record this?
- In pairs, get pupils to experiment with this using different types of measure: sand timer, clapping, stopwatch, etc.

Unit 7.4 Telling the time

- Draw a circle on the board to represent the clock face and write in the numbers 1 to 12 in the appropriate places. Ask pupils where the minute hand would point to for o'clock and write this in above the twelve. Ask pupils where the minute hand would point to for half past and write this in under the six.
- Now ask pupils if they know why it is called 'half past'. What is half? Half of what?
- Discuss with pupils the fact that there are 60 minutes in an hour and half past is half of that hour, which is half of 60, which is 30 minutes past. Show this in digital form to highlight the connection.
- Ask pupils if they know any other fractions that relate to time. Discuss the fact that quarter of an hour is 60 minutes divided into 4 equal parts. Ask pupils to tell you if they know what 60 divided by 4 would be.
- Draw a line down the middle of the clock face you have on the board to show the 2 halves.
- Now draw a line across the middle of the clock face to split into four equal sections.

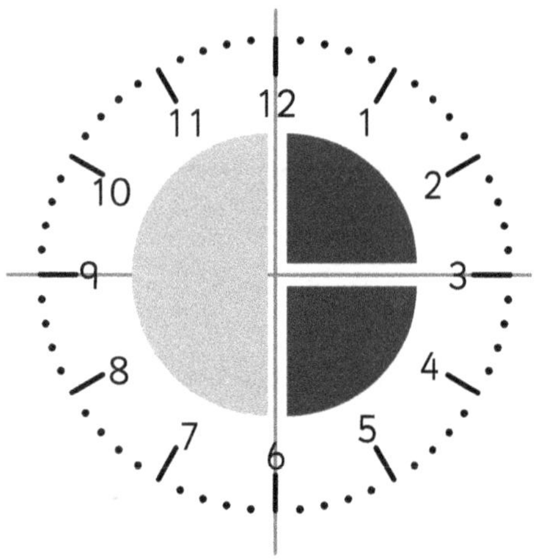

Explain to pupils that the half hour is equal to 2 quarter hours.

- Now explain to pupils that the dark grey section represents minutes past the hour and the light grey section minutes to the hour.
- Using the blank clock face that they have previously created, they can label their own clock face for reference.
- Ask pupils to: **Show where the minute hand would point to for 'quarter past'.** Next ask them: **Which number represents 'quarter past' on the clock face?** Do the same for 'quarter to'.
- Now, ask pupils to: **Write down how you would record 'quarter past' and 'quarter to' in digital.**

Unit 7.5 Five minute intervals

- Draw a circle on the board to represent the clock face and write in the numbers 1–12 in the appropriate places.
- Ask pupils to list all the time facts they know about the clock face. Possible answers could be

60 minutes

1 hour

$2\frac{1}{2}$ hours or 2 hours 30 minutes

$4\frac{1}{4}$ hours or 4 hours 15 minutes

Minute hand

Hour hand

Analogue

5-minute intervals between each number

- Using the clock face that they have each created, point to the 12 and get pupils to count around the clock face saying – 5, 10, 15, 20, 25, 30… up to 60.
- Emphasise that the hour is made up from 12 lots of 5 minutes.
- Now, go back around the clock face with pupils saying – *5 past, 10 past, 15 minutes past/ $\frac{1}{4}$ past, 20 past, 25 past, 30 minutes past/ $\frac{1}{2}$ past, 25 to, 20 to, 15 minutes to/$\frac{1}{4}$ to, 10 to, 5 to and o'clock.*
- Using their own clock face, ask pupils to show you different times to assess their understanding.

Time 1C

Section overview

Textbook 1C units	Review units	Prior learning	Benchmarks/Es&Os
Unit 7.1 Use a calendar to plan events	**1B** Unit 7.2	• I know basic time facts including days of the week and months of the year. • I can recognise different ways to record and measure time. • I can use appropriate vocabulary to sequence and order time – before, during, after…	**MNU 1-10b** • Uses and interprets a variety of calendars and 12-hour timetables to plan key events. • Knows the number of seconds in a minute, minutes in an hour, hours in a day, days in each month, weeks and days in a year. • Orders the months of the year and relates these to the appropriate seasons.
Unit 7.2 Recording time	**1B** Unit 7.3	• I understand time durations. • I can recognise and identify different ways of recording time. • I can use appropriate vocabulary to discuss periods of time.	**MNU 1-10a** **MNU 1-10b** **MNU 1-10c** • Tells the time using half past, quarter past and quarter to using analogue and digital 12-hour clocks. • Records 12-hour times using am and pm and is able to identify 24-hour notation; for example, on a mobile phone or computer. • Records the date in a variety of ways, using words and numbers. • Uses and interprets a variety of calendars and 12-hour timetables to plan key events. • Knows the number of seconds in a minute, minutes in an hour, hours in a day, days in each month, weeks and days in a year. • Orders the months of the year and relates these to the appropriate seasons. • Selects and uses appropriate timers for specific purposes.

Unit 7.3 Convert digital to analogue	**1B** Units 7.4 and 7.5	• I can recognise and identify analogue and digital time. • I understand that analogue and digital time both give us the same information. • I can use appropriate vocabulary to discuss periods of time.	**MNU 1-10a** • Tells the time using half past, quarter past and quarter to using analogue and digital 12-hour clocks. • Records 12-hour times using am and pm and is able to identify 24-hour notation; for example, on a mobile phone or computer. • Records the date in a variety of ways, using words and numbers.
Unit 7.4 Use a.m. and p.m. correctly		• I can recognise and identify analogue and digital time. • I understand the difference between a.m. and p.m. • I can use appropriate vocabulary to discuss periods of time.	**MNU 1-10a** • Tells the time using half past, quarter past and quarter to using analogue and digital 12-hour clocks. • Records 12-hour times using a.m. and p.m. and is able to identify 24-hour notation; for example, on a mobile phone or computer. • Records the date in a variety of ways, using words and numbers.
Unit 7.5 12-hour and 24-hour time	**1C** Unit 7.4	• I can recognise and identify analogue and digital time. • I understand the difference between a.m. and p.m. • I can use appropriate vocabulary to discuss periods of time.	**MNU 1-10a** • Tells the time using half past, quarter past and quarter to using analogue and digital 12-hour clocks. • Records 12-hour times using a.m. and p.m. and is able to identify 24-hour notation; for example, on a mobile phone or computer. • Knows the number of seconds in a minute, minutes in an hour, hours in a day, days in each month, weeks and days in a year. • Orders the months of the year and relates these to the appropriate seasons. • Selects and uses appropriate timers for specific purposes.

Conceptual context

This chapter will deepen the pupils' understanding of time by looking at it as a dimension in which events can be ordered from the past through to the present and into the future. In addition, it is also the measurement of durations of events and the intervals that exist between them.

Explain to pupils that time is not an object or substance they can touch or see. Time has many aspects and represents different things to different people in a variety of different circumstances. People use the word time in a multitude of ways to express a number of different things. There are numerous saying that relate to time. For example: *Time seemed to stand still. Do you have the time? It will take a very long time! This is not the first time you have done that. It's time for dinner. I don't have time today. Sing in time to the music.*

As students become confident at reading and telling the time they can begin to solve problems such as estimating, measuring and calculating how long both single and multiple events take. This can be extended to reading information from timetables written in 24-hour clock and using this information they can plan journeys and other events. Linking with schools overseas will lead naturally to an exploration of the time zones.

Resources

- 24-hour number line (see Resource sheet 7I)
- Analogue and digital clock faces (see Resource sheet 7G)
- Analogue clock faces (see Resource sheet 7E)
- Blank calendar template (see Resource sheet 7H)
- Blank timetable (see Resource sheet 7C)
- Blue and red crayons/coloured pencils
- Clock face (see Resource sheet 7D)
- Days of the week cards (see Resource sheet 7A)
- Digital clock faces (see Resource sheet 7F)
- Individual whiteboards and whiteboard pens
- Paper fasteners – to attach hands onto the clock face
- Sand timers
- Scissors
- Stopwatches
- Subject post-its (see Resource sheet 7B)

Key vocabulary

- **Analogue**
- **Device**
- **Digital**
- **Durations**
- **Estimate**
- **Interval**
- **Least**
- **Most**
- **Quarter**
- **Timetable**

Misconceptions

Potential misconception	Addressing the misconception
Units 7.1, 7.2, 7.3 and 7.4 Pupils might confuse the minute hand and the hour hand.	Using an analogue clock, ensure that pupils are aware that the shorter hand points to the hour and the longer hand points to the minute.
Units 7.1, 7.2, 7.3 and 7.4 Pupils might not be confident about the direction that the clock hands rotate around the clock face.	Using an analogue clock, explain that the hands move in a clockwise direction, which means that they move towards the left-hand side, down and around the face of the clock.
Units 7.1, 7.2, 7.3 and 7.4 Pupils may think that time can only be measured using a clock and in seconds, minutes and hours.	Through questioning and quality discussion, ensure that pupils are familiar with the many different **instruments of measure** that are used: clock, watch, stopwatch, sundial, calendar, diary, clapping hands, sand timer… Also, ensure that pupils are familiar with the different **units of measure** that are used: seconds, minutes, hours, days, weeks, years, decades, etc.

Teaching ideas

Unit 7.1 Use a calendar to plan events

- Start a discussion with pupils by asking them what device would you use to measure, plan and record events on. Explain that, by using a calendar, you can look at a week, month and year.
- Ask pupils to write down examples of what they might use a calendar for and give them time to share their answers.
- Print out blank calendar templates (Resource sheet 7H) and write the current month at the top. Ask pupils to tell you what day was the 1st of the month and fill in the rest of the dates. Identify if there are any special dates to record for this month – holidays, trips, birthdays and so on. Use the calendar to establish pupils' confidence with time facts – how many days is it until…?
- Look at the 'Let's Learn' section of Unit 7.1 and then begin the unit with pupils.

Unit 7.2 Recording time

- Ask pupils to tell you as many different ways they can think about to measure time and record these on the board.
- Hopefully you will get some of the following:
    - o Clock – digital and analogue
    - o Sand timer
    - o Calendar
    - o Stopwatch
    - o Diary
    - o Sundial

- Now, ask them for each of the instruments of measure that they have named, what the unit of time would be and record them on the board.

Clock – digital and analogue	seconds, minutes, hours
Sand timer	seconds, minutes
Calendar	days, weeks, months, years
Stopwatch	milliseconds, seconds, minutes
Diary	days, weeks, months, years
Sundial	minutes, hours

- Finally, ask pupils for an example of activities that they would measure with each one and record them also.
- Ask them to write on their whiteboards the answers to the following questions: What instrument of measure would you use to time someone hopping 20 times? Why? What would be the most accurate device to use for timing someone swimming? What makes you say that? Would I use a sand timer to calculate how long a film is on for? Explain your answer.

Unit 7.3 Converting digital to analogue

- Start off by asking pupils what time it is. How do they know this? Discuss with pupils the different ways in which they can identify what time it is. They may know that you have numeracy after break therefore it will be around 11 o'clock. They may have looked at the clock in the classroom. They may have a watch on. Some pupils may have absolutely no idea what time of the day it is. If you have a clock in the classroom, ask pupils what kind of clock this is. What makes them say this? Encourage the use of mathematical language related to the concept: clock face, minute hand, hour hand, analogue, digital, etc.
- Write analogue and digital on the board and ask pupils to explain what they mean:

- Write down 8 o'clock on the board and ask pupils what they do at this time.
- Through discussion you can establish their understanding of a.m. and p.m. time.
- Ask them how they know if the time is in the morning or the afternoon/evening?
- Look at the 'Let's Learn' section of Unit 7.3 before starting pupils with the activities.

Unit 7.4 Use a.m. and p.m. correctly

- Ask pupils to write down the different things that they are going to be doing for the rest of the day on their whiteboards.
- Now, ask them to draw a line between the activities they will be doing before 12 o'clock (noon) and after 12 o'clock (noon).

Numeracy Music Lunchtime Art PE	Numeracy Music ~~~~~~ 12 o'clock Lunchtime Art PE

- Ask **What will you be doing in the morning? What will you be doing in the afternoon?**
- Explain that all activities before 12 o'clock are morning or a.m. and all activities after 12 o'clock are afternoon/evening or p.m.
- Look at the 'Let's Learn' section of Unit 7.4 to expand this discussion.

Unit 7.5 12-hour and 24-hour time

- Begin this section by asking the pupils: **How many hours are in a day?** Next, ask: **How many numbers are there on an analogue clock face? How do you know if the time is morning/a.m. or afternoon/evening/p.m.?** Now ask them: **What is the difference between 12-hour and 24-hour time?**
- Look at the number line in the 'Let's Learn' section of the unit as the basis of your discussion.

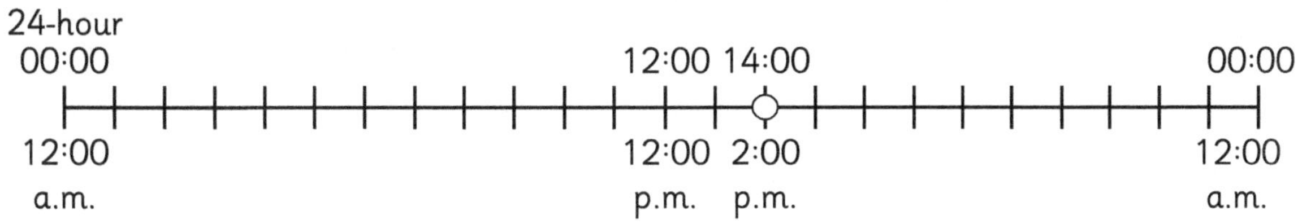

- Ask pupils to identify on the number line midnight and midday.
- Give pupils the blank number line (Resource sheet 7I) and get them to fill it in showing both 12-hour and 24-hour time so that they will have a reference sheet to use when completing the 'Let's practise' section.

8 Measurement

Measurement 1A

Section overview

Textbook 1A units	Review units	Prior learning	Benchmarks/Es&Os
Unit 8.1 Comparing and ordering lengths and heights	**Early** Units 7.2 and 7.3	• Understand and use appropriate language to describe length, e.g. short and tall. • Compare lengths / heights using appropriate language, e.g. longer and shorter.	**MNU 1-11a** • Uses knowledge of everyday objects to provide reasonable estimates of length, height, mass and capacity.
Unit 8.2 Comparing and ordering mass	**Early** Units 7.2 and 7.3	• Understand and use appropriate language to describe mass, e.g. light and heavy. • Compare mass using appropriate language, e.g. lighter and heavier.	**MNU 1-11a** • Uses knowledge of everyday objects to provide reasonable estimates of length, height, mass and capacity.
Unit 8.3 Comparing and ordering area	**Early** Units 7.2 and 7.3	• Understand and use appropriate language to describe area, e.g. small and large. • Compare area using appropriate language, e.g. smaller and larger.	**MNU 1-11b** • Uses knowledge of everyday objects to provide reasonable estimates of length, height, mass and capacity.
Unit 8.4 Comparing and ordering capacity	**Early** Units 7.2 and 7.3	• Understand and use appropriate language to describe capacity, e.g. empty and full. • Compare capacity using appropriate language e.g. more and less.	**MNU 1-11a** • Uses knowledge of everyday objects to provide reasonable estimates of length, height, mass and capacity.
Unit 8.5 Estimating and measuring length (non-standard units)	**1A** Unit 8.1	• Compare and order lengths and heights. • Estimate and measure length using non-standard units.	**MNU 1-11a** • Uses knowledge of everyday objects to provide reasonable estimates of length, height, mass and capacity.
Unit 8.6 Estimating and measuring mass (non-standard units)	**Early** Unit 7.4 **1A** Unit 8.2	• I can compare and order mass. • Estimate and measure mass using non-standard units.	**MNU 1-11a** • Uses knowledge of everyday objects to provide reasonable estimates of length, height, mass and capacity.
Unit 8.7 Estimating and measuring area (non-standard units)	**Early** Unit 7.4 **1A** Unit 8.3	• I can compare and order area.	**MNU 1-11b** • Uses knowledge of everyday objects to provide reasonable estimates of length, height, mass and capacity.
Unit 8.8 Estimating and measuring capacity (non-standard units)	**Early** Unit 7.4 **1A** Unit 8.4	• I can compare and order capacity. • Estimate and measure capacity using non-standard units.	**MNU 1-11a** • Uses knowledge of everyday objects to provide reasonable estimates of length, height, mass and capacity.

Conceptual context

Measurement is a vital area of mathematics as through it we develop an understanding of the physical world around us. It should not be regarded as a discrete subject; an add-on that we try to fit in as a block of learning every year. Measurement provides a context in which pupils can continuously apply their developing sense of number.

Pupils bring a number of established measurement skills to formal education, but many find it difficult to translate this knowledge into formal understanding. It is vital that we support children to develop a conceptual basis of measurement and not just focus on the procedural aspects.

Initially, children have a relational understanding of measurement and develop language to describe differences in size (big/small, etc). Pre-school children use their perception to decide on size: who is taller, or can I fit under that table? They then begin to use direct comparison. Direct comparison is a valid but limiting form of measurement. Only items that can be moved or lifted can be compared. Children often need help to understand that the ends must be lined up for a fair comparison. Often called matching, children can now order items in size by direct comparison.

'Conservation' of measurement is a key aspect of a child's understanding. Young children often believe that if an object is moved its size changes. They need plenty of experience to observe that length, area and volume can be conserved.

The next step that children take is to use a third object to compare two others. This can be achieved by using string or body parts, for example. This helps children to understand that measurement not only compares but that this can be achieved by using some 'unit'. This is still a comparison skill, but children are building a repertoire of units or objects that they can use in the future to compare and estimate. By developing the skills of comparison, both direct and indirect, children are developing a conceptual sense that measurement helps to determine size.

Once we begin to use indirect measurement, we soon realise that there needs to be some element of uniformity in measurement to help us communicate with others. Non-standard units of measurement help children to compare objects and share their answers. The following key principles are introduced:

- Measurements are expressed by counting the total number of units used;
- the unit must not change during the measurement activity; and
- the units of measure used are not absolute but are chosen for their appropriateness.

This section focuses on developing pupils' ability to compare and order length, mass, area and capacity before exploring the need to estimate and measure each using non-standard units.

Resources

- Toys, teddy bears, action figures, etc.
- Feely bags / boxes
- Funnels
- Items to be measured (plastic bottles, jugs, cereal boxes, shopping bags, bin bags, toy box, etc.)
- Non-standard units of capacity (cups, yoghurt pots, bowls, etc.)
- Non-standard units of length (pencils, cubes, paper clips, etc.)
- Non-standard units of weight (marbles, beanbags, 100 blocks, etc.)
- Pan balance (multiple sets)

Key vocabulary

- **Area**
- **Capacity**
- **Compare**
- **Estimate**
- **Heavier / heaviest**
- **Height**
- **Larger / largest**
- **Length**
- **Less**
- **Lighter / lightest**
- **Longer / longest**
- **Mass**
- **More**
- **Order**
- **Shorter / shortest**
- **Smaller / smallest**
- **Taller / tallest**
- **Weight**

Misconceptions

Potential misconception	Addressing the misconception
Units 8.1 and 8.5 Pupils may fail to understand that when measuring length, units are measured from the start of the first unit. They may also fail to line up objects correctly when comparing lengths of objects and/or leave gaps when measuring length using non-standard units.	Demonstrate measuring length accurately and provide varied opportunities for pupils to practise this.
Units 8.1 and 8.5 Pupils fail to appreciate the conservation of measurement, e.g. the length of the string remains the same even when we twist it; the amount of water remains the same when transferred to a different container; etc.	Provide opportunities for pupils to experiment with and investigate conservation through the activities and questions detailed in this chapter.
Units 8.2 and 8.6 When comparing the mass of objects, pupils may assume that larger objects must be heavier than smaller objects.	Provide opportunities for pupils to predict and compare objects of varying size and mass.

Potential misconception	Addressing the misconception
Units 8.3 and 8.7 Pupils may fail to understand conservation of area, i.e. that the area remains constant when we rearrange the shape.	Provide opportunities for pupils to investigate area by cutting up paper shapes.
Units 8.4 and 8.8 Pupils may fail measure capacity accurately using non-standard units as a result of not ensuring that these are equal.	Demonstrate measuring capacity accurately and provide varied opportunities for pupils to practise this.

Teaching ideas

Unit 8.1 Comparing and ordering lengths and height

- Organise pupils into groups and provide them with a range of action figures, teddy bears, etc. (ideally provide some figures that are taller but lighter; smaller but wider; etc.)
- Challenge groups to sort their toys in order of height from tallest to shortest. Ask questions, such as: **Which toy is the tallest? Can you find a toy that is smaller than this? Can you prove that this toy is shorter than this one?** (Ensure that pupils stand the toys together so that they can be correctly compared).
- Repeat the above activity using lengths of objects (for example, pupils could be asked to collect twigs, leaves, etc. or be provided with objects from around the classroom to sort in order of length)
- Show pupils two figures, side by side, and ask them to compare their heights:

- Place the smaller figure on a box and ask them to discuss which is taller now:

- Through discussion, ascertain that standing on the box has no impact on how tall the figure is. The top of the human's head may be higher from the surface than the robot's but their heights remain unchanged. The robot is still taller than the human, regardless of how they are positioned.
- Provide pupils with multilink cubes. Use a timer and give them, for example, 30 seconds to build a tower. Ask questions, such as: **Who has built the tallest tower? How many cubes tall is your tower? How much taller / smaller is your tower than your partner's? Can you put your towers in order at your group from smallest to tallest?** (This activity could be varied by, for example, instructing the pupils to work in pairs where they can only use one hand each.)
- Line up the whole class (or groups of pupils) and challenge them to order themselves by height (this could be done as a silent task). Ask questions, such as: **How accurately can we compare everyone's height in the class? Can we do anything to make it more accurate?** i.e. stand back-to-back, stand up straight, take shoes off, etc.

Unit 8.2 Comparing and ordering mass

- You will need a feely bag, a cover or large box and 5 or 6 items of varying weights (it may also help to have/ sketch a picture of each item).
- Organise pupils in a circle and arrange the items in the middle of the circle. Tell pupils to close their eyes while you put one of the items in the bag and cover the remaining items. Ensure pupils cannot see the contents of the bag, then pass it round the circle.
- Once all the pupils have held the bag, ask them to discuss which item it could be and justify their responses (it may be useful to display a picture / sketch of the items as a reminder).
- Reveal the contents and repeat with another item (it may be best to choose a mid-weight item first so that they can use this as a comparison for the next).
- Ask questions, such as: **Is this heavier or lighter than the last item? Which item could it be?**
- Display the following statement: **Larger objects are heavier than smaller objects; sometimes, always or never?**
- Ask pupils to discuss and justify their thoughts, e.g. *We think it is sometimes true because…*
- Display 4 or 5 items, e.g. a balloon, a large water bottle (empty), a small water bottle (full), a teddy bear and a small bag of marbles.
- Organise pupils into pairs and challenge them to order (write or draw) the items from lightest to heaviest.
- Share pupils' ideas with class then allow them to hold each item before allowing them to change their answer if they want.
- Provide pupils with pairs of items of similar mass and ask them to decide which they think is heavier. Ask questions, such as: **Is it easy to tell which is heavier? How could we tell for sure?** *We can use balance scales to compare.*
- Place items on the balance scales and ask: **Which is heavier? How do we know?**
- Show two objects (e.g. water bottle and pencil case) to pupils then place them in two separate bags (unseen by pupils). Place the bags on the balance scales then ask pupils to predict the contents of each bag. Encourage pupils to justify their thoughts, e.g. *I think the bottle of water is on the lower pan because it is heavier than the pencil case.*
- Repeat with other pairs of objects.

Unit 8.3 Comparing and ordering area

- Prepare the following paper shapes (ideally using different coloured paper for each):

- Organise pupils into pairs / groups and challenge them to put them in order of size from smallest to largest.
- Ask questions, such as: **How could we prove that we have them in the correct order?** *The shapes could be folded or cut in order to make better comparisons.*
- Explain that we use the word *area* to describe the amount of surface space of a shape or object. Elicit through discussion that the size (or area) of each shape remains exactly the same, even when we cut it up and rearrange the parts to form different shapes.
- Challenge pupils to fold or cut up the shapes to make more accurate comparisons. **Has this changed your original order?**
- Set up 4 or 5 'feely boxes' at the front of the class (cut out the front panel of each box so that the class can see the contents but not the pupil being challenged).
- Insert a different sized cardboard rectangle in each box and challenge a pupil to feel each and order from smallest to largest. Mix up the order and repeat with other pupils.
- Provide pupils with scrap paper or card.
- Display one smaller and one larger cut out shapes and challenge groups to:

  o cut out a shape with an area between the two shapes; and

  o cut out a shape with an equal area to either the smaller or larger shape.

Unit 8.4 Comparing and ordering capacity

- Show pupils an empty water bottle and cup and ask: **Which will hold more water? How could we check?** (*We can check by filling the one we predict to hold less and pouring it into the other.*) This could be repeated using a balloon and a water bottle to demonstrate that the balloon has the capacity to expand to hold more water.
- Show pupils a plastic bin bag and school bag (leave the bin bag folded up) and ask: **Which will hold more? How could we check?** Unfold the bag and ask if the pupils have changed their minds. (Use toys, classroom items, shopping, etc.)
- Provide a range of containers, bags, etc. and challenge pupils to order them from smallest to largest capacity. Pupils could be challenged to investigate using something suitable to fill (depending on the size), e.g. sand, water, cubes, counters, etc. Ask questions, such as: **What should we use to compare the capacity of these containers?**

- Pupils could be challenged to determine which would hold more; for example:
  - o Three plastic shopping bags or one bin bag?
  - o Four glasses of water or one jug?
  - o Five bowls of cereal or one box?

Unit 8.5 Estimating and measuring length (non-standard units)

- Organise pupils into pairs / groups and decide on an item to be measured e.g. gym mat, table, bench, etc. Ask: **How long is this?** Give pupils time to discuss and investigate. Pupils may decide to use parts of the body to measure (e.g. hands or feet) or classroom items (e.g. jotters, textbooks, trays, etc). For any groups struggling, ask questions, such as: **What could we use to measure the length of the gym mat?**
- Bring the class together and compare results. Ask questions, such as: **Why might our measurements be different?** Ask different groups to demonstrate how they took their measurements. Challenge pupils to identify differences in how measurements are taken. For example, pairs may have used different units (hands or feet); there may be inconsistencies when measuring (e.g. leaving gaps, not starting from the very edge or not measuring in a straight line; different sized hands or feet, etc.).
- Ask pupils to estimate the length of the mat using their feet then demonstrate measuring using these inconsistencies i.e. don't start from the corner, leave gaps in your steps and don't measure in a straight line. Ask pupils: **How can I take a fair (or accurate) measurement of length?**
- Elicit through discussion, how an accurate measurement can be made and demonstrate this.
- Ask a pupil to demonstrate measuring the length accurately. Ask: **Why are our measurements different?** *Different sized feet.*
- Discuss the fact that the unit used must be consistent if we are to compare lengths accurately. Discuss what could be used to do this, i.e. a cut out could be taken of one pupil's foot and duplicated or a standard sized item could be used (e.g. jotters, Cuisenaire rods, cubes, etc.)
- Challenge pupils to measure the item once again using a consistent non-standard unit for all groups and compare results once again (hopefully, this time, they should be the same or at least very close!).
- Set up stations with an item to be measured and non-standard units. For example:
  - o a length of string to be measured using hands (paper cut-out)
  - o a pencil to be measured using unifix cubes or counters
  - o a cupboard to be measured using pencils
  - o a rug to be measured using jotters or textbooks.
- Encourage groups to estimate lengths and record before measuring accurately.

Unit 8.6 Estimating and measuring mass (non-standard units)

- Organise pupils into groups and provide them with a set of balance scales and a range of objects of varying weights. Challenge groups to make the scales balance (without using exactly the same object at either side). Allow time to investigate.
- Note that if pupils can't find single objects to balance with each other they should be encouraged to investigate multiple items. Ask questions, such as: **What if we tried to balance two beanbags with the jotter?** Etc.
- Compare groups' results with the class. For example, we found that two jotters balanced with seven bean bags. Invite groups to demonstrate and prove their findings. Ask pupils questions, such as: **Are they exactly the same weight? How do we know?**
- Set up a set of balance scales at the front of the class. You will need an item to be weighed (e.g. a pencil case, lunchbox, etc.) and sets of non-standard units to measure with (e.g. beanbags, marbles, dominoes, wooden 100 blocks, etc.).
- Ask pupils questions, such as: **How many beanbags do you estimate the pencil case weigh? How many marbles will it weigh? How can we check?** *Using the scales.* **How will we know?** *The pans will be aligned exactly.*
- Set up stations with an item to be weighed and non-standard units, for example:
    - o a water bottle to be weighed using marbles
    - o a lunchbox to be weighed using wooden 100 blocks
    - o a pencil case to be weighed using post-it pads
    - o a hole-punch to be weighed using beanbags.
- Encourage groups to estimate weights and record before measuring accurately.

Unit 8.7 Estimating and measuring area (non-standard units)

- Show pupils the following:

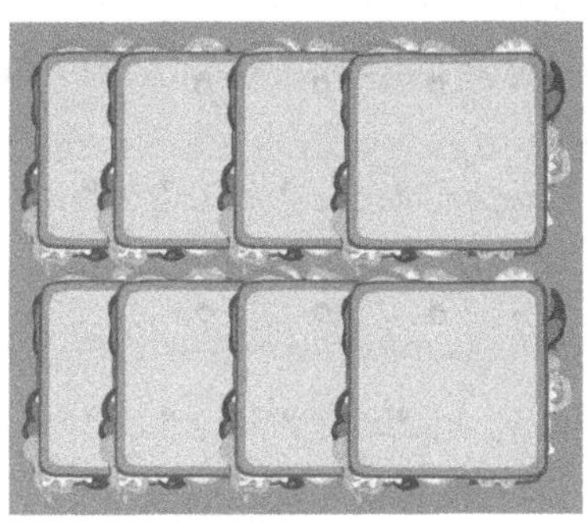
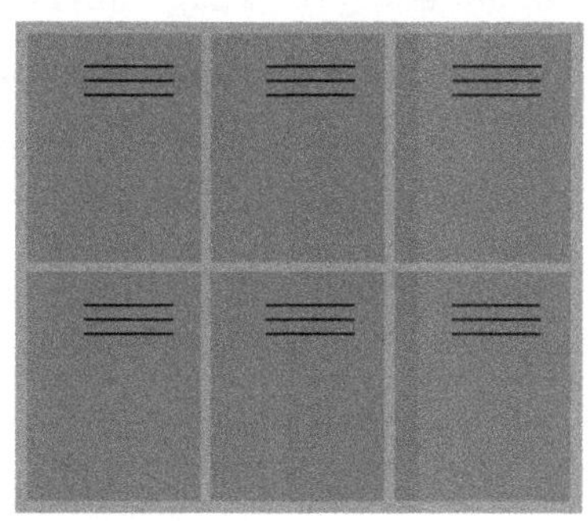

- Challenge pupils to discuss and justify whether the following statements are true or false:
    - o The newspaper fits exactly four pairs of shoes.
    - o The area of the tray is eight sandwiches.
    - o The desk fits exactly six jotters.

- Elicit through discussion that when measuring area, there should be no gaps or overlaps.
- Organise pupils into groups and set up stations where they have to estimate then find *how many fit*, for example:
    - pairs of shoes on a newspaper
    - playing cards on a jotter
    - textbooks on a desk
    - beanbags on a plate.
- Show pupils sets of items, for example:
    - 10 jotters
    - 8 schoolbags
    - 13 stickers
    - 9 paint bottles.
- Provide groups with tape, string or chalk and challenge them to mark out shapes on the floor big enough to fit each of the sets of items.
- Allow pupils to check how accurate their areas are by attempting to fit the items inside their shapes.

Unit 8.8 Estimating and measuring capacity (non-standard units)

- Show pupils a large empty bottle of water. Ask: **What could we measure?** Elicit through discussion that we can measure the height of the bottle (using cubes for example), the weight of the bottle (using beanbags for example) and that we can measure how much it holds. Explain that we use the word *capacity* to measure this.
- Ask the pupils: **What could we use to measure the capacity of the bottle?** (Perhaps give some examples and ask if they would make a sensible unit of measurement, e.g. cubes, beanbags, cups, jam jars, tea spoons, etc.)
- Fill the bottle with water and set out several cups, jars, etc. of different sizes. Ask questions, such as: **Will this give us an accurate measurement? Why not?** Elicit through discussion that the cups need to be of equal size.
- Set out equal-sized cups and pour out the water until the bottle is empty (fill each cup to different levels).
- Ask pupils: **True or false: the bottle holds *X* number of cups of water?**
- Allow pupils to discuss and justify their thoughts then discuss the fact that the cups must have an equal (full) amount in order to accurately determine the capacity of the bottle.
- Organise pupils into groups.
- Set up stations with a container to be measured and non-standard units, for example:
    - a box of cereal to be measured using bowls (the cereal could be replaced by foam 'peanuts')
    - a bottle (or jug) of water to be measured using cups
    - a large jar of counters (or marbles) to be measured using yoghurt pots
    - a box of toys to be measured using school bags.
- Encourage groups to estimate capacities and record before measuring accurately.

Measurement 1B

Section overview

Textbook 1B units	Review units	Prior learning	Benchmarks/Es&Os
Unit 8.1 Estimating, measuring and recording length (standard units)	**1A** Units 8.1 and 8.5	• I can compare and order lengths and heights. • I can estimate and measure length (non-standard units).	**MNU 1-11a** • Makes accurate use of a range of instruments including rulers, metre sticks, digital scales and measuring jugs when measuring lengths, heights, mass and capacities using the most appropriate instrument for the task.
Unit 8.2 Estimating, measuring and recording mass (standard units)	**1A** Unit 8.2 and 8.6	• I can compare and order mass. • I can estimate and measure mass (non-standard units).	**MNU 1-11a** • Makes accurate use of a range of instruments including rulers, metre sticks, digital scales and measuring jugs when measuring lengths, heights, mass and capacities using the most appropriate instrument for the task.
Unit 8.3 Estimating, measuring and recording area (squares)	**1A** Units 8.3 and 8.7	• I can compare and order area. • I can estimate and measure area (non-standard units).	**MNU 1-11b** • Uses square grids to estimate then measure the areas of a variety of simple 2D shapes.
Unit 8.4 Estimating, measuring and recording capacity	**1A** Unit 8.4 and 8.8	• I can compare and order capacity. • I can estimate and measure capacity (non-standard units).	**MNU 1-11a** • Makes accurate use of a range of instruments including rulers, metre sticks, digital scales and measuring jugs when measuring lengths, heights, mass and capacities using the most appropriate instrument for the task.
Unit 8.5 Converting standard units of length / height	**1B** Units 2.10 and 8.1	• I can count in hundreds, tens and ones. • I can estimate, measure and record length (standard units).	**MNU 1-11a** • Uses knowledge of relationships between units of measure to make simple conversions; for example, 1 m 58 cm = 158 cm.
Unit 8.6 Converting standard units of mass	**1B** Units 2.10 and 8.2	• I can count in hundreds, tens and ones. • I can estimate, measure and record mass (standard units).	**MNU 1-11a** • Uses knowledge of relationships between units of measure to make simple conversions; for example, 1 m 58 cm = 158 cm.
Unit 8.7 Reading scales – length	**1B** Unit 8.1	• I can estimate, measure and record length (standard units).	**MNU 1-11a** • Reads a variety of scales on measuring devices including those with simple fractions; for example, $\frac{1}{2}$ litre.
Unit 8.8 Reading scales – mass	**1B** Unit 8.2	• I can estimate, measure and record mass (standard units).	**MNU 1-11a** • Reads a variety of scales on measuring devices including those with simple fractions; for example, $\frac{1}{2}$ litre.
Unit 8.9 Reading scales – capacity			**MNU 1-11a** • Reads a variety of scales on measuring devices including those with simple fractions; for example, $\frac{1}{2}$ litre.

Conceptual context

The focus of Book 1A was to foster pupils' developing understanding of measurement through the ability to:

- identify attributes, i.e. appreciate that objects have different attributes that can be measured (length, mass, capacity, area, etc.)
- compare and order, i.e. use language to describe these attributes (longer, shorter, heavier, lighter, etc.) and
- measure using non-standard units, i.e. give a value to these attributes.

The aim of Book 1B is to continue to foster this understanding through the introduction of standard units in order to allow pupils to communicate measurements accurately and promote an increasing sense of consistency.

Throughout this book, pupils will become familiar with metric units, the quantity involved in each unit, the associated language for naming and writing units, and the use of relevant symbols.

As learners use measuring devices, they learn the following skills and concepts: understanding the measurement of single units with units represented on a scale, the importance of not leaving gaps between repeated units, understanding the accumulation of distance as units are added, aligning the zero on the scale to the start point of the measure and the meaning of the numerals on the ruler. With this experience, the learners can convert between related units of measurement and estimate using standard units of measure.

As pupils develop their understanding of measure using standard units, they will develop the ability to estimate measurements with increasing accuracy. It is important that pupils develop a sense of when it is appropriate to estimate and when there is a need to measure accurately and are able to choose appropriate units.

Resources

- 1cm square paper
- Base 10 materials
- Feely bags
- Funnels
- Measuring jugs
- Metre sticks
- Plastic bottles
- Post-its (or paper squares)
- Rulers
- Scales – balance, kitchen, hanging, bathroom
- Tape measures
- Unifix cubes
- Weights (one kilogram and 100 grams)

Key vocabulary

- **Area**
- **Capacity**
- **Centimetre**
- **Gram**
- **Height**
- **Kilogram**
- **Length**
- **Mass**
- **Metre**
- **Metre stick**
- **Volume**

Misconceptions

Potential misconception	Addressing the misconception
Units 8.1, 8.5 and 8.7 Pupils may fail to line up the measuring device with the object being measured correctly. They may also include the starting increment when measuring using a ruler, therefore incorrectly adding 1 to the actual length.	Demonstrate measuring length accurately and provide varied opportunities for pupils to practise this. Use the 'broken ruler' activity to ascertain misconceptions about counting units. See Unit 8.7. Use a counting stick to develop understanding of counting on from one number to another. *Counting on from 7 to 11 we need to make four jumps, so we have counted on four.* i.e. We count the jumps (7 to 8, 8 to 9, 9 to 10 and 10 to 11 to get 4), *not* all of the numbers (7, 8, 9, 10 and 11 to get 5).
Unit 8.3 Pupils may fail to line up squares correctly when measuring area, i.e. they may leave gaps or overlap.	Use 'true or false' activities to challenge and draw out misconceptions. For example, *Isla has measured the area of this shape accurately?* (see picture on page 141 of the textbook).
Unit 8.3 Pupils may fail to understand conservation of area, i.e. that the area remains the same when we change the shape.	Provide opportunities for pupils to investigate making and drawing different shapes with the same area.
Unit 8.4 Pupils may confuse the terms capacity and volume.	Teach these terms together, providing lots of opportunities for pupils to investigate and differentiate between the two.
Units 8.5 and 8.6 Pupils may struggle to appreciate that, when converting units of measurement, the actual measurement remains unchanged, i.e. *same value, different appearance*.	Provide practical opportunities where measurements are taken using alternative units (for example, centimetres and metres and centimetres) rather than relying on an abstract conversion.
Unit 8.8 and 8.9 Pupils may struggle to appreciate the value of each increment when reading scales.	Provide opportunities for pupils to work out the value of each increment on a range of number lines (i.e. with increments of 2, 5, 10, 50, 100, etc.)

Teaching ideas

Unit 8.1 Estimating, measuring and recording length (standard units)

- Draw the following image (or use a strip of paper) and tell pupils that you are going to measure the length using cubes (do not show them the size of the cubes):

- Challenge pupils to estimate how many cubes long the bar will be. Ask questions, such as: **Why are our estimates different? Do you need more information before you can estimate?** *They will need to know the size of the cubes.*

  Show pupils the following sizes of cubes and explain that you are going to measure the bar using both:

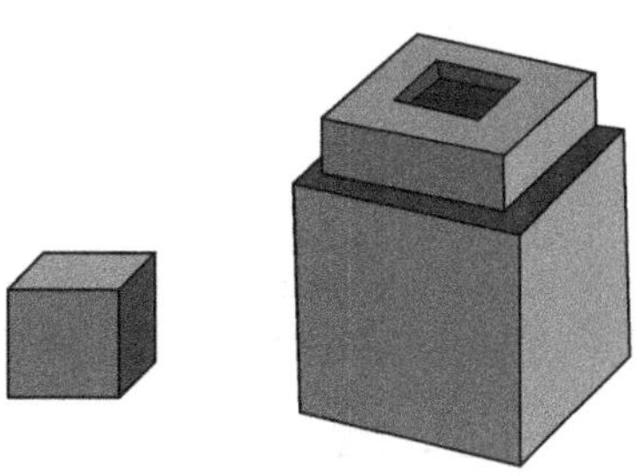

Ask pupils to provide an estimate for both sizes of cube and demonstrate measuring the bar accurately.

Alternatively, groups of pupils could be given different sizes of cubes to measure the same items and compare the results.

- Elicit through discussion the need for a standard unit of length so that we can make and compare measurements consistently.
- Show pupils a ruler and demonstrate how to measure the length of the bar accurately in centimetres, i.e. line the zero up with the start of the bar; keep the ruler straight along the edge, etc.

  Organise pupils into pairs / groups and provide with rulers and items to be measured (organised at stations). Challenge groups to estimate the length of each item then measure accurately.
- Show pupils a metre stick and ask questions, such as: **How many centimetres long is this? What does *centi* mean at the start?** Etc.

  Demonstrate how to measure accurately using a metre stick by measuring, for example, the length of a table.

  Challenge pupils to identify items in the classroom or playground that they would measure with either a ruler or a metre stick, estimate their length then measure accurately.

Unit 8.2 Estimating, measuring and recording mass (standard units)

- Show pupils the following weights:

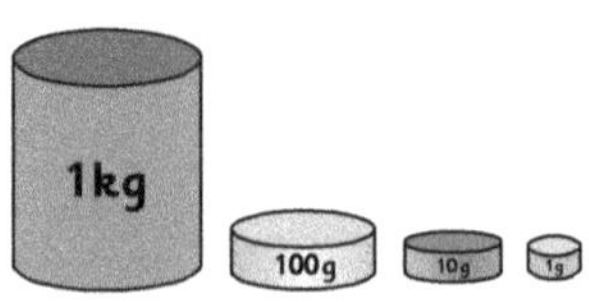

  Ask questions, such as: **How many 10 g weights is the same as 100 g? How many 100 g weights is the same as 1 kg?** Etc.

  Pupils could check this using the balance scales.
- Organise sealed paper bags with weights inside and labels on the outside stating how many weights have been used, for example:

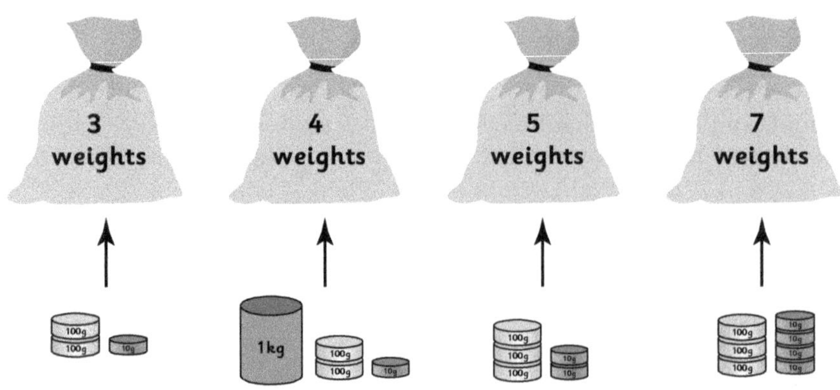

  Organise the bags at stations with balance scales, weights and an empty paper bag. Challenge groups to use the paper bag, weights and balance scales to work out the weights hidden in each bag (pupils should put their attempts inside the other paper bag to cancel out any weight difference).

- Set up stations with an item to be weighed and weights, for example:
    - o a packet of post-its
    - o a box of staples
    - o a dictionary
    - o a block of modelling clay
    - o etc.

  Encourage groups to estimate weights and record before measuring accurately.
- Display 5 or 6 different items and write their actual weights on the board. Challenge pupils to match the items with their weights. Pupils could then check using the balance scales.

Unit 8.3 Estimating, measuring and recording area (standard units)

- Show pupils the following image and ask them to estimate how many squares it would take to cover the rectangle:

Show pupils the following and ask them to discuss:

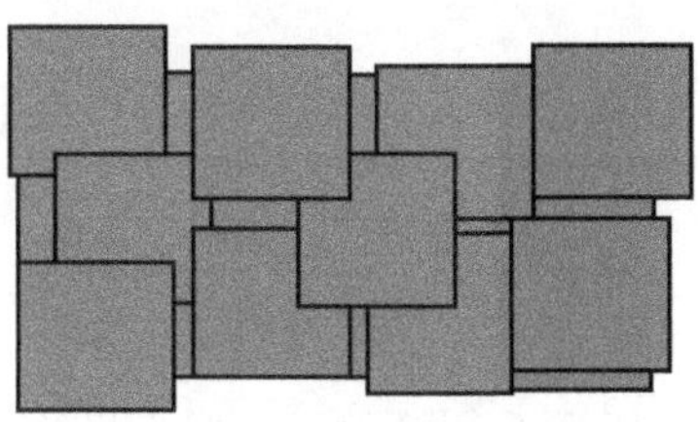

Elicit through discussion that when measuring area, there should be no gaps or overlaps.

Demonstrate that it would take exactly eight squares to cover the rectangle:

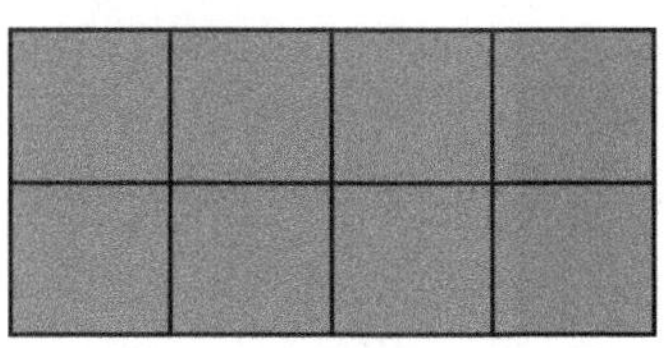

- Organise pupils into pairs / groups and provide with paper squares (e.g. post-its) and shapes to be measured (e.g. different sized paper shapes or suitable classroom items):

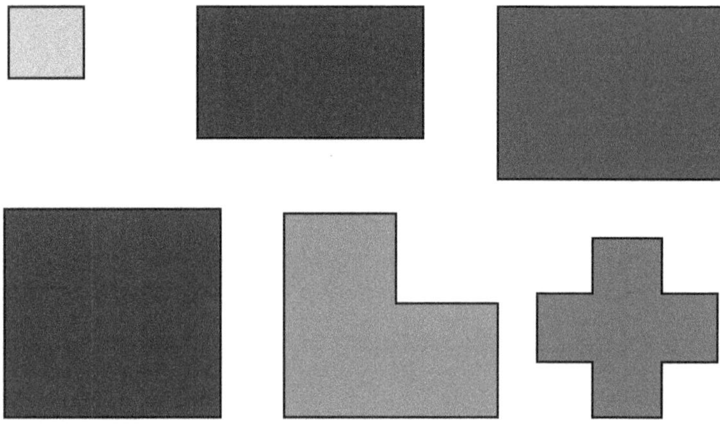

Ask questions, such as: **What is the area of each shape?** *The answer should be given in squares.* **What can we do if the squares don't fit exactly?** *The squares could be cut to fit more accurately.*

- Provide pupils with large sheets of blank paper and a ruler. Challenge them to create shapes with an area of:
  - o 6 squares
  - o 9 squares
  - o 12 squares
  - o 16 squares

  Pupils should then check their attempts using the squares.
- Challenge pupils to find how many different shapes they could make with, for example, 6 squares (these could be drawn on squared paper as an alternative to creating the shapes with post-its).

Unit 8.4 Estimating, measuring and recording capacity

- You will need four identical measuring jugs (larger than 1 litre) and a 5-ml plastic syringe (most children's medicine bottles come with these).

  Fill the syringe with 1 ml and three of the measuring jugs with 100 ml, 500 ml and 1 litre of water, respectively.

  Ask pupils to compare the amount of water in the syringe with the amount in each of the measuring jugs and challenge them to estimate how many syringes they would need to fill each jug to the same level.

  Elicit through discussion that we can use millilitres to measure small volumes of water and litres for larger volumes.
- Display various containers, e.g. teaspoon, tablespoon, yoghurt pots, plastic cups, plastic bottles of various sizes, cans, pots, etc.

  Challenge pupils to sort them into groups of containers that will hold:
  - o less than 100 ml
  - o between 100 ml and 500 ml

- o between 500 ml and 1 litre
- o over 1 litre

Elicit through discussion a method for checking their predictions. For example, each of the containers could be filled and poured into the fourth measuring jug, which could then be compared directly with the original three jugs.

- Display a range of containers with labels (hidden from view) e.g. drinks cans, cartons, bottles, etc and challenge pupils to estimate their capacities.

  Alternatively, provide groups with paper labels with the actual capacities written on them. Challenge each group to place the correct label beside each container (provide each group with a different colour of paper labels in order to track their predictions easily).

  Groups could be allowed to make changes based on the number they have got correct so far; for example, *Yellow group, five of your labels are matched correctly and three are incorrect.*

Unit 8.5 Converting standard units of length/height

- Organise pupils into pairs / groups and provide with masking tape (or string) and a metre stick.
  Challenge pupils to use the metre sticks to set out lengths of tape on the floor that are:
  - o 1 m
  - o 3 m
  - o $2\frac{1}{2}$ m
  - o $\frac{1}{2}$ m

  Groups could check the accuracy of each others' attempts.
  Ask questions, such as: **How else can we write each measurement?** *100 cm, 300 cm, 250 cm and 50 cm.*
- Challenge pupils to identify 3 or 4 objects whose lengths measure more than and less than a certain length; for example, 2 m: *We think the length of the desk is less than 2 metres. We think the bench is more than 2 metres long.*

  Challenge pupils to estimate the length of each object then check using the metre stick. Ask questions, such as: **Can you state their length in two ways?** For example: *the bench is 350 cm long or 3 m 50 cm.*
- Challenge pupils to estimate the heights of each member of their group in both *metres* and *metres and centimetres*.

  Ask questions, such as: **How could me measure each person's height accurately?** *It may be easier to mark their height by standing against the wall or lying on the floor and measuring to the mark rather than trying to measure the actual person. (A tape measure could be used instead of a metre stick.)*
- Challenge pupils to measure out lengths of masking tape that they estimate to be, for example:
  - o 154 cm
  - o 1 m 75 cm
  - o 237 cm
  - o 2 m 85 cm

  Pupils should then choose a suitable measuring device to measure each length accurately and state each in two ways.
- Challenge pupils to work out how close they are with each attempt by finding the difference between estimated and actual lengths (the differences could be totalled to give them an overall 'score' with the lowest being the winner).

Unit 8.6 Converting standard units of mass

- Show pupils a set of scales, balancing by placing a 1 kg weight in each pan:

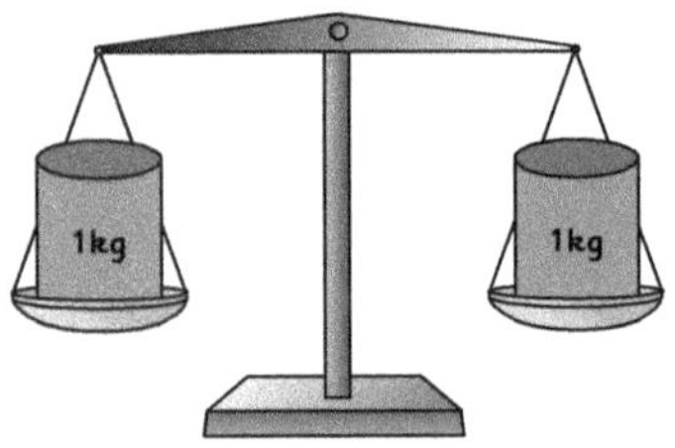

Organise pupils into groups and provide with pan scales and weights.

Challenge them to find other ways of balancing the 1 kg weight using alternative weights (i.e. they could use ten 100 g weights or a 500 g weight and five 100 g weights or nine 100 g weights and ten 10 g weights, etc)

Ask questions, such as: **How many grams is the same as 1 kg? What does 'kilo' mean at the start of a word? What other words start with 'kilo'?** For example: kilometre, kilobyte, etc. **What do each of these words mean?** Etc.

- Set out stations with different items to be weighed (each item should weigh more than 1 kg) and provide pupils with weights (make sure the 1 kg weights are removed).

  Challenge pupils to estimate the mass of each object in grams and then measure accurately using the scales (pupils could draw the weights required to balance each item). *The school bag weighs 1540 grams.*

  Provide pupils with the 1 kg weights and challenge them to use the fewest possible number of weights to measure each item (i.e. by replacing ten 100 g weights with a 1 kg weight).

- Ask pupils to state each object's weight using kilograms and grams. *The school bag weighs 1 kilogram 540 grams.*
- Provide groups with a bag each and various items to fill the bag (or items could be identified from around the classroom).

  Challenge pupils to estimate what combination of items will total a mass of between, for example:

  - 1 kg and $1\frac{1}{2}$ kg
  - $1\frac{1}{2}$ kg and 2 kg
  - 2 kg and $2\frac{1}{2}$ kg
  - $2\frac{1}{2}$ kg and 3 kg

  Pupils should fill the bag with each combination of items, measure accurately using the scales and state each mass in both *grams* and *kilograms and grams.*

Unit 8.7 Reading scales – length

- Display the following (or demonstrate measuring similar items in the same way). See Resource sheet 8B: Reading scales (length).

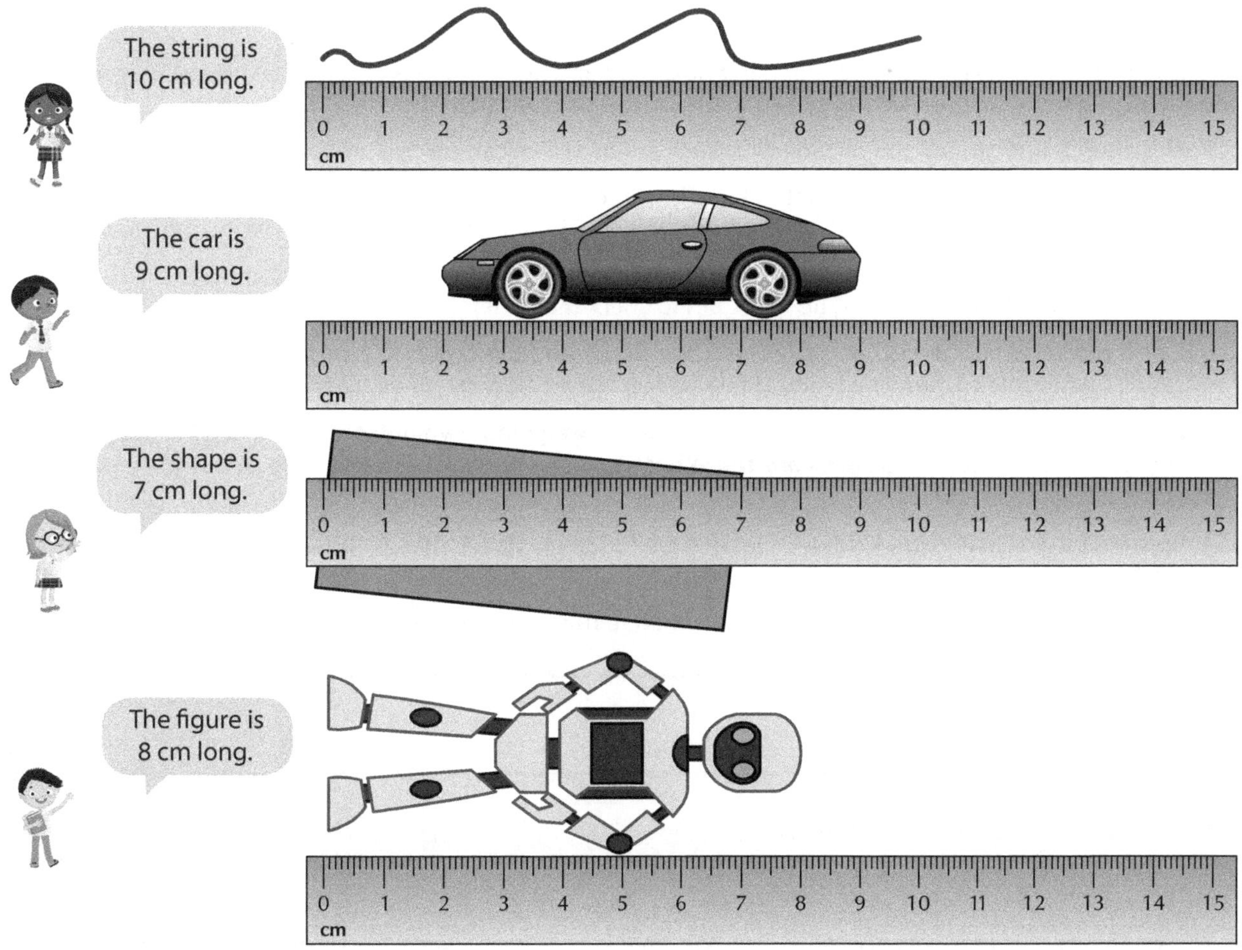

Ask pupils to discuss whose measurements are accurate and whose are not. Encourage them to justify their responses. For example:

- o *Nuria's measurement is not accurate because the string is not straight.*
- o *Amman's measurement is not accurate because the zero must be lined up with one end of the car.*
- o *Isla's measurement is not accurate because the ruler is not lined up with the edge of the shape.*
- o *Finlay's measurement is accurate because the ruler has been lined up correctly.*

Organise pupils into groups and provide them with the items and a ruler.

Challenge pupils to measure the items accurately.

- Display the following and ask pupils to discuss the length of the caterpillar:

An answer of 11 suggests a lack of understanding of units.

'6' suggests that the pupil counted 6, 7, 8, 9, 10, 11 so 6.

'5' is the correct answer; most will count the gaps but how many will find the difference of 11 and 6?

Provide pupils with 'broken rulers' to measure a range of objects.

Unit 8.8 Reading scales - mass

- Demonstrate measuring out a 1 kg bag of marbles (or any other suitable items) using a pan balance.

  Show pupils a set of kitchen scales and / or a set of hanging scales. Explain that these can measure the mass of the marbles without the need for weights.

  Transfer the bag to the kitchen (and / or hanging) scales and ask the pupils to read the display. Remove or add marbles so that the children can see how the dial moves in response to the change in mass.

- Organise pupils into groups and provide with kitchen / hanging scales, a bag and suitable items to be weighed.

  Challenge pupils to measure out exactly 1 kg of the items. Ask questions, such as **How will you know when you have exactly 1 kg?** *The dial will line up exactly with the 1.* **How could we check?** *The measurement could be checked using a pan balance.*

  A pan balance and 1 kg could be set up for pupils to check their attempts.

- Look at the display on the kitchen scales with the pupils and ask questions, such as: **What items would be suitable / unsuitable to measure using these scales? How could we measure the mass of heavier items?**

- Show pupils a set of bathroom scales and demonstrate weighing a volunteer (to the nearest kilogram). Ask questions, such as: **What differences are there between the displays of each type of scale? What do you think the reason is for this?**

- Set up stations with a different kind of scales at each (i.e. hanging, kitchen, bathroom) and suitable items to be measured using each.

  Challenge pupils to measure the items at each station to the nearest kilogram.

Unit 8.9 Reading scales - capacity

- Display the following number lines (for example) and challenge pupils to identify the missing numbers:

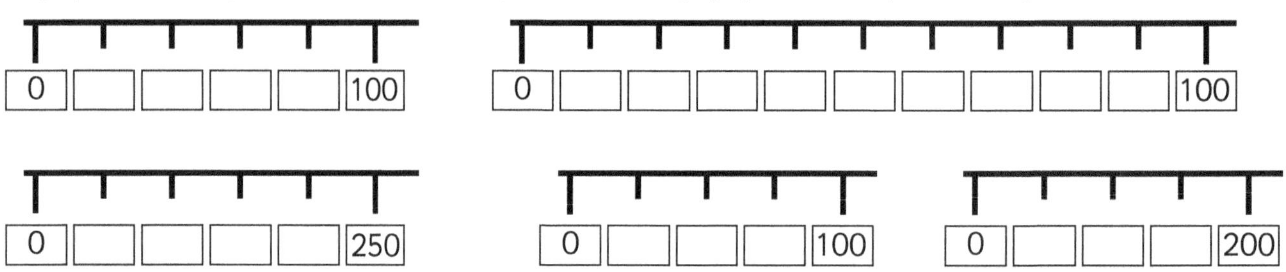

  You will need a filled 500 ml bottle of water and a measuring jug (that holds at least one litre).

  Without letting them know the capacity of the bottle, ask pupils to discuss where they think the bottle will fill the jug to.

  Pour the water into the measuring jug and ask pupils: **How much water is there?** (allowing them to read the scale).

  Fill the bottle again and explain that you are going to pour this into the measuring jug also. Ask questions, such as: **What level will the jug be filled to then? How much water will there be in the jug**. *1000 ml or 1 litre.*

  Pour the water into the jug and check the pupils' predictions with them.

Review the scale on the measuring jug with the pupils and challenge them to work out the value of each increment. Note that it would be worth looking at 2 or 3 measuring jugs with different increments to demonstrate that they are not always the same.

- Organise pupils into groups and provide with various containers, a funnel and a measuring jug.

  Challenge groups to fill the containers with various volumes, for example:

  - 100 ml
  - 300 ml
  - 500 ml
  - 800 ml

  Groups could then pair up with another group to check each other's accuracy, i.e. use their measuring jug to measure the volume of each container.

  Look at various containers with the pupils, e.g. soft drinks cans, milk cartons, washing up liquid, etc. (online if unavailable) and challenge pupils to identify on a measuring jug where each would fill to.

Measurement 1C

Section overview

Textbook 1C units	Review units	Prior learning	Benchmarks/Es&Os
Unit 8.1 Reading and recording measurements – length	**1A** Unit 5.3 **1B** Units 8.1 and 8.7	• I can count in halves and quarters. • I can estimate, measure and record length (standard units). • I can read measurements on a ruler.	**MNU 1-11a** • Reads a variety of scales on measuring devices including those with simple fractions; for example, $\frac{1}{2}$ litre.
Unit 8.2 Measuring and recording length – millimetres	**1B** Unit 8.7 **1C** Unit 8.1	• I can read measurements on a ruler. • I can read and record measurements (cm). • I can estimate and measure mass (non-standard units).	**MNU 1-11a** • Records measurements of length, height, mass and capacity to the nearest standard unit; for example, millimetres (mm), centimetres (cm), grams (g), kilograms (kg), millilitres (ml), litres (l).
Unit 8.3 Converting length – millimetres and centimetres	**1B** Unit 8.5 **1C** Units 8.1 and 8.2	• I can convert standard units of length (cm and m). • I can measure and record length (mm and cm).	**MNU 1-11a** • Uses knowledge of relationships between units of measure to make simple conversions; for example, 1 m 58 cm = 158 cm.
Unit 8.4 Reading and recording measurements for mass	**1A** Unit 5.3 **1B** Units 8.2 and 8.8	• I can count in halves and quarters. • I can estimate, measure and record mass (standard units). • I can read scales (mass).	**MNU 1-11a** • Reads a variety of scales on measuring devices including those with simple fractions; for example, $\frac{1}{2}$ litre.
Unit 8.5 Reading and recording measurements for capacity	**1A** Unit 5.3 **1B** Units 8.4 and 8.9	• I can count in halves and quarters. • I can estimate, measure and record capacity. • I can read scales (capacity).	**MNU 1-11a** • Reads a variety of scales on measuring devices including those with simple fractions; for example, $\frac{1}{2}$ litre.
Unit 8.6 Converting standard units	**1B** Units 8.5 and 8.6 **1C** Unit 8.3 and 8.5	• I can convert standard units of length (mm, cm and m). • I can convert standard units of mass (g and kg). • I can read and record measurements for capacity (ml and l).	**MNU 1-11a** • Uses knowledge of relationships between units of measure to make simple conversions; for example, 1 m 58 cm = 158 cm.
Unit 8.7 Area of shapes	**1B** Unit 8.3 **1C** Unit 5.2	• I can estimate, measure and record area (squares). • I can make a whole.	**MNU 1-11b** • Uses square grids to estimate then measure the areas of a variety of simple 2D shapes to the nearest half square.
Unit 8.8 Creating areas	**1B** Unit 8.3 **1C** Unit 5.2 Unit 8.7	• I can estimate, measure and record area (squares). • I can make a whole. • I can measure area in squares and half squares.	**MNU 1-11a** • Creates shapes with a given area to the nearest half square using square tiles or grids.
Unit 8.9 Area and arrays	**1B** Unit 4.3 Unit 8.3	• I can multiply using an array. • I can estimate, measure and record area (squares).	**MNU 1-11a** • Uses square grids to estimate then measure the areas of a variety of simple 2D shapes to the nearest half square.

Conceptual context

The aim of Book 1B was to develop pupils' understanding of measurement through the ability to estimate, measure and record using standard units. Furthermore, the concept of converting between standard units was introduced, encouraging pupils to make decisions about the most relevant unit of measurement, i.e. *Should we measure the length of the gym hall in metres or centimetres?*

Book 1C aims to extend pupils' understanding of the range of standard units in the metric system and make further connections between related units, i.e. 1 centimetre is equal to 10 millimetres and 1000 millilitres is equal to 1 litre. Pupils should understand that any 'large' unit can be broken down into smaller units in order that attributes can be measured with greater accuracy. In our decimal system this usually means tenths, hundredths and thousandths. However, decimal notation is not introduced at this stage as this is likely to be in advance of the pupils' number skills and will require careful explanation and handling. As such, pupils will develop the ability to convert, for example, 1345 g into 1 kg 345 g (and not 1·345 kg as this may confuse them at this stage). Conversion of standard units should be represented visually (using bar models) to support pupils' understanding of equivalence i.e. when converting four centimetres into millimetres, pupils understand that for every 1 centimetre we count ten millimetres. Pupils should not rely solely on abstract calculations, such as *multiply the number of centimetres by ten to find the number of millimetres*, because the use of *multiplication* implies that the value is increasing in size.

Measurement continues to be a practical and physical exercise that enables children to connect units to quantity. It is vital that pupils continue to develop their understanding of measurement through practical investigations and challenges. As such, the written questions in these units should only be tackled once pupils have had the opportunity to experiment with practical measuring equipment.

The final three units develop understanding of area using squares, half squares and then link the area of a rectangle to arrays. This visual approach will support pupils as they progress to calculating area of composite shapes at second level as opposed to relying on more abstract formulae.

Resources

- 1 cm square paper
- Base 10 materials
- Counting stick
- Feely bags
- Funnels
- Measuring jugs
- Metre sticks
- Plastic syringe
- Post-its (or paper squares)
- Range of containers, e.g. cups, plastic bottles, yoghurt pots, teaspoons, etc.
- Resource sheet 8A: Reading scales (capacity)
- Scales – balance, kitchen, hanging, bathroom
- String
- Tape measures
- Unifix cubes
- Weights

Key vocabulary

- **Area**
- **Array**
- **Capacity**
- **Centimetre**
- **Gram**
- **Height**
- **Kilogram**
- **Length**
- **Mass**
- **Metre**
- **Metre stick**
- **Millimetre**
- **Volume**

Misconceptions

Potential misconception	Addressing the misconception
Unit 8.5 Pupils may fail to understand conservation of volume, i.e. that the volume of liquid remains the same when we pour from one container to another of a different shape.	Provide opportunities for pupils to investigate volume through the use of different shaped containers, i.e. pouring from a narrow into a wider container to understand that the volume of water remains unchanged.
Units 8.3 and 8.6 Pupils may struggle to appreciate that, when converting units of measurement, the actual measurement remains unchanged, i.e. *same value, different appearance*.	Provide practical opportunities where measurements are taken using alternative units, e.g. 132 cm and 1 m 32 cm. Use bar models and counting sticks to represent relationships between converted units (rather than relying on multiplication or division, i.e. *multiply the number of kilograms by 1000 to calculate the number of grams*) as multiplication implies that the measurement is getting bigger and division implies that it is getting smaller.
Units 8.4 and 8.5 Pupils may struggle to appreciate the value of each increment when reading scales or struggle to estimate a value if the measure sits between two increments.	Provide opportunities for pupils to work out the value of each increment on a range of number lines (i.e. with increments of 2, 5, 10, 50, 100, etc.) Provide opportunities for pupils to estimate measurements when sitting between increments.
Units 8.7, 8.8 and 8.9 Pupils may confuse area with perimeter and therefore incorrectly assume that the area of one square is four because they count the four edges.	Use post-it notes or paper squares initially to create shapes with a specific area in order that pupils have something tangible to count before progressing to pictorial representations.
Unit 8.9 Pupils may confuse the formula for calculating area with perimeter (and become over reliant on the formula area = length × width as this is only applicable for the area of a rectangle).	Avoid emphasis on formulas with little or no conceptual understanding. Develop conceptual understanding through the use of arrays to calculate area, i.e. pupils may find it easier to find the number of squares in one row then calculate this by the number of rows.

Teaching ideas

Unit 8.1 Reading and recording measurements - length

- Count on and back in halves using slides (showing number lines and pizza portions) referred to in *Teacher Guide 1A: Unit 5.3*

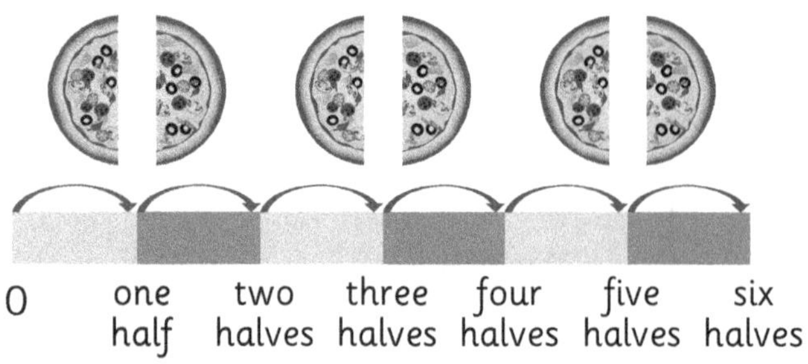

- Repeat the activity referred to in *Teaching Guide 1B: Unit 5.7, Counting in fractions*: Draw or display the following counting stick:

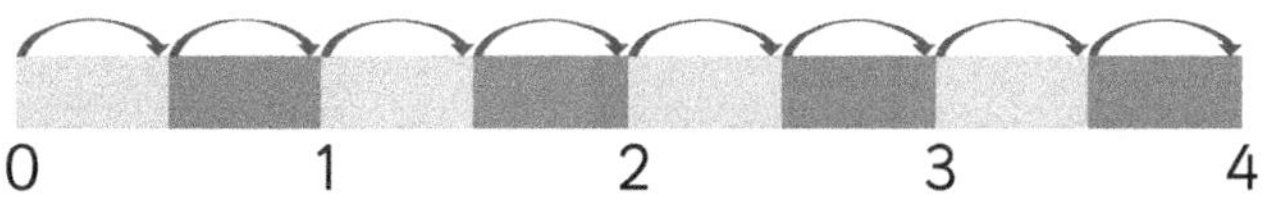

Ask questions, such as: **How many jumps are there between each whole number?** *Two.* **What must be the value of each jump?** *One half.* Fill in the missing jumps as follows:

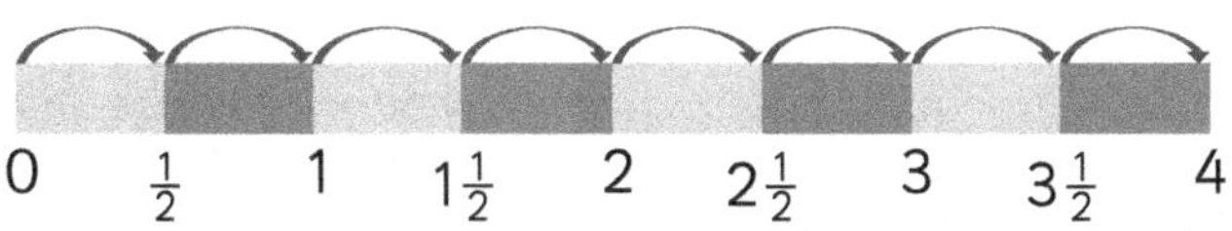

Use a range of contexts for counting in, e.g. glasses of water, bars of chocolate, etc. before introducing the context of length, i.e. counting in half centimetres.

- Provide pupils with rulers and ask them to identify the half centimetre increments:

  Count on and back in half centimetres, using the ruler as the counting stick (pupils should use their finger to keep track of the count on the ruler).

- Challenge pupils to draw lines that are:
  - o four centimetres long
  - o four and a half centimetres long
  - o half a centimetre long
  - o seven and a half centimetres long.

  Challenge pupils to extend each line (using a coloured pen or pencil) to make the total length of each line ten centimetres:

Ask questions, such as: **Can you calculate the length of the coloured line? How did you work it out?** *Subtraction / counting on / counting back.*

Challenge pupils to measure accurately to check.

Unit 8.2 Measuring and recording length – millimetres

- Discuss pupils' understanding of term 'tenth'.

  Elicit through discussion that to find one tenth of an object, we must split it into ten equal-sized parts. (The activity outlined in *Teaching Guide 2C, Unit 6.2* could be demonstrated to create tenths.)

  Look at the markings on a ruler with pupils and elicit through discussion that there are ten equal intervals between each centimetre. Ask questions, such as: **What fraction of a centimetre are each of these intervals?** *One tenth.*

  Explain that one tenth of a centimetre is called a millimetre. Ask questions, such as: **Why might they be called millimetres? What does milli mean at the start of a word?** *One thousandth.* **How many millimetres are there in one centimetre?** *Ten.* **How many centimetres are there in one metre?** *One hundred.* **So how many millimetres are there in one metre?** *One thousand.*

- Challenge pupils to draw lines that are:

  - o 12 mm
  - o 19 mm
  - o 25 mm
  - o 37 mm

  Pupils can swap their attempts with a partner to check.

  Challenge pupils to extend each line (using a coloured pen or pencil) to make the total length of each line 50 mm:

  Ask questions, such as: **Can you calculate the length of the coloured line? How did you work it out?** *Subtraction / counting on / counting back.*

  Challenge pupils to measure the coloured line accurately to check.

Unit 8.3 Converting length – millimetres and centimetres

- Ask pupils to draw a line exactly 5 cm long. Ask: **Can we describe the length of the line using different units?** Elicit through discussion that we can state the length of the line using millimetres.

  The link between centimetres and millimetres could be illustrated by drawing the following bar:

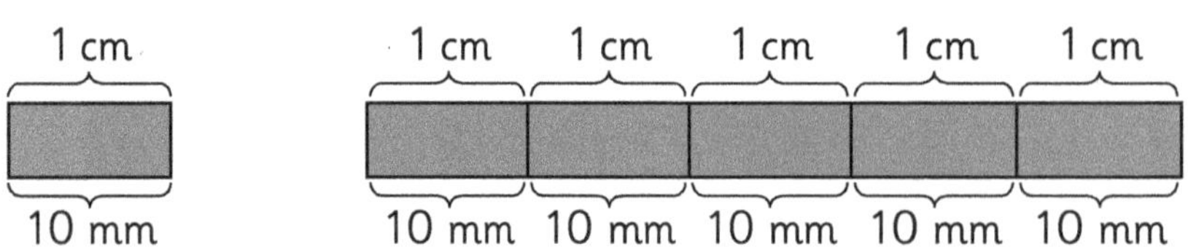

1 cm = 10 mm so 5 cm = 50 mm

Challenge the pupils to convert the following measurements into millimetres:

- o 3 cm
- o 7 cm
- o 10 cm
- o $9\frac{1}{2}$ cm

Note: avoid phrases such as 'add a zero' as it's mathematically incorrect and does not support conceptual understanding. This could be demonstrated using a counting stick:

For every jump of one centimetre:

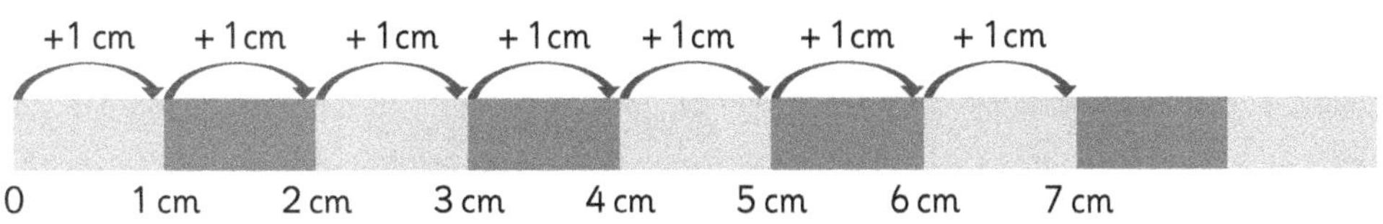

We count ten millimetres:

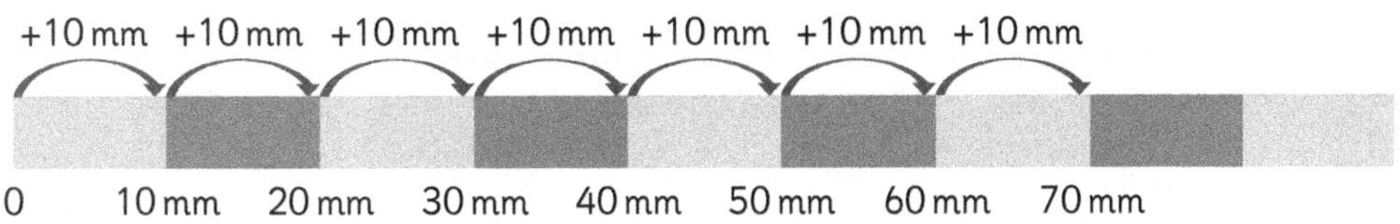

So, 7 centimetres is the same as 70 millimetres.

Challenge pupils to draw lines that are the following lengths and convert them into millimetres:

- o 4 cm and 3 mm
- o 5 cm and 5 mm
- o 7 cm and 9 mm
- o 10 cm and 1 mm

Challenge pupils to draw lines that are the following lengths and convert them into centimetres and millimetres:

- o 38 mm
- o 51 mm
- o 66 mm
- o 111 mm

Challenge pupils to draw lines (or cut lengths of string) they estimate to be the following (i.e. without the use of a ruler):

- o 46 mm
- o 6 cm and 3 mm
- o 84 mm
- o 12 cm and 5 mm

Pupils could then measure each other's lines to check how accurate they were.

Unit 8.4 Reading and recording measurements for mass

- Count on and back in halves and quarters using slides (showing number lines and pizza portions) referred to in *Teaching Guide 1A, Unit 5.3*:

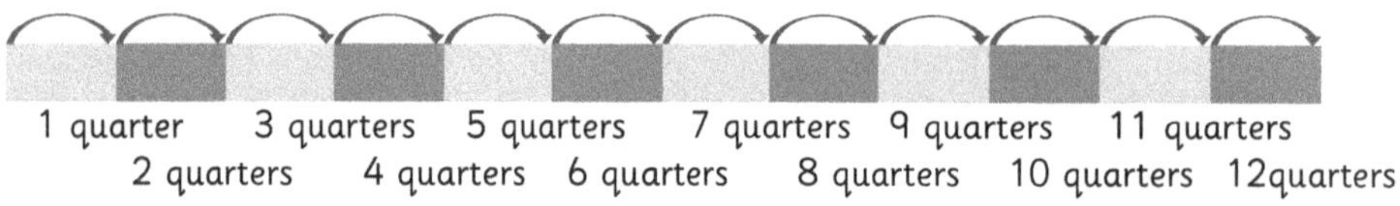

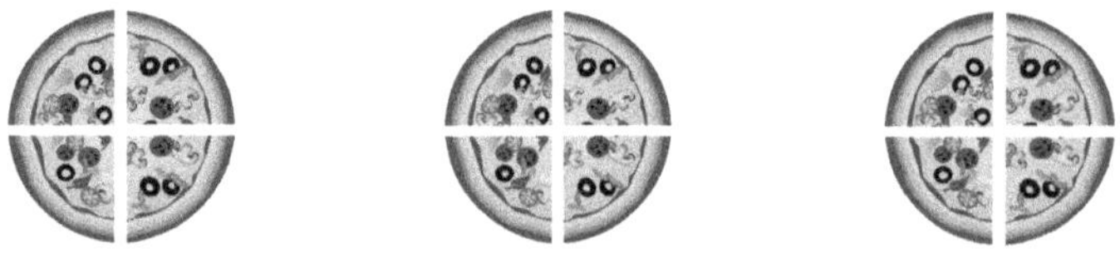

- Repeat the activity referred to in *Teaching Guide 1B, Unit 5.7*. Draw or display the following counting stick:

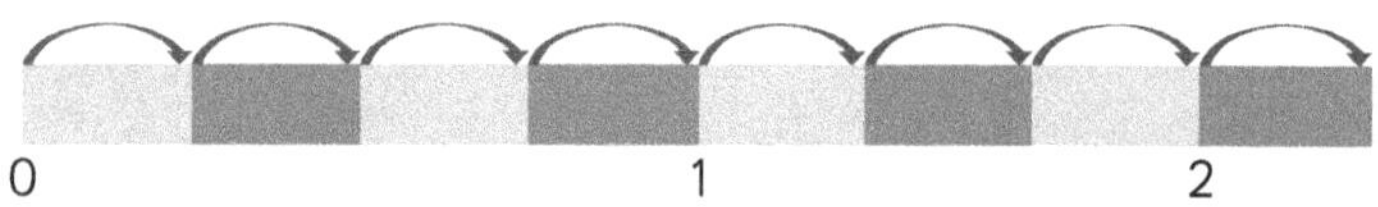

Ask questions, such as: **How many jumps are there between each whole number?** *Four*. **What must be the value of each jump?** *One quarter*. Fill in the missing jumps as follows:

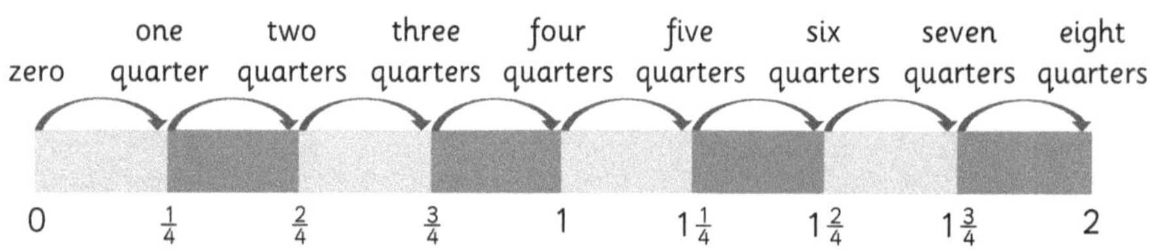

Use a range of contexts for counting in (for example, glasses of water, bars of chocolate, etc.) before introducing the context of mass i.e. counting in half kilograms and quarter kilograms.

- Use a set of kitchen scales to measure out 1 kg of, for example, sand. Ask pupils to read the scales. Pour out half of the sand and ask them to discuss what mass the scales are now displaying: $\frac{1}{2}$ *kg*.

  Pour out half of the remaining sand. Challenge pupils to identify the mass of the sand now. Discuss the fact that the scale is halfway between 0 kg and $\frac{1}{2}$ kg and that half of a half is one quarter, so the mass of sand is now $\frac{1}{4}$ kg.

  Ask pupils questions, such as: **How many grams are there in one kilogram? How many grams are there in half a kilogram? How many grams are there in a quarter of a kilogram? How can we work this out?** *Half kilogram: half of 1000 g = 500 g. Quarter kilogram: half of 500 g = 250 g.*

- Organise pupils into pairs / groups. Provide them with kitchen scales and weights (1 kg, 500 g, 100 g and 50 g) Challenge pupils to identify where the pointer will settle for each of the following:

  - $1\frac{1}{2}$ kg
  - $2\frac{1}{4}$ kg
  - $\frac{3}{4}$ kg
  - $1\frac{3}{4}$ kg

  Challenge pupils to use the weights to measure out each of the above. Ask questions, such as: **What weights did you need to put on the scale for each measurement?** *For example, $1\frac{1}{2}$ kg: 1 × 1 kg and 1 × 500 g.*

Unit 8.5 Reading and recording measurements for capacity

- Repeat the counting stick activities (counting in halves and quarters) outlined in the previous unit.
- See Resource sheet 8A: Reading scales (capacity). Display the number lines (for example) and challenge pupils to identify the missing numbers.
- Fill a one litre measuring jug and draw the following bar to represent it:

Ask pupils, **How many millilitres does this represent?** *1000 ml*

Draw the following below the 1 litre bar:

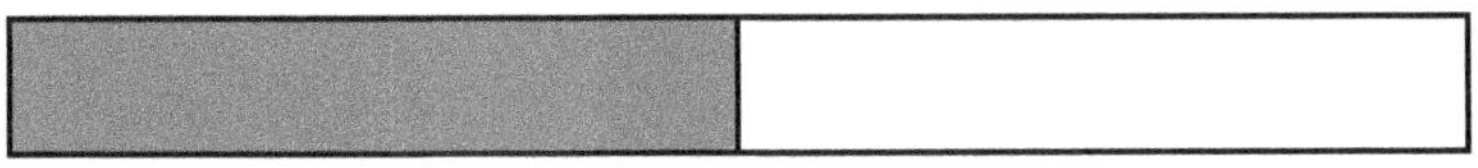

Ask pupils: **What fraction of a litre does this represent?** *Half a litre.* **How many millilitres does this represent?** *500 ml*

- Challenge pupils to measure out half a litre of water.

Draw the following below the half litre bar:

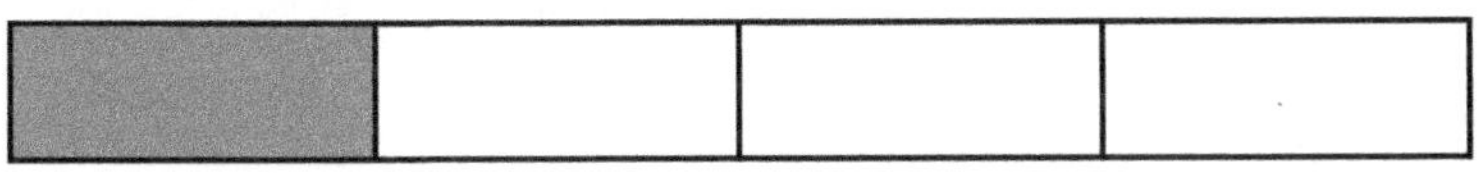

Ask pupils: **What fraction of a litre does this represent?** *Quarter of a litre.* **How many millilitres does this represent?** *250 ml.*

Challenge pupils to measure out one quarter of a litre of water.

- Challenge pupils to draw bar models to represent the following volumes:
  - one and a half litres
  - one and a quarter litres
  - three-quarter of a litre
  - one and three-quarter litres.

For example:

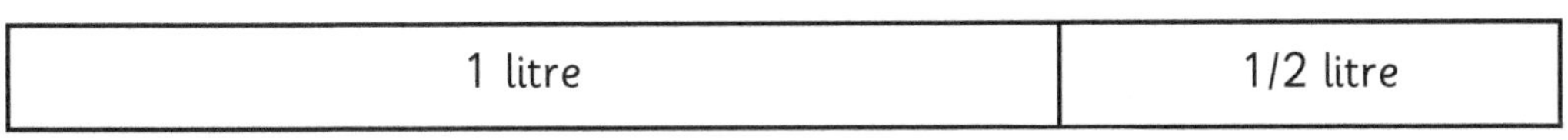

- Organise pupils into groups and provide with various containers, a funnel and a measuring jug.

Challenge groups to identify the fill levels for each of the volumes above. Fill the containers with each of the volumes.

Groups could then pair up with another group to check each other's accuracy, i.e. use their measuring jug to measure the volume of each container.

Unit 8.6 Converting standard units

- Ask pupils: **What standard units can we use to measure:**
  - **Length?** *Metres, centimetres and millimetres*
  - **Mass?** *Kilograms and grams*
  - **Capacity or volume?** *Litres and millilitres*
- Show pupils a metre stick, a kilogram weight and a one litre measuring jug and draw the following bars to represent them:

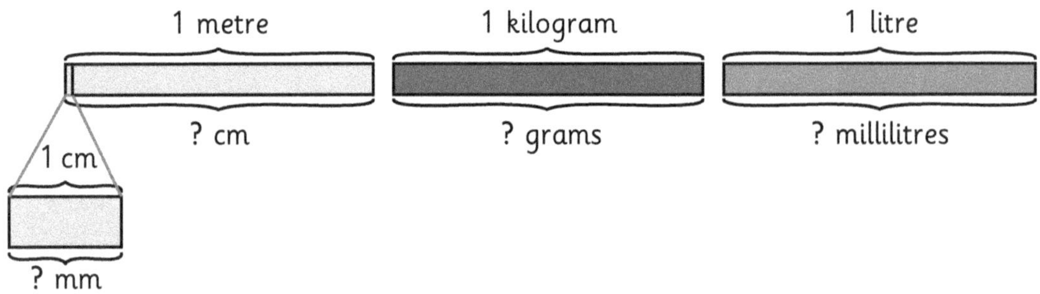

Ask pupils to identify the missing numbers.

- Use the counting stick activity outlined in *Teaching Guide, Unit 8.3* to convert 4 kg 700 g into grams:

For every jump of one kilogram:

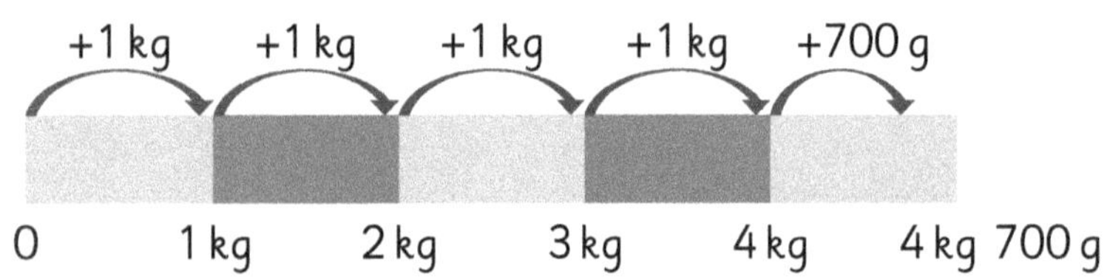

We count one thousand grams:

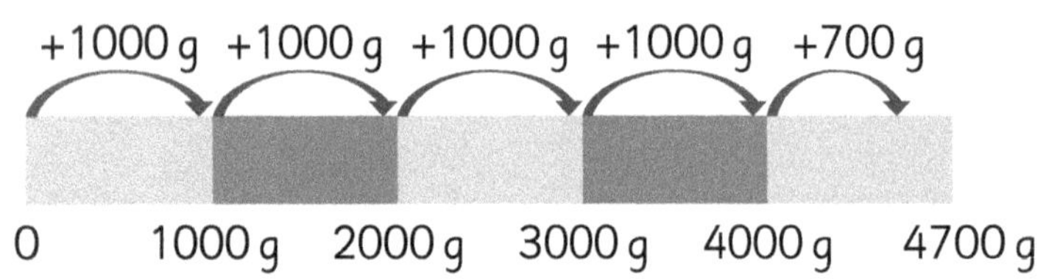

So, 4 kilograms and 700 grams is the same as 4700 grams.

- Challenge pupils to draw bar models (or counting sticks) to convert the following measurements:
  - o 3 metres and 42 centimetres into centimetres
  - o 4 metres and 7 centimetres into centimetres
  - o 2 kilograms and 538 grams into grams
  - o 4 kilograms and 60 grams into grams
  - o 1 kilograms and 9 grams into grams
  - o 5 litres and 763 millilitres into millilitres
  - o 2 litres and 84 millilitres into millilitres
  - o 6 litres and 5 millilitres into millilitres.

- Challenge pupils to draw bar models (or counting sticks) to convert the following measurements:
  - o 297 centimetres into metres and centimetres
  - o 301 centimetres into metres and centimetres
  - o 1803 grams into kilograms and grams
  - o 2070 grams into kilograms and grams
  - o 3002 grams into kilograms and grams
  - o 4217 millilitres into litres and millilitres
  - o 2010 millilitres into litres and millilitres
  - o 5008 millilitres into litres and millilitres.

Unit 8.7 Area of shapes

- Display the following:

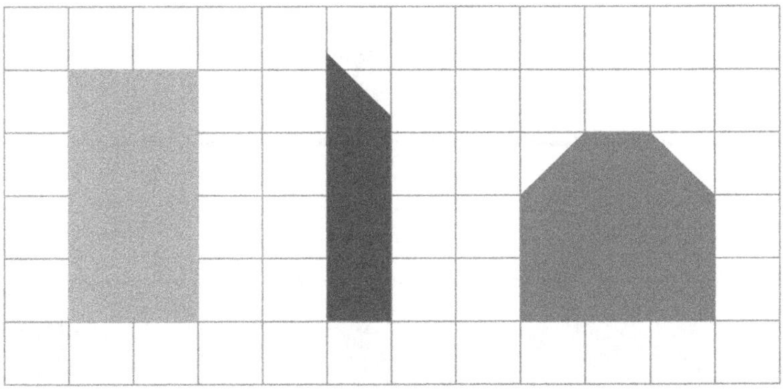

See Resource sheet 8B: Area of shapes. Make (or write) the following statements – True or false:

- o The green shape has an area of six squares.
- o The red shape has an area of three squares.
- o The blue shape has an area of seven squares.

Ask pupils to discuss their thoughts and justify their responses.

Organise pupils into pairs and provide them with copies of the shapes (or alternatively ask them to draw the shapes on squared paper) and scissors and challenge them to measure the area of each (pupils should be asked to prove their results, i.e. by cutting the shape up).

Demonstrate that a square can be cut in half in two ways that will help us measure the area of each shape:

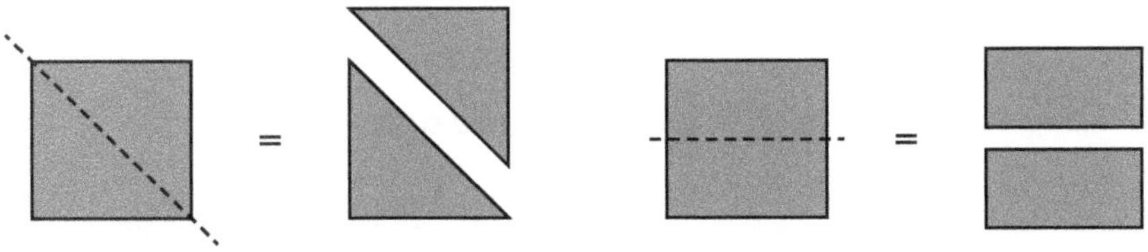

Elicit through discussion that we can now use these to accurately measure the areas of seven squares, three and a half squares, and eight squares, respectively.

- Display (or provide pupils with) the following and challenge them to measure the area of each:

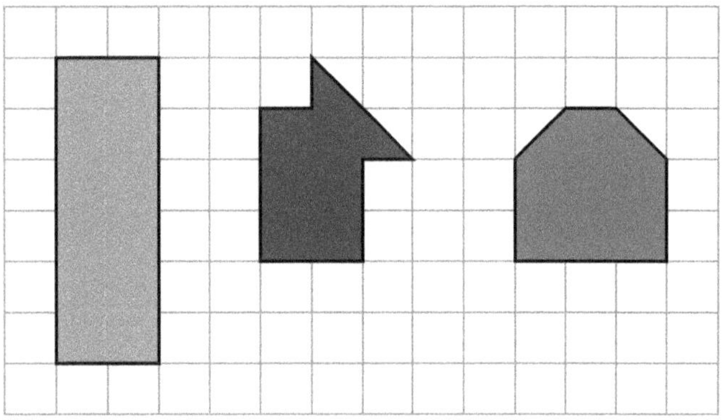

- Provide pupils with post-it notes (or paper squares) and challenge them to create shapes (containing at least one half square) with the following areas:
    - o five and a half squares
    - o six squares
    - o seven and a half squares
    - o nine squares

  Alternatively, pupils could be provided with squared paper and challenged to find as many shapes as they can (using the above criteria).

Unit 8.8 Creating areas

- Provide pupils with post-it notes (or paper squares) and challenge them to create as many shapes as they can with an area of four squares, for example:

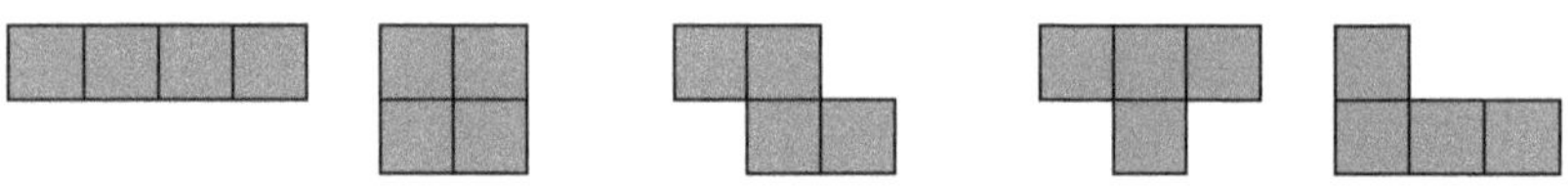

  Provide pupils with scissors and ask them how many more shapes they can create if they are allowed to cut one or more of the squares in half (creating both triangular or rectangular halves), for example:

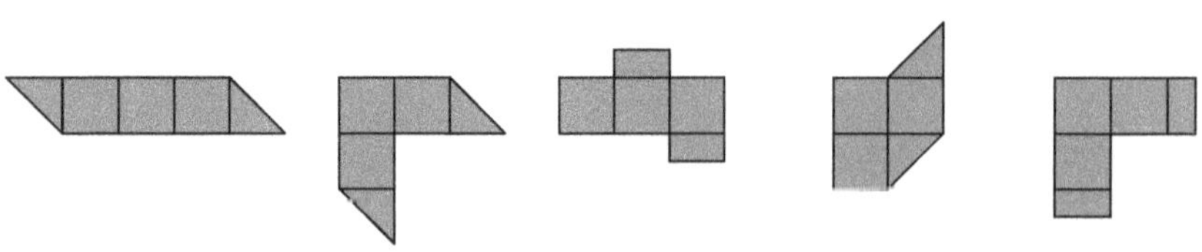

- Organise pupils into pairs / groups. Roll a dice to generate the number of whole squares, for example:

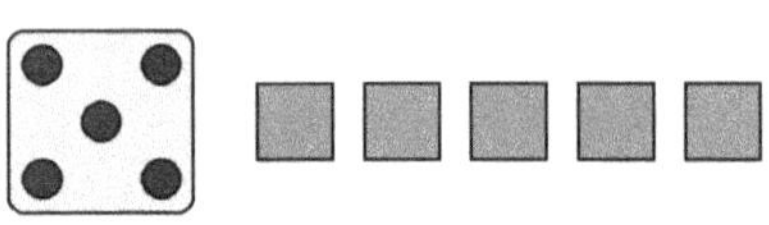

Roll a second dice to generate the number of half squares, for example:

Challenge pupils to draw (or create) a shape using the same combination and measure the area, for example:

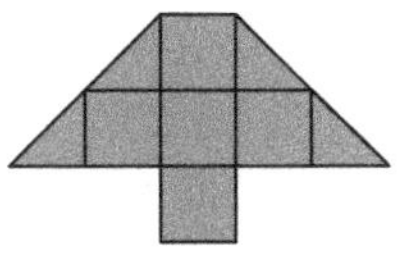

7 squares

- Provide pupils with eight squares. Challenge them to make shapes with specific criteria; for example, make a shape that must contain:
    - o at least one side that is five squares long
    - o exactly seven sides
    - o six half squares
    - o more half squares than whole squares

Unit 8.9 Areas and arrays

- Challenge pupils to draw arrays making a total of:
    - o 12
    - o 16
    - o 20
    - o 24

For example:

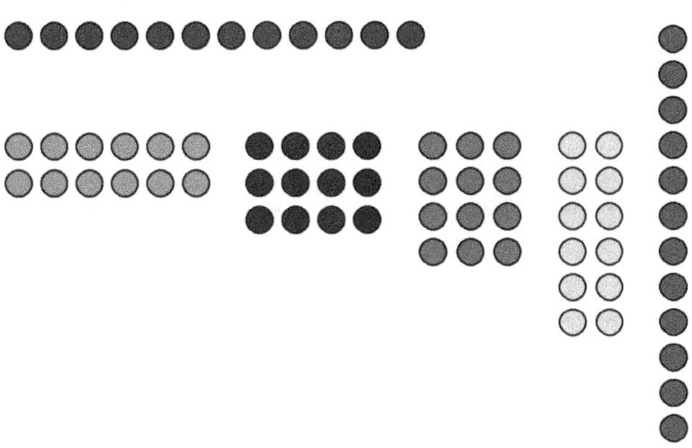

Ask questions, such as; **How many different arrays can you draw for each?** *6, 5, 6, 8.* **What multiplication number stories can you write for each array?** *E.g.* $1 \times 12 = 12$, $2 \times 6 = 12$, $3 \times 4 = 12$, $4 \times 3 = 12$, $6 \times 2 = 12$ *and* $12 \times 1 = 12$. **What shape is each of the arrays you have drawn?** *Rectangle.* For example:

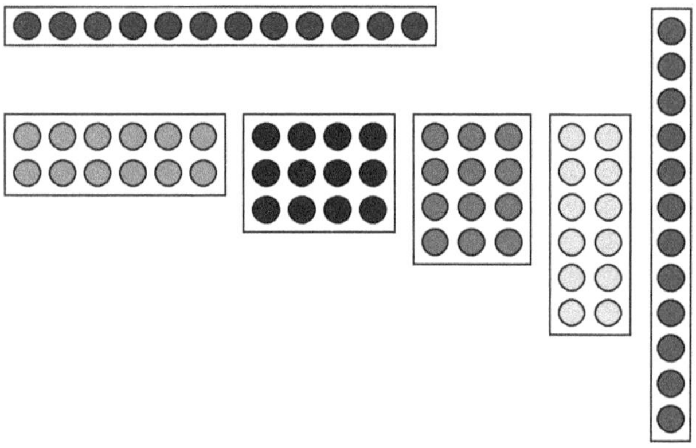

Demonstrate that the same arrays can be represented using squares:

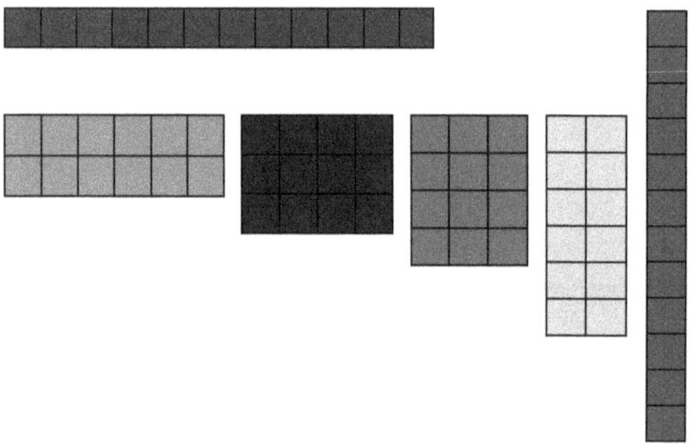

Ask pupils: **How can we measure the area of each of these rectangles (arrays)?** *We can count the total number of squares OR we can use the multiplication story for each array, e.g. 2 rows of 6 squares =* 2×6 *squares = 12 squares.*

Challenge pupils to draw rectangles (arrays) that represent the following number stories and calculate the area of each:

- o $3 \times 5 = ?$
- o $4 \times 6 = ?$
- o $5 \times 5 = ?$
- o $7 \times 3 = ?$

9 Mathematics, its impact on the world, past, present and future

Mathematics, its impact on the world, past, present and future 1A

Section overview

Textbook 1A units	Review units	Prior learning	Benchmarks/Es&Os
Unit 9.1 Ways numbers are used in real life		• I recognise numbers are used every day. • I can identify different ways we use numbers. • I know that numbers have been used by many cultures and civilisations. • I know that numbers are represented in different ways.	**MTH 1-12a** • Investigates and shares understanding of the importance of numbers in learning, life and work. • Investigates and shares understanding of a variety of number systems used throughout history.

Conceptual context

The study of mathematics has led to great inventions that have raised standards of living and created the modern society that we live in today. Famous mathematicians litter history and their lives and discoveries are still discussed today. People such as Lovelace, Einstein, Aryabhatta, Nightingale, Pythagoras and Turing, have all contributed to the development of human thinking and their ideas are celebrated in the mathematics community.

Interestingly, the study of mathematics was often undertaken alongside other disciplines or not even thought of as mathematics. Many historical figures that we recognise for mathematics often considered themselves as philosophers. For Example Isaac Newton (1642 – 1727) published his famous laws of motion in the book entitled, 'Philosophiæ Naturalis Principia Mathematica' (Mathematical Principles of Natural Philosophy).

Engaging with the history of mathematics and the colourful figures from the past (and present) that have led to our current understanding of mathematics can help to build motivation in pupils and identify cross-curricular links.

The textbook unit presents a section on numbers used in everyday life and encourages pupils to look at their environment and daily experiences and routines to identify the many areas in which numbers are featured. Encourage pupils to recognise that mathematics is a worldwide phenomenon and that mathematics is a universal language. From simple tally marks on a stick to complex written number systems that could be used to perform many types of calculations, people in the ancient world developed and used a wide variety of number systems.

Resources

- Number cards (Resource sheet 9B)
- Picture cards (Resource sheet 9A)

Key vocabulary

- **Mathematician**
- **Numerical notation**
- **Research**

Misconceptions

Potential misconception	Addressing the misconception
Unit 9.1 Pupils may think that number systems must contain digits.	Pupils might think that due to the word 'number', that a number system should contain a digit. Explain that a number system measures a quantity that can be represented using letters, tally marks, diagrams, symbols, etc.

Teaching ideas

Unit 9.1 Ways numbers are used in real life

- Before starting this unit, a broad discussion about what pupils think mathematics actually is might be interesting. For example, ask: **What are numbers? Why are numbers important in your daily life? What do you use numbers for outside of your school day?**
- Through discussion you can explore pupils' knowledge and understanding of how they perceive numbers in relation to their lives and daily routine.
- Ask pupils to think of as many different ways they use numbers on a daily basis. (Keeping a list on the wall of the classroom that gets added to every week can be a fun challenge for the whole class.)
- Ask pupils how they know what each of the numbers mean? How can they check or clarify this?
- Either in pairs or groups, give pupils a copy of the picture cards and the number cards (Resource sheets 9A and 9B).
- Explain to pupils that numbers are used in everyday life. Ask them to look at the pictures and identify the different ways numbers are being used. Alternatively, this activity can take place during a visit to a local supermarket.

Mathematics, its impact on the world, past, present and future 1B

Section overview

Textbook 1B units	Review units	Prior learning	Benchmarks/Es&Os
Unit 9.1 Ways numbers are used in work	**1A** Unit 9.1	• I understand people use numbers every day. • I can identify different ways we use numbers. • I know that numbers are represented in different ways.	**MTH 1-12a** • Investigates and shares understanding of the importance of numbers in learning, life and work. • Investigates and shares understanding of a variety of number systems used throughout history.

Conceptual context

The study of mathematics has led to great inventions that have raised standards of living and created the modern society that we live in today. Famous mathematicians litter history and their lives and discoveries are still discussed today. People such as Lovelace, Einstein, Aryabhatta, Nightingale, Pythagoras and Turing, have all contributed to the development of human thinking and their works are celebrated in the mathematics community.

Interestingly, the study of mathematics was often undertaken alongside other disciplines or not even thought of as mathematics. Many historical figures that we recognise for mathematics often considered themselves as philosophers. For example, Isaac Newton (1642 – 1727) published his famous laws of motion in the book entitled, 'Philosophiæ Naturalis Principia Mathematica' (Mathematical Principles of Natural Philosophy).

Engaging with the history of mathematics and the colourful figures from the past (and present) that have led to our current understanding of mathematics can help to build motivation in pupils and identify cross-curricular links.

The textbook unit presents a section on the way numbers are used in a variety of different workplace settings. By learning about different number systems, pupils can start to recognise that mathematics is a worldwide phenomenon and that numbers are used universally as a means of communication. Number systems have been used for years to communicate amounts of things and these have evolved over the years to the modern base 10 system we use today. A number system is a way of recording and expressing numbers using digits, letters or symbols in a consistent way.

Finally, by studying the impact of mathematics on the world, pupils will begin to see how much of our lives are connected with mathematics. Every financial purchase or transaction relies on a mathematical analysis to make a good choice. Everyday risk is informed by chance and uncertainty and the way information is presented and used requires a sound statistical grounding, to ensure that facts are separated from falsehoods.

Resources

- Profession cards (resource sheet 9D)
- Recipe card (Resource sheet 9C)

Key vocabulary

- **Civilisation**
- **Invention**
- **Mathematician**
- **Numerical notation**
- **Profession**
- **Research**

Misconceptions

Potential misconception	Addressing the misconception
Unit 9.1 Pupils may think that numbers and maths are only important in school.	Pupils might think that numbers are only for calculations and used during school activities. Take time to discuss the importance of numbers in our environment and how they are everywhere.

Teaching ideas

Unit 9.1 Ways numbers are used in work

- Give pupils copies of Resource sheet 9D and ask them to discuss with their shoulder partner/group the different professions and where they will use numbers in their jobs.
- Tell pupils to be as creative as they can and to think about all areas of the jobs each one has. You could give pupils post-its and get them to record their ideas and this could form a display for the Numeracy Wall.
- Ask pupils to generate a list of other professions and discuss how numbers will play a part in their daily lives. Alternatively, save this activity for a 'bring a parent to school' day and quiz the adults on how they use numbers and mathematics as part of their job.
- Show pupils the recipe card (Resource sheet 9C) and ask them to identify the different ways in which numbers are used. Discuss how they would make the recipe without the specific quantities listed. Using 'no-cook' recipes can make this into a practical activity. The amounts of each ingredient can be measured using scales or cups. Some no-cook recipes include peppermint creams, truffles, cheesecake, ice cream and raw strawberry jam.

Mathematics, its impact on the world, past, present and future 1C

Section overview

Textbook 1C units	Review units	Prior learning	Benchmarks/Es&Os
Unit 9.1 Mathematicians and early number systems	**1B** Unit 9.1	• I understand people use numbers every day. • I can identify different ways we use numbers. • I know that numbers are represented in different ways.	**MTH 1-12a** • Investigates and shares understanding of the importance of numbers in learning, life and work. • Investigates and shares understanding of a variety of number systems used throughout history.

Conceptual context

The study of mathematics has led to great inventions that have raised standards of living and created the modern society that we live in today. Famous mathematicians litter history and their lives and discoveries are still discussed today. People such as Lovelace, Einstein, Aryabhatta, Nightingale, Pythagoras and Turing, have all contributed to the development of human thinking and their ideas are celebrated in the mathematics community.

Interestingly, the study of mathematics was often undertaken alongside other disciplines or not even thought of as mathematics. Many historical figures that we recognise for mathematics often considered themselves as philosophers. For example, Isaac Newton (1642 – 1727) published his famous laws of motion in the book entitled, 'Philosophiæ Naturalis Principia Mathematica' (Mathematical Principles of Natural Philosophy).

Engaging with the history of mathematics and the colourful figures from the past (and present) that have led to our current understanding of mathematics can help to build motivation in pupils and identify cross-curricular links.

The textbook unit presents a section on mathematical number systems and ends with a challenge to research a famous historical figure. By learning about different number systems, the pupil can start to recognise that mathematics is a worldwide phenomenon and that mathematics is a universal language. Number systems have been used for years to communicate amounts of things and these have evolved over the years to the modern base 10 system we use today. A number system is a way of recording and expressing numbers using digits, letters or symbols in a consistent way. From simple tally marks on a stick to complex written number systems that could be used to perform many types of calculations, people in the ancient world developed and used a wide variety of number systems. Around 3000 BCE, the ancient Egyptians used a system of numerical notation or 'hieroglyphs' based on a combination of shapes and marks.

When challenged to research a historical figure, pupils can also develop skills in literacy, history and ICT. By creating a presentation, they are developing their ability to communicate and share ideas.

Finally, by studying the impact of mathematics on the world, pupils will begin to see how much of our lives are connected with mathematics. Every financial purchase or transaction relies on a mathematical analysis to make a good choice. Everyday risk is informed by chance and uncertainty and the way information is presented and used requires a sound statistical grounding, to ensure that facts are separated from falsehoods.

Resources

- Famous mathematician fact cards (see Resource sheet 9E)

Key vocabulary

- **Civilisation**
- **Invention**
- **Mathematician**
- **Numerical notation**
- **Research**

Misconceptions

Potential misconception	Addressing the misconception
Unit 9.1 Pupils may think that number systems must contain digits.	Pupils might think that due to the word 'number' that a number system should contain a digit. Explain that a number system measures a quantity that can be represented using letters, tally marks, diagrams, symbols, etc.

Teaching ideas

Unit 9.1 Mathematicians and early number systems

- Write the following question on the board and ask pupils to discuss with their shoulder partner: **What is a mathematician?**
- Encourage pupils to share their ideas with one another thinking about all the people who use maths in their daily lives. They could also draw a picture of what they think a mathematician looks like and the tools they would use.
- Give pupils the famous mathematician fact cards (Resource sheet 9E). There are four cards, so pupils could have one per pair/group. Each pair has to become an expert and describe their mathematician to other pupils.
- Now quiz the class on the cards by asking questions, such as: **Which two mathematicians were alive at the same time? Which two were involved in the development of computing? Who wrote the first maths textbook? Who was a nurse as well as a mathematician? What was she famous for?**
- On the board, put up the following:

- Ask pupils what this represents and if they know what it is called.
- Discuss the fact that tally marks are in fact an example of a number system and a way to represent a value or quantity. Ask pupils if they know any other different ways that they can write numbers? Note that a simple list can include digits, words, dots, pictures (such as the ancient Egyptian system) and computers system numbers, such as binary.
- Continue to the 'Let's Practise' section of Unit 9.1.

10 Patterns and relationships

Patterns and relationships 1A

Section overview

Textbook 1A units	Review units	Prior learning	Benchmarks/Es&Os
Unit 10.1 Continuing patterns	**Early – B** Units 8.1 and 8.2	• I understand the terms patterns, sequence, repeat and continue. • I can copy and continue repeating patterns. • I can use concrete materials to represent patterns and sequences.	**MTH 1-13a** I can continue and devise more involved repeating patterns or designs, using a variety of media. **MTH 1-13b** Through exploring number patterns, I can recognise and continue simple number sequences and can explain the rule I have applied. • Counts forwards and backwards in 2s, 5s and 10s from any whole number up to 1000. • Describes patterns in number; for example, in the multiplication tables and hundred square. • Continues and creates repeating patterns involving shapes, pictures and symbols. • Describes, continues and creates number patterns using addition, subtraction, doubling, halving, counting in jumps (skip counting) and known multiples.
Unit 10.2 Recognise and continue number sequences		• I understand the terms patterns, sequence, repeat and continue. • I can recognise number patterns. • I can use concrete materials to represent patterns and sequences.	**MTH 1-13a** I can continue and devise more involved repeating patterns or designs, using a variety of media. **MTH 1-13b** Through exploring number patterns, I can recognise and continue simple number sequences and can explain the rule I have applied. • Counts forwards and backwards in 2s, 5s and 10s from any whole number up to 1000. • Describes patterns in number; for example, in the multiplication tables and hundred square. • Continues and creates repeating patterns involving shapes, pictures and symbols. • Describes, continues and creates number patterns using addition, subtraction, doubling, halving, counting in jumps (skip counting) and known multiples.

Conceptual context

Patterns of numbers and patterns of shapes are everywhere in mathematics. Some patterns are repeating, and some are sequential. Patterns and relationships provide the foundations for a variety of the strategies that pupils are being taught to solve number calculations. Patterns in simple terms are relationships that exist between various elements. A sequential pattern needs to have a starting point and a rule to explain the consistent growth of the pattern. Pupils should be challenged to identify patterns and relationships in their environment and be encouraged to use different strategies to record patterns and relationships including in pictures, diagrams and tables. Other differentiators you could use to introduce pupils to patterns include size, texture, temperature, flavour and smell.

Pupils have looked at how patterns and sequences can be made up by using the four operations. Within this unit, pupils' understanding is developed by asking them to identify and explain a pattern or sequence. Pupils may recognise familiar numbers and sequences without fully understanding mathematically the relationship between the digits. For example, if pupils have rote-learned their 2 times table (2, 4, 6, 8…) then they will recognise a sequence that uses multiples of 2 without being able to articulate that it is increasing by 2 each time. Providing pupils with the correct vocabulary and framework to articulate the relationship within a pattern or sequence is a vital part of deepening their understanding.

Resources

- Lego
- Unifix cubes (different colours)

Key vocabulary

- **Elements**
- **Exploring**
- **Extending**
- **Pattern**
- **Recur**
- **Relationship**
- **Repeating**
- **Sequence**
- **Term**

Misconceptions

Potential misconception	Addressing the misconception
Unit 10.1 Pupils may think that patterns or sequences only contain numbers.	Provide pupils with lots of examples of patterns or sequences that contain letters, shapes, colours and numbers to highlight that it is not only numerical.
Unit 10.1 Pupils may think that patterns or sequences cannot have two of the same thing next to one another – ABB, Blue Red Red…	Introduce pupils to a wide variety of repeating patterns to highlight how they can contain duplicate letters, numbers, shapes and so on and still form a pattern – A, B, B, C, D, D, etc.

Teaching ideas

Unit 10.1 Continuing patterns

- In front of pupils, start to join unifix cubes using a 2-colour pattern.

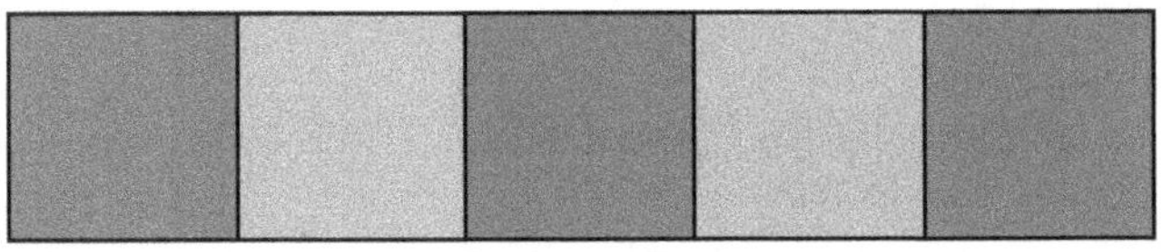

- Ask pupils to describe what you are doing and to explain what they see. Give them the opportunity to discuss with a shoulder partner and then feed back. Ask pupils if it is a coincidence that the cubes have been joined red, blue, red, blue…
- Now, ask pupils to copy this pattern. It is important that pupils can both copy the original pattern and compare their own with the original to demonstrate their pattern awareness. This can then be extended by asking them what colour of cube they would add next and why. Some pupils will copy a pattern accurately but will be unable to continue it. Understanding the 'unit of repeat' leads to multiplicative thinking. This involves counting groups of items and not just single items, which is important when understanding number composition.
- Introduce pupils to a variety of repeating patterns using different shapes, objects and numbers.
- Looking at the 'Let's Learn' section with pupils, emphasise with pupils the fact that patterns are created as a result of the relationship between a variety of different things including shapes, pictures, letters, numbers and actions. Highlight the importance of being able to discuss the relationship as the key mathematical thinking.

Unit 10.2 Recognise and continue number sequences

- Write the first 5 odd numbers on the board: 1, 3, 5, 7, 9.
- Ask pupils to look at the number sequence and to explain what they see. Discuss the relationship between the numbers before asking pupils to write down the next 2 numbers in the sequence.
- Challenge pupils to create a number sequence of their own that has at least 5 numbers.
- Discuss the sequences that they have created and the relationship between the numbers.
- Encourage dialogue using the following questions: **What is the relationship between the numbers in your sequence? Are the numbers getting bigger or smaller? Are the numbers increasing/decreasing by the same amount each time? Can you find a pattern? Can you write the previous/next two numbers?**
- Before starting the unit, ensure that pupils are familiar with the idea that number sequences can get larger and smaller and involve +, −, × and ÷.

Patterns and relationships 1B

Section overview

Textbook 1B units	Review units	Prior learning	Benchmarks/Es&Os
Unit 10.1 Investigate repeating patterns	**1A** Unit 10.1	• I understand the vocabulary: patterns, sequence, repeat and continue. • I can continue a repeating pattern or sequence. • I can use concrete materials to represent patterns and sequences.	**MTH 1-13a** **MTH 1-13b** • Counts forwards and backwards in 2s, 5s and 10s from any whole number up to 1000. • Describes patterns in number; for example, in the multiplication tables and hundred square. • Continues and creates repeating patterns involving shapes, pictures and symbols. • Describes, continues and creates number patterns using addition, subtraction, doubling, halving, counting in jumps (skip counting) and known multiples.
Unit 10.2 Recognise and continue number sequences	**1A** Unit 10.2	• I can continue a repeating pattern or sequence. • I can use concrete materials to represent patterns and sequences. • I can explain simple number patterns.	**MTH 1-13a** **MTH 1-13b** • Counts forwards and backwards in 2s, 5s and 10s from any whole number up to 1000. • Describes patterns in number; for example, in the multiplication tables and hundred square. • Continues and creates repeating patterns involving shapes, pictures and symbols. • Describes, continues and creates number patterns using addition, subtraction, doubling, halving, counting in jumps (skip counting) and known multiples.

Conceptual context

Patterns and relationships exist in numbers, shapes, letters and in the world around us. Pupils who can recognise and use these are better problem solvers, have deeper understanding of mathematics and are more able to engage in algebraic thinking, which involves recognising mathematical features, identifying the relationship between elements and noting regularities. Developing this pattern-based thinking is very important and leads to a greater appreciation of how functions are used to describe relationships. Recognising, constructing and extending and classifying objects and identifying rules are key features of pattern based thinking.

Pupils should be given the opportunity to recognise, construct and extend patterns using blocks, sticks, cubes and other concrete materials developing the tools to become better learners of mathematics and better problem solvers, making connections between maths and other curricular areas.

Resources

- Buttons
- Hundred square
- Unifix cubes
- Whiteboards
- Whiteboard pens

Key vocabulary

- **Element**
- **Exploring**
- **Extending**
- **Formula**
- **Pattern**
- **Recur**
- **Relationship**
- **Repeating**
- **Sequence**
- **Symbol**
- **Term**

Misconceptions

Potential misconception	Addressing the misconception
Unit 10.1 Pupils may expect patterns to always increase in size.	Ensure that pupils encounter a range of different patterns that have increasing and decreasing rules.
Unit 10.1 Pupils may expect patterns to always change by the same amount each time.	Ensure that the pupils meet patterns created by all four operations and also patterns that are created according to shape (square and triangular numbers) or patterns that have a multi-step rule, such as the Fibonacci sequence.
Unit 10.1 Pupils may not realise that they can strategise to work out the rule for generating the pattern, instead they expect the 'rule' to pop into their head.	Ensure that you explain your reasoning for continuing a pattern and encourage them to do the same. Show the pupils that you look for the gaps between numbers, you use your number facts, like multiplication facts and also your knowledge of special sequences such as square and triangular numbers and the Fibonacci sequence.

Teaching ideas

Unit 10.1 Investigate repeating patterns

- Ask pupils to look around the classroom and to identify any patterns they can see. For example, the way the desks are joined together or the window panes, or the carpet tiles, etc.
- Once they have had time to record their observations, give pupils time to discuss their ideas and encourage them to think about the relationship between the patterns and sequences they have found.

- Using a hundred square and the counters, ask pupils to create patterns and to explain the relationships to each other. Pupils can place the counters over numbers to show their patterns and sequences.

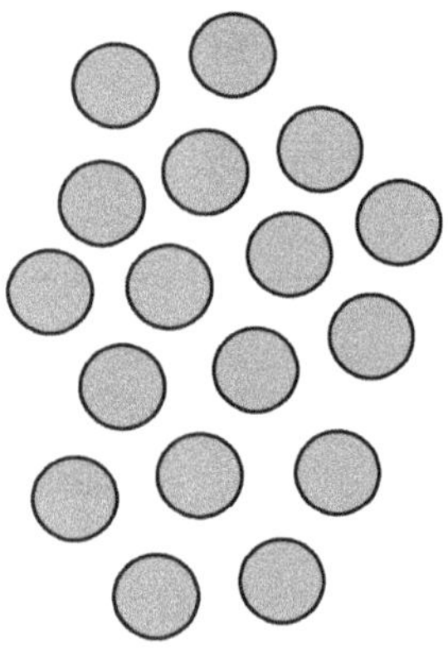

1	2	3	4	5	6	7	8	9	10
11	12	13	14	15	16	17	18	19	20
21	22	23	24	25	26	27	28	29	30
31	32	33	34	35	36	37	38	39	40
41	42	43	44	45	46	47	48	49	50
51	52	53	54	55	56	57	58	59	60
61	62	63	64	65	66	67	68	69	70
71	72	73	74	75	76	77	78	79	80
81	82	83	84	85	86	87	88	89	90
91	92	93	94	95	96	97	98	99	100

- Possible examples could be numbers ending in one or numbers decreasing by 11, e.g. 100, 89, 78…
- Ask pupils to create a repeating pattern of their own using 2D shapes. Encourage them to share their pattern with their shoulder partner, explaining how they have created it.

Unit 10.2 Recognise and continue number sequences

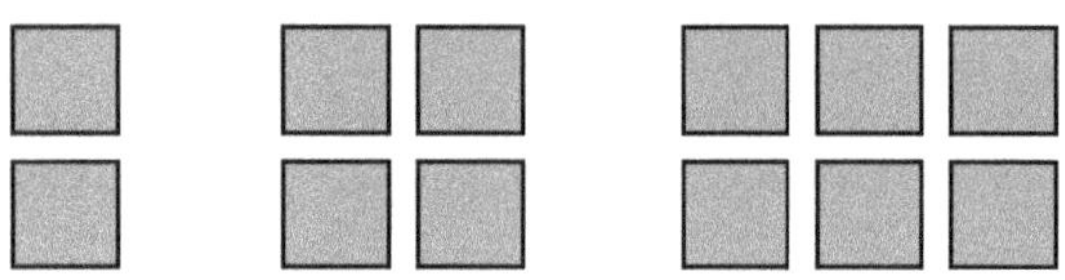

- Show the above pattern to pupils and ask them to explain what they see. Encourage them to be specific in their descriptions. Develop the discussion using the following questions: **What do you see? How many squares are in each group of the pattern? Is the pattern increasing or decreasing? By how much is the pattern increasing? How many squares are in the next group in the pattern?**
- Ask pupils to create their own number pattern and encourage them to describe it to their shoulder partner using the appropriate vocabulary.

Patterns and relationships 1C

Section overview

Textbook 1C units	Review units	Prior learning	Benchmarks/Es&Os
Unit 10.1 Continue number patterns and sequences	**1B** Unit 10.1	• I understand the vocabulary: patterns, sequence, multiple, increasing and decreasing. • I can identify and continue a repeating pattern or sequence. • I can use concrete materials to represent and expand patterns and sequences.	**MTH 1-13a** **MTH 1-13b** • Counts forwards and backwards in 2s, 5s and 10s from any whole number up to 1000. • Describes patterns in number; for example, in the multiplication tables and hundred square. • Continues and creates repeating patterns involving shapes, pictures and symbols. • Describes, continues and creates number patterns using addition, subtraction, doubling, halving, counting in jumps (skip counting) and known multiples.
Unit 10.2 Explain the rules for simple number sequences	**1B** Unit 10.2	• I understand and can continue a repeating number sequence. • I can use concrete materials to represent number patterns and sequences. • I can identify and explain simple number patterns.	**MTH 1-13a** **MTH 1-13b** • Counts forwards and backwards in 2s, 5s and 10s from any whole number up to 1000. • Describes patterns in number; for example, in the multiplication tables and hundred square. • Continues and creates repeating patterns involving shapes, pictures and symbols. • Describes, continues and creates number patterns using addition, subtraction, doubling, halving, counting in jumps (skip counting) and known multiples.

Conceptual context

Finding patterns in number, shapes, colour and the many other examples that can be found in our lives will support students to recognise, describe and continue sequences. We should realise that patterns can be used to analyse and predict real-life situations and through this process we will make links with algebraic concepts such as formulae, gradient and the equations for a straight line.

Investigating patterns in an organised and systematic way develops pattern-based thinking and encourages problem solving. This leads to an appreciation of how functions can be used to describe relationships between number and number patterns. Pupils should use manipulatives to investigate what happens in a pattern as the number of terms is extended or as the beginning of a number is changed. As pupils look at square numbers and triangular numbers, they will study patterns that involve multiplication and division. As categories become more complex, more than one attribute is used to categorise and classify objects. Pupils will work to organise their study of patterns more carefully and systematically by learning to use tables more effectively to record, identify and extend their findings. When pupils start to collect data and look for a pattern in an attempt to solve a problem, they can often be unsure as to what they are looking for. By organising this data into a chart or a table, patterns can begin to appear that will help pupils to determine a solution.

Resources

- Dice
- Pens
- Whiteboards

Key vocabulary

- **Element**
- **Exploring**
- **Extending**
- **Formula**
- **Multiple**
- **Pattern**
- **Recur**
- **Relationship**
- **Repeating**
- **Sequence**
- **Square number**
- **Symbol**
- **Term**
- **Triangular number**

Misconceptions

Potential misconception	Addressing the misconception
Unit 10.1 Pupils may think that a multiple of one number cannot be a multiple of another.	When discussing the multiples of 3 within the 'Let's learn' section, take time to discuss multiples of other numbers so that pupils understand that there will be an overlap.
Unit 10.1 Pupils may expect patterns to always increase in size.	Ensure that pupils encounter a range of different patterns that have increasing and decreasing rules.
Unit 10.1 Pupils may expect patterns to always change by the same amount each time.	Ensure that the pupils meet patterns created by all four operations, patterns that are created according to shape (square and triangular numbers), and patterns that have a multi-step rule, such as the Fibonacci sequence.
Unit 10.1 Pupils may not realise that they can strategise to work out the rule for generating the pattern, instead they expect the 'rule' to pop into their head.	Ensure that you explain your reasoning for continuing a pattern and encourage them to do the same. Show the pupils that you look for the gaps between numbers, you use your number facts, such as multiplication facts.
Unit 10.2 Number patterns or sequences need to be multiples.	Ensure that pupils are clear that a pattern or sequence can be created starting at any number and increasing or decreasing by any given number. Encourage them to think about all possibilities.

Teaching ideas

Unit 10.1 Continue number patterns and sequences

- Introduce this unit by establishing prior knowledge of key terms that will be used – patterns, sequences, forwards, backwards, multiplication and division.
- Ask pupils to share their knowledge and understanding using whiteboards. Ask pupils to write down a definition for each of the terms and an example of each one.
- Ask pupils to create their own number pattern that counts forwards using multiples, giving them the opportunity to get their shoulder partner to work out the pattern and continue by adding the next two numbers.
- Show the pupils this cutting from a hundred square:

35	36	37
45	46	47
55	56	57

- Ask the pupils to describe the patterns that they can see. Encourage the pupils to look for diagonal patterns and patterns that decrease as well as increase. Show the next cutting:

74	75	76
84	85	86
94	95	96

- Again, ask the pupils to describe the patterns. Ask pupils: **What is the same and what is different from the first diagram?**
- Now show the following diagrams and challenge pupils to complete the missing numbers from these cuttings from a hundred square.

	29	

		83

93		

Unit 10.2 Explain the rules for simple number sequences

- In pairs, ask pupils to get a whiteboard, a pen and a dice.
- Put the following numbers on the board: 1, 10, 100.
- Ask each pair to create their own number sequences by selecting one of the numbers on the board as a starting number, rolling the dice and using the number from the dice to increase or decrease. Each sequence should have at least four numbers.
    - Select 1 as the starting number.
    - Roll 5 on the dice.
    - 1, 6, 11, 16, 21.
- Encourage pupils to discuss their sequences and to look for patterns. For example, the above sequence ends in 1 or 6 each time.

11 Expressions and equations

Expressions and equations 1A

Section overview

Textbook 1A units	Review units	Prior learning	Benchmarks/Es&Os
Unit 11.1 Equations	**Early – B** Units 3.12, 3.15, 3.16, 3.18 and 3.19	• I recognise the terms 'equal to', 'not equal to', 'less' and 'more'. • I can demonstrate an understanding of basic number relationships. • I can use = in a number sentence.	**MTH 1-15a** **MTH 1-15b** • Understands and accurately uses the terms 'equal to', 'not equal to', 'less than', 'greater than' and the related symbols (=, ≠, <, >) when comparing quantities. • Applies understanding of the equals sign as a balance, and knowledge of number facts, to solve simple algebraic problems where a picture or symbol is used to represent a number; for example, ____ + 17 = 30 and ____ × 6 = 30.

Conceptual context

In mathematics, the terms 'expression' and 'equation' are used frequently but people often misunderstand an expression for an equation. However, these two mathematical terms are not the same; the main difference is in how they are arranged. The simplest way to identify an expression or equation is that if it contains an 'equal to' sign (=), it is an equation. If it does not contain an 'equal to' (=) sign, it is an expression.

Pupils have simplified expressions and have solved equations when they were asked to add and subtract. They probably didn't know that 5 + 3 is an expression and that 7 + 2 = 9 is an equation. It is important for pupils to understand these terms to clearly understand the similarities and differences between equations and expressions. They will begin to use algebraic expressions that feature variables as well. By employing their addition and subtraction skills, they will be simplifying expressions and evaluating algebraic expressions. Stress the progression from an expression to an equation by demonstrating how equal expressions are found on either side of an 'equals' sign.

Resources

- Blocks
- Cubes
- Whiteboards and pens

Key vocabulary

- **Balance**
- **Equal**
- **Equation**
- **Expression**
- **Greater than**
- **Less than**
- **Statement**
- **Symbols**
- **Terms**
- **Values**

Misconceptions

Potential misconception	Addressing the misconception
Unit 11.1 Pupils may think an equation and a number sentence are not the same thing.	Make sure that pupils are clear when you are talking about equations and number sentences that they are the same. Interchange the language to expose pupils to the different terminology used for the same thing.
Unit 11.1 Pupils may think that the value of a symbol will always remain the same in every equation or expression: ● + 2 = 8 ∴ a grey circle will always be equal to 6.	Make sure that pupils are clear that they need to read each question and each example as the symbol being used will have different values in different questions. In addition, ensure that pupils know that the symbol could not only be replacing a digit; it could also be replacing a sign: –, +, ×, ÷ or =. A simple way to encourage this thinking is to create a worksheet of number sentences and paint over some of the numbers or signs. This way the pupils can see there is something tangible covering up the thing they are trying to identify.

Teaching ideas

Unit 11.1 Equations

- Write $3 + 2 = 6$ on the board and ask pupils to tell you about the number sentence.
- Ask them if this equation is correct. How do they know this?
- Discuss what would need to change to make this number sentence correct.
- Introduce the concept of 'balance' by asking what the = sign means when used in an equation.
- Ask pupils to look at $6 + 3 = 9$ and consider what is on the left side of the equals sign and what is on the right side.
- Write $6 = 3 + 3$ on the board and explain that it is called an equation and that the left side of an equation equals the right side.
- Show them an example, such as the one below.

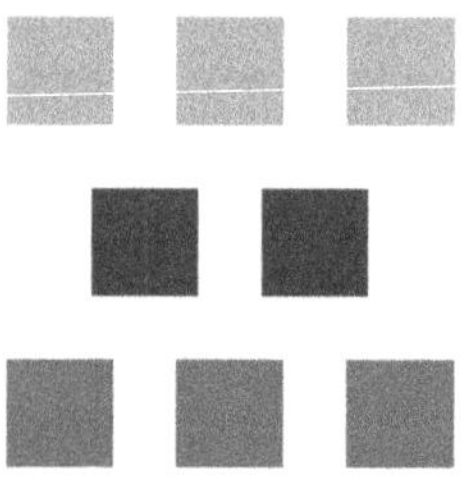

$= 8$

- Through questioning, see if the pupils can see that this could be written as: $8 = 8$ or $3 + 2 + 3 = 8$ or $5 + 3 = 8$ or similar.
- Using concrete or pictorial materials, ask pupils to create different examples of equations to clarify their understanding. Share these on the main whiteboard and ask the pupils who created the equation to explain how they know it is balanced and therefore an equation.

Expressions and equations 1B

Section overview

Textbook 1B units	Review units	Prior learning	Benchmarks/Es&Os
Unit 11.1 Solving simple equations	**1A** Unit 11.1	• I use the terms 'equal to', 'not equal to', 'less than' and 'more than'. • I can recognise the term 'greater than'. • I can demonstrate an understanding of simple number relationships. • I understand that the 'equals sign' is used to show balance.	**MTH 1-15a** **MTH 1-15b** • Understands and accurately uses the terms 'equal to', 'not equal to', 'less than', 'greater than', and the related symbols (=, ≠, <, >) when comparing quantities. • Applies understanding of the equals sign as a balance, and knowledge of number facts, to solve simple algebraic problems where a picture or symbol is used to represent a number; for example, ____ + 17 = 30 and ____ × 6 = 30.

Conceptual context

In mathematics, the terms 'expression' and 'equation' are used frequently but people often misunderstand an expression for an equation. However, these two mathematical terms are not the same; the main difference is in how they are arranged. The simplest way to identify an expression or equation is that if it contains an 'equal to' sign (=) it is an equation. If it does not contain an 'equal to' (=) sign, it is an expression.

Pupils have simplified expressions and have solved equations when they were asked to add and subtract. They probably didn't know that 5 + 3 is an expression and that 7 + 2 = 9 is an equation. It is important for pupils to understand these terms to clearly understand the similarities and differences between equations and expressions. They will begin to use algebraic expressions that feature variables as well. By employing their addition and subtraction skills, they will be simplifying expressions and evaluating algebraic expressions. Stress the progression from an expression to an equation by demonstrating how equal expressions are found on either side of an 'equals' sign.

Key vocabulary

- **Balance**
- **Equal**
- **Equation**
- **Expression**
- **Greater than**
- **Less than**
- **Statement**
- **Symbols**
- **Terms**
- **Values**

Misconceptions

Potential misconception	Addressing the misconception
Unit 11.1 The pupil may think an equation and a number sentence are not the same thing.	Make sure that pupils are clear when you are talking about equations and number sentences that they are the same. Interchange the language to expose pupils to the different terminology used for the same thing.
Unit 11.1 The value of a symbol will always remain the same in every equation or expression: ● + 2 = 8 ∴ a grey circle will always be equal to 6.	Make sure that pupils are clear that they need to read each question and each example as the symbol being used will have different values in different questions. In addition, ensure that pupils know that the symbol could not only be replacing a digit; it could also be replacing a sign; -, +, ×, ÷ or =. A simple way to encourage this thinking is to create a worksheet of number sentences and paint over some of the numbers or signs. This way, the pupils can see there is something tangible covering up the thing they are trying to identify.

Teaching ideas

Unit 11.1 Solve simple equations

- Write 2 × 2 = 3 + 1 on the board and then ask a pupil to read the equation aloud.
- Discuss what the pupils' understanding of this number statement is.
- Pupils may respond by stating that one side is multiplication and the other is addition, they may say that each side has the same answer and so on.
- Emphasise the importance of the '=' and how each expression that is on either side needs to have the same value for the equation to balance.
- Give pupils the total '10' and ask them to find as many different expressions as they can to go on either side of an equals sign.
- Challenge more able pupils to use multiplication and division if they are capable.
- Show pupils the following expressions:

2 × 4	3 × 2
10 – 1	10 ÷ 2
2 + 2 + 2	8 + 0
10 – 5	3 × 3

- Ask pupils to match the expressions so that if they add an = in between each one they will have an equation with both sides having the same/equal answer.
- Now that pupils are familiar with the concept that each side of the '=' sign must match, introduce the concept of balancing the equation. Ask pupils what happens when they sit on a seesaw.

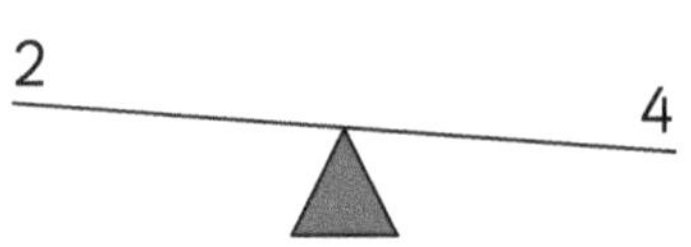

- Discuss the idea that the heavier/bigger person causes the seesaw to go down at one side; it is not balanced. Think about having an adult on one side and two children on the other to balance the weight.

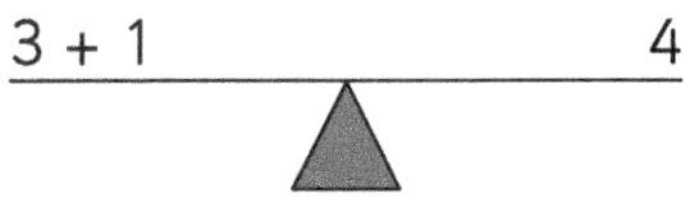

- To balance the equation, what number is missing?

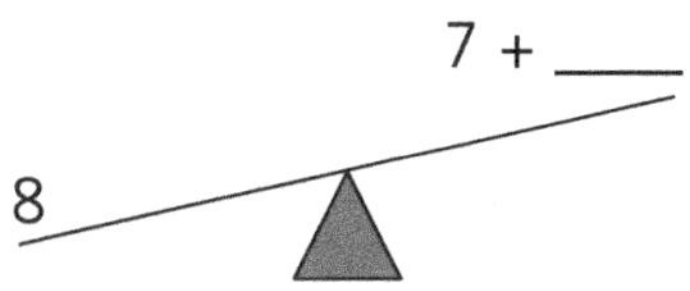

- Ask pupils to identify what you need to add to 7 to make 8.

Expressions and equations 1C

Section overview

Textbook 1C units	Review units	Prior learning	Benchmarks/Es&Os
Unit 11.1 Completing number sentences	**1B** Unit 11.1	• I recognise the terms 'equal to', 'not equal to', 'less' and 'more'. • I can demonstrate an understanding of basic number relationships. • I can use = in a number sentence.	**MTH 1-15a** **MTH 1-15b** • Understands and accurately uses the terms 'equal to', 'not equal to', 'less than', 'greater than', and the related symbols (=, ≠, <, >) when comparing quantities. • Applies understanding of the equals sign as a balance, and knowledge of number facts, to solve simple algebraic problems where a picture or symbol is used to represent a number; for example, ____ + 17 = 30 and ____ × 6 = 30.

Conceptual context

Equations are mathematical sentences created when two expressions are related to one another. In an equation, the two expressions are equal and this is shown by the equal to '=' symbol. For example: *5 = 3 + 2 or 5 is equal to 3 add 2.*

Mathematics is not always about 'equals'. Sometimes we only know that something is greater than or less than something else. This links to the estimation and measurement sections where lengths, masses or capacities are being compared. An inequality is where the two expressions (amounts) are not necessarily equal, which is shown by the symbols: *is greater than* > or *is less than* <.

$9 > 7$ 9 is greater than 7

$5 < 10$ 5 is less than 10

An equation or an inequality that contains at least one variable is called an 'open sentence'.

When you substitute the variable in an open sentence with a number, the resulting statement is either true or false. If the statement is true, the number is a solution to the equation or inequality. When you solve inequalities it is the same as solving equations and we do most of the same things but we must also pay attention to the direction of the inequality.

Resources

- Crocodile puppet
- Whiteboards and pens

Key vocabulary

- **Balance**
- **Equal**
- **Equation**
- **Expression**
- **Greater than**
- **Inequalities**
- **Less than**
- **Statement**
- **Symbols**
- **Terms**
- **Values**

Misconceptions

Potential misconception	Addressing the misconception
Unit 11.1 Pupils may think an equation and a number sentence are not the same thing.	Make sure that pupils are clear when you are talking about equations and number sentences that they are the same. Interchange the language to expose pupils to the different terminology used for the same thing.
The value of a symbol will always remain the same in every equation or expression: ● + 2 = 8 ∴ a grey circle will always be equal to 6.	Make sure that pupils are clear that they need to read each question and each example as the symbol being used will have different values in different questions. In addition, ensure that pupils know that the symbol could not only be replacing a digit; it could also be replacing a sign; −, +, ×, ÷ or =. A simple way to encourage this thinking is to create a worksheet of number sentences and paint over some of the numbers or signs. This way the pupils can see there is something tangible covering up the thing they are trying to identify.
A number sentence always has an '=' sign in the middle and as such always need to balance.	Explain to pupils that they can complete a number sentence by inserting <, >, = and ≠.

Teaching ideas

Unit 11.1 Completing number sentences

- Introduce the concept by asking pupils to look at the following number statements and getting them to write down 'true' or 'false' for each one.

  $2 + 2 + 2 = 10 - 4$

  $15 \div 5 = 2 + 2$

  $9 \times 2 = 8 + 9 + 1$
- Ask them to explain each answer.
- Show them the '≠' sign and ask them if they know what this means. Ask pupils in which of the above number sentences they would use the '≠' sign and why.
- Now, ask pupils to create their own number sentences that have '≠'.
- For each one, ask them if the expression on the left hand side is 'less than' or 'greater than' the expression on the right hand side.
- Show pupils the '<' and '>' signs and ask them to re-write their number statements replacing the '≠' with the appropriate sign. If you have a crocodile puppet then you can make the puppet 'act out' the inequality. The crocodile is always hungry to eat the bigger amount!

12 2D shapes and 3D objects

2D shapes and 3D objects 1A

Section overview

Textbook 1A units	Review units	Prior learning	Benchmarks/Es&Os
Unit 12.1 2D shapes	**Early – A** Unit 9.1 **Early – B** Unit 9.1	• Recognise common 2D shapes. • Describe and sort 2D shapes according to various criteria including straight and curved.	**MTH 1-16a** • Names, identifies and classifies a range of simple 2D shapes and 3D objects and recognises these shapes in different orientations and sizes. • Uses mathematical language to describe the properties of a range of common 2D shapes and 3D objects including side, face, edge, vertex, base and angle.
Unit 12.2 Sorting 2D shapes	**Early – A** Unit 9.1 **Early – B** Units 9.2, 9.3 and 9.5	• Recognise common 2D shapes. • Describe and sort 2D shapes according to various criteria including straight and curved.	**MTH 1-16a** • Names, identifies and classifies a range of simple 2D shapes and 3D objects and recognises these shapes in different orientations and sizes. • Uses mathematical language to describe the properties of a range of common 2D shapes and 3D objects including side, face, edge, vertex, base and angle.
Unit 12.3 Sorting 3D objects	**Early – A** Unit 9.1 **Early – B** Units 9.4 and 9.5	• Recognise common 3D objects. • Describe and sort common 3D objects according to various criteria, including straight, round, flat and curved.	**MTH 1-16a** • Names, identifies and classifies a range of simple 2D shapes and 3D objects and recognises these shapes in different orientations and sizes. • Uses mathematical language to describe the properties of a range of common 2D shapes and 3D objects including side, face, edge, vertex, base and angle. • Identifies 2D shapes within 3D objects and recognises 3D objects from 2D drawings.
Unit 12.4 3D objects	**Early – B** Units 9.4 and 9.5	• Recognise common 3D objects. • Describe and sort common 3D objects according to various criteria, including straight, round, flat and curved.	**MTH 1-16a** • Names, identifies and classifies a range of simple 2D shapes and 3D objects and recognises these shapes in different orientations and sizes. • Uses mathematical language to describe the properties of a range of common 2D shapes and 3D objects including side, face, edge, vertex, base and angle. • Identifies 2D shapes within 3D objects and recognises 3D objects from 2D drawings.

Conceptual context

Pupils will start school with little knowledge of shapes and their properties so they will need many opportunities to play with shapes and objects and learn the associated vocabulary. Pupils should be able to visualise, draw and model shapes and to think and reason geometrically. This will initially involve investigating, exploring and experimenting with everyday objects and manipulatives. Before naming an object or idea, pupils should experience 2D shapes, 3D objects and their representations in many different forms and orientations. This supports visualisation, an essential skill that pupils need to develop for geometrical understanding. The world of young children is filled with 3D objects such as building blocks, cardboard boxes and toys; to make links between 3D objects and 2D shapes, the faces of cuboids and prisms as printing blocks can be used to create shapes to discuss. Subsequently, pupils will see figures, 2D shapes and 3D objects as collections of properties. They will be able to recognise and name properties of geometric figures, 2D shapes and 3D objects, and see the relationships between these properties and where they are used in the wider environment. It is vital, at this stage, that pupils discuss the names and characteristics of 2D shapes and 3D objects to clarify mathematical understanding.

Without understanding concepts such as edges, sides, corners and faces, the definitions of shapes are meaningless. When describing and naming shapes and objects, pupils should identify and discuss their similarities **and** differences using properties such as sides, whether they have straight or curved faces, the number of corners/vertices, etc.

Resources

- A selection of shapes with only straight sides, only curved sides and both straight and curved
- A selection of 3–4 different squares, rectangles, triangles and circles. These should be different colours, sizes and orientations.
- A solid cylinder, a cylindrical container without its lid and the centre of a kitchen roll.
- Resource sheet 12A 'Let's Practise' Q1.
- Resource 12B 'Let's Practise' Q2.
- Selection of different 3D objects to manipulate: cone, square-based pyramid, cylinder, sphere, cube, cuboid
- Selection of different triangles to manipulate: scalene, isosceles, equilateral and right-angled
- Selection of non-regular 2D shapes, e.g. crosses, hearts, etc. These can be commercially produced games/materials or shapes that have been made. 'Homemade' shapes can also be used to print shapes for matching games.

Key vocabulary

- **Circle**
- **Cone**
- **Corners**
- **Cube**
- **Cuboid**
- **Curved**
- **Cylinder**
- **Dotted lines**
- **Edges**
- **Faces (flat and curved)**
- **Length**
- **Opposite**
- **Rectangle**
- **Roll**
- **Sides**
- **Sphere**
- **Square**
- **Square-based pyramid**
- **Triangle**

Misconceptions

Potential misconception	Addressing the misconception
Units 12.1 and 12.2 Pupils may experience prototypical visual images of shapes, which limits their understanding of shapes to the examples they are shown, e.g. regular pentagons, shapes always orientated with their base along the horizontal.	Teachers must expose pupils to shapes of varying sizes, orientations and type (regular and irregular).
Unit 12.1 Pupils may confuse shapes with three curved sides as triangles or parallelograms/trapeziums as rectangles.	It is usually around the age of six when a child's definition of a shape stabilises and they are able to use criteria to define shapes rather than 'triangles are pointy shapes'. Six-year-olds found it more difficult to identify triangles and rectangles within a set of shapes with included circles and squares. Drawing pupils' attention to the properties, similarities and differences of shapes and giving them plenty of experience exploring shapes of different sizes and types will help this.

Potential misconception	Addressing the misconception
Unit 12.2 Pupils may only identify scalene triangles as a 'triangle'.	Giving pupils different types of triangle – scalene, isosceles, equilateral and right-angle – to sort and identify will help develop the understanding that a triangle is a shape (polygon) with three sides. Later, pupils may add that it has three sides and three angles.
Unit 12.2 Pupils may not think that 2D shapes can have rounded corners.	Ensure that, if pupils are drawing around 3D representations of a 2D shape, their finished product does not have rounded corners. Sharp corners can be achieved by drawing a pencil along one side at a time.
Units 12.1 and 12.2 Pupils may think that a circle has only one side.	How many sides a circle has depends on how one defines a 'side'. If a side is defined as a straight-line segment, then a circle has no sides. If a side is defined as a curved boundary, a circle could have one curved side. A circle could also be defined as having an infinite number of sides as a polygon with an infinite number of sides approximates a circle. It is important to include the word 'curved' and more useful to describe a circle as having a curved edge rather than side. This will provide a rich source of discussion and argument.
Units 12.3 and 12.4 Pupils may be confused with the large variety of ways 2D shapes and 3D objects can be defined.	While it is important for pupils to know, describe and name shapes according to their various properties, they must be given ample opportunity to discover and understand the relationships *within* and *between* shapes, noticing their similarities and differences. Pupils should be able to discuss the properties of a square and not simply state it is a shape with 4 equal sides. Asking pupils to share their observations allows them to hear different definitions/properties noticed by others, which they possibly have not.

Teaching ideas

Unit 12.1 2D shapes

- Use a Venn diagram to sort shapes into those with 'straight sides', curved sides' and both where the circles overlap. Ask: **Are there any 2D shapes that have both curved and straight sides? Are there any 2D shapes that have neither curved nor straight sides?**
- When introducing the shapes *square, rectangle, triangle* and *circle* to the pupils, it is best to introduce these as objects to the pupils. If images are used, ensure that the base is parallel with the horizontal. Draw their attention to the properties of each shape. Ask: **What do you notice about each of these shapes? What makes them the same as and different to each other?** If pupils are focusing on the colour of the shapes, direct their attention to the sides, encouraging them to count the sides and to notice if they are straight, curved or both. Ensure that the pupils are shown different sizes and colours of the same shape to reinforce that it is a shape's properties that gives it its name.
- Match a selection of 2D shapes (either as objects or images, e.g. square, triangle, rectangle and circle) with their shape word. Ensure these shapes are orientated differently to the shapes they have seen before.
- Give pupils a selection of 3 or 4 different types of square, rectangle, triangle and circle so they are different colours, sizes and orientations. Ask them to sort the 2D shapes into groups according to the name of shape.
- Display a square, rectangle, triangle and circle. Ask one pupil to secretly choose a shape, then give the others in the group a clue in order to guess the shape they have chosen. Again, encourage pupils to think about the properties of the shape and not the colour or where it is on the page/paper/interactive whiteboard.
- Play 'Guess the Shape' using squares, rectangles, circles and triangles where most of the shape is hidden and can be slowly revealed. This can be done by either covering part of a shape on paper or using interactive whiteboard screening options.

Unit 12.2 Sorting 2D shapes

- Using the context of 'Which shape will fit in the hole?' can allow for a rich discussion of 2D shape properties. Use resources that are available, such as games where the aim is to fit different shapes into holes. Alternatively, get the pupils to construct their own matching games, using paint on shapes or cut-outs to match the print to the shape that made it.
- Using Venn or Carroll diagrams, ask pupils to sort a variety of shapes (with straight and curved sides). Ask: **Can you guess how these shapes have been sorted?** to encourage discussion around the properties of the shapes.

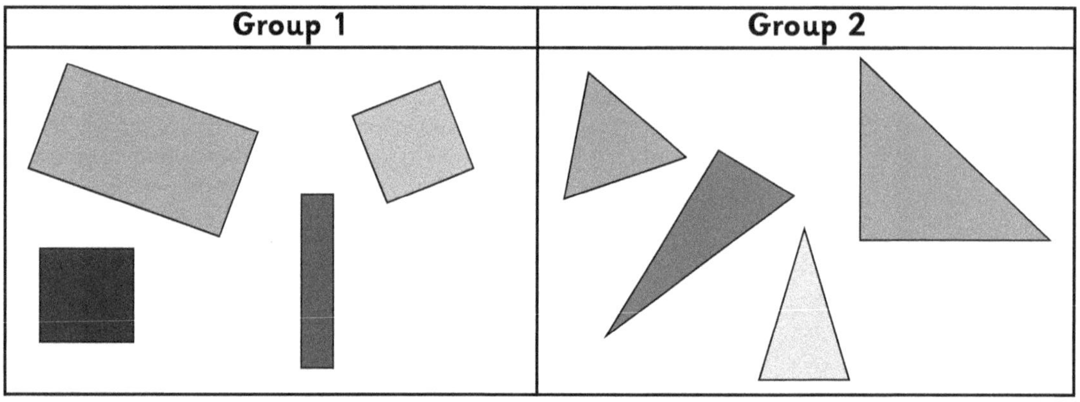

- Before the 'Challenge' part of the textbook, give pupils a selection of triangles and ask: **What can you tell me about the number of sides and the number of corners you can see with these shapes?** Focusing the discussion on the number of sides being the same as the number of corners may help support pupils to complete the 'Challenge' section more easily.

Unit 12.3 Sorting 3D objects

- Show pupils a cone, square-based pyramid and cylinder similar to that in the 'Before we start' section. Introduce the terms **faces, edges** and **corners** to help support pupils in their explanations. It may need to be explained to pupils that the 'face' of a 3D object does not have any of the extra bits and bumps that human faces do!
- Introduce the 3D objects *cylinder, cube, sphere and cuboid* and this new vocabulary to the pupils. Encourage pupils to say 'sphere' instead of 'si-feer'. Play 'Guess the Object' using these four objects and a feely bag. Encourage pupils to focus on the properties of the 3D objects and using vocabulary *flat/curved faces, edges and corners* and how a flat surface feels different from a curved surface.
- Show pupils a solid cylinder, a cylindrical container without its lid and the centre of a kitchen roll. Ask: **What is the same about these three objects? What is different? Which are solid and which are hollow?** Solid and hollow objects may be challenging for some pupils to grasp. It can be helpful to submerge the three different 3D objects in water to allow pupils to observe the results.
- For the 'Let's Practise' part of the textbook, it is useful to have the six 3D objects the pupils have to identify on their tables so they can pick them up and count the number of faces and edges. Question 2 in the 'Let's Practise' section (on page 162) will also support this learning.
- Find approximate 3D objects in pupils' local environment or in real life for 'Hunt the Shape'. Some examples include:
    - cereal packets
    - cans are cylinders
    - some ice-creams are in cones
    - lighthouses have a variety of approximate shapes – pyramids and cones

Unit 12.4 3D objects

- Use a cone, cube, cylinder and sphere on a ramp (or sloped surface) for the 'Before we start' section of the textbook (page 163). There may be discussion around the cube and, if pupils are familiar with dice, its ability to 'roll'. Placing the cube on the sloped surface should demonstrate that the cube may slide but not roll on its own.
- Ask pupils to write clues for one of the following 3D objects: cube, cylinder, sphere, cone, cube, cuboid, square-based pyramid. Concentrate on encouraging using *faces, edges, flat, curved, sides*. Ask others to match the clue with the correct 3D object, e.g. 'If you look at me you will see a circle and just one point. What am I?'
- Ensure pupils understand that the dotted line indicates the part of the 3D object that we cannot see. Use 3D objects to model this and provide a 2D example of the 3D object in question. Draw attention to the part of the shape they could not see and how dotted or broken lines are used to show this.

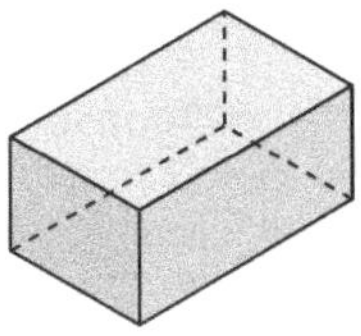

2D shapes and 3D objects 1B

Section overview

Textbook 1B units	Review units	Prior learning	Benchmarks/Es&Os
Unit 12.1 Properties of 2D shapes	**1A** Units 12.1 and 12.2	• Identify square, circle, rectangle and triangle. • Describe and sort these shapes according to their sides and corners. • Identify and name a right angle.	**MTH 1-16a** • Names, identifies and classifies a range of simple 2D shapes and 3D objects and recognises these shapes in different orientations and sizes. • Uses mathematical language to describe the properties of a range of common 2D shapes and 3D objects including side, face, edge, vertex, base and angle. **MTH 1-17a** • Knows that a right angle is 90°. • Uses informal methods to estimate, compare and describe the size of angles in relation to a right angle. • Finds right angles in the environment and in well-known 2D shapes.
Unit 12.2 2D shapes in 3D objects	**1A** Unit 12.3	• Identify and describe a variety of 2D shapes including circle, square, rectangle, triangle, hexagon and pentagon. • Describe 3D surfaces as curved or flat. • Identify and describe a cone, cylinder, cube, cuboid, pyramid according to their properties.	**MTH 1-16a** • Names, identifies and classifies a range of simple 2D shapes and 3D objects and recognises these shapes in different orientations and sizes. • Uses mathematical language to describe the properties of a range of common 2D shapes and 3D objects including side, face, edge, vertex, base and angle. • Identifies 2D shapes within 3D objects and recognises 3D objects from 2D drawings.
Unit 12.3 Recognising 3D objects	**1A** Units 12.3 and 12.4	• Identify and describe a variety of 2D shapes including circle, square, rectangle, triangle, pentagon and hexagon. • Describe 3D surfaces as curved or flat. • Identify and describe a cone, cylinder, cube, cuboid, pyramid according to their properties.	**MTH 1-16a** • Names, identifies and classifies a range of simple 2D shapes and 3D objects and recognises these shapes in different orientations and sizes. • Uses mathematical language to describe the properties of a range of common 2D shapes and 3D objects including side, face, edge, vertex, base and angle. • Identifies 2D shapes within 3D objects and recognises 3D objects from 2D drawings.
Unit 12.4 Tiling patterns	**1A** Units 12.1 and 12.2	• Describe 2D shapes according to their properties – sides and corners.	**MTH 1-16b** • Identifies examples of tiling in the environment and applies knowledge of the features of 2D shapes to create tiling patterns incorporating two different shapes.

Conceptual context

Pupils will start school with little knowledge of shapes and their properties so they will need many opportunities to play with shapes and objects and learn the associated vocabulary. Pupils should be able to visualise, draw and model shapes and to think and reason geometrically. This will initially involve investigating, exploring and experimenting with everyday objects and manipulatives. Before naming an object or idea, pupils should experience 2D shapes, 3D objects and their representations in many different forms and orientations. This supports visualisation, an essential skill that pupils need to develop for geometrical understanding. The world of young children is filled with 3D objects such as building blocks, cardboard boxes and toys; to make links between 3D objects and 2D shapes, the faces of cuboids and prisms as printing blocks can be used to create shapes to discuss. Subsequently, pupils will see figures, 2D shapes and 3D objects as collections of properties. They will be able to recognise and name properties of geometric figures, 2D shapes and 3D objects, and see the relationships between these properties and where they are used in the wider environment. It is vital, at this stage, that pupils discuss the names and characteristics of 2D shapes and 3D objects to clarify mathematical understanding.

Without understanding concepts such as edges, sides, corners and faces, the definitions of shapes are meaningless. When describing and naming shapes and objects, pupils should identify and discuss their similarities **and** differences using properties such as sides, whether they have straight or curved faces, the number of corners/vertices, etc. When describing, sorting and comparing prisms and pyramids, highlight and discuss the similarities and differences between their properties.

Resources

- Cubes, cuboids, cylinders, cones, triangular-based prism and square-based pyramid
- Geoboards
- Matchsticks, lolly sticks or small straws – 20 for each pupil or pair
- Multilink cubes (4 per pupil or pair)
- Rectangles to be used for tiling patterns
- Resource 1B 12.1 'Let's Practise' Q1
- Right angles in a variety of orientations
- Right-angle testers
- Triangular, square, pentagonal and hexagonal-based pyramids

Key vocabulary

- **Base**
- **Circle**
- **Corners**
- **Curved**
- **Hexagon**
- **Pentagon**
- **Rectangle**
- **Right angle**
- **Right-angled triangle**
- **Repeating patterns**
- **Semi-circle**
- **Sides**
- **Square**
- **Square corner**
- **Straight**
- **Tile/tiling**

Misconceptions

Potential misconception	Addressing the misconception
Units 12.1 and 12.4 Pupils experience prototypical visual images of shapes, which may limit their understanding of shapes in relation to the examples they are shown, e.g. regular pentagons, shapes always orientated with their base along the horizontal.	Teachers must expose pupils to shapes of varying sizes, orientations and type (regular and irregular).
Unit 12.1 Pupils may believe that squares and rectangles are two discrete shapes.	Discussing the similarities and differences between square rectangles and non-square rectangles (oblongs) and allowing pupils to discover the special properties of a square, instead of asking them to repeat 'It has four sides the same length and four corners which are the same'. Sorting exercises focusing on squares and non-square rectangles may also help pupils with these distinctions.
Unit 12.1 Pupils may not identify right angles when the arms of the angle are not of equal length.	Ensure that pupils are given examples of right angles in various orientations and with arms of various lengths.
Units 12.2 and 12.3 Pupils may be confused by the large variety of ways that 2D shapes and 3D objects can be defined.	While it is important for pupils to know, describe and name shapes according to their various properties, they must be given ample opportunity to discover and understand the relationships *within* and *between* shapes, noticing their similarities and differences. Pupils should be able to discuss the properties of a square and not simply state it is a shape with 4 equal sides. Asking pupils to share their observations allows them to hear different definitions/properties noticed by others, which they possibly have not.
Unit 12.3 Pupils may be unable to identify a 3D object from different perspectives.	Pupils need rich and varied experiences to be able to visualise 3D objects in their 'mind's eye' and to identify the object from different perspectives. Asking pupils to visualise shapes and objects after observing them will also help their attempts to view it from a different direction.

Teaching ideas

Unit 12.1 Properties of 2D shapes

- During the discussion of the 'Before we start' section, ensure that replicas of the angles and their orientation are displayed on a screen or on paper and are able to be rotated. Pupils may justify that the right angle is the one 'pointing right' or 'on the right' amongst other ideas. It is helpful to be able to rotate all angles so that they can be compared easily. A right angle can be described as a name of special kind of angle that is in the corners of squares.
- Show examples of right angles in a variety of orientations and with the arms of the angle being different lengths. Ask: **Are these all right angles? How do we know? How can we check?**
- Create right-angle testers by tearing the corners of a sheet of card. Pupils can then search for right angles in the classroom and the school grounds. Ask: **Did you find any right angles in natural materials/nature?**
- Using a square, rectangle, circle, hexagon, pentagon, right-angled triangle and semi-circle, ask pupils to sort the shapes. How many different ways can we sort them? Encourage the use of vocabulary such as corners, straight and curved sides and square corners. Introduce the vocabulary pentagon, hexagon and semi-circle. Link these names to their etymology – *pent* meaning 'five', *hex* meaning 'six' and *semi* meaning 'half'.
- Using a large Geoboard or a large piece of square dotty paper, create shapes with three or four sides. How many different ways can we make a three-sided shape?

Unit 12.2 2D shapes in 3D objects

- Using a cube, cuboid, cone and cylinder, discuss the 2D shapes the pupils see on the faces of the 3D objects. Place the 2D shapes on the 3D objects to check.
- Have a cube, cuboid, cone and cylinder available during the 'Let's Practise' section of the textbook for the pupils to hold when they are discussing the similarities and differences between the objects. Encourage use of the terms *faces, edges and corners.*
- Use Resource 1B 12.2 'Let's Practise' question 2 to support the completion of the table on page 172.
- Use Resource 1B 12.2 'Challenge' to support the completion of the table on page 173. Have triangular, square, pentagonal and hexagonal-based pyramids available to support pupils in identifying the number of triangular faces and number of edges.
- Discuss the results of the pupils' tables to identify the relationship between the number of faces and edges (double the number of triangular faces). Ask: **Which pyramid is the odd one out?** The triangular pyramid is the only one with all triangular faces.

Unit 12.3 Recognising 3D objects

- Ensure pupils can identify and name sphere, cube, cuboid, cylinder, cone, square-based pyramid and triangular-based pyramid. Discuss the properties of these objects and the different ways in which they could be sorted.
- Give each pupil a 3D object to hold in their hands for the 'Let's Learn' section of page 174. Ask: **What happens to the shapes you can see when you turn the 3D object around? Do we all see the same shapes?**
- Give pupils a camera and ask them to take photos of a 3D object from unusual angles. Collate these and share with the group. **Can you identify each 3D object from the photo? Did anyone photograph the same shape but from different angles?** This type of activity will support the work on pages 174 and 175.
- Create a model using three multilink cubes. Ask: **What shape do you see from above** (bird's eye view)? **What shape do you see from the side and front?**

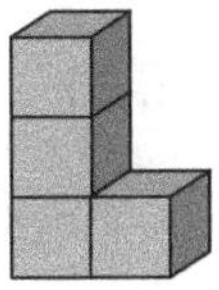

Unit 12.4 Tiling patterns

- Use whiteboards to allow pupils to sketch the shape in the 'Before we start' section. Ask: **How did you decide on which shape to draw? What was the biggest clue Amman gave?**
- When discussing what 'tiling' means, ask: **Where have you seen tiling patterns?** Pupils can explore their classroom, school and school grounds to take photos, sketch or write a list of the tiling patterns they can see.
- Using a variety of 2D shapes, ask pupils to predict which ones they think will tile. Ask: **Why do you think that? What properties does this shape have that makes you think it will tile so there are no gaps or overlaps?**

2D shapes and 3D objects 1C

Section overview

Textbook 1C units	Review units	Prior learning	Benchmarks/Es&Os
Unit 12.1 Sorting 3D objects	**1B** Unit 12.2	• Name a cube, cuboid, sphere, cone, square-based pyramid, triangle-based pyramid, cylinder. • Sort 3D objects according to their properties: corners, edges, faces. • Describe the properties of 3D objects.	**MTH 1-16a** • Names, identifies and classifies a range of simple 2D shapes and 3D objects and recognises these shapes in different orientations and sizes. • Uses mathematical language to describe the properties of a range of common 2D shapes and 3D objects including side, face, edge, vertex, base and angle. • Identifies 2D shapes within 3D objects and recognises 3D objects from 2D drawings.
Unit 12.2 Plan drawings	**1B** Unit 12.3	• Name a cube, cuboid, various types of pyramid, cylinder, cone, sphere and triangular prism. • Identify, describe and sort 3D objects by their properties: edges, vertices and faces.	**MTH 1-16a** • Identifies 2D shapes within 3D objects and recognises 3D objects from 2D drawings.
Unit 12.3 Tiling patterns	**1B** Unit 12.4	• Identify examples of tiling in the environment. • Make tiling patterns by repeating a single shape. • Know that for a shape to tile there must be no overlaps or gaps.	**MTH 1-16a** • Identifies examples of tiling in the environment and applies knowledge of the features of 2D shapes to create tiling patterns incorporating two different shapes.

Conceptual context

Pupils will arrive at school with little knowledge of shapes and their properties so they will need many opportunities to play with shapes and objects and to learn the associated vocabulary. Pupils should be able to visualise, draw and model shapes and to think and reason geometrically. This will initially involve investigating, exploring and experimenting with everyday objects and manipulatives. Before naming an object or idea, pupils should experience 2D shapes, 3D objects and their representations in many different forms and orientations. This supports visualisation, an essential skill that pupils need to develop for geometrical understanding. The world of young children is filled with 3D objects such as building blocks, cardboard boxes and toys; to make links between 3D objects and 2D shapes, the faces of cuboids and prisms as printing blocks can be used to create shapes to discuss. Subsequently, pupils will see figures, 2D shapes and 3D objects as collections of properties. They will be able to recognise and name properties of geometric figures, 2D shapes and 3D objects, seeing the relationships between these properties and where they are used in the wider environment. It is vital, at this stage, that pupils discuss the names and characteristics of 2D shapes and 3D objects to clarify mathematical understanding.

Without understanding concepts, such as edges, sides, corners and faces, the definitions of shapes are meaningless. When describing and naming shapes and objects, pupils should identify and discuss their similarities **and** differences using properties such as sides, whether they have straight or curved faces, number of corners/vertices, etc. When describing, sorting and comparing prisms and pyramids, highlight and discuss the similarities and differences between their properties.

Drawing and construction

Pupils will initially draw shapes freehand or by tracing around templates and actual objects. But as their understanding of measurement and the properties of shapes and objects grow, they will need to represent these properties accurately. Creating equal and parallel sides as well as right angles requires pupils to master tools such as rulers and protractors. Using squared or dotty paper can support them in recreating 2D shapes and angles accurately.

Resources

- Resource 1C 12.1, 'Let's Practise' Q2
- Triangular prisms, hexagonal-based pyramid, cylinders, triangular-based pyramid, cuboids, square-based pyramids, cubes and cones

Key vocabulary

- **Cuboids**
- **Curved surface**
- **Edges**
- **End face, front/side/top/plan view**
- **Faces**
- **Octagon**
- **Prisms**
- **Vertices**
- **Venn diagrams, triangular, rectangular**
- **Tile**

Misconceptions

Potential misconception	Addressing the misconception
Units 12.1 and 12.3 Pupils may experience prototypical visual images of shapes, which limits their understanding of shapes to the examples they are shown, e.g. regular pentagons, shapes always orientated with their base along the horizontal.	Teachers must expose pupils to shapes of varying sizes, orientations and type (regular and irregular).
Units 12.1, 12.2 and 12.3 Pupils may be confused with the large variety of ways 2D shapes and 3D objects can be defined.	While it is important for pupils to know, describe and name shapes according to their various properties, they must be given ample opportunity to discover and understand the relationships *within* and *between* shapes, and notice their similarities and differences. Pupils should be able to discuss the properties of a square and not simply state it is a shape with 4 equal sides. Asking pupils to share their observations allows them to hear different definitions/properties noticed by others, which they possibly have not noticed.
Unit 12.2 Pupils unable to identify 3D object from different perspectives.	Pupils need rich and varied experiences to be able to visualise 3D objects in their 'mind's eye' and to identify the object from different perspectives. Asking pupils to visualise shapes and objects after observing them will also help their attempts to view them from a different direction.

Teaching ideas

Unit 12.1 Sorting 3D objects

- During the 'Before we start' section, ask which 3D objects could *not* be the ones Amman and Isla are describing. Doing this exercise without the 3D objects available to the pupils helps with the visualisation process and their recall of the names of the 3D objects. If pupils are struggling with some of the vocabulary, objects can be provided.

- Explain that 'vertices' is a better word for 'corners' when describing the properties of 3D objects. A vertex is a point where two or more lines meet. 'Corner' is also used in social contexts where the word is less mathematically accurate (e.g. the corner of the chair may be rounded) and is often used in contexts involving a right angle. Vertex or vertices do not need to be right angles.
- Show pupils a solid cylinder, a cylindrical container without its lid and the centre of a kitchen roll. Ask: **What is the same about these three objects? What is different? Which objects are cylinders? Which are solid and which are hollow?** The concept of solid and hollow objects may be challenging for some pupils to grasp. It can be helpful to submerge the three different 3D objects in water to allow pupils to observe the results.
- Provide triangular prisms and hexagonal-based pyramids for pupils to explore. Ask: **What is different about these 3D objects? One is a pyramid and one is a prism – which do you think is the pyramid and which is the prism? Why?** Draw pupils' attention to the fact that, if you take a 'slice' from the object, prisms having the same cross-section, and are named after the 2D shape on its 'top' (for example, a pentagonal prism has a base and top that are both pentagons).

  Remind pupils about dotted/broken lines in drawings of 3D objects and how they are used to show the parts of the object that cannot be seen from a front view.

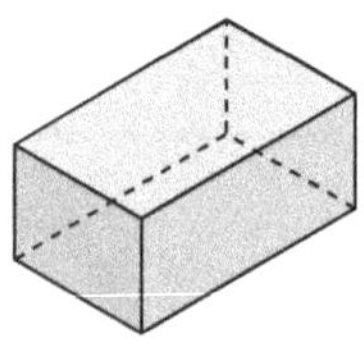

- Resource 1C 12.1, 'Let's Practise' Q2 can be used to support the completion of the table. Having triangular prisms, hexagonal-based pyramid, cylinders, triangular-based pyramid, cuboids, square-based pyramids, cubes and cones available for pupils to use may be of use to some pupils.
- Resource 1C 12.1, 'Challenge' can be used to support the completion of the table on page 167.

Unit 12.2 Plan drawings

- Give pupils a camera and ask them to take photos of a 3D object from unusual angles. Collate these and share them with the group. **Can you identify each 3D object from the photo? Did anyone photograph the same shape but from different angles? Are the photos/sketches showing the front, side, top or plan view of the object.** Ask: **Why do you think it is called a plan view?** A plan view is the view/image when the three other views – front, side and top are combined. Designers, engineers, builders and architects all can have access to computer software (CAD – computer-aided design) to help them draw plans and views from measurements they have taken.
- Use a cuboid to draw the front, side and top views together as a group.
- Ensure multilink cubes are available for pupils to construct the front, side and top views of the objects in the 'Challenge' question on page 170.

Unit 12.3 Tiling patterns

- Ask pupils to share their predictions for the 'Before we start' question and ask them to explain their thinking. Ask pupils if they would need another shape for the hexagon to tile correctly. What might that shape be?
- Make a tiling pattern by drawing round a regular pentagon. Ask: **Could this shape tile? If not, what other shape would we need to make it tile? What combinations of two 2D shapes will tile?**

13 Angles, symmetry and transformation

Angles, symmetry and transformation 1A

Section overview

Textbook 1A units	Review units	Prior learning	Benchmarks/Es&Os
Unit 13.1 Using positional language	**Early – B** Unit 10.1	• Know which is my left hand and which is my right hand. • Understand the language of position and direction, including in front, behind, above, below, left, right, to solve simple problems in movement games. • Use the language of position and direction to solve simple problems in movement games.	**MTH 1-17a** • Uses technology and other methods to describe, follow and record directions using words associated with angles, directions and turns including, full turn, half turn, quarter turn, clockwise, anticlockwise, right turn, left turn, right angle.
Unit 13.2 Using directions	**Early – B** Unit 10.1	• Know which is my left hand and which is my right hand. • Understand the language of position and direction, including in front, behind, above, below, left, right, to solve simple problems in movement games. • Use the language of position and direction to solve simple problems in movement games.	**MTH 1-17a** **MTH 1-18a** • Uses technology and other methods to describe, follow and record directions using words associated with angles, directions and turns including, full turn, half turn, quarter turn, clockwise, anticlockwise, right turn, left turn, right angle.
Unit 13.3 Symmetry	**Early – B** Unit 10.2	• Identify pictures with one line of symmetry.	**MTH 1-19a** • Identifies symmetry in patterns, pictures, nature and 2D shapes.

Conceptual context

Position and orientation

As children develop their language skills, they will use increasingly accurate descriptions to describe position. For example, children may describe a toy as being 'over there' or 'next door' but, with experience, will use words such as far, near, above, below, in front or behind, first or last, on the left or right. The language associated with direction will include to the left or right, forwards, backwards and straight. Teachers should model this language and be mindful of the words they use when talking to children.

As the children build their spatial awareness, they will be able to give instructions to others to guide them around familiar locations or along simple journeys. Initially, a lot of the detail in these instructions will be personal to the children (for example, 'go past the display with my report on it'). With experience, they will learn to tailor their explanations for others.

Maps do not always have to be drawn to scale. An informal map from the school to the nearest shop can take the form of a line drawing that highlights notable sights, such as the play park and telephone box. The pupils should learn which form of map or plan is suitable for the circumstances.

Grids are the precursor to coordinates and build the skills that learners will need in order to read coordinates such as moving along the horizontal then the vertical. There are many contexts for grids (for example, cinema seats, games such as battleships or chess, and spreadsheets).

The phrase 'along the corridor…' is often used to explain the order to read and plot coordinates. However, not all grid systems fit with this phrase so very careful consideration must be given to your explanations. For early learners, the explanation and the context must fit together along with the focus on the horizontal movement first followed by the vertical. Remember that at third level, negative values will be introduced so we do not always go right, then up. In ICT applications, cell and cursor coordinates use the top left-hand side of the window as the origin, so as you look at the screen you move along then down!

Transformation

From the very early stages of learning, children will need to develop the ability to visualise what will happen if a shape or object is moved or changed. Questions such as 'Will the box fit on the shelf?', 'What will it look like if we turn it over?' along with the opportunity to play and experiment with a range of shapes and objects will help children develop the ability to *predict* what an object will look like after a transformation. There are many activities that can be used to develop this skill: jigsaws, matching games, tangrams, etc. Then, as children begin to focus on specific skills, such as line symmetry, we can ask them to visualise and predict what the shape will look like and then reflect on the result of the transformation.

Symmetry

Pupils learn about three inter-related transformations throughout Curriculum for Excellence including line symmetry, rotational symmetry and translation. These can be considered as three types of congruence; although the shape has been transformed, the length of its sides remain the same, as do the size of the angles and the orientation of the sides and the angles.

Reflective or line symmetry is the first kind of symmetry that children will experience. In mathematics it is a broader idea than just mirror images. A shape that has reflective symmetry has two or more matching parts. it is important that pupils experience reflecting and folding shapes in many ways to understand the differences between horizontal and vertical lines of symmetry.

We have to be careful in our explanations of symmetry and reflection. Initial experiences will focus on symmetry and recognising symmetrical shapes and pictures. In this case, symmetry is seen as a 'whole' and is not dynamic. Beautiful faces are said to be symmetrical and humans, generally, enjoy art, decoration or architecture that is symmetrical. So, when we create a butterfly by painting one half of a sheet of paper and then folding and pressing to transfer the paint to the other half, the result is seen as the final completed picture of the butterfly. Initially though, we are creating or completing a picture to make it symmetrical using a fold line or a flip.

Reflection is a dynamic movement or translation. When we reflect an object, it is moved to a new position to create an 'image'.

Resources

- Blank symmetry grid
- Colouring pencils
- Counters
- Counters and two dice with 1R, 2R, 3R, 1L, 2L and 3L on the faces
- 3D shapes small enough to place on the grid – cube, sphere, cylinder, square-based pyramid
- Resource sheet 13A
- Resource 1A 13.2, 'Challenge'
- Resource 1A 13.2, 'Let's Practise' Q1
- Resource 1A 13.1, 'Let's Practise' Q2
- Resource 1A 13.2, 'Let's Practise' Q2
- Resource 1A 13.1, 'Let's Practise' Q3 or squared paper

Key vocabulary

- Above
- Backward
- Between
- Below
- Forward
- Left
- Not symmetrical
- Opposite
- Right
- Symmetrical

Misconceptions

Potential misconception	Addressing the misconception
Units 13.1 and 13.2 Pupils may confuse left and right.	Pupils are unable to turn left or right correctly if they do not understand the position of left and right in relation to their bodies. Complexity arises as left and right are relative to your position and orientation. Time spent on activities and demonstrations involving pupils in body actions, following instructions and using appropriate vocabulary will help consolidate 'left' and 'right' as will being involved in mirroring activities with partners to see that their left will be another person's right.
Unit 13.2 Pupils may be unfamiliar with the terms 'forward' and 'backward'.	If pupils are struggling to apply this vocabulary to grids, spend some more time working with physically moving forward and backward and using this vocabulary to describe movements (e.g. in dances).
Unit 13.3 Pupils may find identifying lines of symmetry challenging.	Using a mirror helps unite whatever perceptions of symmetry and reflection develop as pupils' understanding grows. Using mirrors to check pupils' predictions helps to hone their skills in identifying lines of symmetry. Pupils may initially find it easier to identify vertical lines of symmetry than horizontal.

Teaching ideas

Unit 13.1 Using positional language

- During the 'Before we start' section, ask questions such as: **How do you know that is Finlay's left hand? How can we describe Finlay's other hand? Do the words 'left' and 'right' have any other meanings that we know of?**
- If pupils are struggling with left and right, playing a game with three pupils, 10 counters each and two dice with 1R, 2R, 3R, 1L, 2L and 3L on the faces may help. Three pupils sit in a circle, having 10 counters each and take it in turns to roll the dice. What appears on the faces indicates the number of counters each pupil has to give to the other two in their group. For example, if one pupil rolls 2L and 3R they must give 2 counters to the pupil on their left and 3 counters to the pupil on their right. The first pupil who has no counters left is the winner.
- In preparation for 'Let's Learn' activities, arrange pupils' chairs in a rectangular block (either in the classroom or in an open space). Pupils can then state where they are in relation to the others, e.g. Abbie can say 'I am behind Callum, to the right of Karen, to the left of Mark (between Karen and Mark) and under the big light'. This could then be extended to drawing where some pupils were sitting onto large squared paper and sharing a short summary of each pupil using the vocabulary *left, right, between, below* and *above*.

- In preparation for 'Let's Practise' and 'Challenge' complete a 3×3 grid with different coloured 2D shapes. Ask pupils to pick one shape and write/share clues for its position so that the rest of the pupils can guess which shape they have chosen. Encourage the use of *below, one/two squares, right, left, above, between.* If some pupils are not secure with naming 2D shapes, allow them to draw and colour the shape/s in question instead of writing/sharing the name of it. For example:

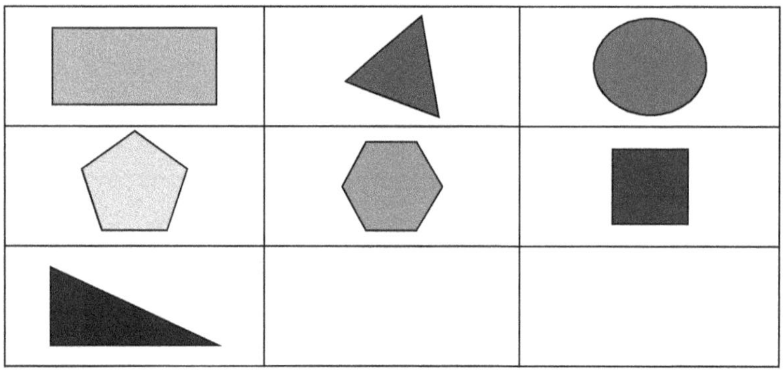

Unit 13.2 Using directions

- Giving instructions to pupils that involve touching their right ear with their left hand, their left knee with their right elbow, their right palm with their left shoulder, etc. can further consolidate 'left' and 'right'. Giving the whole group/each pupil the names of two objects in the room (for example, 'window' and 'whiteboard') and asking each pupil to state where they are in relation to each object (*'The window is behind me and the whiteboard is on my left'*) may help consolidate positioning and perspective.
- A large version of the Jollytown plan (page 169) can be recreated in a large space using masking tape/chalk and labels. Pupils can then physically stand on a square and step forward/backward/left/right one space, then report where they are now standing.
- Enlarging question 2 on page 170 may help demonstrate the usefulness of rotating a book or piece of paper so that the pupil is orientated correctly to follow the instructions given. Ask: **Why is rotating the page/paper like this helpful?**
- Creating a large grid on the floor of the classroom, hall or outdoor space with masking tape/chalk allows pupils to experience physically moving forward/backward/turning left/right. Obstacles can be placed on this grid with pupils working in pairs to guide each other through the course accurately. Or places such as "loch', 'forest', 'mountain' can be added to the grid with a specific order in which to visit the different parts of the landscape.

Unit 13.3 Symmetry

- In preparation for the 'Let's Learn' section of the textbook, provide pupils with a selection of objects that fly on Resource sheet 13A, so they can sort them into those which are 'symmetrical', 'nearly symmetrical' and 'not symmetrical'.
- Use the local environment or school grounds to identify symmetry in nature before embarking on creating symmetrical pictures using natural materials. Chalk lines or man-made objects such as rulers can be used to make the line to demonstrate symmetry.
- The Blank Symmetry Grid worksheet can be used for the 'Challenge' section on page 172.

Angles, symmetry and transformation 1B

Section overview

Textbook 1B units	Review units	Prior learning	Benchmarks/Es&Os
Unit 13.1 Making turns	**1A** Units 5.2 and 5.4 Units 13.1 and 13.2	• Use positional language to locate objects. • Fllow and give directions using left, right, forward and backward.	**MTH 1-17a** • Uses technology and other methods to describe, follow and record directions using words associated with angles, directions and turns including, full turn, half turn, quarter turn, clockwise, anticlockwise, right turn, left turn, right angle.
Unit 13.2 Right angles	**1B** Unit 12.1	• Identify a quarter, half or full turn.	**MTH 1-17a** • Knows that a right angle is 90°.
Unit 13.3 Grid references	**1A** Units 13.1 and 13.2	• Match shapes and images that are the same	**MTH 1-17a** **MTH 1-18a** • Identifies where and why grid references are used. • Describes, plots and uses accurate two figure grid references, demonstrating knowledge of the horizontal and vertical location.
Unit 13.4 Symmetry	**1A** Unit 13.3	• Create a design with one line of symmetry.	**MTH 1-19a** • Identifies symmetry in patterns, pictures, nature and 2D shapes. • Creates symmetrical pictures and designs with more than one line of symmetry.

Conceptual context

Angles

Angle is a measurement: a measure of rotation. A key conceptual understanding of angles is that they exist as both dynamic and static. For example, the movement involved in opening and closing a pair of scissors is the dynamic aspect of angle (demonstrating the size of rotation); the final position of the handle or blades is a static representation of this turn. Thinking of angle as the difference in direction between two lines helps to link the dynamic view of angle with the static view.

When pupils are asked to define an angle, they may suggest it is a corner that is pointy or sharp, a place where two lines meet, the space between two lines, or the difference between the slope of the two lines. These are not correct. Angles can be defined as 1) intersections of two or more lines; 2) corners of shapes; 3) bends; 4) slopes; 5) limited rotation (e.g. a door handle); 6) unlimited rotation (e.g. a wind turbine). To deepen conceptual understanding of angle, it is important that pupils have extensive experience of all six contexts.

Position and orientation

As the children build their spatial awareness, they will be able to give instructions to others to guide them around familiar locations or along simple journeys. Initially, a lot of the detail in these instructions will be personal to the children (for example, 'go past the display with my report on it'). With experience, they will learn to tailor their explanations for others.

Maps do not always have to be drawn to scale. An informal map from the school to the nearest shop can take the form of a line drawing that highlights notable sights, such as the play park and telephone box. The pupils should learn which form of map or plan is suitable for the circumstances.

Grids are the precursor to coordinates and build the skills that learners will need in order to read coordinates such as moving along the horizontal then the vertical. There are many contexts for grids (for example, cinema seats, games such as battleships or chess, and spreadsheets).

The phrase 'along the corridor...' is often used to explain the order to read and plot coordinates. However, not all grid systems fit with this phrase so very careful consideration must be given to your explanations. For early learners, the explanation and the context must fit together along with the focus on the horizontal movement first followed by the vertical. Remember that at third level, negative values will be introduced so we do not always go right, then up. In ICT applications, cell and cursor coordinates use the top left-hand side of the window as the origin, so as you look at the screen you move along then down!

Transformation

From the very early stages of learning, children will need to develop the ability to visualise what will happen if a shape or object is moved or changed. Questions such as 'Will the box fit on the shelf?', 'What will it look like if we turn it over?' along with the opportunity to play and experiment with a range of shapes and objects will help children develop the ability to *predict* what an object will look like after a transformation. There are many activities that can be used to develop this skill: jigsaws, matching games, tangrams, etc. Then, as children begin to focus on specific skills, such as line symmetry, we can ask them to visualise and predict what the shape will look like and then reflect on the result of the transformation.

Symmetry

Pupils learn about three inter-related transformations throughout Curriculum for Excellence including line symmetry, rotational symmetry and translation. These can be considered as three types of congruence; although the shape has been transformed, the length of its sides remain the same, as do the size of the angles and the orientation of the sides and the angles.

Reflective or line symmetry is the first kind of symmetry that children will experience. In mathematics it is a broader idea than just mirror images. A shape that has reflective symmetry has two or more matching parts. it is important that pupils experience reflecting and folding shapes in many ways to understand the differences between horizontal and vertical lines of symmetry.

We have to be careful in our explanations of symmetry and reflection. Initial experiences will focus on symmetry and recognising symmetrical shapes and pictures. In this case, symmetry is seen as a 'whole' and is not dynamic. Beautiful faces are said to be symmetrical and humans, generally, enjoy art, decoration or architecture that is symmetrical. So, when we create a butterfly by painting one half of a sheet of paper and then folding and pressing to transfer the paint to the other half, the result is seen as the final completed picture of the butterfly. Initially though, we are creating or completing a picture to make it symmetrical using a fold line or a flip.

Reflection is a dynamic movement or translation. When we reflect an object, it is moved to a new position to create an 'image'.

Resources

- Interlocking square tiles
- Mirrors
- Tracing paper
- Red pencils
- Resource 1B 13.3, 'Challenge', squared paper, large grids, chairs, selection of 2D shapes
- Resource 1B 13.4, 'Let's Practise'
- Right-angle tester from a corner of a piece of paper or card
- Rulers
- Tracing paper

Key vocabulary

- **Anti-clockwise**
- **Clockwise**
- **Degrees**
- **Half turn**
- **Full turn**
- **Horizontally**
- **Line of symmetry**
- **Quarter turn**
- **Right angle (90 degrees)**
- **Symmetrical**
- **Vertically**

Misconceptions

Potential misconception	Addressing the misconception
Unit 13.1 Pupils may confuse clockwise/anti-clockwise with left/right.	Clockwise and anti-clockwise are used to describe moving in a circular path; right and left are generally used for only one movement.
Unit 13.2 Pupils may only recognise angles, such as right angles, when both arms of the angle are the same length and/or pointing in a standard direction.	Ensure that, when drawing and measuring angles, pupils experience them with unequal arm lengths and in various positions, e.g. the angle pointing to the right, left, up and down.
Unit 13.3 Pupils may confuse the order of two-figure grid references.	Use the term 'Along the corridor, then up in the lift' along with physically doing this on a large grid to help pupils internalise this process.
Unit 13.4 Pupils may have problems identifying lines of symmetry.	Pupils are more able to identify and work with vertical lines of symmetry than horizontal. Pupils should be encouraged to rotate their jotters, textbooks, etc. so that the line of symmetry is made vertical. Some may also think that a line dividing a shape into two parts or two equal parts must be line of symmetry. Experiences with mirrors being placed along lines of symmetry and exploring this is key to move pupils beyond this reasoning.

Teaching ideas

Unit 13.1 Making turns

- When explaining 'clockwise' and 'anti-clockwise' with an analogue clock, ask the pupils: **What other objects turn clockwise or anti-clockwise? Is there a reason why they turn in the direction that they do? Would everyone here say the object turns clockwise/anti-clockwise or does it depend on where you are standing?**
- Ask: **Where have you heard the word 'turn' before? Does it have other meanings than the one we are using just now?**
- Using two identical shapes, place both side-by-side on a surface. Screening one, ask a pupil to rotate it either a half or quarter turn clockwise or anti-clockwise. Ask the other pupils to state how the shape has been moved.

- After completing the 'Challenge' part of the textbook on page 180, ask pupils to sketch the journey Finlay would have taken before and after one of his quarter turns. Ask pupils: **What angle does Finlay's quarter turn remind you of?** It is important pupils make the link between quarter turns and right angles as an angle is a measurement of *turn*.

Unit 13.2 Right angles

- Use a shape, such as a heart or an arrow, to play 'Guess where it started?'. Pupils close their eyes while one pupil chooses the starting point of the shape and then turns it a quarter turn clockwise or anti-clockwise. Pupils then have to guess what the starting point of the shape was before it was turned clockwise/anti-clockwise.
- Question 2 on page 182 may need to be enlarged to support pupils in checking for right angles.
- Use the discussion from Unit 13.1 linking quarter turns to 90 degrees to help support pupils in the 'Challenge' part of the textbook on page 182 in working out how many degrees are in a half and full turn.

Unit 13.3 Grid references

- In preparation for the pupils' introduction to grid references, chairs can be laid out in a grid format with large letters labelling each column and large numbers labelling each row. Pupils can be given a card or post-it instructing them where to sit. This can be written as 'Column C, Row 5' in the beginning or 'C5' if pupils are comfortable with 'walking along the corridor, going up in the lift' analogy.

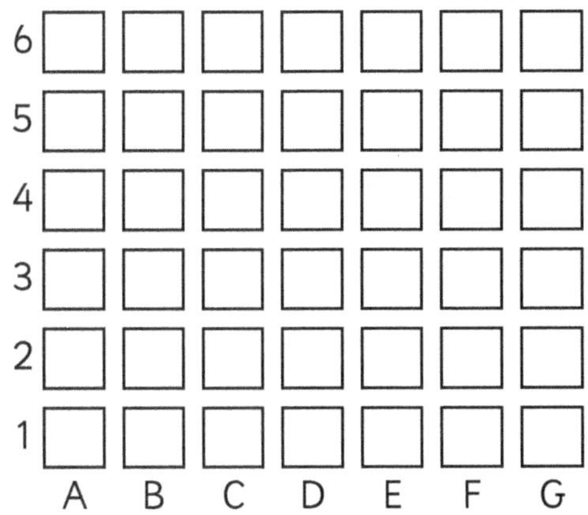

- Large grids can be constructed, either on large pieces of paper, on table tops or on the floor with the columns labelled A – G and the rows numbered 1 – 6. Give instructions to the pupils on where to place a selection of 2D shapes, either verbally, or in written form.
- Resource 1B 13.3, 'Challenge' is required for the game of Battleships.

Unit 13.4 Symmetry

- The grid on the 'Before we start' section of the textbook on page 186 is a good opportunity to begin discussions around vertical *and* horizontal lines of symmetry. Until now, pupils have formal experience of vertical lines of symmetry. Using mirrors to allow them to 'see' their symmetrical patterns may help, as will asking guiding questions such as: **Is this the only way we can hold the mirror to show symmetry?** if pupils are hesitant to explore holding the mirror in a horizontal orientation.
- Use Resource 1B 13.4 'Let's Practise' Q3, or tracing paper and a ruler to explore lines of symmetry in a variety of 2D shapes. Ask pupils to explain which shapes could be folded in more than one way to show more than one line of symmetry. Ask: **How can we check these are lines of symmetry?**

Angles, symmetry and transformation 1C

Section overview

Textbook 1C units	Review units	Prior learning	Benchmarks/Es&Os
Unit 13.1 Identifying angles	**1B** Unit 13.2	• Identify a right angle. • Know that a right angle measures 90 degrees.	**MTH 1-17a** • Uses technology and other methods to describe, follow and record directions using words associated with angles, directions and turns including, full turn, half turn, quarter turn, clockwise, anticlockwise, right turn, left turn, right angle. • Knows that a right angle is 90°. • Finds right angles in the environment and in well-known 2D shapes.
Unit 13.2 Half and quarter turns	**1B** Unit 13.3	• Make a quarter, half or full turn. • Say whether an object or person has made a quarter, half or full turn. • Say in which direction an object or person will be pointing after making a quarter, half or full turn. • Read two-figure grid references.	**MTH 1-17a** **MTH 1-18a** • Uses technology and other methods to describe, follow and record directions using words associated with angles, directions and turns including, full turn, half turn, quarter turn, clockwise, anticlockwise, right turn, left turn, right angle. • Describes, plots and uses accurate two figure grid references, demonstrating knowledge of the horizontal and vertical location.
Unit 13.3 Using compass points	**1B** Units 13.2 and 13.3	• Give and follow directions in the form of left, right, forward, backward. • Identify a quarter turn, a half turn and a full turn. • Say whether a turn is clockwise or anticlockwise.	**MTH 1-17a** **MTH 1-18a** • Knows and uses the compass points, North, South, East and West. • Identifies where and why grid references are used. • Describes, plots and uses accurate two figure grid references, demonstrating knowledge of the horizontal and vertical location.
Unit 13.4 Grid references	**1B** Unit 13.3	• Read two-figure grid references. • Know the meaning of the words horizontal and vertical. • Give directions using forward, backward, left, right, quarter turn, half turn, clockwise and anti-clockwise.	**MTH 1-17a** **MTH 1-18a** • Knows and uses the compass points, North, South, East and West. • Describes, plots and uses accurate two figure grid references, demonstrating knowledge of the horizontal and vertical location.
Unit 13.5 Symmetry	**1B** Unit 13.4	• Find the mirror line. • Create designs with one line of symmetry.	**MTH 1-19a** • Identifies symmetry in patterns, pictures, nature and 2D shapes. • Creates symmetrical pictures and designs with more than one line of symmetry.

Conceptual context

Angles

Angle is a measurement: a measure of rotation. A key conceptual understanding of angles is that they exist as both dynamic and static. For example, the movement involved in opening and closing a pair of scissors is the dynamic aspect of angle (demonstrating the size of rotation); the final position of the handle or blades is a static representation of this turn. Thinking of angle as the difference in direction between two lines helps to link the dynamic view of angle with the static view.

When pupils are asked to define an angle, they may suggest it is a corner that is pointy or sharp, a place where two lines meet, the space between two lines, or the difference between the slope of the two lines. These are not correct. Angles can be defined as 1) intersections of two or more lines; 2) corners of shapes; 3) bends; 4) slopes; 5) limited rotation (e.g. a door handle); 6) unlimited rotation (e.g. a wind turbine). To deepen conceptual understanding of angle, it is important that pupils have extensive experience of all six contexts.

Position and orientation

As the children build their spatial awareness, they will be able to give instructions to others to guide them around familiar locations or along simple journeys. Initially, a lot of the detail in these instructions will be personal to the children (for example, 'Go past the display with my report on it'). With experience, they will learn to tailor their explanations for others. Maps do not always have to be drawn to scale. An informal map from the school to the nearest shop can take the form of a line drawing that highlights notable sights, such as the play park and telephone box. The pupils should learn which form of map or plan is suitable for the circumstances.

Grids are the precursor to coordinates and build the skills that learners will need in order to read coordinates such as moving along the horizontal then the vertical. There are many contexts for grids (for example, cinema seats, games such as battleships or chess, and spreadsheets).

The phrase 'along the corridor…' is often used to explain the order to read and plot coordinates. However, not all grid systems fit with this phrase so very careful consideration must be given to your explanations. For early learners, the explanation and the context must fit together along with the focus on the horizontal movement first, followed by the vertical. Remember that at third level, negative values will be introduced so we do not always go right, then up. In ICT applications, cell and cursor coordinates use the top left-hand side of the window as the origin, so as you look at the screen you move along then down!

Transformation

From the very early stages of learning, children will need to develop the ability to visualise what will happen if a shape or object is moved or changed. Questions such as 'Will the box fit on the shelf?', 'What will it look like if we turn it over?', along with the opportunity to play and experiment with a range of shapes and objects will help children develop the ability to *predict* what an object will look like after a transformation. There are many activities that can be used to develop this skill: jigsaws, matching games, tangrams, etc. Then, as children begin to focus on specific skills, such as line symmetry, we can ask them to visualise and predict what the shape will look like and then reflect on the result of the transformation.

Symmetry

Pupils learn about three inter-related transformations throughout Curriculum for Excellence including line symmetry, rotational symmetry and translation. These can be considered as three types of congruence; although the shape has been transformed, the length of its sides remain the same, as do the size of the angles and the orientation of the sides and the angles.

Reflective or line symmetry is the first kind of symmetry that children will experience. In mathematics, it is a broader idea than just mirror images. A shape that has reflective symmetry has two or more matching parts. It is important that pupils experience reflecting and folding shapes in many ways to understand the differences between horizontal and vertical lines of symmetry.

We have to be careful in our explanations of symmetry and reflection. Initial experiences will focus on symmetry and recognising symmetrical shapes and pictures. In this case, symmetry is seen as a 'whole' and is not dynamic. Beautiful faces are said to be symmetrical and humans, generally, enjoy art, decoration or architecture that is symmetrical. So, when we create a butterfly by painting one half of a sheet of paper and then folding and pressing to transfer the paint to the other half, the result is seen as the final completed picture of the butterfly. Initially though, we are creating or completing a picture to make it symmetrical using a fold line or a flip.

Reflection is a dynamic movement or translation. When we reflect an object, it is moved to a new position to create an 'image'.

Resources

- Access to coding programmes
- Camera
- Compass showing N, E, S, W
- Counters
- Cubes or tiles in a variety of colours
- Large grid (at least 4x4)
- Mirrors
- Resource Sheet 13C
- Resource 1C 13.3 'Let's Practise' Q2
- Resource 1C 13.3 'Let's Practise' Q3
- Resource 1C 13.3 'Challenge'
- Resource 1C 13.4 'Let's Practise' Q1 & Q2
- Resource 1C 13.4 'Challenge'
- Right-angle testers
- Variety of 2D shapes (square, rectangle, regular pentagon, Regular hexagon, trapezium, parallelogram)

Key vocabulary

- **Anti-clockwise**
- **Compass**
- **East**
- **Horizontal grid reference**
- **Line of symmetry**
- **More/less than a right angle**
- **North**
- **Quarter turn = 90 degrees**
- **South**
- **Two quarter turns = 180 degrees**
- **Vertical grid reference**
- **West**

Misconceptions

Potential misconception	Addressing the misconception
Unit 13.1 Pupils may only recognise angles, such as right angles, when both arms of the angle are the same length and/or pointing in a standard direction.	Ensure that, when drawing and measuring angles, pupils experience them with unequal arm lengths and in various positions e.g. the angle pointing to the right, left, up and down.
Unit 13.1 Pupils may order angles incorrectly.	Pupils may be focusing on the length of the arms of the angle or the size of the arc of the angle when asked to order a set of angles. Experiencing angles with unequal arm lengths, unequal arcs and in various positions, e.g. the angle pointing to the right, left, up and down, and discussing why these features do not alter the actual size of the angle is important in identifying this misconception and moving beyond it.
Unit 13.4 Pupils may confuse the order of two-figure grid references.	Use the term 'Along the corridor then up the stairs/up in the lift' along with physically doing this on a large grid to help pupils internalise this process.
Unit 13.4 Pupils may have problems identifying lines of symmetry.	Pupils are more able to identify and work with vertical lines of symmetry than horizontal and diagonal. Pupils should be encouraged to rotate their jotters, textbooks, etc. so that the line of symmetry is made vertical. Some may also think that a line dividing a shape into two parts or two equal parts must be line of symmetry. Experiences with mirrors being placed along lines of symmetry and exploring this is key to move pupils beyond this reasoning.

Teaching ideas

Unit 13.1 Identifying angles

- Ask pupils: **What is special about a right angle? How can we identify one?** Ask pupils to identify right angles in their environment as part of 'Before we start'. Remind pupils that angles are a measurement of turn. Observe whether the pupils are noticing *static right angles* or instances where the right angle is more dynamic e.g. *the opening of a pair of scissors so that the scissor blades make a right angle; the turning of a door knob; the right-angled turn to go from one place to another on a route.*
- Distribute the angle cards (see Resource sheet 13C) to pupils to allow pairs to compare their angles. These angles purposefully have different arm lengths and different size of arcs (the part showing the angle). This will potentially allow any misconceptions in these areas to be uncovered. **Who has the larger angle? Whose is smaller?** If they work with another pupil, do they still have the smaller/larger angle? **Who has the largest/ smallest angle?**

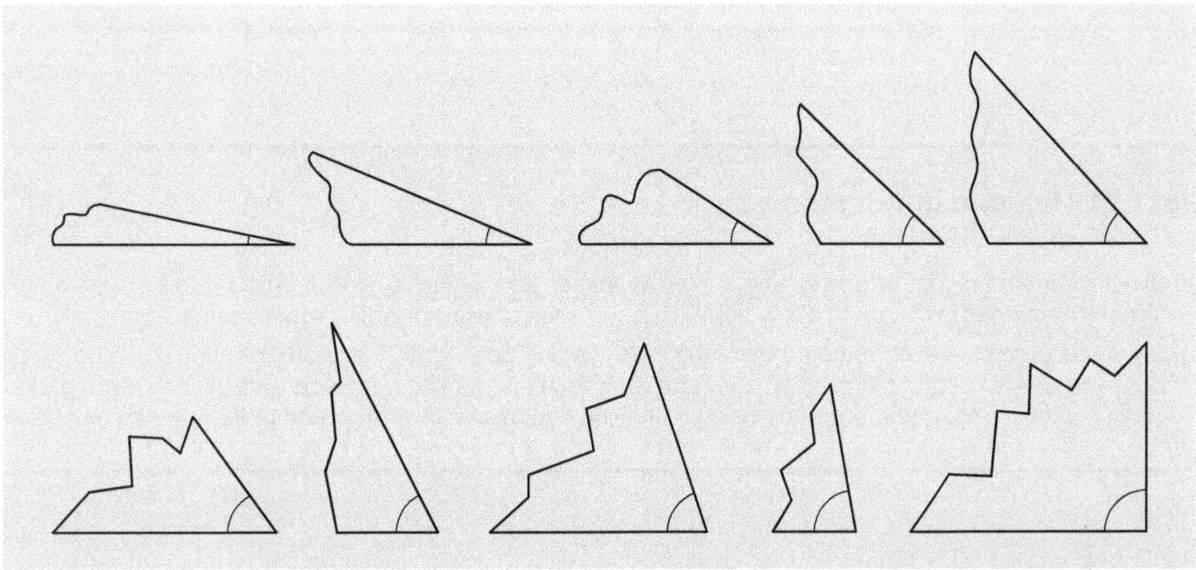

- The pizzas on question 1 and the angles on question 3 for the 'Let's Practise' section on pages 173–4 of the textbook may need to be enlarged in order for pupils to check whether the angles are more than or less than a right angle.
- Ask pupils to draw what the missing angle could be on Resource sheet 13C: Missing angles. Notice if the pupils are turning the angles around so the angle is at the 'bottom' instead of the 'top' as they are on the Resource sheet. Are they sketching on top of the right angle or obtuse angle to compare them more easily? Can they easily visualise the type of angle that is missing without any support? Discuss why the pupils have drawn those angles to allow them to share their strategies and reasoning. As an extension task, the square boxes around angles on the Resource sheet could be cut out and the pupils asked to order the angles according to size. Pupils can then be asked to draw angles on whiteboards or post-its that would fit in between the angles they have ordered from the worksheet.

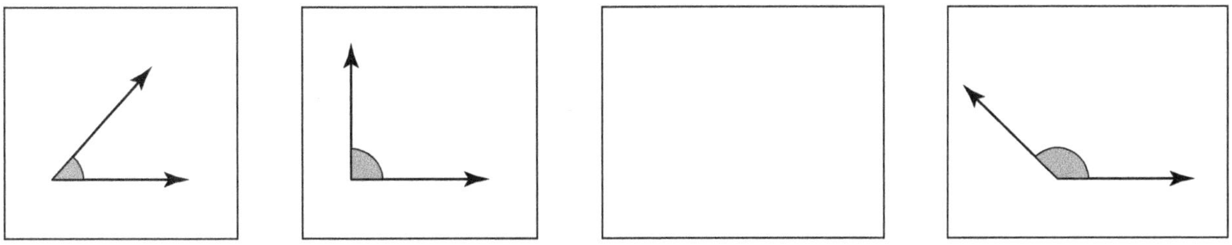

- In preparation for the 'Challenge' part of page 174 in the textbook, distribute a variety of 2D shapes (a square, rectangle, regular pentagon, regular hexagon, trapezium and parallelogram are a good starting point) to be sorted into 'Shapes with angles less than a right angle', 'Shapes with angles more than a right angle' and 'Shapes with right angles'. Ask: **Could any shape fit into more than one sorting set?** If using an interactive whiteboard to display shapes, the 'infinite cloner' function can be used to allow pupils to drag shapes into more than one set.

Shapes with angles less than a right angle	Shapes with angles more than a right angle	Shapes with right angles

Unit 13.2 Half and quarter turns

- Use a square made out of one yellow, green, blue and red multilinks, as well as the grid for 'Before we start' (possibly enlarged in colour) to allow pupils to justify their choices of which square is incorrect.
- Online or computer programming materials, such as Bee-Bot, Pro-Bot and other online software that allow pupils to use the Logo coding system, can be used to allow pupils to develop their skills in writing direction code. Tasks such as writing pupils' names or following a route are all appropriate tasks at this stage of learning.

Unit 13.3 Using compass points

- When introducing compasses, ask: **How do magnets work?** Use a large compass or one online to show all pupils that the red arrow or needle points to 'N' meaning 'north'. Explain that a compass contains a magnet that lines up with the Earth's magnetic field so that it always points north. **What do you think the letters 'S', 'E' and 'W' stand for?** Distribute compasses so that each pupil can explore how a compass works, practise turning the compass to line up the red arrow/needle with N and that, no matter which direction you are walking, the red compass arrow/needle always points north. If there is a weather-vane nearby, you may want to take pupils and their compasses to this so they can check that the 'north' on their compass matches the 'north' on the weather vane.
- A large grid can be created with chalk or masking tape in the classroom, hall or outside space. A game of cat and mouse can be played with up to 4 pupil 'mice' being placed on the grid and one pupil 'cat'. Each pupil on the grid has a partner outside the grid giving them directions to escape or catch. Instructions should be given for one movement and using the terms *square/squares, north, south, east* and/or *west*. The 'mice' may only move one square at a time, while the 'cat' may move two squares. Variables such as number of pupils, size of grid, time and number of total instructions can be introduced to alter the complexity of the activity.
- Use Resource 1C 13.3, 'Let's Practise' Q2 to support page 179 in the textbook and Resource 1C 13.3, 'Let's Practise' Q3 and Resource 1C 13.3, 'Challenge' to support page 180.

Unit 13.4 Grid references

- Using a large grid either on a large piece of paper, on the floor or on an interactive whiteboard, allow pupils to practise plotting a two-figure grid reference by finding the horizontal reference first, then the vertical. This will prepare pupils for the 'Let's Learn' section on page 181.

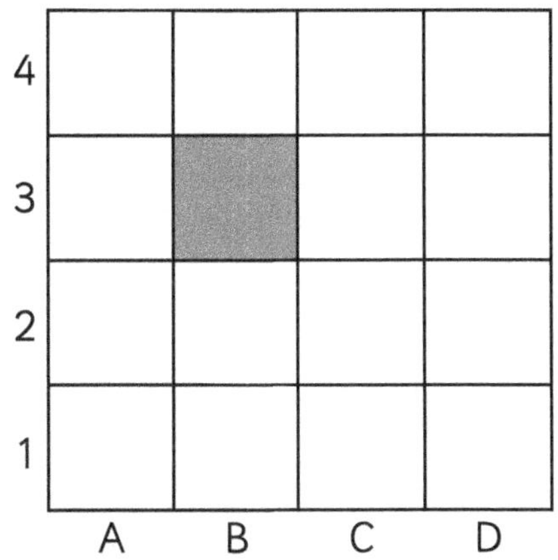

- Use Resource 1C 13.4, 'Let's Practise' Q1 and Resource 1C 13.4, 'Let's Practise' Q2 to support pupils in completing page 182.
- Using grids to allow pupils to draw treasure maps, maps of the local area, etc. will help consolidate skills in locating and reading two-figure grid references. Pupils can create their own questions and give these to other pupils to solve.
- Use Resource 1C 13.4, 'Challenge' to support completion of page 183.

Unit 13.5 Symmetry

- Use mirrors to check pupils' responses to the 'Before we start' question. Ask: **How did you work out which shapes were symmetrical?**
- Explore two lines of symmetry using art and craft materials, e.g. creating snowflakes with paper and scissors, pegboards or coloured beads to make a necklace.
- Explore symmetry in the local environment, recording these with a camera. The images can be printed off and the pupils have to draw the line(s) of symmetry on.
- Flags and logos are worth exploring to spot one or two lines of symmetry. Challenge the pupils to create a class flag with exactly one or two lines of symmetry.

14 Data handling and analysis

Data handling and analysis 1A

Section overview

Textbook 1A units	Review units	Prior learning	Benchmarks/Es&Os
Unit 14.1 Understanding data and information	**Early – B** Units 11.2 and 11.4	• I know different ways to collect information. • I can ask basic questions to collect information. • I am familiar with picture diagrams.	**MNU 1-20b** • Selects and uses the most appropriate way to gather and sort data for a given purpose, for example, a survey, questionnaire or group tallies.
Unit 14.2 Understanding data and information	**Early – B** Units 11.1 and 11.3	• I know key vocabulary – information, data, graph. • I understand pictures can be used to represent a quantity.	**MNU 1-20a** • Asks and answers questions to extract key information from a variety of data sets including charts, diagrams, bar graphs and tables.
Unit 14.3 Using data	**Early – B** Units 11.1 and 11.3	• I know key vocabulary – information, data, graph. • I understand pictures can be used to represent a quantity. • I recognise that information can be represented in different ways.	**MNU 1-20a** **MTH 1-21a** • Uses a variety of different methods, including the use of digital technologies, to display data, for example, as block graphs, bar graphs, tables, Carroll diagrams and Venn diagrams.

Conceptual context

Data handling and analysis should not be considered as a mathematical concept in isolation and where possible should be used in a cross-curricular way. Pupils should be encouraged to display and discuss information with the main purpose being communicating information. Prior to commencing these units, pupils will have had experience of sorting objects, selecting criteria for sorting and choosing criteria for sorting and recording data. In addition, pupils should be familiar with a variety of methods of recording basic data. Pupils are used to sorting, classifying and analysing data on a daily basis when they play with building blocks, select teams for a game, choose coloured pens, collect football cards and so on. Within the classroom setting, we use different forms of data to order our daily activities: ability groupings, social groupings, gender groupings, and packed lunches to name a fraction of them; thus, pupils are familiar with this process.

Resources

- Blank bar chart (see Resource sheet 14b)
- Favourite colours bar chart (see Resource sheet 14a)
- Post-its
- Whiteboards and pens

Key vocabulary

- **Chart**
- **Column**
- **Data**
- **Diagram**
- **Graph**
- **Heading**
- **Row**
- **Survey**
- **Table**
- **Tally**
- **Value**

Misconceptions

Potential misconception	Addressing the misconception
Units 14.1, 14.2 and 14.3 Pupils may think that all data is numerical.	Ensure pupils are aware that data collection and analysis can include concrete objects, pictorial materials and numerical data.
Units 14.1, 14.2 and 14.3 Pupils may think that all data is accurate.	The data is only as accurate as the methods used to gather and collect it. If the person or people responsible for recording the data are not careful, the information collected might not be correct.

Teaching ideas

Unit 14.1 Understanding data and information

- Ask pupils how they would find out what is the most popular flavour of ice cream in the class?
- Give them the opportunity to discuss their ideas with a shoulder partner before sharing with the class.
- Ask pupils to tell you the different types of ice cream that they like and write them down, e.g. chocolate, vanilla, strawberry, mint choc chip. Now, ask pupils to choose one flavour as their favourite and record the numbers beside each flavour using tally marks. Go over with pupils that when they reach 5, they cross through:

- Ask pupils to look at the information gathered and answer the following questions: **What is the most popular flavour? What is the least popular flavour? What is the difference between the most popular flavour and the least popular flavour?**
- Go through the 'Let's Learn' section with pupils.

Unit 14.2 Understanding data and information

- Show pupils the favourite colours bar chart (Resource sheet 14a).
- Ask them what information they can tell you from the bar chart and record them on the board.
- Ask pupils the following questions: **What is the most popular colour? What is the least popular colour? How many people liked red? How many people voted altogether? How do you know?**
- Using the blank bar chart (see Resource sheet 14b) get pupils to create their own chart to represent the class's favourite colours.
- Discuss with pupils how you will gather the information to put into the chart; how will you record the colours and the total amount of pupils?
- Encourage pupils to think about how they will collect the data and ensure that it is accurate.
- How will they check that everyone has participated?
- Ask them to predict what colours will be the most/least popular and why.
- Once all pupils have collected their data, before they complete their bar charts, go over the colours they have chosen and the total for each one. Ask pupils why it is important to have accurate data.

Unit 14.3 Using data

- Write the months of the year on the board and ask the pupils what month their birthday is in. Record their names next to the appropriate month.
- Ask pupils what this data can tell them. Answers could include: how many pupils were born in each month, the month in which most pupils were born, the oldest pupils, the youngest pupils and so on.
- Ask pupils if there are any other ways that they could gather this information and different ways that they could display the information.
- For each of their suggestions, discuss why they think this would be a good way to display the data.
- Discuss with pupils if they think it is important to have their names listed in the month of their birthday or if simply having tally marks to show how many have a birthday in each month. **What difference does this make to how the information is used?**
- Ensure that pupils have a good understanding of the different ways that data can be used before moving onto the 'Let's Practise' section within the unit.

Data handling and analysis 1B

Section overview

Textbook 1B units	Review units	Prior learning	Benchmarks/Es&Os
Unit 14.1 Surveys and questionnaires	**1A** Units 14.1, 14.2 and 14.3	• I collect information in different ways. • I can ask relevant questions to collect information. • I am familiar with different types of charts and diagrams.	**MNU 1-20a** **MNU 1-20b** • Asks and answers questions to extract key information from a variety of data sets including charts, diagrams, bar graphs and tables. • Selects and uses the most appropriate way to gather and sort data for a given purpose, for example, a survey, questionnaire or group tallies.
Unit 14.2 Bar graphs	**1A** Units 14.1, 14.2 and 14.3	• I can understand how to gather data. • I can ask relevant questions to collect and interpret data. • I am familiar with different types of charts and diagrams.	**MNU 1-20a** **MTH 1-21a** • Uses a variety of different methods, including the use of digital technologies, to display data, for example, as block graphs, bar graphs, tables, Carroll diagrams and Venn diagrams.
Unit 14.3 Investigate and interpret information	**1A** Units 14.1, 14.2 and 14.3	• I can recognise data in tables, charts and diagrams. • I can ask relevant questions to understand and interpret data. • I am familiar with different types of charts and diagrams.	**MNU 1-20a** • Asks and answers questions to extract key information from a variety of data sets including charts, diagrams, bar graphs and tables
Unit 14.4 Drawing conclusions from data and graphs	**1A** Units 14.1, 14.2 and 14.3	• I can recognise data in tables, charts and graphs • I can ask relevant questions to understand and interpret data. • I am familiar with different types of charts and diagrams.	**MNU 1-20a** **MNU 1-20b** **MTH 1-21a** • Asks and answers questions to extract key information from a variety of data sets including charts, diagrams, bar graphs and tables. • Selects and uses the most appropriate way to gather and sort data for a given purpose, for example, a survey, questionnaire or group tallies. • Uses a variety of different methods, including the use of digital technologies, to display data, for example, as block graphs, bar graphs, tables, Carroll diagrams and Venn diagrams.

Conceptual context

Data handling and analysis should not be considered as a mathematical concept in isolation and where possible should be used in a cross-curricular way. Pupils should be encouraged to display and discuss information with the main purpose being communicating information. Prior to commencing these units, pupils will have had experience of collecting data, selecting criteria for collecting data and recording data. In addition, pupils will be familiar with a variety of methods of recording and displaying basic data. Pupils are familiar with collecting information on a daily basis when asking each other about their favourite sports, how many pets they have, who has siblings and so on. Within the classroom setting, pupils are surrounded by different forms of data used to order our daily activities: ability groupings, social groupings, gender groupings, packed lunches to name a fraction of them, but they may not be familiar with the different ways that this data is used to make decisions and impact further actions.

Resources

- Blank bar chart (see Resource sheet 14b)
- Favourite colours bar chart (see Resource sheet 14a)
- Our pets (see Resource sheet 14c)
- Post-its
- Unifix cubes
- Whiteboards and pens

Key vocabulary

- **Carroll diagram**
- **Chart**
- **Column graph**
- **Data**
- **Datum**
- **Diagram**
- **Graph**
- **Heading**
- **Questionnaire**
- **Row**
- **Survey**
- **Table**
- **Tally**
- **Value**
- **Venn Diagram**

Misconceptions

Potential misconception	Addressing the misconception
Units 14.1, 14.2, 14.3 and 14.4 Pupils may think that all data is numerical.	Ensure pupils are aware that data collection and analysis can include concrete objects, pictorial materials and numerical data.
Units 14.1, 14.2, 14.3 and 14.4 Pupils may think that all data is accurate.	The data is only as accurate as the methods used to gather and collect it. If the person or people responsible for recording the data are not careful then the information collected might not be correct.

Teaching ideas

Unit 14.1 Surveys and questionnaires

- Tell pupils that you want to find out what their favourite colour is in the class.
- Label each corner of the room a different colour; red, blue, green and yellow.
- Ask pupils when you tell them they will go and stand in the corner that represents their favourite colour.
- Once everyone has made a choice, ask them what they can tell you. By looking at the different corners, pupils should be able to draw conclusions about which colour is the most/least popular. Discuss whether or not this is the best way to gather information; ask them to explain their thoughts.

- By giving pupils only four colours to choose from, does this give us the most accurate information?
- **Is there a better way to find this information out? What other ways can we gather information?**
- Ask pupils to think about how they would create a survey to find out what pets they have in the class and what they will need to consider when creating their survey/questionnaire.
- Think about the following: **Do you want to simply know how many pupils have a pet? Do you want to know what types of pets pupils have? Do you want to know how many of each type of pet pupils have in total?**
- Explain to pupils that in order to make sure they get the correct information, they will need to spend time planning the types of questions that they will ask.
- Look at the 'Let's Learn' section within the unit and explore the different types of information that you can collect.

Unit 14.2 Bar graphs

- Give pupils a copy of Our Pets (Resource sheet 14c) and ask them to collect the data from their peers about the pets that they have within the class. Discuss with pupils whether or not they should include their own pets in the survey and how this might impact the results.
- Once they have completed their own sheets, ask them to tell you the different pets they have surveyed and write down the information on the board, for example:

		Total
Dogs	𝍸 ||	7
Cats	𝍸 𝍸 ||	12
Rabbits	||||	4

- Ask pupils to check that their information is the same as yours and discuss why it is important that the information is accurate.
- Ask pupils how they could show this information visually and discuss the benefits of this. They may suggest a bar graph or a pictogram.
- Look at the 'Let's Learn' section of the units and talk about the examples shown, pointing out the layout of them both and the importance of the labelling to ensure that the person who is reading the information understands what they are looking at.
- Using a copy of the blank bar chart (see Resource sheet 14b) get pupils to create a bar chart to display the information they have gathered about their pets.

Unit 14.3 Investigate and interpret information

- With pupils, look at the 'Before we start' section of the unit and ask them to record their answers on a whiteboard.
- Discuss their answers with them, asking them to give an explanation to clarify their understanding.
- Ask pupils who uses graphs and charts? Where do they see graphs and charts being used?
- In pairs, get pupils to discuss how graphs and charts can make it easier to understanding data and information.

Unit 14.4 Drawing conclusions from data and graphs

- With pupils, look at the 'Before we start' section and ask them to write down four pieces of information that they have taken from the graph about pasta shapes.

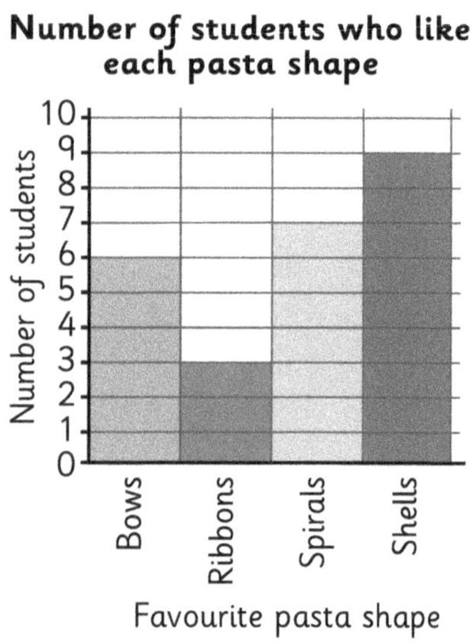

- Ask the pupils: **How many students were questioned? How do they know? What 2 pasta shapes account for ½ of the votes? Prove it. Can you tell if all pupils voted? What makes you say that? Do you know from the data if all pupils like pasta?**
- Discuss with pupils the importance of understanding what the data and graphs are telling us and what information is NOT there. Emphasise the importance of really looking at the data before drawing conclusions.

Data handling and analysis 1C

Section overview

Textbook 1C units	Review units	Prior learning	Benchmarks/Es&Os
Unit 14.1 Collect, organise and display data	**1B** Units 14.1, 14.2, 14.3 and 14.4	• I collect information in different ways. • I can ask relevant questions to collect information. • I can organise information using tables and charts. • I am familiar with different types of charts and diagrams.	**MNU 1-20b** **MTH 1-21a** • Selects and uses the most appropriate way to gather and sort data for a given purpose, for example, a survey, questionnaire or group tallies. • Uses a variety of different methods, including the use of digital technologies, to display data, for example, as block graphs, bar graphs, tables, Carroll diagrams and Venn diagrams. • Includes a suitable title, simple labelling on both axes and an appropriate scale where one unit represents more than one data value in graphs.
Unit 14.2 Use data to create Carroll and Venn diagrams	**1B** Units 14.1, 14.2, 14.3 and 14.4	• I can ask relevant questions to collect information. • I can organise information using tables and charts. • I am familiar with different types of charts and diagrams.	**MTH 1-21a** • Uses a variety of different methods, including the use of digital technologies, to display data, for example, as block graphs, bar graphs, tables, Carroll diagrams and Venn diagrams.
Unit 14.3 Use data to check and verify information	**1B** Units 14.1, 14.2, 14.3 and 14.4	• I can ask relevant questions to using information. • I can organise data into tables and charts. • I am familiar with different types of charts and diagrams.	**MNU 1-20a** • Asks and answers questions to extract key information from a variety of data sets including charts, diagrams, bar graphs and tables.
Unit 14.4 Solve problems using data, graphs and diagrams	**1B** Units 14.1, 14.2, 14.3 and 14.4	• I can ask relevant questions to using information. • I can organise data into tables and charts. • I am familiar with different information represented on charts and diagrams.	**MNU 1-20a** • Asks and answers questions to extract key information from a variety of data sets including charts, diagrams, bar graphs and tables.

Conceptual context

Data handling and analysis should not be considered as a mathematical concept in isolation and where possible should be used in a cross-curricular way. Pupils should be encouraged to display and discuss information with the main purpose being communicating information. Prior to commencing these units, pupils will have had experience of collecting data, selecting criteria for collecting data and recording data. In addition, pupils will be familiar with a variety of methods of recording and displaying basic data. Pupils are familiar with collecting information on a daily basis when asking each other about their favourite sports, how many pets they have, who has siblings and so on.

Within the classroom setting, pupils are surrounded by different forms of data used to order our daily activities; ability groupings, social groupings, gender groupings, packed lunches to name a fraction of them but they may not be familiar with the different ways that this data is used to make decisions and impact further actions. Moving onto collecting and recording their own information and then presenting this in a bar chart will help pupils to grasp this concept as they tend to find producing their own bar charts tricky and need plenty of help to draw a set of axes and then work out how to draw bars all of equal width and evenly spaced. Pupils will look at both discrete and continuous data. Discrete data is information that can only take on certain values; for example, numbers of pupils (you can't have half a pupil). Continuous data can take any value within a range; for example, a measurement like a person's age, a cat's weight and time taken to get to school.

All too often, too much time is spent on drawing graphs, and not enough time on actually finding out what the graph/chart is telling us (interpreting).

There are many elements to consider; for example: What data do we need to collect and why? How will we collect, organise and represent the data? What is the best way to represent the data? Is the data reliable? What 'story' does this data tell us?

When planning data handling opportunities for pupils it is important to ensure a balance of activities are prepared, including: collecting, organising, representing, interpreting and discussing data.

At First Level, this process is formalised as:

1. Ask the question (what are we finding out?)
2. Make a plan (what do we need to know?)
3. Collect the data (how do we do this?)
4. Present the data
5. Interpret the data

Pupils are also encouraged to develop 'I notice' statements to *interpret* and draw conclusions from the data and then 'I wonder' statements from data gathered to allow them to create predictions based on data gathered and to suggest other data they would like to collect to help deepen their understanding of the big question.

Resources

- Blank bar chart (see Resource sheet 14b)
- Favourite colours bar chart (see Resource sheet 14a)
- Our pets (see Resource sheet 14c)
- Post-its
- Unifix cubes
- Whiteboards and pens

Key vocabulary

- **Carroll diagram**
- **Chart**
- **Column graph**
- **Data**
- **Datum**
- **Diagram**
- **Graph**
- **Heading**
- **Questionnaire**
- **Survey**
- **Table**
- **Tally**
- **Row**
- **Value**
- **Venn Diagram**

Misconceptions

Potential misconception	Addressing the misconception
Units 14.1, 14.2, 14.3 and 14.4 Pupils may think that all data is numerical.	Ensure pupils are aware that data collection and analysis can include abstract, concrete and pictorial materials.
Units 14.1, 14.2, 14.3 and 14.4 Pupils may think that all data is accurate.	The data is only as accurate as the methods used to gather and collect it. If the person/people responsible for recording the data are not careful then the information collected might not be correct.

Teaching ideas

Unit 14.1 Collect, organise and display data

- Write the following on the board: **What is a question?**
- Give pupils 5 minutes in pairs to discuss their thoughts. Explain that there is no right or wrong answer and you just want them to write down all their ideas.
- Encourage learners to consider the questions they will use to collect the data. Use questions such as: **Who shall we ask?** Discuss if it would it be fair to only ask the boys. **How many pupils shall we ask?**
- Pupils should understand that asking too few pupils may not give a fair picture of the situation, and that asking too many pupils may be more difficult to manage.
- **When/Where shall we carry out our survey?**
- Is the end of lunch time a good time to conduct the survey and should we conduct the survey on more than one day to see if there are any differences? It is important to phrase questions carefully so that the data collected is clear.
- For example, if an internet provider was to ask 'Do you use the internet?' and only give a choice of 'Yes' or 'No' as answers, it would be quite difficult to analyse the results. When you think about it, an answer of 'yes' has a range of meanings so you could consider offering multiple choice answers.
- Look at the 'Let's Learn' section to go over open-ended and closed questions in more detail.

Unit 14.2 Use data to create Carroll and Venn diagrams

- Introduce a Carroll diagram and explain that is used to organise data and group it according to whether it fits certain criteria.
- Write down the following numbers on the board:
- 1, 2, 3, 4, 5, 6, 7, 8, 10, 12, 15, 16, 20, 24, 25, 28, 30
- Now ask pupils to sort these numbers using the following criteria:
    - o can be divided by 2 and 5
    - o can be divided by 2 but not by 5
    - o cannot be divided by 2 but can be divided by 5
    - o cannot be divided by 2 or 5.

	Can be divided by 2	Cannot be divided by 2
Can be divided by 5	10, 20, 30	5, 15, 25
Cannot be divided by 5	2, 4, 6, 8, 12, 16, 22, 24, 26, 28	1

- Go over answers with pupils, discussing why they have placed each number in the places that they have. Ask them about the benefits of sorting the numbers in this way.
- Look at the example in the 'Let's Learn' section.

Unit 14.3 Use data to check and verify information

- Ask pupils to create a diagram or graph to show the number of pupils who have brown hair and the number of pupils who do not. Tell pupils to present it in such a way that the names of the children in each category can be identified. Discuss different ways of collecting the data; for example, interviews, surveys and so on.
- Once all the data has been collected, ask different groups to display it in different ways: bar graph, pictogram, names written in two groups are possible suggestions. Give pupils the opportunity to present their work to each other and encourage them to ask each other questions about the data, such as: **How many children have brown hair? How many children do not have brown hair? How many children were asked altogether? What colour of hair does Antoinette have?**
- Encourage pupils to check that on each occasion the answers are the same and the data collected across all of the groups, although presented differently, is the same.
- Discuss the advantages and disadvantages of each method of presentation, drawing conclusions about the most useful.

Unit 14.4 Solve problems using data, graphs and diagrams

- Across all curricular areas, look for opportunities to pose a problem that requires data collection to arrive at an answer. Encourage pupils to decide what data they require, the method they will use to collect it and the form they choose to present it in.
- Provide the pupils with a problem to solve: **How many pupils eat packed lunches on a daily basis?**
- Ask pupils to predict what they think the answer will be and get them to think about how they will find out if their prediction is correct. Split the pupils into groups and ask them to design a method of data collection, undertake the task of collecting the data and decide the best way to present their findings.
- Once they have finished, give all groups the opportunity to present their work including the conclusions they have drawn from the data. Encourage the pupils to use *I notice* and *I wonder* questions. Discuss how they will be able to verify their results.

15 Ideas of chance and uncertainty

Ideas of chance and uncertainty 1A

Section overview

Textbook 1A units	Review units	Prior learning	Benchmarks/Es&Os
Unit 15.1 Understanding chance		• Informal language associated with uncertainty, particularly around the weather and events that may happen today or soon. • Sequencing of events into a logical order.	**MNU 1-22a** • Uses mathematical vocabulary appropriately to describe the likelihood of events occurring in everyday situations including: probable, likely/unlikely, certain/uncertain, possible/impossible and fair/unfair. • Interprets data gathered through everyday experiences to make reasonable predictions of the likelihood of an event occurring.

Conceptual context

In mathematics, probability is a measurement just like any other measurement. The difference is probability is applied to the likelihood of whether or not an event will occur. We are teaching pupils to explore doubt and uncertainty by understanding the vocabulary that is used and the different situations where they might use this as a measurement.

In probability, we discuss 'events' and 'outcomes' with an event being anything that happens and an outcome being the result of what happens. For example, when you toss a coin it can have two possible results, either heads or tails. Therefore, tossing the coin is the event and the outcome is either heads or tails.

Using probability you can measure which outcome is more likely to occur as the result of any given event. By dividing the number of times that the outcome has occurred by the total number of events you can start to predict the probability of the outcome.

Resources

- Coins
- Counters
- Dice
- Probability scale (Resource sheet 15a)

Key vocabulary

- **Certainty**
- **Chance**
- **Doubt**
- **Likely**
- **Likelihood**
- **Predicting**
- **Probability**
- **Uncertainty**
- **Unlikely**

Misconceptions

Potential misconception	Addressing the misconception
Unit 15.1 Pupils may think that events are thought of as being together and not individually.	If you ask pupils how likely it is to roll a 6 on a dice they will make their mind up based on their most recent experience. So, if they have just rolled the dice 4 times and each time it was a 6 they may say 'very likely'. If they have rolled the dice 4 times and got a different number each time, they will likely have a different answer despite the probability remaining the same in both cases. This needs to be clearly explained to pupils: that the probability is one out of six ($\frac{1}{6}$) regardless.
Unit 15.1 Pupils may think that personal experience and belief can influence an individual's ability to think about probability and chance.	If a pupil's frame of reference is that you win every time you play a game, then their perception of the likelihood an event will occur will be very different from a pupil who has experienced losing every game they have played. This needs to be explored to explain that the chances are the same for each game; this might be a difficult concept for some pupils to take on board.

Teaching ideas

Unit 15.1 Understanding chance

- Start this section by asking pupils to name some of their favourite stories. Discuss their suggestions; ask them what each story is about and ask them how do they know. Ask them if they have heard the story about Goldilocks and the Three Bears. From the title of the story, what can they be certain that the story will be about? Ask them if there is a possibility that there could be more than three bears? Now, start to read the story to the point where she is in the house looking at the three bowls of porridge. Ask the pupils how many bowls there are. How do they know? Discuss the fact that Goldilocks can see the three bowls of porridge, this is certain. However, does she know if the porridge if too hot? Is it possible that it is cold? Use the language from the probability scale to challenge their thinking.
- Introduce the key vocabulary to pupils so they understand what each of the terms means to ensure when they use them, they are clear why they have selected a specific word to describe the event.
- Put the following words up on the board and ask the pupils to discuss with a partner what each of them mean:

  Certain Even Chance Possible Impossible
- Ask pupils, either individually or in pairs, to write down an example of an event. For each one, tell them that they will need to be able to explain their answer. This will provide the opportunity to clarify understanding and any misconceptions that pupils may have.
- Give pupils a copy of the probability scale (see Resource sheet 15a) and a set of the probability cards (see Resource sheet 15b) and ask them to work with a partner to place each card along the scale. Tell them that they will have to have a reason for placing each card. When asking pupils to explain their answers, ensure that they are using the correct vocabulary to reinforce their understanding.
- Encourage the pupils to play games involving chance, such as Snakes and Ladders and Frustration.
- As the pupils are working, ask: **What makes you say that? What weather would you expect at this time of the year? What would make you give me a different answer?**

Understanding chance and uncertainty 1B

Section overview

Textbook 1B units	Review units	Prior learning	Benchmarks/Es&Os
Unit 15.1 Understanding chance and uncertainty	**1A** Unit 15.1	• I can use the vocabulary *certain* and *uncertain* correctly. • I can predict if an event might happen based on prior knowledge.	**MNU 1-22a** • Uses mathematical vocabulary appropriately to describe the likelihood of events occurring in everyday situations including: probable, likely/unlikely, certain/uncertain, possible/impossible, and fair/unfair. • Interprets data gathered through everyday experiences to make reasonable predictions of the likelihood of an event occurring.

Conceptual context

We come across many different events on a daily basis that we are interested in finding the chance of happening. This forms the basis of the concept of probability. Pupils need to understand what events are and the different kinds of events that this may apply to.

A random event is one where the outcome is unknown. For example, when we toss a coin we do not know if it will land heads up or tails up so tossing a coin is considered an action that will produce a random event.

Events can be independent (with each event being unaffected by other events); dependent or conditional (where an event is affected by other events); and mutually exclusive (where events can't happen at the same time).

An *independent* event is not affected by any other events and the past outcomes will not affect the next one.

Dependent events are affected by previous events (for example, when you select a card from a deck). Once you have taken one card from the deck there are fewer cards available; consequently, the probabilities change. However, if we put each card back after drawing it, or replace it, then the chances don't change, as the events are independent.

Key vocabulary

- **Certainty**
- **Chance**
- **Doubt**
- **Likely**
- **Likelihood**
- **Predicting**
- **Probability**
- **Uncertainty**
- **Unlikely**

Misconceptions

Potential misconception	Addressing the misconception
Unit 15.1 Pupils may think that events are thought of as being together and not individually.	If you ask pupils how likely it is to roll a 6 on a dice they will make their mind up based on their most recent experience. So, if they have just rolled the dice 4 times and each time it was a 6 they may say 'very likely'. If they have rolled the dice 4 times and got a different number each time, they will likely have a different answer despite the probability remaining the same in both cases. This needs to be clearly explained to pupils that the probability is one out of six (⅙) regardless.
Unit 15.1 Pupils may think that personal experience and belief can influence an individual's ability to think about probability and chance.	If a pupil's frame of reference is that you win every time you play a game, then their perception of the likelihood an event will occur will be very different from a pupil who has experienced losing every game they have played. This needs to be explored to explain that the chances are the same for each game; this might be a difficult concept for some pupils to take on board.

Teaching ideas

Unit 15.1 Understanding chance and uncertainty

- Explain to pupils that there are some things that we know are certain and do not rely on the influence of anything else to happen. Things that are certain can include: there are 12 months in a year. Things that are uncertain can include: it will be sunny today.
- Ask pupils if they know what a random event might be. Introduce the concept of going for a walk and the different events that might take place. Read the story 'We're Going on a Bear Hunt' and talk about each event and whether or not this would certainly happen, if there is a possibility and so on.
- Extend the conversation by asking them to explain why they think that.
- Ask pupils: **What is the probability of someone in their class being born in the same year as them?** Ask them why they have given that answer. Extend this by asking them what the possibility is of someone in their school being born in the same year as them. Have the pupils given a different answer? You are looking for pupils to have recognised that within their own class, the probability is higher as they are all around the same age but across the school there is a wider range of ages, therefore the probability is lower. Tell them that this is an example of the outcome being dependent on the information being considered.
- Extend this activity by asking about the chances of them being born on the same day of the week, month or year as their peers. A good activity to illustrate this is by lining pupils up and asking them to order themselves from oldest to youngest. This also promotes teamwork and can be used for groupings before a task.
- Give pupils a set of cards numbered 1–6 (see Resource sheet 15c) and ask them to shuffle them and place them face down. Write the following questions on the board and ask pupils to discuss the answers with a partner:
    - **What is the possibility that they pick a card with an even number?**
    - **What is the chance that they will pick a card with an odd number?**
    - **What is the likelihood that they pick a card with 7 on it?**
    - **How likely is it that they select a card with 4 on it?**
- For each of these questions, although the selection is random, there is a specific set of parameters within which pupils have to work (as there are only 6 cards): there is only one of each number, there are only numbers 1–6 and this will not change. Therefore, they have an even or 50/50 (50%) chance of selecting either an odd or an even number, a zero chance of selecting a 7 and a 1 in 6 chance of selecting a 4. Explore the vocabulary of chance and the different numerical ways that chance can be expressed.

Understanding chance and uncertainty 1C

Section overview

Textbook 1C units	Review units	Prior learning	Benchmarks/Es&Os
Unit 15.1 Using data to predict the outcome	**1B** Unit 15.1	• I can use the vocabulary *certain, possible, unlikely, uncertain* and *impossible* correctly. • I can predict if an event might happen based on prior knowledge.	**MNU 1-22a** • Uses mathematical vocabulary appropriately to describe the likelihood of events occurring in everyday situations, including: probable, likely/unlikely, certain/uncertain, possible/impossible, and fair/unfair. • Interprets data gathered through everyday experiences to make reasonable predictions of the likelihood of an event occurring.

Conceptual context

Predicted probability has to do with how probability is calculated and what the outcomes mean. Thus, a predicted probability is, essentially, the probability of an event that is calculated from available information or data.

There is a wealth of information available about natural occurrences (e.g. the weather), or statistics (e.g. football results) that can be used to develop this concept. But there are also many opportunities to use practical experiments to deepen pupils' understanding.

Collecting local weather information can lead to questions, such as 'How likely is it to rain in June?'. We can start to say if it is likely to rain more in June or in January and we can predict how many days rain we might get in June. However, we cannot say if it will rain on sports day!

When we want to make predictions, it is a good strategy to make an organised list. If we can identify what could happen, we can begin to work out how likely it is to happen. If pupils are able to make a list of all the possible outcomes, they can then make predictions and give numerical values to the probability of an event occurring.

Pupils find making an organised list difficult, particularly in ensuring that they have all the possibilities listed. The initial focus should therefore be on ensuring that all the possible outcomes have been found rather than any numerical analysis.

Key vocabulary

- **Certainty**
- **Chance**
- **Doubt**
- **Likely**
- **Likelihood**
- **Predicting**
- **Probability**
- **Uncertainty**
- **Unlikely**

Misconceptions

Potential misconception	Addressing the misconception
Unit 15.1 Pupils may think that events are thought of as being together and not individually.	If you ask pupils how likely it is to roll a 6 on a dice they will make their mind up based on their most recent experience. So, if they have just rolled the dice 4 times and each time it was a 6 they may say 'very likely'. If they have rolled the dice 4 times and got a different number each time, they will likely have a different answer despite the probability remaining the same in both cases. This needs to be clearly explained to pupils that the probability is one out of six ($\frac{1}{6}$) regardless.
Unit 15.1 Pupils may think that personal experience and belief can influence an individual's ability to think about probability and chance.	If a pupil's frame of reference is that you win every time you play a game, then their perception of the likelihood an event will occur will be very different from a pupil who has experienced losing every game they have played. This needs to be explored to explain that the chances are the same for each game; this might be a difficult concept for some pupils to take on board.

Teaching ideas

Unit 15.1 Using data to predict the outcome

- Ask pupils: **How did you decide if you wore a waterproof jacket or not today?** It may be that their parents made the decision, but you can rephrase the question to ask why the parent chose a waterproof jacket or not. Do the pupils realise that they are using their understanding of chance and uncertainty if they picked a particular jacket because they predicted it was going to rain? **When else do you make predictions?** Do you choose what table to sit at in the lunch hall based on where you think your friends will sit? Many choices made are based on a prediction of how likely they think an event is to happen.
- Ask pupils to think about their daily timetable. If they come to school Monday to Friday and they know that PE is on the timetable two days that week, **what is the probability that PE will be on any given day?** (You can adapt this for other curricular areas.)

  Write on the board:

Monday	Tuesday	Wednesday	Thursday	Friday
? ? ? ? ?				

  Discuss with pupils how they could work this out…

  It would be 2 out of 5, because there are two desired outcomes (PE) and five possible outcomes (days of the school week).
- **As the week continues, however, do the chances change? If PE is not on Monday, what is the probability of it being on Tuesday? Is it still 2 out of 5?** Ask pupils to discuss this with a partner.

Monday	Tuesday	Wednesday	Thursday	Friday
X	?	? ? ?		

- **If there is no PE on Tuesday, how will this change their prediction?**

Monday	Tuesday	Wednesday	Thursday	Friday
X	X	? ? ?		

- **If PE is then on Wednesday, what can they predict for the rest of the week?**

Monday	Tuesday	Wednesday	Thursday	Friday
X	X	PE	? ? ?	

- A possible follow-up to this activity is for the pupils to make a list or tally of regular predictions and events. For example, which will be the most popular lunch, what will the weather be tomorrow and will the school team win? The class can then discuss which activities are easier to predict? Is it lunches, because we all like sausages, the weather because we know about the seasons or the school team because we know how good our players are?